OPENING DOORS

Volume Two

OPENING DOORS
The Life and Work of Joseph Schumpeter
Volume Two: America

Robert Loring Allen

Foreword by
Walt W. Rostow

Transaction Publishers
New Brunswick (U.S.A.) and London (U.K.)

Library of Congress Catalog Number: 90-34813
ISBN: 0-88738-380-7
Printed in the United States of America

Library of Congress Cataloging-in-Publication Data

Allen, Robert Loring.
    Opening doors : the life and work of Joseph Schumpeter / Robert
Loring Allen.
        p. cm.
    Includes bibliographical references (p.).
    ISBN: 0-88738-362-9 (v. 1)
    ISBN: 0-88738-380-7 (v. 2)
    ISBN: 0-88738-381-5 (2 vol. set)
    1. Schumpeter, Joseph Alois, 1883-1950. 2. Economist—United
States—Biography. I. Title.
HB119.S35A64 1990
330'.092—dc20
    [B]   90-34813
                                                                      CIP

Dedicated to
Jeanne Miriam Allen

Contents

Foreword Walt Rostow   ix
Preface   xix

1.	Embracing America and Abandoning Europe (1933-1935)	1
2.	Research and Romance (1935-1936)	17
3.	Teaching and Marriage (1936-1937)	35
4.	The Secret Life (1937-1938)	51
5.	*Business Cycles*: The Amplified Vision (1939)	71
6.	Alienation and Isolation (1939-1942)	87
7.	Capitalism's Fate (1942)	115
8.	Toil and Turmoil (1942-1945)	137
9.	A New and Uncomfortable World (1945-1947)	157
10.	Effort Rewarded, Contradictions, and Solace (1947-1948)	181
11.	Reviewing the Troops (1942-1949)	203
12.	Reunion with the *Hasen* (1948-1950)	219
13.	Epilogue	243

Appendix A	Chronology of Joseph Alois Schumpeter	265
Appendix B	Bibliographies of Schumpeter's Writings	269
Appendix C	Personal Interviews	273
Appendix D	The Schumpeter Papers	277
Appendix E	Bibliography	281
Name Index		323
Subject Index		333

Photographs follow page   156

Foreword

W. W. Rostow

Loring Allen's study of Joseph Schumpeter is a distinguished addition to a small set: biographies of major economists. And this is not surprising. The art of biography and professional knowledge of a scientific field are only rarely combined in the same individual. There is even a generalized warning against the effort to make that combination. Sir Peter Medawar has written: "The lives of scientists, considered as Lives, almost always make dull reading. . . . their private lives may be unhappy, strangely mixed up or comic, but not in ways that tell us anything special about the nature or direction of their work."[1]

Nevertheless, we have not only David Hume's terse, charming autobiography but also several substantial accounts of his life.[2] Hume, however, was a figure whose wide-ranging grandeur was widely perceived in his own time and transcends his underrated place in the history of economic thought. There are several accounts of Adam Smith, but none penetrates his prototypical Medawar surface or significantly links his life and his economics except, perhaps, for his dislike of Oxford.[3] Again, we know something of Malthus[4] and Ricardo and their remarkable friendship,[5] but there are no efforts to explore their personalities deeply.

John Stuart Mill and Karl Marx are a different case. For quite different reasons, they did generate substantial biographical literatures that I shall not attempt to annotate here. Mill's *Autobiography*, with his eccentric education, psychological and intellectual crisis, and intriguing tie to Harriet Taylor, invited intensive exploration, including a small book on Mill and Mrs. Taylor by Friederich von Hayek. Marx's effort to shape history with a theory of economic and societal dynamics, and his egomaniacal, obsessed private life, have challenged a good many analysts.

Alfred Marshall generated Keynes's superb memorial essay, one of the most successful efforts to illuminate a body of economic thought through an understanding of its creator.[6] And, as with Mill and Marx, Keynes himself has triggered a biographical cottage industry: notably, the works of R.F. Harrod and Robert Skidelsky. I could, of course, cite many memorial essays, including Schumpeter's *Ten Great Economists*. But essentially, that's about it.

I believe Loring Allen's study of Schumpeter belongs mighty close to the top of this class. In dealing with Schumpeter's life, he exhibits a rare consciousness of the extraordinary complexity and only limited penetrability of the human personality. At each stage of Schumpeter's life, one is reminded of David Hume's youthful dictum:[7] "What is man but a heap of contradictions."

Loring Allen provides no grand explicit Freudian (or other) theory to "explain" Schumpeter. But, as Schumpeter's closely interwoven personal and professional life unfolds, Allen develops without dogmatism a pattern of linkages for the reader to contemplate. And, in a splendid final passage, he provides a memorable summation of "a multifaceted man of paradox" whose great professional career left him "frustrated and despairing."

Despite Schumpeter's complexity as a personality, however, there is a remarkable shapeliness and consistency in his work as an economist. From first to last, he was an erudite scholar of the history of economic theory who developed into a teacher with an ability to transmit the fascination and excitement he himself found in the field. He believed that it was in one's third decade that a scholar defined the "vision" whose elaboration dominated his or her subsequent professional life. He not only lived by this insight but it suffused with a kind of reverence his relations with the host of talented students whose lives and careers he touched. As for paradox, who else would have challenged a university librarian to a duel because he was not sufficiently liberal in providing books to his students?

In his evaluation of fellow economists, past and contemporary, he exhibited a rare capacity to capture with sympathy their perspectives, even when they differed from his own, and to suppress substantially, not wholly, his often strongly held prejudices. And, in dealing with students, he systematically avoided using his influence to generate disciples. He encouraged the talented young economists who gathered around him to pursue their own visions.

On the other hand, Schumpeter's vision was defined early with singular clarity and pursued relentlessly to the end of his life. His first book, published when he was twenty-five, was *Das Wesen und der Hauptinhalt der theoretischen Nationaloekonomie* (1908). A study of static economic theory, with Léon Walras at its center, it nevertheless foreshadows the central, obsessive theme in Schumpeter's career: the effort to produce a coherent formal theory to explain the dynamics of capitalism. In *Das Wesen*, he asserted that statics and dynamics are completely different fields, and concluded: "Dynamics, still in its infancy, is a 'Land of the Future'."[8]

By 1909, he was hard at work in that land: He had worked out the substance of *The Theory of Economic Development*, published two years later when he was still within his "sacred decade." And, in the final phase of his career, he was still struggling to find a definitive formulation of his view of the dynamics of capitalism in *Business Cycles* (1939), *Capitalism, Socialism and Democracy* (1942), and *History of Economic Analysis* (1953).

Capitalism, Socialism and Democracy, the most accessible of Schumpeter's books, argued that the social and political conditions generated by the success of capitalism would inevitably lead to the throttling of innovation and a transition to socialism. (Schumpeter would have been amazed at the relative repute of capitalism versus socialism as the 1980s came to a close.)

Business Cycles sought to capture the dynamics of capitalism and its evolution since the end of the eighteenth century by combining his theory of innovation with historical and statistical materials. It remains a respected but ultimately unpersuasive (and largely unread) monument to Schumpeter's quest.

His *History of Economic Analysis* was meant to serve as a prelude to a definitive synthesis of dynamic analysis. The book was incomplete when he died, despite nine years of arduous labor. He never found a way to fulfill his vision, which can be defined as rendering dynamic Walras's static model of general equilibrium by embracing endogenously major structural innovations. As he grew older, Schumpeter expressed regret on some occasions that he had not become an economic historian; on others that he had not learned more mathematics. In an industrious but essentially amateur way, he tried to reach his goal by both routes, and they both failed him.

Why?

Schumpeter's aim was to expound and present in terms of formal theory the process central to the dynamics of modern societies. What distinguishes the world economy since the late eighteenth century is that, for the first time in recorded history, invention and innovation became a flow, not a series of sporadic, widely spaced events. In part, that flow was incremental and, in some sectors, reasonably steady—geared, as Adam Smith perceived, to the widening of the market. But invention and innovation also took the form of major revolutionary events with great creative and destructive power, altering irreversibly the structure of economies and the contours of social and political life. As they were brought into the world economy, these great innovations also set in motion in many directions phases of increasing returns.

Adam Smith, almost uniquely, made the distinction that lay at the heart of Schumpeter's insight. Both in his *Lectures* and his *Wealth of Nations,* Smith evoked not merely inventions contrived by those who actually operated the machines—a kind of incremental learning by doing—but those created by "philosophers" (scientists) that involved "new powers not formerly applied."[9] Looking back from his own time, Smith noted that such major innovations were occasional events. But, in his last decade (the 1780s), in one of the great watersheds of history, the rhythm of innovations incorporating "new powers" radically altered: Watt's steam engine, factory-manufactured cotton textiles, and coke-manufactured iron came on stage as operational innovations in that decade. Over the next two centuries, they were followed (among other innovations) by railroads, cheap steel, electricity, the internal combustion engine, a flow of new chemicals, microelectronics, genetic engineering, lasers, and a widening group of new industrial materials in a sequence of, roughly, four batches.

Down to about 1870, Adam Smith's successors dealt with the revolutionary changes in technology in a straightforward way linked endogenously to the economic process as a whole. Deep in the eighteenth century, David Hume had enunciated the most fundamental linking principle: "Necessity ... is the great spur to industry and invention."[10] In the troubled wake of the Napoleonic wars, Malthus and Ricardo debated the impact of the new machines on the level of employment, exports, and national income. Influenced by John Rae and Charles Babbage, J.S. Mill dealt not only with the technological revolution of his time but with its roots in science and with ways to strengthen the scientific foundations of a technologically dynamic economy.[11] Marx, also greatly influenced by Babbage, derived from Ricardo's judgment that there were cases where the introduction of machinery could reduce the level of employment, one of his central propositions; that is, to contain money wage rates, the entrepreneur introduced machinery to maintain an ample "reserve army of the unemployed."

The marginal revolution and the seduction of mainstream economics by the possibility of formally defining microequilibrium and general equilibrium via the differential calculus, changed this easy acceptance of ever-expanding technology, creative and disruptive, as an inescapable reality of economic life and analysis. Innovation was pushed aside or down the hall to some eccentric, off-beat member of the economics department.The reasons was simple: Increasing returns, with its falling supply as well as demand curves, did not permit the formal definition of equilibrium positions. And Walras's elegant general equilibrium could only be defined with the structure of the economy given and unchanging.

Alfred Marshall, with the best grasp on mathematics of any of the economists of his time, understood the dilemma with a special clarity. He explicitly separated short- and long-period analyses; dramatized in two appendixes the problem posed for formal theory by the pervasive case of increasing returns; refined the techniques of equilibrium microanalysis under short-period assumptions; wrestled manfully but with little success to formalize long-period microanalysis; and fell back on history and institutional analysis to deal with long-period change. It was out of this experience that he concluded:

> The theory of stable equilibrium of normal demand and supply helps indeed to give definiteness to our ideas; and in its elementary stages it does not diverge from the actual facts of life, so far as to prevent its giving a fairly trustworthy picture of the chief methods of action of the strongest and most persistent group of economic forces. But when pushed to its more remote and intricate logical consequence, it slips away from the conditions of real life. In fact we are here verging on the high theme of economic progress; and here therefore it is especially needful to remember that economic problems are imperfectly presented when they are treated as problems of statical equilibrium, and not of organic growth. For though the statical treatment alone can give us definiteness and precision of thought, and is therefore a necessary introduction to a more philosophic treatment of society as an organism; it is yet only an introduction.
>
> [I]t is barely even an introduction to the study of the progress and development of industries which show a tendency to increasing return. Its limitations are so constantly overlooked, especially by those who approach it from an abstract point of view, that there is a danger in throwing it into definite form at all.[12]

Marshall's awareness that he could not solve in formal mathematical terms the problem of long-period analysis did not particularly trouble him. He judged economics to be essentially a biological subject rather than an offshoot of neo-Newtonian physics. And, much to Schumpeter's annoyance, Marshall and his followers were ultimately not seeking to develop a pure economic science but to improve the level and quality of life of the poor. Indeed, almost all the British economists in the tradition of Hume and Smith were men who accepted from the beginning that, in the service of policy, economic analysis had to be merged with social and political analysis and with any other insight history and the social sciences could provide. They were, therefore, much less concerned than Schumpeter to elevate economics to scientific parity with neo-Newtonian physics.

In a sense, Schumpeter's romantic effort to produce an elegant, dynamic version of the Walras general-equilibrium model was an impossible, perhaps even a misguided, dream. On his great effort in *Business Cycles,* he concluded:

> I took longer than I thought to turn that scaffolding [*The Theory of Economic Development*] into a house, to embody the results of my later work, to present the historical and statistical complement, to expand old horizons. Nevertheless I doubt whether the result warrants that simile. The house is certainly not a finished and furnished one—there are too many glaring lacunae and too many unfulfilled desiderata. The restriction to the historical and statistical material of the United States, England, and Germany, though serious, is not the most serious of all the shortcomings. The younger generation of economists should look upon this book merely as something to shoot at and to start from—as a motivated program for further research. Nothing, at any rate, could please me more.[13]

The drifting off of his *History of Economic Analysis* before completion, despite nine years of labor, was probably, in part at least, a consequence of his frustration and sense of failure.

Loring Allen has pointed out to me that if the mathematics of nonlinear dynamics and chaos theory had been available to Schumpeter, his inner gloom might have been lifted to a degree. Indeed, the introduction of a succession of major innovations renders economic growth a profoundly nonlinear process, with passages of (bounded) creative-destructive turbulence that might well yield chaotic outcomes if we had the requisite data. Even without an econometric filling of empty boxes, the emergence of nonlinear dynamics might well have resolved the schizophrenic conflict in Schumpeter's mind between the elegance of Walrasian equilibrium and an awareness that economic life was inherently in perpetual disequilibrium, and convinced him that he was on the right track. For, indeed, he was.

Starting with Walras's concept of general equilibrium under fixed conditions of supply, Schumpeter introduced a broadly-defined concept of major innovations as "The Fundamental Phenomenon of Economic Development."[14] And he did so in language that clearly foreshadows nonlinear dynamics:

> Development in our sense is a distinct phenomenon, entirely foreign to what may be observed in the circular flow or in the tendency toward equilibrium. It is spontaneous and discontinuous change in the channels of the flow, disturbance of equilibrium, which forever alters and displaces the equilibrium state previously existing.[15]

Here we have a process built into the system—endogenous, not exogenous. It yields irreversible results and is inherently in disequilibrium so long as the process persists. Schumpeter was quite conscious that his assumption that the major economic changes of the capitalist epoch occurred in an irreversible, revolutionary way rather than by continuous incremental adaptation was theoretically explosive. He referred, for example, to Marshall's failure to overcome "the difficulties which surround the problem of increasing return."[16] But, to the end, he sought courageously to explore the implications of his proposition and to wrap up his findings in a neat theory.

Schumpeter's proposition is, of course, not a complete theory of growth. It deals with only one component of the production function: that is, the role of major technological change in sustaining the increase of production and inducing cyclical fluctuations. His structure lacks, for example, a theory relating birth and death rates to development, including population-related investment in housing, infrastructure, and agriculture. It lumps the opening of a new source of supply for food or raw materials with technological and institutional change without examining its special features, including prior shifts in relative prices and typically longer periods of gestation than industrial investment. It does not deal with the stages of and limits to growth. But, taken on its own terms and in its own time, *The Theory of Economic Development* is a powerful, creative landmark in the history of economic thought. Subsequent mainstream economics is a good deal less than it might have been had its practitioners not acted in accordance with a *bon mot* attributed to Winston Churchill: "Men often stumble over the truth, but most manage to pick themselves up and hurry off as if nothing had happened."[17]

There has been, of course, a great deal of further work done on innovation in the Schumpeterian tradition. But, down to the present day, mainstream economic theory has gone to great pains to avoid what might be called the Schumpeter Problem by rendering structural innovations exogenous or by burying them in one kind of highly aggregated black box or another, such as capital-deepening, intermediate production, the capital-output ratio, or the residual. Its practitioners have, in effect, preferred to go on playing equilibrium games with differential calculus rather than face up to the central characteristic of the dynamic economies for which they have pretended to offer analysis and prescription: Economies are always in the process of irreversible change, never in equilibrium. Surely, as Marshall understood, equilibrium analysis had a useful pedagogical role and was helpful in the preliminary phase of examining a serious economic problem. But it could not deal with the complexities of "organic growth."

I believe Schumpeter's sense of failure derived, in part, from his inability to translate his powerful, correct understanding of the significance of innovation into either an elegant mathematical formulation in the style of Walras or a neat historical pattern. But the limitations of equilibrium analysis and the inherent messiness of history were bound to deny him success in the romantic terms he set for himself. And the reader of this book will find other sources—personal and professional—for the dark undertone of his apparently sprightly life, including a compulsion to be recognized as the greatest economist of his day, an image perhaps imposed by a widowed mother's search for fulfillment through her *wunderkind*; successive failures in politics and business; the traumatic triple tragedy of 1926 that, in Loring Allen's phrase, "imprisoned him for the rest of his life"; recognition (in his view) denied him by publications of John Maynard Keynes and, in the case of his two most important books, by the timing of the First and Second World Wars; and, finally, the defeat of Germany and Japan in the Second World War, countries with which he sympathized for reasons he could not wholly understand.

So far as his professional life is concerned, Schumpeter's knowledge of the history of his craft was unsurpassed and his capacity to stimulate the talented young and to earn their lasting gratitude was remarkable. And if he did not wholly fulfill his youthful vision, neither did David Hume or Adam Smith, Karl Marx or Alfred Marshall. To use a vivid image of F.H. Hahn and R.C.O. Matthews, Schumpeter did not devote his energies to strengthening and polishing the links in the chain that were already relatively strong.[18] What he did was boldly to dramatize the fact that post-1870 mainstream economics, systematically ignoring or evading the innovational process, was Hamlet without the prince. On a grand scale, he not only explored the innovational process but also began the long, hard, still unfinished task of rendering it an endogenous component of dynamic economics, thus linking it to the main body of theory.

Few of his predecessors, contemporaries, or successors could claim to have done more. He certainly deserves this respectful, candid, and sensitive portrait of his life and work.

Notes

1   Sir Peter Medawar, *Pluto's Republic* (New York: Oxford University Press, 1982), 263.
2   See, for example, Ernest Campbell Mossner, *The Forgotten Hume, Le bon David* (New York: Columbia University Press, 1943) and John Vladimir Price, *The Ironic Hume* (Austin: Texas University Press, 1965). See also William Bell Robertson's introduction to Hume's *Political Discourses* (London: Walter Scott Publishing, 1906).
3   See, for example, John Rae, *Life of Adam Smith* (London: MacMillan, 1895).
4   See, for example, Patricia James, *Population Malthus, His Life and Times* (London: Routledge & Kegan Paul, 1979).
5   See, notably, P. Sraffa and M. Dobb, eds., *Biographical Miscellany*, vol. 10 of *Works and Correspondence of David Ricardo* (Cambridge, England.: at the University Press, 1955).

6   J.M. Keynes, "Alfred Marshall: 1842-1824," in A.C. Pigou, ed., *Memorials of Alfred Marshall* (London: MacMillan, 1925).
7   David Hume, *Philosophical Works*, eds. T.H. Green and T.H. Grose (London: Longman's Green, 1912) vol. III, p. 238.
8   J.A. Schumpeter, *Das Wesen und der Hauptinhalt der theoretischen Nationaloekonomie* (Muenchen and Leipzig, Germany: Duncker and Humblot, 1908), 182-3.
9   Adam Smith, *Wealth of Nations*, ed. Edwin Cannan, with an introduction by Max Lerner (New York: Random House, 1937), 9-10.
10 David Hume, *Writings on Economics*, edited and with an introduction by Eugene Rotwein (Madison: University of Wisconsin Press, 1955), 17-18.
11 J.S. Mill, *Principles of Political Economy*, ed. V.W. Bladen and H.M. Robson (Toronto: University of Toronto Press, 1965), 969.
12 Alfred Marshall, *Principles of Economics*, 8th ed. (London: MacMillan, 1930), 461.
13 J.A. Schumpeter, *Business Cycles* (New York: McGraw-Hill, 1939), 1:v.
14 The quoted designation is the title of chapter 2 of Schumpeter's *The Theory of Economic Development* (Cambridge: Harvard University Press, 1934).
15 Ibid., 63.
16 Ibid., n.1.
17 Alexander B. Trowbridge, *Private Leadership and Public Service* (Washington, D.C.: National Academy of Pubic Administration, 1985), 14-15.
18 F.H. Hahn and R.C.O. Matthews, "The Theory of Economic Growth: A Survey," *Economic Journal* 74, no. 296 (December 1964): 890.

Preface

This study of Joseph Alois Schumpeter originated in the conviction that the life and work of this great social scientist instructs us in the workings of the human mind and the ways of the human soul. It also informs us of how progress in the analysis of society and the economy takes place, and tells the story of a vital, multifaceted man.

Economists and other social scientists have used and neglected the work of their great men. They have rediscovered only now and again some previously ignored contributor. But, aside from anecdotal knowledge, they have ignored the whole man. Almost the only exception to this observation in recent times is John Maynard Keynes, the best-known economist of the twentieth century.

Beginning as a Harvard graduate student in 1947, I was one of many students of Schumpeter. Although I took his courses in advanced economic theory and the history of economic literature, I was never an intimate nor one of his inner circle of students. Over the years, in my work in economic development and history, my appreciation of Schumpeter grew. In a 1980 conversation with my colleague, Joseph McKenna, also a student of Schumpeter, we both lamented the lack of biographies of great economists. This book evolved from that conversation. That summer and the following six summers I studied the Schumpeter papers in the Harvard University Archives.

I owe staggering debts to many of Schumpeter's students and colleagues, as well as those in America, Germany, and Austria who are interested in his life and work. Among the former are Gottfried Haberler, Wassily Leontief, Arthur Smithies (deceased), Edward Mason, Paul Sweezy, Paul Samuelson, Nicholas Georgescu-Roegen, Toni Stolper (deceased), Herbert Furth, Redvers Opie (deceased), Fritz Machlup (deceased), Paul Rosenstein-Rodan (deceased), Herbert Zassenhaus (deceased), Steffy Browne, Eduard Maerz (deceased), Lucia Krassnigg, Guenther Harkort (deceased), Christa Hasenclever, Hans Singer, Emily Schumpeter, and many others. I must mention especially the many stimulating conversations I have had with Wolfgang Stolper, professor emeritus of the University of Michigan, one of the students closest to Schumpeter and a Schumpeter scholar of the first order. Dr. Alfred Goessl of the German Department of the University of Missouri-St. Louis has aided me immensely with German texts and translations. Many of those named above have read some or all of earlier versions of the manuscript, resulting in its improvement. Ms. Marla Schorr, an experienced writer and editor, formerly of the University of Missouri-St. Louis, did much to improve the readability of the manuscript.

I have visited Schumpeter's birthplace in Czechoslovakia and am most grateful to Methodej Burian, mayor of Třešť, Dr. Karel Brazda, student of the Schumpeter family, and others for their help. I also visited Schumpeter's home in Taconic, Connecticut, his beloved Vienna, as well as Graz and Bonn, and owe much to the helpful people in all those places. Notes, correspondence, manuscripts, and diaries abound in the Harvard University Archives, and archives in Graz and Vienna preserve many documents. Still, the wartime destruction of most of his notes, diaries, and correspondence from childhood and early Vienna days to 1932 leaves a void.

Financial assistance for this study came from many sources. My own Department of Economics at the University of Missouri-St. Louis helped with money and time off. On two occasions I received money from the University of Missouri Weldon Springs Fund for Research. The College of Arts and Sciences and the Center for International Studies also provided some funds, as did the National Endowment for the Humanities.

This book's purpose is not to convince readers of the greatness of Schumpeter or the merits or lack of merit of his scientific or policy views. Rather, it is to tell the story of his life in relation to his work and the development of his ideas. No "Schumpeter school" exists, nor are there Schumpeterians contending with Keynesians and monetarists since none exist. This is as he wanted it, for, as he told his students many times, "Only fish run in schools, not economists." Many economists and social scientists continue to study and use his analysis while others criticize it.

In 1986, students of Schumpeter initiated a scholarly society—the International J. A. Schumpeter Society in Augsburg. Its purpose is to encourage and sponsor continued scientific work along lines suggested by Schumpeter. Wolfgang Stolper of the United States was the first president; Arnold Heertje of the Netherlands is president at present. In the late 1980s and 1990, many scholars have begun to take an interest in Schumpeter's work; the number of books and articles is increasing rapidly. In this work, I have tried to state his position accurately and sympathetically, although not without criticism. For those who wish to pursue Schumpeter's thinking in more detail and on a more technical level, and to learn of the thinking of those who would promote or denigrate, attack or defend, and comment or elaborate upon his work, the Bibliography is a generous sampling of the critical literature.

ROBERT LORING ALLEN

Nashua, New Hampshire
September, 1989

1

Embracing America and Abandoning Europe (1933-1935)

Toward the end of his first academic year at Harvard, Schumpeter pondered his future. Should he stay in the United States or return to Europe? He had already decided to visit Europe in the summer of 1933. But did he want to go back and stay in a Germany with Hitler now in power, or did he want to return to an United States with Roosevelt in charge? Taussig reminded him that, with the Nazis currently in control of university appointments, Schumpeter could probably not keep an appointment even if he got one. The demanding nature of National Socialism was becoming apparent. Its antisemitism had opened up many university posts, but if the Jews could not last in Nazi Germany, could Schumpeter? At least in the United States, the ability to speak and write as he chose, his personal freedom, and his economic position were secure. Even if the United States remained that "uncomfortable" country, Germany, for all its attraction, was forbidding.

The democracy of the United States at once attracted and repelled Schumpeter, who regarded the country as too democratic. He thought its political system was unusually sensitive to the greed of pressure and self-seeking economic groups, while its political leadership in the 1930s seemed bent on reinstalling the mercantilist policies of the seventeenth and eighteenth centuries—policies that modern nations had phased out in the nineteenth century. Still, the United States was free, with no one telling others what to do, say, or think. Cambridge was an exception to uncomfortable America.

Schumpeter in these early days of his tenure delighted in Harvard, especially its young; and Cambridge, much more than Bonn or Berlin, was a beehive of intellectual activity, not only in economics but in every field. Hundreds of men, untrammeled by politics and unimpeded by worldly worries, pursued knowledge for its own sake. Despite an attraction for some of Hitler's ideas, despite the lingering fondness for things European, Schumpeter knew that he could not survive under the Nazis. On 3 May 1933, Schumpeter, a resident only seven months, took a taxi to the Federal Building in downtown Boston where he declared his intention to become a citizen of the United States.

1

On Sunday morning, 28 May 1933, Schumpeter boarded the steamship *Scythia* in Boston, bound for England. His announced purpose in returning to Europe that summer, as well as the two subsequent summers, was to study the architecture of French cathedrals, a life-long interest that needed nourishment. Someone once quipped, only half jokingly, that Schumpeter's greatest book would be on French architecture. The trip thus combined a holiday with the renewal of old friendships, since he planned to meet Mia. Schumpeter did not work in the ordinary sense of that word on these trips, but he did plan and think through problems. At every opportunity, wherever he was, he looked up the local economists for conversation and stimulation. He argued, to himself and to others, that he needed this time of looking away from the deadly seriousness of economic theory day by day in order to confront it the better back in his study.

His itinerary began with a two-week stay in England, where he visited London, Cambridge, and Oxford. In London, he usually stopped at the art galleries, the London School of Economics, and the British Museum, sitting in the latter, as he had before, where Marx had worked. In Cambridge and Oxford, the dons and professors absorbed his attention, especially at lunches and dinners with the greats, near-greats, and students—from Maynard Keynes to that bright young R. F. Kahn and the brilliant Joan Robinson whose new book was stirring up economists. On occasion, he spoke before a group of students or teachers. He loved every minute of it since England was almost a second home to him. By 11 June 1933, he was in Rouen, France; a week later in La Rochelle. He next travelled down to Biarritz for two weeks, and then to Avignon, Nimes, and other sites in France, including Grenoble and Chartres—to see the cathedrals, of course. Finally, in mid-August, he was in Paris. At night, in hotels all over France, he studied Joan Robinson's new book, *The Economics of Imperfect Competition*, in preparation for writing his review.[1]

Schumpeter's tastes in art and architecture were catholic, with a preference for the Gothic. He wandered through French cathedrals for hours, making sketches of windows and spires. From nearby shops, he bought photographs; from the cathedral archives, he learned about the building's history and construction. Although amateur, he was expert. He also bought photographs of great art and recorded his impressions of it in his diary. The Louvre was a special favorite. But. whatever city he was in, he visited the local church or cathedral and the art gallery. Not an art critic, Schumpeter was more of an enthusiastic yet knowledgeable consumer of art whose favorites included portraits of individuals and paintings of groups of people.[2]

In August, Schumpeter met Mia, who still lived in Juelich and worked in Bonn. After relaxing at a German spa for a couple of weeks, they returned to Bonn in September and early October. For both, it was a pleasant interlude with no strings attached since they knew by this time that they had both accepted that marriage was out of the question. In the early fall, Schumpeter stayed with Mia's family in nearby Juelich for a few days before moving on to London, Oxford, and Cambridge again for another round of meetings with economists. In October, he left England on the *SS Laconia* and was soon back in Cambridge, ready for the new academic year. Nothing had happened during the summer that impelled him to consider returning to Europe permanently.

2

In the fall of 1933, Schumpeter had a heavy teaching load. Along with Taussig and J. R. Walsh, an instructor, he taught the theory of value and distribution, but his participation consisted of only a few lectures. He continued to teach economic trends and fluctuations, along with money and banking. The most interesting teaching that year was his experiment in mathematical economics, a course called Introduction to the Mathematical Treatment of Economics. But it did not go too well. Schumpeter was not a mathematician and had never taken a course in mathematics. What he knew of the subject was self-taught. He had a historical, literary, and even romantic outlook, not a mathematical turn of mind, and he could did not embrace all that stern symbolic logic, nor could he impart it to others.

Mathematics requires a special talent to understand it fully, and an even rarer talent to teach it properly—talents not possessed by Schumpeter. Its teaching allows no grand Schumpeterian flourishes, important but oft-neglected facts, startling hypotheses, interesting paradoxes, intricate verbal analyses, and profound conclusions—all standard parts of Schumpeter's teaching repertoire. The department decided that, as soon as possible, someone with more training in mathematics (for example, Wassily Leontief or E. B. Wilson) should teach the course. Still, all was not lost, for Schumpeter had jarred the department into introducing and continuing a course in mathematical economics, even if he would not teach it, which was never his intention anyway. And not everyone thought Schumpeter had wasted his time and effort. Edward Mason, a junior faculty member in economics, attended the class and later said that he had learned something from it.[3]

By the fall of 1933, Schumpeter had become a permanent fixture in the Yard, where he began in earnest to try to influence the young people. He had given up, without expending much effort, on the old men and his contemporaries. In his diary, he wrote contemptuously of the three Bs— Bullock, Black, and Burbank. But he thought the young group at Harvard held promise. After all, since the years between twenty and thirty were the most important ones for a scholar, Schumpeter felt a responsibility to guide these young economists through those years.

In 1932, he had formed another informal group of those interested in theory called the Cournot Group, named after Antoine Augustin Cournot, the famous seventeenth-century French economist best known for his mathematical formulations. The group met to stimulate its members in the study of economics.

This new group overlapped the Seven Wise Men and yet another group, often referred to by Schumpeter in his diary as the Inner Circle, as well as the occasional Friday Seminar. All these groups were informal, intermittent, and direct descendants of the Chance, Love, and Logic Society of the 1920s. When active, a group typically met once a month, though sometimes more frequently. The usual Friday night meeting place might be Lochobers, the Oyster House, or some other good restaurant in Cambridge or Boston. After a few drinks and a good meal, followed by some brandy and talk, the group retired to the house, apartment, or rooms of a participant. When it was Schumpeter's turn to host the group, it met most often in the upstairs room of the Harvard Faculty Club. Although discussions of economics ruled these evenings, all was not serious. The members initiated Schumpeter into the joys of American burlesque by attending the Old Howard, with its striptease, at Scollay Square in Boston. These gatherings were later followed by more drinks and even more talk long into the night.[4]

The purpose of these groups was not to accomplish anything tangible, even though results sometimes ensued. For example, the book *The Economics of the Recovery Program* was a product of the Seven Wise Men to which each Wise Man contributed a chapter. Leontief presented a paper on "Composite Commodities and the Problem of Index Numbers" at a group meeting in the fall of 1933. In 1936, after many revisions, *Econometrica* published the paper. Still, the real purpose was to exchange ideas and learn. Schumpeter's motives were clear. He wanted to soak up the intelligence and insights of lively young people, as well as to experience the intellectual excitement that only a group of young minds on the move can provide. In addition, he wanted to promote the interests of these young colleagues and students. Schumpeter also needed an audience for his own musings and the admiration of a group that regarded him as mentor. The groups substituted for family life, a combination social and intellectual occasion that got him out of the library and away from the Taussig household. Outside these groups, he had only a limited social life.

Above all, Schumpeter's groups in the 1930s at Harvard were not an effort to establish a school, that is, an informal group of scholars who share a common economic vision and who are followers of a great scholar. Schumpeter remained as much opposed to schools at Harvard as he had been at Bonn. He did not seek to dominate the young people, to teach them his brand of economics, to inculcate any particular way of thinking about economics or anything else. No homogeneity existed in his groups. Instead, he wanted to make each person strong in whatever that person did best. If Paul Sweezy wanted to be a Marxist, then Schumpeter wanted him to be the best Marxist in the United States. Seldom speaking of his own theories, Schumpeter addressed himself to the concerns of the groups' members and otherwise threw out ideas for all to chew on.

While a new school was no part of his intention, Schumpeter did enjoy and bask in the attention of these young people. Because he was the oldest and most intellectually mature member, all the younger men looked to him for guidance, suggestions, and ideas. Seymour Harris, at the time a young instructor at Harvard, tells of having lunch with Schumpeter,

> I always dreaded these lunches, though Schumpeter was always a most interesting and convivial companion ... lunch with him was an exhausting experience. It would not be long before he knew more about the subject than the expositor, and soon he would begin sticking pins into the arguments, offering suggestions and debating every point with vigor. After one of these luncheons, I was of no use for the afternoon, though the net gain was large; but Schumpeter was almost certain to return to the classroom or spend arduous consultation hours with his students.[5]

He made strenuous efforts to get to know and help the graduate students, and his office at Holyoke 42 became the center of gravity for many of the more able young men. His table at Dunster House was regularly filled with economics students engaged in earnest talk of economics. As he walked through the Yard and around the Square, like a magnet he attracted the most inquisitive. He always seemed to have a spare half-hour for conversation in his office or down at Merle's, a coffee shop on Massachusetts Avenue opposite the Widener Library rear entrance. Unlike many of the professors, Schumpeter would even talk to fools and show-offs, believing even one of them might sometime have an idea.[6]

3

Schumpeter's special rapport with graduate students, young instructors, and assistant professors stands in stark contrast to his inability to get along well with some of his contemporaries. He was on good enough terms with the associate and full professors, but no closeness prevailed with most of them. To them, he seemed an idiosyncratic Austrian gentleman—perhaps a brilliant economist, but a little off the beaten track, and not a leader in economics. They respected him and his ideas, but did not look to him for either friendship or leadership. With a few of the mature scholars, such as Taussig and some others, he got along famously, lunching frequently with Abbot Payson Usher, the economic historian. Arthur H. Cole, another economic historian, later joined the business school and became interested in the historical counterpart of Schumpeter's theoretical entrepreneur. Schumpeter also got along with William Leonard Crum, and the two eventually coauthored a book. Leontief, already a world-class economist, was still a junior member of the staff, as was Gottfried Haberler when he later joined Harvard. Aside from these colleagues, Schumpeter did not interact with many of the full professors in the department except on a superficial level. Outside of economics, Schumpeter had limited contacts, getting acquainted with a few history and sociology people but not establishing any lasting connections. An exception was Talcott Parsons who, before moving over to sociology, had studied economics.

Partly because of this disinterest in most of his colleagues, especially those outside economics, Schumpeter exercised little influence within the university. He had small fondness for institutions and bureaucracies such as universities. Although useful vehicles for sponsoring his work, he thought them unworthy of his time and attention for their own sake. He never attended general faculty meetings, nor did he serve on university committees or participate in university politics and governance. Believing that institutions existed to serve professors, not the other way around, he felt that those who had no scientific talents to hone or work to do should serve the institution. His scrupulous attention to departmental and full professors' meetings he felt was justified because their work determined the economics curriculum and personnel.[7]

Schumpeter showed little interest in undergraduates, except for the most talented. He never fully understood Harvard's emphasis on undergraduates since his view of a university's role left little room for such education. In his conception of the ideal university, no "students" existed, only master scholars and apprentice scholars working together in a more or less medieval arrangement. As the masters and apprentices educated one another, they mutually pushed forward the frontiers of knowledge. His university also had no room for those attending to please their fathers or to satisfy family tradition. No babysitter or haven for growth between puberty and maturity, the university existed to serve the intelligent, the dedicated, and the scientific and intellectual worker.[8]

To achieve this mutual learning experience and bring him closer to students, he employed the same device he had used at Graz and Bonn: the consultation. Schumpeter continued his practice of holding regular office hours, but, unlike most professors who made little effort to make students feel welcome, Schumpeter went out of his way to encourage students to come and talk, often handing out a slip of paper in class for them to sign up for reserved times during his consultation afternoons. Hardly a graduate student in economics got through Harvard without at least some personal contact with Schumpeter. He awed many of these students. With his strong Austrian accent and aristocratic mannerisms, he seemed foreign to most of them, but his obvious interest in students nevertheless attracted them.

While many students were drawn to his unusual behavior, some of his colleagues were put off. Schumpeter's actions during oral examinations, for example, sometimes led to controversy when he would interrupt a student's answer to ask the questioner, a fellow faculty member, what he meant and then proceed to examine the professor. He seemed to take pleasure in riling his colleagues, just for fun. Edwin Frickey, who taught statistics, refused to sit on examinations with Schumpeter because he did not want to face such an interrogation.[9] Others served with him reluctantly. Still, Schumpeter socialized with those colleagues he liked and respected and was welcome company to many. He frequently had dinner with the Leontiefs, the Masons, the Sorokins, the Ushers, the Carl Snyders, the Robert Blakes, Crane Brinton (the last two of the History Department), and many others. In May 1934, he went to East Rindge, New Hampshire, for a weekend at the Seymour Harris's, who had their summer home there. Despite many social invitations during the academic year, Schumpeter lived almost exclusively a scholastic life, devoting most of his time to study, discussion, and writing about economics. In Cambridge, he lived largely in a man's world since women graduate students and instructors at Harvard were few and most of them too immature for Schumpeter, now fifty. But, with the women faculty and graduate students at Radcliffe, Schumpeter occasionally sought female companionship, though such social outings infrequently impinged on what seems to have been a solitary intellectual life dedicated to his own work and the development of his students.

4

Another break in this routine came in the summer of 1934. Schumpeter once again travelled to Europe to study French cathedrals. Sailing for

England on 10 June, he went immediately to the London School of Economics, always his first stop in England, to find that he had arrived on the day of the annual outing of the economics professors and graduate students. Lionel Robbins later reminisced about the excursion:

> The last time I saw Schumpeter was on a river picnic in the middle thirties. He had turned up unexpectedly from the United States on the day of our annual seminar outing at the [London] School [of Economics]; and he was immediately co-opted as an honorary member, so to speak, and pressed into joining the excursion. It was a lovely day in June; and, as we glided down the Thames between Twickenham and Datchet, I can still see him, cheerily esconced in the prow of our ship, surrounded by the eager spirits of the day, Nicky [now Lord] Kaldor, Abba Lerner, Victor Edelberg, Ursula Hicks—Webb, as she then was, the master-organizer of the party—the four fingers and thumb of each hand pressed against those of the other, discoursing with urbanity and wit on theorems and personalities.[10]

Schumpeter then visited other friends in London, Cambridge, and Oxford, and took a holiday to see Winchester, Salisbury, and Wellington Hill.

A few days later, Schumpeter crossed the Channel and spent some time in Ostende, Belgium, then went on to Beauvois, Paris, Nice, and other cities in France. Mia met him early in the trip for an auto tour of the French countryside in a rented car with her behind the wheel.[11] She returned to Bonn while Schumpeter remained in France and then journeyed to Italy. At the end of July, he picked Mia up in Bonn so they could spend much of August in a German spa where they swam, played tennis, took outings, and had a glorious time. But all was not vacation for Schumpeter on this trip. A former Bonn student, Herbert Zassenhaus, visited them at the spa and listened to Schumpeter relate his troubles with his research in their long talks that lasted well into the night.[12]

In the spring of 1934, Schumpeter had a great deal of difficulty with the cycles book, on which he worked intermittently along with the money book. In the cycles book, he desperately wanted to state and analyze mathematically his development theory, which includes cycles, and to test it statistically as a formal model, but he had thus far failed. After his discussions with Zassenhaus and some serious thinking, he decided to recast his research program, putting aside the money book, intractable so far, for the time being in order to concentrate all his effort on cycles. In his diary, he recorded his plans to complete the cycles book in mid-1935, then return to the money book, which he hoped to finish in another year. That schedule would make him ready to begin work on a major study of economic theory in mid-1936. The depression that afflicted the industrial countries in part impelled the decision. He also wanted to get back to his theory of economic development, which underlaid his ideas on business cycles. But his failure with the money book was also part of the reason. With this decision made, Schumpeter returned to Harvard for another hectic academic year.

5

In the fall of 1934, Schumpeter once again taught the mathematical treatment of economics, though this was his last effort to teach that course since Wassily Leontief took it over the next year. Schumpeter also offered his advanced course in economic theory and another in business cycles. Three classes was a heavier teaching load than usual for Harvard professors, but throughout his career Schumpeter frequently taught three courses each semester. As the principal teacher of economic theory, he played a key role in the education of nearly every economics Ph.D. at Harvard during the 1930s, and he frequently chaired doctoral candidates' general examinations. Yet Schumpeter directed only a small number of doctoral dissertations; rarely did anyone write in economic theory, since students considered it the most difficult thesis field for making an original contribution to knowledge. In 1934-35, one student, Arthur Smithies, wrote on the theory of production, and several, especially those working in cycles and money, had Schumpeter on their committees and consulted him.

Teaching was still not so time and energy consuming that it slowed down Schumpeter's round of talks or his consultations. Before the end of 1934, he talked to at least eight groups, and in the spring term at least six more, including a series of lectures, all listed in his diary. Schumpeter regarded his speech-making as an essential and thoroughly enjoyable part of his work. Preparing each talk separately, he had no canned or regular speeches. As always, he spoke without notes, although he had prepared them in detail and studied them carefully prior to speaking. The word "Annie" or "Annerl" headed most sets of these prepared, and then ignored, notes. His subjects ranged over a wide spectrum, from narrow technical issues to broad topics beyond the scope of economics. His speech-making facility bespeaks a man with great confidence in his vast knowledge and no doubts about what he thought, but his notes show that he continued to depend on the *Hasen*.

During the 1934-35 academic year, the Harvard University Press published Redvers Opie's translation of *Die Theorie der wirtschaftlichen Entwicklung* as *The Theory of Economic Development*. Its ideas were already well known to U.S. economists through the English articles that had discussed Schumpeter's ideas. But English-speaking scholars up to this time had lacked the opportunity to sample his personal style before. Now, because Schumpeter had a strong hand in the translation, making the book a sort of revised fourth edition of the earlier *Entwicklung*, Americans got a good look at his writing. Since the original book had been published many years earlier, many journals did not review it, but those that did reviewed it favorably.

R. S. Howey, in the *American Economic Review*, said that it was "worth reading in English ... a notable work of a contemporary Continental economist who gives a brilliant and unconventional picture of the economic process.... The translation ... preserves the author's lively style of exposition." In *Social Research*, Hans Neisser wrote "The main significance of Schumpeter's famous book ... is to be found ... in the close analysis of a concept that is fundamental for all good economic theory, namely the concept of *homo aeconomicus*." Alvin Hansen of the University of Minnesota, later of Harvard, wrote in the *Journal of Political Economy* that

> nowhere else does one find so penetrating a treatment as here of the significant characteristics of the process of development, of economic dynamics, in contrast with the "circular flow" of an essentially static society.... What is quite impossible to convey is the vivid imagination with which the "vision" is conceived, and the dramatic marshaling of ideas which give the book a quality all its own.[13]

Even though Schumpeter had abandoned work on the money book, Harvard University Press advertised it as forthcoming. Meanwhile, his work on cycles went slowly. With his writing on these two projects having consumed so much of his time, his published output in 1934 was quite limited, and most of his 1933-34 research and writing would not appear for many years. He did write an article entitled "The Analysis of Economic Change" for the one of the Harvard economic journals.[14] A popular book of readings on business cycles later included Schumpeter's article as chapter 1, part 1.[15] Although presenting no ideas he had not already introduced, he painted the entire process of economic development, business cycles, and evolutionary change, in just a few pages.

6

Once in a while, when the mind tires of pounding away on the same subject, a researcher will seek refuge in writing of a different nature. So it was with Schumpeter, who several times tried his hand at writing novels. Usually such attempts did not go beyond scribbling a few sentences or a paragraph in his diary, but his papers preserve more extensive notes for one projected novel that he entitled *Ships in the Fog*. Some notes are in English, but much of it also is in shorthand. The manuscript, in longhand, runs as follows:

> Now backgrounds, racial and social, are essential in order to understand what a man is.

Well he—let us call him Henry—was an Englishman by birth. But by race only on his mother's side. His father, before he acquired English citizenship called himself an Italian.... The family belonged to the fringe end of the commercial and financial set of Trieste which racially was a mixture defying analysis. Greek, German, Serb, and Italian elements and presumably all of them contributed towards making our hero's paternal ancestry. His father had emigrated to England as a representative of Triestan shipping interests and married an English girl with a great pedigree and absolutely no money.

Their only child was four years old, when, well on the way to a considerable financial position, the father was killed on the hunting field. And the mother was henceforth the one great human factor in Henry's life. She was an excellent woman, strong and kind and amply provided with the delightful blinders of English society.... To make him an English gentleman was her one aim in life.

She had not much money ... but she had connections which she resolutely exploited for her darling—that was among other reasons why to her dying day he belonged to one of the four or five best clubs ... though, at the time of this story, he had ceased to frequent them and the corresponding county houses. But I want to make this quite clear—the social world was open to him from the beginning and shut only when he did not trouble to go and that meant much. No complexes. No faked contempt. No hidden wistfulness.

Where was he at home? Not really in England! Often he had thought so but ancestral past had asserted itself each time. But neither in France or Italy though he found himself drifting to both whenever he had a week or a month. Certainly not in Germany or what had been the Austro-Hungarian Empire.

But that was not the salient point. More important than country means class—but he did not with subconscious allegiance belong either to society or the business class or the professions or the trade union world, all of which provided such comfortable homes for everyone he knew. Yes—his mother's corner of society had been his as long as she lived.

And for modern man his work is everything—all that is left in many cases.... Doing efficient work without aim, without hope.

No family. No real friends. No woman in whose womanhood to anchor.[16]

From this and the scattered notes, it is impossible to determine the precise plot and development of the story. We can tell that Henry's mother wanted him to become a politician and that Henry seems to have some success until he discovers he cannot pursue that career. For several years, he is undecided about his future, but he finally goes to the United States to enter business. His purpose in entering business is not necessarily to make money but rather to wrestle with its intellectual problems. At one point in the notes, Henry tells his assistant to buy up a business. When the assistant points out that Henry has scant respect for its directors, he replies, "How good must be a business that can stand such directors?" What role the heroine plays, the later influence of the mother, and how the story ends are not delineated in Schumpeter's notes.

The autobiographical echoes are clear. The importance of the mother and mother love, the father's death at the same age as that of Schumpeter's father, the confusion about racial and social background, about which Schumpeter knew but little in his own case, the interest in and then abandonment of politics, the move to the United States, the remark about work, the interest in a subject for its intellectual content, the acceptance of class—all these resonate in Schumpeter's own life. Noteworthy also are omitted parts of his real life. Since this was to be a novel (public property), he could say nothing of the tragic deaths of his loved ones and his resulting obsession. Great romantic love, denied by death, is missing from his novel, as is religion, private or public. The story of Henry tells only a part of what Schumpeter would have us believe of him, even in the disguise of a novel. He worked no more than one working session—several hours—on this novel. The notes, kept in one neat clump, tail off into shorthand for later writing in English, but Schumpeter abandoned *Ships in the Fog*. On several later occasions, he tried his hand at fiction again, showing his interest in the idea that he had something to say through stories.

7

When summer vacation came in 1935, Schumpeter was off again for Europe, first to England, then the Continent, where he had his fill of French cathedrals, and ending up in Bonn and Juelich with Mia. But things seemed different to him on the 1935 visit. The new German Luftwaffe and the Italian war against Abyssinia demonstrated signs of violence and the threat of more to come. Hitler had promoted a blood bath in Germany in 1934, ordering the assassination of many of his opponents. The Nazis in 1934 had slain the Austrian Chancellor Engelbert Dollfuss and met with his successor, Kurt von Schuschnigg. Schumpeter, always opposed to Austro-German *Anschluss*, now feared the worst, not believing that Hitler would keep his word to continue to recognize the sovereignty of Austria. He was right. Germany absorbed Austria in 1938.

In a plebiscite, Hitler became the Fuhrer of the German Reich, proving his popular support. Schumpeter was by this time less concerned about Hitler's 1935 repudiation of the Treaty of Versailles and his taking back of the Saarland than he was about the growing threat of the Soviet Union, which

Schumpeter believed only Germany could hold in check. He applauded German conscription and the rebuilding of the *Wehrmacht* (the armed forces) as signs of rebuilding the country's strength. At the same time, Schumpeter became well aware that Europe was becoming a less desirable place to live or even visit.[17] The flood of intellectual migrants from Europe to the United States had perhaps suggested that he may have just completed his last trip to Europe when he boarded the *SS Scythia* in Liverpool on 14 September 1935. The lights of Germany were beginning to dim, perceptible even to one like Schumpeter who sought to justify Germany's actions.

Another change was in Mia. Neither she nor Schumpeter had deluded themselves about marriage. Although they had discussed it many times, it was not to be since Schumpeter had simply decided it would not work, despite his fondness for Mia and the temptation to marry her. He based his decision only partly on his continuing devotion to his second wife; in large measure, he did not regard Mia as a suitable mate. She was demanding of his time and energy and made no positive contribution to his intellectual life. At this point, Schumpeter measured everything by its effect upon his work, and he did not believe Mia would fit into his Cambridge routine.[18]

Increasingly restive with a one-month-in-twelve fling with an aging lover who lived an ocean away, Mia would gladly have followed Schumpeter to Cambridge, either as wife or mistress. She had turned down many opportunities to marry, but in the summer of 1935 she was not so sure her decision had been correct. Schumpeter urged her to marry, knowing that nothing would come from their annual visits. After another summer passed, a summer when he did not go to Europe, Mia decided to marry. But she and Schumpeter remained friends and corresponded regularly all through the rest of the 1930s. Finally, the war cut off communications.[19]

By the mid-1930s, one aspect of Schumpeter's troubled European life came under control. Before moving to the United States, he had paid some of his principal obligations, but other debts lingered. By 1935, he had paid them all, with the exception of one debt of 100,000 schillings (about $15,000 today), written off by the authorities when the Biedermann Bank collapsed. The lifting of the burden of debt was a great relief to Schumpeter, although in his years in the United States it had preoccupied him but little. His salary at Harvard reassured him that he could pay the debt in due course. When he had paid the last of it, he breathed a sigh of relief and turned his back on the entire unpleasant episode.[20] He didn't know it at the time but, in a way, he was turning his back on Europe.

Notes

1   Some of this chapter is based on the diary material in the Schumpeter papers in the Harvard University Archives. Schumpeter kept a separate diary for his summer trips. The entries began with the date and place, and he frequently recorded with whom he talked and what he did. His summer diary was often more detailed than at other times because he was travelling and staying in hotels with time for writing. Some of the diary, however, is not written in notebooks but rather on scraps of paper, sometimes hotel stationery, and notepads. In the Schumpeter papers in the Harvard University Archives, these papers are often disorganized and in disarray.

2   He expressed these preferences and his ideas about painters and their subjects often in great detail in his diary.

3   Wassily Leontief and Edward Mason told me of Schumpeter's teaching of mathematical economics. Schumpeter readily admitted that he was not at his best in teaching mathematical economics, but he thought that the subject was so important that it was better that he teach it than not to have it taught.

4   These comments are based on conversations with people who participated in these events.

5   Harris's introduction to Seymour Harris, ed., *Joseph Schumpeter, Social Scientist*.

6   These remarks are a composite of what was told to me by John Kenneth Galbraith, Edward Mason, Wassily Leontief, and others.

7   Schumpeter served on department committees and was an active participant in the meetings of the department, but he had no interest in college or university matters.

8   Some of Schumpeter's most scathing remarks in his diary are aimed at faculty members who neglected their scholarly duties, and at the educational establishment, including Harvard, for not taking science and scholarship more seriously.

9   Joseph McKenna, who was his assistant, told me of Frickey's refusal and his antipathy to Schumpeter.

10   *Quarterly Journal of Economics* 69 (1955): 1-22.

11   The Schumpeter papers in the Harvard University Archives include a score of photographs of Schumpeter, Mia, and the car they rented for touring France. Mia drove, since Schumpeter did not know how.

12   Herbert Zassenhaus, a former official of the International Monetary Fund and former Schumpeter student told me of this visit with Schumpeter in Europe.

13   The Neisser review appears in *Social Research* and the Hansen review in the *Journal of Political Economy*.

14   *Review of Economic Statistics* 17 (May 1935): 2-10.

15   Gottfried Haherler, *Readings in Business Cycle Theory* (Philadelphia: Irwin and the American Economic Association, 1944).

16   The manuscript is on scraps of paper in the Schumpeter papers in the Harvard University Archives. It is not a part of the diary and is written on yellow pad paper. The exact date of the manuscript is not known, but probably about 1934.

17   There are many entries in the early 1930s about Germany and other European matters.

18   While Schumpeter was considering the move to Harvard, the wives of Harvard

faculty let it be known that a Harvard professor should not have a mistress, even if he were not married. The professors told Schumpeter that if he wanted to bring Mia to Cambridge, he should marry her.

19   This correspondence is in the Schumpeter papers in the Harvard University Archives.

20   In his diary after he came to America, Schumpeter did not often mention his financial condition, indicating that much of the pressure was off. When all his indebtedness was finally paid in 1935, there is an exultant remark of relief, and thereafter no mention of the debt problem and indeed little mention of financial matters.

2

Research and Romance (1935-1936)

By 1935, Schumpeter was an old hand at Harvard, seen frequently in the Yard on his way between the Taussig home and the department in Holyoke House on Massachusetts Avenue, in the Yard, and at Dunster House. The depression dampened his spirits, but for Schumpeter it made the study of the economy all the more interesting. Why was the economy behaving in this way? What causes cycles and depressions? Always, for Schumpeter, the question was why? For many economists, the question was not why but rather what to do? "Why" was of academic interest; "what to do" was a burning public policy issue.

Across the Atlantic, an English economist, the best-known economist in the world at the time—John Maynard Keynes—thought that he knew what to do and that, by knowing that, knew also why the economy was in the fix. He wrote *The General Theory of Employment Interest and Money*, published at the end of 1935, that told economists that the economy could not generate enough private investment to use up the savings of people. Solution: People should save less and the government should invest (spend) more, especially by borrowing. He dressed up his policy with theoretical justifications, initiating what economists call the Keynesian Revolution—a change in the way economists, as well as other people, think about the economy.

Schumpeter disagreed with Keynes's proposed policy and rejected Keynes's theoretical justification, taking particular offense at his starting with policy and then developing a theory to support the policy. Schumpeter stood with the old guard.

17

Schumpeter's personal life was becoming more interesting. After three summers in Europe, it became clear that nothing would come of his affair with Mia. On this side of the Atlantic, Schumpeter had some girlfriends, especially a young lady who was working on her doctorate in economics in Cambridge. After attending seminars together and working together on research projects, the occasional date blossomed into a romance and an affair. Marriage was still down the road, but the object of his affections—Elizabeth Boody Firuski, a divorcee—had already decided that Schumpeter was her man.

1

By the fall of 1935, on the eve of the publication of *The General Theory of Employment Interest and Money* by John Maynard Keynes, economists continued to struggle to understand the depression still devastating the country. The start of the depression in 1929 didn't surprise Schumpeter because his analysis had led him to expect the economy's ups and downs. But the depth and length of the Great Depression did take him, and all other economists, by surprise. According to the analysis accepted by most economists, the depression should have been over and the economy fully recovered long before 1935. But the economic doldrums continued despite the government's frantic efforts. The economy's failure to bounce back in a short time did not conform to accepted analysis and prevailing economic theories, including those of Schumpeter.

With accepted analysis offering no clues, economists could only speculate on the reasons for continued hard times. In the decade following 1929, economists indulged in a great deal of theoretical speculation, as many spun new theories in search of an explanation for a new phenomenon. But an explanation remained elusive since most economic theory in 1935 did not deal with the problems of the economy as a whole or the level of production and income. Macroeconomics, the study of the economy's operation in its entirety—that is, the behavior of aggregate magnitudes, such as national product and income, consumption, savings, and investment—did not even exist, nor did statistical measures of most of these aspects of the economy. No economist had yet proposed a theory that showed how the economy's operation determined the level of real production and income. Indeed, most economic theory dealt with the behavior of individual consumers and producers, how particular markets were organized and behaved, the analysis of prices and costs of a product, as well as the allocation of resources and the distribution of goods. The economist usually extracted just a few elements from the whole complex economy and examined them while assuming that everything else remained constant. A typical analysis examined price, the quantities consumers wanted to buy, and the quantities producers wanted to sell. This analysis assumed that preferences, expectations, other prices, production methods, income, and, indeed, everything else, stayed the same.[1]

General-equilibrium analysis, in which everything—prices and production, as well as other variables—was free to change, was for the most part mathematical. Because of their innocence of mathematical analysis, economists had drawn but few implications about how the economy as a whole functioned from general analysis. Only the simplicity of Say's Law, dating back to the classical economists, bridged the gap between individual prices and quantities and the aggregate economy of all prices and all production and income. Jean Baptiste Say, basing his work on that of Adam Smith, had argued early in the eighteenth century that producers, as they made goods of a given value, hired the services of the factors of production—labor, resources, capital, and management—and paid them an amount having the same value. The incomes earned by workers, resource owners, capitalists, and managers—incomes paid by enterprises making goods—were therefore exactly the right amount to buy all the goods they produced—no more, no less.

The cliche, "Supply creates its own demand," summarized the proposition that consumers, as owners of productive factors, earn precisely the amount of income needed to buy the products that they produce. Say's Law is a theorem, a true statement about a theoretical economy in equilibrium, and does not necessarily apply in a real economy away from equilibrium. Economists often forgot this, believing that Say's Law necessarily prevailed in the real economy.

When all markets and all consumers and producers are in equilibrium, no general glut is possible. The ever-active equilibrium forces—Schumpeter and other economists of the neoclassical orthodoxy believed—inexorably returned the real economy to equilibrium, as in the theoretical model. The adjustments of prices, including wages, and quantities in all markets would therefore prevent a prolonged depression, just as changes in interest rates would necessarily bring a balance between savings and investment. Schumpeter, along with others, assumed that the real economy, although seldom in an equilibrium position, constantly struggled toward it, as the general-equilibrium theory suggested. If the forces of equilibrium were always moving the economy toward equilibrium, a condition which Say's Law postulated, then depression could disable the economy only temporarily. Imagine the doll of yesteryears that had a rounded bottom with a heavy weight in the bottom's center. If the doll is tipped over on its side and then released, it will come erect again. It can be tossed about and kicked around the room, but when external force is removed, it always come upright. That was how most economists thought the economy operated.[2]

2

Schumpeter's mid-1934 research plan had called for the completion of the cycles book, which would explain the depression, by 15 June 1935. His optimistic estimate reflected the length of time necessary to complete his books and articles before and during the First World War, in his "sacred decade." But, by mid-1935, the book was far from finished. The writing of the book's analytical first part had gone well enough, since he wrote only a slight modification of the theoretical work that he had done more than two decades earlier. In the earlier work, he had dealt extensively with the development process, while this new book elaborated particularly on the cycles part of the theory. Despite great effort, he had been unable to make a significant improvement in the theory, nor had he succeeded in putting it in mathematical form.

Schumpeter's purpose in the book, in addition to improving the theory, was to test his theory, to verify or prove it wrong. But a deep methodological chasm separated his scientific stance and the problem of testing his theory. Since he had an historical-evolutionary theory, not a determinate one, he had no satisfactory formal statistical test. Schumpeter finally tried to solve the problem by confronting his evolutionary theory with historical developments over a long period of time. If the detailed course of history did not conform to the way the theory said history should develop, then a prima facie case existed for denial of the theory. If history and the theory's predictions seemed to conform, then he reasoned that the theory could and might be correct. The best this procedure can do is indicate whether a presumptive case for denial or acceptance of the theory exists, but Schumpeter realized that in this sort of test an analyst could selectively use facts and thus distort the results.

The review of history over a long span, and its comparison with how the economy would function in theory, required a great deal of time and effort, not only because Schumpeter was a fastidious scholar but also because he wanted to avoid the charge that he had rigged the case. Still, he was in a hurry, hoping to complete his book in a short time. Unfortunately, his research on the history of cycles extended far beyond what he had originally intended. Although his optimism and wishful thinking sometimes led him to expect an early completion, in the fall of 1935 more than three years' work remained.[3]

His research in the fall and winter of 1935 and into 1936 addressed economic theory and its testing, not economic policy. Schumpeter had views about where depressions came from and why the present depression was so severe and had lasted so long, but his analysis sought theoretical explanations, not a remedy. Although he refused to include his policy sentiments in the book, he was telling his friends that he thought that irresponsible and often speculative borrowing, condoned by the banking system, helped account for the depression. Also arguing that monetary mismanagement and government attacks on business partly explained the continued hard times, he felt that government should avoid measures that would interfere with the economy's natural restorative powers. With ad hoc remedies for restoring prosperity, he favored government emergency policies and government cooperation with business. Unlike many economists, he also urged massive government emergency spending, a shot in the arm to stimulate enterprises.[4] But after this one-time remedy and for the long haul, Schumpeter, along with other economists, parroted the promise of Say's Law that, in equilibrium, when recovery arrived, the harmful effects of the depression would vanish. But these matters found no voice in the book he was writing.[5]

3

The General Theory of Employment Interest and Money by John Maynard Keynes arrived at Harvard from England in the fall of 1935, even before the book was formally published.[6] Several years in the making, the book had aroused much excitement and anticipation among most of the leading economists, who already knew it would be an important book. Bits and pieces of Keynes's thinking were known through his conversations with visitors, and the articles that he used in his work from the *Economic Journal*, which he edited—notably Kahn's work—provided further hints. As early as 1933, Keynes wrote a letter to President Roosevelt and to the *London Times* that contained many of his conclusions, but not his reasoning or analysis. In the fall of 1935, a graduate student, Robert B. Bryce of Canada, arrived at Harvard with manuscript and notes from the other Cambridge. Because he had been in Keynes's seminar, Bryce's comments were eagerly sought by professors and students alike. Schumpeter presided over one meeting at Winthrop House during which Bryce explained Keynesian theory, and he was in the thick of the discussion at Harvard regarding the new analysis.[7]

Keynes boasted that his new book would revolutionize economics. Writing to George Bernard Shaw on New Year's Day 1935, he asserted, "I believe myself to be writing a book on economic theory which will largely revolutionize—not, I suppose, at once but in the course of the next ten years—the way the world thinks about economic problems."[8] When the book came out, his intention to turn economics on its head was obvious. As Gottfried Haberler would say in 1947 when memorializing Keynes, he "stirred the stale economic frog pond to its depth."[9]

Keynes, the leading British and best-known economist in the world in the 1930s, pondered the English depression that had begun in the 1920s, earlier than the one in the United States. He had written extensively on the economy's behavior, and contributed significantly to the money-price theory, when he wrote *The Treatise on Money* (1930). Still not satisfied, he wanted to develop a theory that would explain the worldwide depression, and he especially hoped to convince the world that his remedy for the depression assaulting Great Britain—enlarged government spending—was correct.

The depression called for a response from government, and Keynes felt his proposed policy needed a justification from economics. The old economics did not provide the justification for what political leaders and the populace had already decided upon as the depression's remedy—government spending. Thus, in the race for a new economics that would justify this intervention, Keynes won. With the assistance of able British economists such as R. F. Kahn (now Lord Kahn), the theory presented in his book, nicknamed *The General Theory*, became the most influential work in economics since Adam Smith's *Wealth of Nations*.

Rejecting the business-cycle approach and the money-price theory, Keynes concentrated on income, which is the other side of the production coin. Changes in income and production, he argued, depend upon decisions about savings and investment, which are separate and independent acts undertaken by different groups for different reasons. By investors, Keynes meant those responsible for decisions about real capital formation, and by investment he meant building something real. If investors want to invest a greater amount than savers want to save, then investors will add to and therefore enlarge the income stream more than savers in withdrawing from it reduce the stream. Savers behave passively, saving (not spending) an amount that depends on how large their income is. Out of a larger income, people want to save more, bringing savings and investment closer to equality. Income increases under the impact of larger investment until the amount that people want to save equals the amount that investors want to invest, and eventually savings and investment become equal. Always expecting profits, investors act independently of savers, as they borrow from banks, which can create money or use accumulated savings. Regardless of motives, savers save simply what they do not consume.

Keynes argued that, although savings and investment were independent decisions, the income of the economy rises or falls so that the amount saved and the amount invested become equal. In the new Keynesian system, production and income—not prices, as in the older orthodoxy—are the equilibrating parts of the economy. In the older theory of the relation of money to prices, which Keynes had earlier contributed to but railed against now, aspects of the economy other than income and production made the adjustment. To Schumpeter and many others, prices, wage rates, and interest rates changed, altering the decisions of consumers to save and investors to invest. To Keynes, prices, wage rates, and interest rates do not decline in a depression, or at least not enough to perform their equilibrating function. Rather, people stop buying, firms restrict production and lay off workers, and people just hold more money with no effect on interest. Keynes, in his new theory, said that the mechanisms of interest rates, prices, and wages—Say's Law—simply did not work, and he assumed that prices, wages, and interest remained constant. Therefore, the adjustment restoring equilibrium to the economy was income instead of prices.[10]

If people persistently want to save more than investors want to invest, then income, and with it savings, must fall until income reaches a level at which investment and savings are equal. This income is an equilibrium level of income and production, which, in the absence of changes in savings and investment decisions, will persist. Each amount of income and production is associated with a specific amount of employment and unemployment. The economy links income, production, employment, and unemployment together, and only one level of income implies full employment; lower levels of income and production imply involuntary unemployment, even though they may be equilibrium levels at which savings and investment are equal. According to Keynes, no mechanism in the economy assures an income at which full employment prevails in the economy, even though income may be in equilibrium. If the economy is in equilibrium at a full-employment income and, for some reason, investors decide not to invest, then income will fall to a lower equilibrium income, giving rise to chronic unemployment that will persist if investment does not recover. Keynes believed this had happened in Britain and the United States: Investment had collapsed, but the propensity to save remained strong. The lower equilibrium income implied large-scale unemployment that would not go away until investment increased or people decided to save less.

This analysis gave Keynes the remedy for persistent depression, which he called an underemployment equilibrium. If private investors will not invest, then the government must do so. The government can make up for the lack of private investment by spending—creating an enlarged income stream—without taking money out of the income stream through taxation. In other words, it can and must run deficits in its operations to restore full employment. The government could increase income somewhat just by spending and then taxing an equivalent amount, since the government would spend all the revenue taken from people who, in the absence of the tax, would spend part and save part of it. But, since balanced-budget spending adds only modestly to income, the restoration and maintenance of full employment in a chronic depression requires large deficits to match the deficiency in private investment.

These few paragraphs hardly do justice to Keynes's contribution. His theory is more complex, more subtle, and more sophisticated, full of insights into how the economy operates and suggestions for measures to improve its performance. In essence, this theory shifted emphasis away from money and prices to income, savings, and investment, as Keynes argued that the equilibrium mechanism that economists believed would insure a full-employment income—prices and the market mechanism—did not work. Neither goods markets nor financial markets functioned, according to Keynes, to bring about a full-employment equilibrium. His theory justified—nay, mandated—government intervention by spending and running deficits. Keynes even proposed, in the last chapter of *The General Theory*, that the government assume responsibility for, or socialize, investment. Although such an extreme position seemed heretical to economists and businessmen in the 1930s, the people and their leaders did come to regard the economy as the government's responsibility.[11]

4

In early 1936, economists all over the world were studying *The General Theory*, either trying to adjust to a new way of thinking or resisting it. *The Journal of the American Statistical Association* asked Schumpeter to write a review of the book, a task made more difficult by the turgid and obscure writing that resulted from both Keynes's stranglehold on his publisher and his incomplete understanding of his own theory. Keynes also placed his reviewers under a heavy psychological burden by strongly attacking those who held what he called the prevailing "classical" views in economics and did not drop them instantly in favor of his new views. Charging all previous economic theory with backwardness, Keynes stated that economists were living in scientific sin with wrong-headed policy prescriptions.

Most of the reviews were negative, even those by many later proponents of Keynesian analysis and policy, for the simple reason that the new theory veered sharply from then current thinking of economists. On first encounter, his ideas repelled most of them, but later reflection and gradually getting used to his ideas produced a more favorable response. For example, Alvin Hansen, Schumpeter's colleague at Harvard, wrote an unfavorable review but later became the chief proponent of Keynesian analysis in the United States.

Schumpeter's review was the strongest and most critical evaluation of another economist's work that he ever wrote. And unlike some reviewers, he never changed his mind. If anything, as time passed, he regarded Keynes's work in an increasingly unfavorable light. Too imbued with the general-equilibrium model, where price and quantity adjustments do take place, Schumpeter saw no merit in making the strong opposite assumptions that Keynes did. Keynes had assumed that the economy's equilibrium forces did not work. At issue partly were questions of fact, not theory. During the 1930s, a time of sticky prices and rigid wages, the facts often seemed to support Keynes, but not completely, not in all sectors, and not at all times. Schumpeter didn't believe that the occasional and partial failure of price adjustments to respond over a short period of time justified the assumption that prices always remained constant.

Recognizing the book as a bold stroke and the work of genius, Schumpeter still objected strongly to its attack upon savings. Keynes held that, if people only spent more and saved less, the government would not find it necessary to spend for them. Schumpeter felt that Keynes could have attacked capitalism's inadequacies in adjusting properly and have made suggestions to improve its performance in ways other than by attacking savings, which Schumpeter saw as the key to capitalist progress. To Keynes, the culprit in the capitalist system as it existed in the 1930s was savings. People saved too much—more than investors wished to invest. Put another way, people didn't consume enough. According to Keynes, capitalism could not generate enough investment to keep the economy fully employed unless people consumed more and saved less. To redress this savings surplus, someone has to find outlets for the excess savings, and that someone is the government. Therefore, inadequate investment and consumer spending give the government an excuse to spend. If people do not spend but save instead, then the government must offset that excess savings by spending more than it takes in.

Schumpeter also objected to Keynes's exclusive concentration on the short run, a period of time so brief that production relations do not change and innovations do not occur. He felt that Keynes's analysis did not consider a time period long enough for price adjustment processes to work, nor did it let entrepreneurs and their innovations play a role in the process. Schumpeter believed that innovations and consequent changes in the structure of production were the essence of the capitalist process, the cause of prosperity and depression, and the origin of economic progress. Keynes had assumed away all that Schumpeter deemed important. In addition, Schumpeter disagreed with Keynes's attempt to tie economic theory to policy. Regarding analysis as the proper work of the economist, Schumpeter relegated policy to the province of the politician. If the economist insists on recommending policy, he at the very least should identify the policy as dependent on political and other values in addition to economic theory. Feeling that Keynes was presenting his political views as analytical conclusions, Schumpeter wrote:

> Mr. Keynes underlines the significance of the words "General Theory" in his title. He professes to address it primarily to his fellow economists and seems to invite purely theoretical discussion. But ... everywhere he really pleads for a definite policy, and on every page the ghost of that policy looks over the shoulder of the

analyst, frames his assumptions, guides his pen. In this sense, it is Ricardo all over again.[12]

In his work on business cycles then underway, Schumpeter was keeping analysis and policy completely separate. His starting point was an effort to understand the economy, not to propose a remedy for its ills. Using a model more complex and subtle, his assumptions, he thought, were more realistic, as he refused to be drawn into the Ricardian trap of making assumptions that supported a predetermined policy position. The difficulty, only faintly recognized by Schumpeter, was that his theoretical position also implied a policy—a policy of not using government spending to influence the economy, or, as some would say, of doing nothing.

The extent of Schumpeter's contempt for Keynes's new theory is perhaps best seen in his 1936 letters to Oskar Lange, a promising young Polish economist and Rockefeller fellow. In answer to Lange's praise of Keynes, he wrote:

> The indulgence you show to Keynes as so many of our best people do is food for psycho-sociological thought.... There is no question in my mind about Keynes's vital personality although I do believe that he squanders the Marshallian inheritance both the analytical and moral part of it. What I find so difficult to understand is that obviously bad workmanship is so readily condoned by people who know what good workmanship is.[13]

Several months later, he wrote to Lange again, saying:

> The book could have been written a hundred years ago and skirts all real problems. It is the reverse of progressive ... it is the dying voice of the bourgeoisie calling out in the wilderness for prophets it does not dare fight for and shifts its ego to the real problems it does not face.[14]

6

While Keynes's new theory began to stir controversy in the fall of 1935, Schumpeter taught for the first time the basic graduate economic theory course, the course taught for so many years by Taussig. Marking the end of an era, the departure of Taussig initiated the age of Schumpeter in teaching theory. By this time, almost all the old hands—Bullock, Carver, Sprague, Ripley, Taussig—were gone. Only Gay remained, but he would be there only one more year.

Schumpeter tried at first to teach basic economic theory the way Taussig had taught it, using the Socratic method. But he soon abandoned this technique and reverted to the lecture method employed in his other courses, which included his advanced theory course, problems of economic theory, and business cycles and economic forecasting.

Another change, more honorific than substantial in Schumpeter's academic life, was his appointment on 1 September 1935, to the George F. Baker Professor of Economics, a chair he held for the rest of his tenure at Harvard. The chair initially paid Schumpeter $10,000 a year, the same that he had been earning.[15]

Outside the classroom, Schumpeter kept his informal seminars going and met frequently with the younger faculty and senior graduate students. To those young people, he made it clear that he took a personal interest in their problems, as he inquired about their difficulties and helped them. The Seven Wise Men also continued to meet occasionally. Paul Sweezy, Schumpeter's assistant, and Wolfgang Stolper, a graduate student who had also studied at Bonn, organized a birthday party with Schumpeter's favorite Moselle and Austrian wines. Schumpeter liked the idea and suggested they make it a monthly birthday party, remarking "All you have to do is supply the birthday and I will supply the wine." Sweezy and Stolper found a few more birthdays, and the practice continued for some months until other matters interfered.[16]

Schumpeter's mind did not permit him to work on only a single project for a protracted period, even though he realized that success for him—carrying a project to completion—came through concentration. In the fall of 1935, despite, or perhaps because of, his trouble with the cycles book, he began detailing his analysis of the fate of capitalism and the economics of socialism that he had worked on intermittently for two decades. When asked to address a U.S. Department of Agriculture seminar in January 1936, Schumpeter decided to speak on the topic "Can Capitalism Survive?" In this and another lecture, he answered, "No, it cannot." Capitalism would not survive because it succeeded too well, creating social and political conditions inimical to its continuation and hospitable to the introduction of socialism. These lectures elaborated on his 1928 article in the *Economic Journal*, which continued a line of thinking initiated in *Die Krise des Steuerstaates* in 1918.

In the mimeographed report of the lectures, Schumpeter said: "The reason, the deepest reason, why I think capitalism won't survive is the rationalizing effect the system has on our minds, the effect the system has of doing away with everything traditional."[17] To Schumpeter, the demise of capitalism had little to do with the Great Depression. Even without the depression, capitalism was foredoomed because of the social and political effects that its performance had on people generally and especially on the entrepreneur, whose stimulus was removed by capitalism's success. The thinking embodied in the Washington lectures provided the foundation for Schumpeter's most important generalizations about capitalism. After mulling over the present and future of capitalism for thirty years, bit by bit he had confirmed his conviction that capitalism was a historical phase that would pass, to be replaced by socialism. In the 1930s, all the mechanisms underlying his conclusion and its full implications were not yet worked out. Still in gestation, the full idea would not be born until the early 1940s in his *Capitalism, Socialism and Democracy.*

7

As his academic life settled into a comfortable routine, Schumpeter's personal life finally started to revive, and serious romance once again entered his world. Shortly after he had arrived in Cambridge, he met Elizabeth Firuski at an informal, extra-academic seminar that both attended. Now fifty, Schumpeter sought a certain maturity, as well as good looks, in women. His attraction to the beautiful, thirty-five-year-old Elizabeth, in the throes of divorcing her husband, is therefore not surprising. But for Joseph she was doubly appealing because, as an economist, she could understand him, his devotion to his work, and his need for concentration. His diary notations about EF and EBF began in 1933 and became numerous in 1934. Then, in 1935, the number of times he saw Elizabeth increased dramatically as they became better acquainted. After learning that she occasionally worked as a research assistant for Harvard professors, he hired her with the small grant he received from the university each year.[18]

As she helped with library work, book and article abstracts, and data compilation, Joseph's attention to Elizabeth increased gradually. At first, the occasional research assistant became the occasional date; the dinner and party date soon became the target for seduction. The seduction accomplished, they then settled into a pleasant routine of dating, at this point with no commitment by either. Initially star-struck with the attention of the mature Austrian economist, Elizabeth's interest in him soon became intensely personal and even partly maternal as their involvement increased. Joseph seemed so inept at so many things at which she was so proficient. She was a competent businesswoman and homemaker; he couldn't keep a checkbook or heat up a can of soup. Soon learning that her talents went considerably beyond her ability in bed and as a research assistant, he grew to depend upon her for many of the little things of living. In return, her admiration and respect for him grew into a deep love.

Born on 16 August 1898 in Lawrence, Massachusetts, Romaine Elizabeth Boody was the only daughter of Maurice and Swedish-born Hilda (Hokansen) Boody. She had two brothers, but both died before she did. Although her most intimate friends called her Lizzie, Joseph typically always called her Elizabeth. And she called him Joseph, despite the fact that many of his U.S. friends and colleagues called him Joe. After graduating summa cum laude (the first in economics) and Phi Beta Kappa from Radcliffe College in 1920, she went on to receive her master's degree from Radcliffe in 1925 and her Ph.D. in economics from Harvard (Radcliffe) in 1934.[19] She was an unusually bright as well as beautiful young lady—perhaps too bright for her own good. She found most Harvard students, even graduate students, dull, dumb, and immature. Although she had her share of college romances, no one really interested her because she preferred older men and someone she could not only respect but who needed her.

While studying for her M.A. degree at Radcliffe, she worked for the Harvard Economic Service from 1922 to 1925. In a seminar on the industrial revolution with Edwin F. Gay, she became interested in eighteenth-century English trade and decided to write her doctoral dissertation on that topic. Spending most of 1925 to 1927 in England on a Whitley Travelling Fellowship from Radcliffe, she first studied at the London School of Economics and then researched English foreign trade in the Public Records Office and the British Museum. After collecting the material needed for her dissertation, Elizabeth returned to the United States in 1927. She did not meet Schumpeter in either England or Massachusetts in 1927-30, although their paths crossed in both places. Still, any trained economist in those days would have at least heard of the Austrian economist.

In 1927-28, she taught economics at Vassar College and did odd jobs around Cambridge, where she became acquainted with the owner of a successful Harvard Square bookstore. In March 1929, she married Maurice Firuski, several years older than she. Something of a bibliophile when they first knew one another, Firuski later bought the Housatonic Book Shop in Salisbury, Connecticut, in the northwestern corner of the state. He also bought a home called Windy Hill in the nearby village of Taconic. Continuing to work toward her doctorate, Elizabeth did not abandon her academic interests when she married. She also practiced her avocation of growing things through a small nursery operated from her Taconic home. The Firuski marriage at first worked well, but broke down a few years later, the result of many problems, including the fact that Elizabeth was smarter and more mature than her husband. In isolated Taconic, she missed the intellectual stimulus of Cambridge and could not remain happy as the operator of a nursery and the wife of a small bookstore owner in northwestern Connecticut.

They were divorced in December 1933 after more than a year of separation. In the divorce settlement, she received the title to the Windy Hill home in Taconic on 8 August 1933. Although much of Elizabeth's time was spent in Cambridge, she kept the home. Her parents, not wealthy but well off, helped her financially while she completed her dissertation, *Trade Statistics and Cycles in England, 1698-1825*. In 1960, Clarendon Press, Oxford, finally published this work under the title *English Overseas Trade Statistics, 1698-1808*, with an introduction by T. S. Ashton and a memoir of Elizabeth by her friend, Dr. Elizabeth W. Gilboy of Cambridge. Elizabeth had worked with Dr. Gilboy, another Radcliffe economist and administrator of the Harvard Social Science Research Committee in the 1930s, on an article entitled "English Prices and Public Finance, 1660-1882" for the *Review of Economic Statistics*, a Harvard economics journal.[20] From 1935 to 1940, Elizabeth also held an appointment at the Bureau of International Research at Harvard. While there, she continued her work on eighteenth-century English trade and researched the industrialization of Japan and Manchukuo in a study sponsored by the Bureau.[21]

Attracted by the Cambridge intellectual milieu, Elizabeth was a Harvard hanger-on, one of the many who would never get a professorial appointment there but who stayed on in Cambridge despite everything. Harvard was not very broad-minded about hiring women, even the first-class professionals it had trained, yet she could obtain minor appointments and jobs as a research assistant sufficient to make Cambridge life possible. After her mother's 1935 death and her father's death three years later, Elizabeth received a modest fortune and had no fear of indigence. Although she had only modest professional jobs in the Harvard-Radcliffe community, she was well known in Cambridge and highly respected by Harvard's economists, all of whom she knew. On a small scale, she continued her horticultural business during these years at Cambridge. Her uncanny ability to grow things, attested to by the magnificently trimmed lawns and gardens of her Taconic home, provided her with part-time work after her divorce. Although her business made money, it more importantly filled a vital part of her life.

8

Having kept steady company for more than a year, Elizabeth decided in 1935 that she wanted to devote her life to Joseph Schumpeter, to take care of him, and to help him realize his goals.[22] She was one of those who are fulfilled by having someone depend upon them. As she learned of his idiosyncrasies and something of his secrets, she became convinced that he desperately needed her, whether he realized it or not. She was willing to do anything to make him happy, from sharing his bed to washing his socks. And she was astute enough to realize that, in addition to doing things for him, her greatest contribution was in leaving him alone. Of course, by 1935 neither of them were young lovers. He was a 5-foot, 8-inch bald man, whose 160-pound, slightly overweight body showed the beginning of a paunch. But he was still a man of immense charm who treated the ladies with great interest and affection. In 1935, Elizabeth became his protector, his helper, his cheering squad, and his mistress; and she made it clear that Joseph was her man. Any time he was invited to a party, she let it be known that she was to be invited also. The few times when that did not happen, she called up and raised hell with the host and hostess and their friends. By the spring of 1936, the two were regarded as a couple in Cambridge. Although she had announced her intention to marry him, Joseph had not made up his mind.

For Joseph, two factors favored the match. He was becoming increasingly restive in the Taussig household. To be sure, he had his freedom, but living in another man's home had disadvantages. Now accepted as a member of the Taussig family, he could not avoid regular conversations with the aging "Pa," whose powers were beginning to abandon him. Sometimes during these conversations, Taussig would lapse into unconsciousness. This upset Schumpeter a great deal, although Taussig's daughter, Dr. Helen Taussig, a well-known physician of Johns Hopkins University, assured him this was normal at her father's age. That consoled Schumpeter only slightly. He admired and respected Taussig greatly and felt a deep sense of gratitude toward him. Even though he wanted out, Schumpeter felt he could not just leave 2 Scott Street without a reason.[23] He remained, moreover, incapable of getting along on his own. He could try living in an apartment, but it would be a shambles in weeks. His small apartment at Dunster House proved unsuitable as living quarters. Who would take care of his clothes, his meals, the housekeeping? He could live in a hotel, but that would insult Taussig and be expensive and stultifying. Marriage to Elizabeth, on the other hand, would provide someone to take care of him and give him an honorable reason for leaving the Taussig home.

Another compelling reason for getting married was Taconic and Windy Hill. Joseph had fallen in love with Mrs. Firuski's home in the Connecticut Berkshires after his first visit there in 1933. In a hilly country setting—a part of the Berkshires—Windy Hill was large and comfortable, isolated and yet a part of the community, just what Joseph wanted.[24] In the extreme northwest corner of Connecticut, Taconic lies less than 120 miles from Boston, a manageable distance from Harvard. The nearest town, Salisbury, with its churches, stores, restaurants, and inns, provided the daily necessities of life. Taconic itself had no stores nor places of business, just some houses hidden here and there in the wooded and hilly terrain. A resident's home at the foot of Windy Hill served as the post office. Taconic, Salisbury, and Lakeville, another small town nearby, all on the fringes of the Berkshires, comprised a small back bedroom and weekend retreat mainly for people from New York City, which is closer to Taconic than is Boston. In the 1930s and 1940s, a rail line connected New Haven, Hartford, and New York City to Millertown, New York, just across the state line from Lakeville.

The house, called Windy Hill, rested close to the hilltop, reached by the winding Twin Lakes Road. On the right side, going up the hill but short of its crest, was a small frame house in which the caretaker of the estate lived, receiving the house and modest pay for his services. Alongside it, next to the road, was a small graveyard, belonging to the family of Loring Bartlett, who built the Windy Hill main house in 1812. On the other side of the road was the Windy Hill house. The brick front part of the house saw the addition, in the early twentieth century, of a frame structure in the rear that nearly doubled the house's size. A large garage quite apart from and behind the big house contained an upstairs apartment. An expansive yard and landscaped area also included, in Schumpeter's time, a tennis court. Elizabeth's skill as a gardener and landscape artist still shows throughout the estate's grounds. In the mid-1930s, only a few houses dotted the area surrounding the Twin Lakes, which are appropriately named. While the Schumpeters lived there, Elizabeth persuaded the local government to move the road so that the caretaker's house and graveyard were on the same side as the main house, which now sits back, almost invisible, from the road and is behind the caretaker's house.[25]

Beginning in 1935, Joseph became a regular visitor of Elizabeth's at Taconic. On long weekends, holidays, and vacations, he and Elizabeth motored down from Boston, Elizabeth driving her car. Sometimes mutual friends came along, including Schumpeter's graduate students, such as Wolfgang Stolper, Aaron Gordon, Peggy Shaughnessy (the future Mrs. Gordon), Phillip Chantler, a British Commonwealth Fellow, and many others. On these trips down to Taconic, Joseph usually brought along some work to pursue in the room Elizabeth assigned him as his study—formerly the front bedroom with the fireplace near the top of the stairs. He also enjoyed the large economics library that Elizabeth had collected and kept in the downstairs federal room and parlor at Windy Hill. Sometimes he played tennis with the other guests. Although Joseph never fully mastered the game, he played with vigor and enthusiasm. For relaxation, he also walked in the nearby woods and down the Between the Lakes Road until he reached the lakes, where he would sit for hours in the comfort of their stillness. On occasion, Joseph and Elizabeth would eat out at the White Hart Inn or some other Salisbury inn, or visit with Elizabeth's friends.

Notes

1   The standard textbook—for example, Paul Samuelson's *Economics*—distinguishes between partial and general equilibrium and different modes of analysis. Some of what is now studied in the beginning courses in economics

were, in the mid-1930s, a part of advanced economics, studied only in graduate schools.

2 Most economists believed that savers saved in order to invest and that financial markets brought savings and investment into equilibrium. This equilibrium system was denoted Say's Law, after Jean Baptiste Say, who was one of the first to make the observation. Great controversy has surrounded Say's Law for more than a century, most of it centering about whether or not it is an empirical observation, true (or nearly true) of the real-life economy, or a theoretical law true only of a model of the economy.

3 Repeatedly in his diary over the next several years he records his intent to finish the book by some future deadline, only to fail to complete the work by the time the deadline arrived.

4 Friends, such as Edward Mason, Wassily Leontief, and Gottfried Haberler, believed that Schumpeter's views were conservative and strongly anti-interventionist except as emergency measures. But colleagues remember that Schumpeter in those days proposed emergency spending in the billions of dollars, more than that proposed by other economists. But he was always careful to point out that these expenditures were one-time emergency projects.

5 He did voice these political views to his colleagues and some of his students. He was strongly opposed to the policies of the New Deal in efforts to "reform" capitalism. He favored even larger temporary and emergency measures than those pursued by the New Deal, but believed that after such temporary intervention the economy would recover and capitalism would need no "reform" that he feared might impair its functioning.

6 (New York: Harcourt, Brace and Co, 1936).

7 In conversation, John Kenneth Galbraith remembers the days when the new Keynesian ideas were hotly debated among students and faculty. Schumpeter was a part of those discussions, standing always with the old guard.

8 Charles Hession, *The Life of John Maynard Keynes* (New York: MacMillan, 1984).

9 See his essay in Seymour Harris, editor, *The New Economics: Keynes' Influence on Theory and Public Policy* (New York: A. A. Knopf, 1947).

10 Seymour Harris, editor, op. cit., produced the first major evaluation of Keynes's work. Today, every economics textbook uses and evaluates Keynesian analysis and policies.

11 Keynesian analysis was a part of a seachange that began during the depression and was still going strong after the second World War.

12 *Journal of the American Statistical Association* December 1936: 791-5.

13 This letter is in the correspondence file of the Schumpeter papers in the Harvard University Archives.

14 This letter is in the correspondence file of the Schumpeter papers in the Harvard University Archives.

15 Schumpeter's appointment to the Baker Chair and his income in this period are in correspondence in the Schumpeter papers of the Harvard University Archives.

16 Wolfgang Stolper told me this story.

17 A copy of the mimeographed report of the paper and the questions and answers of the Washington seminars are on file in the Schumpeter papers at the Harvard University Archives.

18 Some of the information about Elizabeth Firuski and her romance with

Schumpeter comes from conversations with colleagues of Schumpeter as well as his diary.

19 In her thesis, *English Overseas Trade Statistics, 1698-1808* (Oxford: Clarendon Press, 1934), T. S. Ashton in an edition published in 1960 wrote an introduction and Betty Gilboy a personal memoir that included much personal information. The information on Elizabeth comes from the Gilboy memoir, the documents in the Elizabeth Boody Schumpeter papers in the Radcliffe Library, and from conversations with friends.

20 *Review of Economics and Statistics* February 1938.

21 These and other details were given by Betty Gilboy and by documents in Elizabeth's papers at the Radcliffe Archives.

22 Although Elizabeth kept no diary, she made no secret of her attitude toward Schumpeter, telling all her friends and acquaintances, including Friedl Haberler, wife of Gottfried Haberler, about how serious she was in her romance with Schumpeter.

23 According to Edward Mason and others, Schumpeter felt greatly beholden to Frank Taussig for having made a home for him.

24 From the very first day that Schumpeter visited Taconic and Windy Hill, his diary is full of praise for his northwest Connecticut hideaway. He loved it in the summer, away from hot and miserable Cambridge, and even in the winter with its blanket of white. His favorite times were spring and fall, however, when temperate weather allowed him to be outside.

25 Windy Hill, the house and grounds, is still a beautiful estate, kept by the present owner, Mrs. LaVerne Baldwin, in the same condition that Elizabeth insisted upon. The road has been moved and there are now many more houses—mostly of them artfully concealed in the woods—than when Schumpeter visited Windy Hill.

3

Teaching and Marriage (1936-1937)

By 1936, Schumpeter had definitely turned his back on Europe and begun to build a permanent new life in the United States. The Schumpeter era had begun at Harvard when, that year, he became the senior theory teacher for graduate students. Gone at Harvard, and later across the country, was Socrates, as he had been replaced by the erudite Germanic scientific lecturer with a long reading list. However, his research did not go well. In the past, his research and writing had gone quickly; he could write a book in a year. Now, his scholarly instincts required more research, and the writing was painfully slow. The steady invasion of Keynesian ideas, especially among the brighter students, added bitterness to the snail's pace of his own work.

Occasional depression and despair often plagued his personal life. He became increasingly unhappy with his home life—living in a small apartment in the Taussig household. His courtship of Elizabeth Boody Firuski accelerated as she pressed him more and more to get married. Their love affair was a bit one-sided: Her love for him was total, but Schumpeter, still deeply committed to Annie, held back, fearful of making the move. Finally, in late summer, Schumpeter cancelled a planned visit to the Rockies, and he and Elizabeth went to New York to get married.

1

During his first few years in the United States, the depressions that had so plagued Schumpeter in Bonn had eased.[1] The new surroundings, students,

35

and courses, the manifest respect of his colleagues, the stimulation of the young people, and the strong diet of teaching and research had reduced the amplitude of the swings in his temperament, making the periods of depression less severe and shorter. The dark view of life, the future, and everything brightened up a bit. But, although lighter, the weight of depression had by no means completely lifted. Elizabeth also helped make his life more comfortable. After they became intimate, she came to recognize his mood swings, learned something of the causes for his torment, and made deliberate efforts to offset them. When they were together in Taconic or her Cambridge apartment, she could lift his thoughts from those tragedies in the mid-1920s, cheering him up a bit. Still, nothing could permanently relieve the burden of guilt and sorrow that stooped his shoulders and tortured his soul.[2]

Although those who knew him knew some of the facts of what had happened, Joseph could not impart his raw sentiments and deepest feelings to anyone, not even Elizabeth, who knew the consequences but could only guess at their causes or course. When he was in one of these funks, he was not pleasant company. He forgot appointments, ignored friends, and was inconsiderate of others. He had no really intimate male friends with whom he could confide. Wassily Leontief, Gottfried Haberler, and Edward Mason were good friends, all younger. But, while he confided in them somewhat, there were limits. Elizabeth could, sometimes, with a combination of cajolery, concern, and comfort, bring him out of these moods, but often, when depressed, he avoided her.

Their relationship was one-sided. Her love for him was deep, genuine, and all-encompassing. For his part, Joseph was still so deeply in love with his second wife and obsessed by her memory that he could not bestow on Elizabeth the kind of love she had for him and wanted in return. She kept insisting that if they were together all the time—if they were married—his depression would flee. He knew better.

One of the few men in whom Schumpeter could confide, but only to a limited extent, was Irving Fisher of Yale, whom he saw as a kindred soul. First meeting in 1913 on Schumpeter's initial visit to the United States, they later cooperated in founding the Econometric Society in 1930. By the mid-1930s, despite profound theoretical and policy differences, they had become professional friends. Schumpeter had scant sympathy for Fisher's ideas on health and nutrition. Among other attributes Fisher was a nonsmoking teetotaler who drank no coffee or tea and ate no chocolate. He was also an advisor to Roosevelt, and a strong proponent of both the quantity theory of money and the monetary policy based on it. Schumpeter, who indulged in all the minor vices, scoffed at Fisher's purity and rejected his monetary theory and policy ideas.

Still, as an economic scientist, Schumpeter had immense respect for Fisher and visited New Haven several times, especially in those trying days when he was trying to make the cycles book come together. One Sunday, Schumpeter visited Fisher when Ragnar Frisch, the great Norwegian economist, was also visiting the country. The devotion of the three to science is demonstrated by their activities that day. They closeted themselves in Fisher's workshop, which occupied much of his large home at 460 Prospect in New Haven. Only late in the evening, after a long day of animated discussion and exhaustive examination of reams of statistical data, charts, and figures, did one of them note that they had not eaten all day.[3]

Schumpeter was more frank with Fisher about his problem of coping with everyday life than he was with most of his colleagues, partly because Fisher was in New Haven. In March 1936, Schumpeter wrote to Fisher, apologizing for dallying in his duties as a Fellow and Council Member of the Econometric Society:

> It is extremely difficult for me to make clear to so active a man as you are what the trouble is ... I cannot work except by putting my mind entirely on the work at hand and I am very sensitive to disturbances. Each day when I have done with my scientific work and the current duties incident to a professorial chair, I am tired and languid and actually cease to function. The consequence is that current matters are not attended to and letters left unopened for weeks.[4]

Schumpeter then promised to do better, especially after June 1936, when he said he would finish his manuscript on cycles. In another letter to Fisher, this one dated 19 March, he wrote, "My work is my only interest in life," and then explained why he must relax during the summer, interesting himself in nothing more strenuous than tennis and French cathedrals so that he would be in working trim for the beginning of the academic year.[5]

2

In the spring term of 1936, Schumpeter kept up a heavy schedule of teaching basic and advanced theory as well as business cycles, and lecturing in Cambridge and on the road. He spoke several times on the fate of capitalism and the current economic situation. Most of his research time was devoted to the cycles book. His other research plans—primarily his money book—hinged on finishing the cycles book, due originally for completion in mid-1935 but still far from finished in the spring of 1936.

As a fifty-three-year-old widower with an overflowing schedule, Schumpeter lived a quiet life, still in his small comfortable apartment in the Taussig home. He arose early and spent a great deal of time preparing for the day. Dressing was a major operation for Joseph Schumpeter, requiring not only careful thought about the clothes he would wear, but also time to dress properly. His tailor-made suits, expensive shirts, shoes, socks, and accessories had to be just right. By nine o'clock, he was ready for breakfast with the Taussigs. After breakfast, Schumpeter walked the few blocks down Kirkland Street and up Quincy Street past the Faculty Club to Holyoke House just off Massachusetts Avenue in Harvard Square. He often then went to his small study, a carrel, in Widener Library, and either spent the morning working there or behind his closed office door in Holyoke House.

On several days of the week, he had a luncheon date with either Mason, Leontief, Chamberlin, Haberler, Sweezy, or one of the many other senior graduate students or young faculty members. They typically ate at one of the many restaurants in the Square or at the Faculty Club. When he did not have a definite luncheon partner, he walked down to Dunster House and ate with whatever students or young faculty were there. Sometimes research discussions and shop talk made his luncheons last until nearly three, when it was time for him to hold his consultation. Usually held twice a week in the afternoon, frequently by appointment, these consultations enabled Schumpeter to meet with any student who wanted to talk, even those just passing by. Sometime during the afternoon, he had coffee with a student or faculty member in one of several little places along Massachusetts Avenue near Holyoke House.[6]

Often, he stayed in his office until dinner time and once again ate at Dunster House or at a restaurant in the Square. Since he disliked eating alone, Dunster, with its young people, was a favorite place. But he also went back to the Taussig house for supper with his "family." Evenings were typically spent in his apartment, where he read and made notes, or back at Widener for a few quiet hours of work. About once a week, usually on weekends, he went out to a cocktail party at a faculty member's home, had dinner with colleagues, or in the early 1930s kept a date with a senior graduate student or Radcliffe faculty member. By 1934 and 1935, this was usually Elizabeth Boody Firuski. After dinner with her, he would repair to her apartment to talk and eventually perhaps make love, arriving back at the Taussig's in the wee hours.[7]

3

Schumpeter's style perhaps most clearly emerged when he was in the classroom, where his adherence to a rigid routine of research and writing benefitted his students. Paul Samuelson, the first American to win the Nobel Memorial Prize in Economics in 1970, studied with Schumpeter in the mid-1930s. In the most graphic account of Schumpeter as a teacher, Samuelson wrote:

Schumpeter liked to talk too well to be at his best in leading a small seminar. He loved to lecture! And to large audiences. If left to himself, he would probably have swallowed up imperialistically all fields of economics and lectured on all subjects.... After, and not before, the students had assembled for class, in would walk Schumpeter, remove hat, gloves, and topcoat with sweeping gestures, and begin the day's business. Clothes were important to him; he wore a variety of well-tailored tweeds with carefully matched shirt, tie, hose, and handkerchief ... he never told jokes and had no prepared-in-advance booby traps; he was never dead-pan and ingenuous, but somehow made the class itself seem witty, so that even earnest Radcliffe students felt themselves to be engaging in brilliant sortie and repartee. He was free of the congenital vice of the veteran college professor: he never repeated his stories.... He did not lecture in the strict European sense of a unilateral monologue. He called on people in class, and he was constantly interrupted by his audience. If anything, he tolerated too many interruptions from grade-chasers, fools, and exhibitionists.

His 1935 theory course more nearly resembled the courses now being given in every graduate school than did any course then being given in America.... He took you out of the flat dull textbook world and into the three dimensional world of living economics and economists; his enthusiasm over the latest article to appear in the *Review of Economic Studies* on the elasticity of substitution was real and catching.

Though Schumpeter left behind him no band of zealots bent on differentiating his views from those of traditional economic theory, he did leave behind him the only kind of school appropriate to a scientific discipline—a generation of economic theorists who caught fire from his teaching.[8]

Samuelson also recalls that Schumpeter told of the four greatest economists of all time. Ironically, considering his background, three were French—François Quesnay, the Physiocrat; Augustin Cournot, the mathematical economist; and Léon Walras, the Lausanne mathematical economist. To compound the irony, the fourth was the Englishmen whom he did not greatly admire—Alfred Marshall. On other occasions, he preferred Sweden's Knut Wicksell to Marshall.

From my own recollection as a student, in both class and consultation, the flow of comments from Schumpeter was smooth and continuous, apparently spontaneous. He never uttered a sentence that seemed as though it had been said before, although he did paraphrase himself and others, in speaking as well as in writing. Questions answered incorrectly by students did not deter him and he took interruptions in stride. On occasion, he would write a mathematical formula on the blackboard, using it more as a visible focal point for his lecture, as a prop, than as a mathematical tool necessary in developing his argument. He even made mistakes in the mathematics he used in lectures, but the errors made no difference, since the mathematics, as such, were not central to the lecture. Sprinkling his lectures with men, events, and ideas, he stimulated his students by permitting them to observe the gradual unfolding of the logic of a theory, each point following from the one before. While showing the intricacy of theory, he showed its grand simplicity at the same time. He flattered his students by assuming they knew more than they did, making references to people and ideas that students would later hurry to look up in order to insure their understanding. Sitting riveted to their seats, students wanted to know more than he had told them. When Schumpeter was through, the most obscure eighteenth-century Italian economist seemed important and interesting.

At the end of a Schumpeter lecture, most students felt they had witnessed an artist's performance. Take away the asides and interruptions, correct a few minor syntactical errors, organize in paragraph form, and each lecture could become a chapter in a book. In class, he gave the impression that his comments were spontaneous and unrehearsed.[9] Never did he indicate that he had slaved over notes, preparing for that presentation, or that his comments distilled hours and hours of late-night reading and study. Although he never used notes in his class or for any of his other talks, he did prepare them. Nor did he ever use the same class notes twice. At the end of the term, all the notes for a course were bundled into a small package and laid away, never to be touched again. The next year, he might give the same course, but he made a new set of notes for a different lecture series, worked out laboriously before class, studied, and then laid aside. But none of this preparation showed in his presentation. The only notes a student ever saw were those he took during his own lectures. At any moment, Schumpeter might whip out a piece of paper— he always carried little scraps of paper for making notes—and write something down. Then he would continue talking as if nothing had happened.[10]

4

Although popular and intriguing to most students, Schumpeter was not everybody's favorite teacher. Some found him too exotic, too European, too difficult to understand, too Olympian. Because he lectured to those who already knew a great deal of economics, he assumed they had read the material and knew what he was talking about. When he spoke, for example, of Marshall's representative firm, he did not explain in detail what it was, what it meant, and how Marshall had used the tool. Instead, he commented about special aspects to clarify the concept for those with an already well advanced understanding. Perhaps because of this approach, Schumpeter's explanations of elementary notions, theories, and techniques were not always good. Many, if not most, economics teachers could explain the demand curve, the technical aspects of elasticity, and elementary theories better than Schumpeter could. Yet he was superb at evaluating the fundamental meaning of the demand curve, its origin and applicability, and its uses, and at commenting on its strengths and weaknesses. He could examine theoretical interrelationships and impart an understanding of them as only a few could, giving his better students an intense desire to learn more about economic theory.

With his high academic standards, Schumpeter's reading list was long and difficult, requiring a great deal of time to master. Without berating his students, he made it clear that, as embryonic scholars, they would have much reading, studying, and thinking to do. He simply presumed they would do it. After all, were these not his apprentices, inspired by the same dedication to science and knowledge as he? It was unthinkable that a Harvard graduate student in economics would be a shirker or settle for a B if he were capable of an A. But for all his high standards, Schumpeter did not always enforce them on others. He was more generous in his grading than most of his colleagues, and he even rewarded good students with nonexistent grades. He gave Arthur Smithies an A+ in the 1932-33 theory course. He later outdid himself and gave Samuelson an A++, unquestionably deserved. An A+ went to the Canadian Robert B. Bryce, the man who brought Keynes's *General Theory* to Harvard and later became secretary of the cabinet and then deputy minister of finance in Canada. Schumpeter's use of supergrades was not casual; they rewarded genuine merit.[11] The rumor once floated that Schumpeter gave all men an A and all women an A-, regardless of what they wrote on the final examination. This was untrue, although he was not fully convinced that women were as capable of the same sort of intellectual effort and achievement as were men. But, when women did make the effort and did achieve, they received accolades from him. No one more admired the Englishwoman and Cambridge economist Joan Robinson than Schumpeter.

One aspect of his teaching troubled many of his students: They never learned about Schumpeter's theories or ideas from his classes. He did not discuss any of his writings, nor did he mention in class that he had ever written anything; his own writings never appeared on his reading lists. This annoyed those students who had come to Harvard specifically to learn from Schumpeter about his ideas. On rare occasions, students insisted that he address his own work. Fritz Machlup, an Austrian Rockefeller fellow, and Paul Sweezy, an assistant to Schumpeter, once managed to persuade him to speak about his own theories. But he described them blandly and did not invite discussion.[12] Usually, he turned students aside with the comment that all his ideas were in his books and articles for anyone to read. In my recollection, the closest he ever came to mentioning his own work was the remark made in class: "Boehm-Bawerk's theory of interest is very important and instructive, but it was not the final word. Other theories, including that of Professor Fisher, as well as my own, may well be superior." Then he went on to another topic.

His mode of teaching was in keeping with Schumpeter's public image of himself. He had not the slightest doubt about his own ability or his mastery of the subject; he spoke without hesitancy, questioning, or uncertainty. He also saw himself as a worldly man. In the company of men—and almost all his professional and scientific associations were male—he was the suave international connoisseur of wine and women from all climes, telling stories of parties from Vienna to Tokyo. At the same time, he was the consummate scholar, a friend of, or on speaking terms with, every economist of note everywhere in the world, from the ancient Greeks to young men just getting their degrees. Still, paradoxically the private Schumpeter—pen in hand with his wife's or his own diary, praying, praising, and giving thanks—never made a public appearance. Students and colleagues remained unaware of his silent soliloquy with his *Hasen*, his pleadings for help in preparing a manuscript, or his gratitude for assistance in making a speech successful. Even people who knew the cherubic Schumpeter intimately never suspected him to be a profoundly religious man.[13]

5

When the summer of 1936 rolled around, Schumpeter decided not to make his usual trip to Europe. Several reasons governed this decision, including the fact that Mia was not going to meet him. In addition, three summers of looking at French cathedrals had at least temporarily sated his appetite for Gothic churches, arches, windows, doors, and spires. Elizabeth also pressured him to stay and work at Taconic or, if not there, then in Cambridge, where she could see him more frequently. Another major factor was the great political turmoil in Europe. German troops once again occupied the Rhineland, and the country had begun building the fortified Siegfried Line close to the French border. As elections gave Hitler 99 percent of the vote, and his speeches became increasingly strident, the *Wehrmacht*, or German war machine, was growing and consolidating its power. So-called defensive treaties began dividing Europe into two bristling armed camps, while Mussolini's Abyssinian war ended with Italy's absorption of Ethiopia. Schumpeter decided to spend his first summer in the United States.

During part of the summer of 1936, he stayed in Cambridge, working on the business cycles book in either his Holyoke House office or Widener

Library across the street. He frequently lunched with the Austrian Rockefeller scholar, Fritz Machlup, to whom he poured out his difficulties with the cycles book. Wanting only a sympathetic ear, Schumpeter still did not ask for help. They also discussed scientific methodology in economics, a special interest of Machlup, who later became an illustrious professor at Princeton and New York Universities. Often, they reminisced about their mutual homeland, at the time little more than a satellite of Germany. As a Rockefeller fellow, Machlup was part of an important educational experiment undertaken by the Rockefeller Foundation in the 1930s to provide fellowships to young European scholars to study outside their own countries, most often in U.S. universities.[14]

Another smaller group of young professionals came to U.S. universities as British Commonwealth Fellows. Since many of these scholars were economists, most of them studied, at least part of the time, at Harvard, where they naturally sought out Schumpeter. He became life-long friends with most of them, many of whom either stayed in the United States or returned to enrich U.S. and European economics immensely. The impressive list of Rockefeller and British Commonwealth fellows who studied with Schumpeter includes Arthur Smithies of Tasmania; Gottfried Haberler, Oskar Morgenstern, and Machlup of Austria; Oskar Lange of Poland; Abba Lerner, Nicholas (now Lord) Kaldor, Paul Baran, and Eric Roll of England; Robert Bryce of Canada; August Loesch (a student of Schumpeter's from Bonn) and Jacob Marschak of Germany; Nicholas Georgescu-Roegen of Rumania; and others.

Schumpeter also spent some time during the summer of 1936 in Taconic with Elizabeth, along with other occasional house guests. On days when it was not too hot, he played tennis, took long walks down along the lake shore, and sat out in the yard on the cool evenings. But mostly he worked on the cycles book. Although he relaxed, he was so preoccupied with that research during the summer that he missed the celebration of Harvard's Tercentenary. On 12 July 1936, he recorded in his journal that "this kind of summer really suits me best." For a few days during the late summer, he spent some time in Cotuit, south of Boston, with the Taussigs at their summer home. While there, he relaxed in the sun, went swimming, and sailed, but he also continued work on the cycles book. Finally, in September, just before the academic year began, Schumpeter took a genuine vacation, leaving all work behind. For two weeks, in the White Mountains of northern New Hampshire near Franconia, he took long walks, climbed among the rocks, rented a car and driver to take him around and through the mountains, and played some golf—badly, like his tennis. Just before returning to Cambridge in late September, he again recorded in his diary the theme so prevalent since 1927, "not *joy*, but *peace*."[15]

6

In the fall term of 1936, Schumpeter taught the basic economic theory course and his own advanced course, now called Selected Problems in Economic Theory, along with his usual business cycles and economic forecasting. In addition to his review of Keynes's book, published in 1936, he also wrote an essay on "Professor Taussig on Wages and Capital" for a book of essays in honor of Taussig.[16] Now that Taussig was over seventy-five and retired, his students and colleagues sought some other way to honor him in addition to this book. Partly at Schumpeter's instigation they planned a great dinner for December 1936, attended by many of his former students, now illustrious businessmen, professors, and government leaders from up and down the East Coast. This gala affair, which took over the Faculty Club, had all the university worthies in attendance. Schumpeter wrote to one former student, asking for a letter or telegram expressing his sentiments toward the grand old man of Harvard economics. After an exchange of letters in the fall, President Franklin Delano Roosevelt finally accommodated with a letter that Schumpeter read at the dinner. Both the dinner, the accolades, and the Roosevelt letter immensely pleased Taussig.[17]

During this semester, his routine continued as before, filled with the usual rounds of lectures, lunches and dinners with friends and colleagues, and weekends in Taconic with Elizabeth. One incident that occurred during the semester is remembered with amusement by some who were at Harvard. At the request of James Bryant Conant, Harvard's president, Schumpeter wrote a long report on the possible economists that Harvard might hire to improve its position. Although negative about the scientific standing of most economists of the day, Schumpeter did recommend Ragnar Frisch strongly. He also thought highly of John Hicks, an English economist. Without authority, and innocent of the ways of departments and universities, Schumpeter offered a job to Hicks. Everyone breathed a sigh of relief when Hicks turned him down, since the department didn't have the money to pay him.[18]

Throughout the semester, he was disheartened about the lack of progress on the cycles book, and the discouragement spilled over into other areas of his life. On 27 December 1936, the day before leaving for the American Economic Association meeting in Chicago, he wrote in his diary: "I work daily on MS. But with less success. Many useless sources. Free but so miserable." Schumpeter's depression was mounting at year's end, as nothing seemed to be going right. He received word that Mia had married Dr. Stojan Bicanski of Yugoslavia the day after Christmas 1936. Even though he knew that she planned to marry, the event depressed him. At about the same time, the success of Keynes bore down on him; it seemed the whole world of economics was talking about *The General Theory*. Regarding the book as inferior and wrong-headed, he didn't envy what Keynes had done, but he was unhappy that so many of his colleagues paid serious attention to it.

One of Schumpeter's standard methods for coping with depression was to get away. The work he did, the work all scholars do, must be done alone, but his depression struck most strongly when he was alone. Travel, new faces and places, seemed to have a salutary effect. After the AEA meetings in Chicago, Schumpeter decided to take a vacation in an effort to shake the depression, this time flying to Miami (his first flight) and staying at the Pancoast Hotel in Miami Beach. During his three weeks there, he loafed, swam, and laid on the beach, not even attempting to work, but hoping to restore his balance. On 22 January, he was back in Cambridge, ready for the spring term.[19]

7

The spring term of 1937 saw the same round of activities and continued work on the cycles book. He taught, for a change, only two courses: the second part of basic economic theory and the seminar on cycles and forecasting. In the latter, he shared lectures with Gottfried Haberler, whose great book, *Prosperity and Depression*, had come out a short time before. He also attended some class sessions of E. B. Wilson's course in mathematical economics, the course that Schumpeter had taught earlier.[20] After spending the Easter vacation at Taconic, the many oral examinations for doctoral candidates and lectures consumed his time.

By now, Schumpeter had become the official greeter for the Department of Economics. Whenever an outstanding foreign visitor, or in some cases an important colleague from another U.S. university, came to Cambridge, Schumpeter took him in tow. If he didn't already know the visitor, he wanted to make his acquaintance and learn of his work. At this point in his career, Schumpeter was Harvard's most well-known economist and possessed an international aura. Other Americans, such as Yale's Irving Fisher, were better known. But, among economic theorists, Schumpeter's name often headed the list. Taking visitors to lunch or dinner, he also introduced them when they spoke a few words at social gatherings, and presided over the seminars at which the outsiders gave papers.[21]

One such visit was remembered by Professor Kei Shibata, the former young assistant professor at Kyoto University who, in February 1931 in Japan, had spent a whole day sightseeing and talking about economics with Schumpeter. When Schumpeter learned that Shibata was on his way to the United States in 1936, he wired the Japanese professor on board his ship, "Cordially Welcome." Schumpeter assigned one of his graduate students, Shigeto Tsuru, later one of Japan's foremost economists and public figures, to shepherd the professor while at Harvard. In his autobiography, Professor Shibata records that:

> So warm was Professor Schumpeter's welcome with a bouquet of flowers that the way the hotel treated us changed immediately.... He was in the middle of writing his *Business Cycles* (1939) and therefore apologized for not having time to get involved in discussion with me.... Even though pressed, the Professor made time to dine and take a walk with me twice a week.[22]

The flowers were a typical Schumpeterian touch, as were the biweekly conversations after protesting that he was too busy.

The firestorm created by the publication of *The General Theory* still burned in Schumpeter's mind. Telling Professor Shibata that economists should not involve themselves in policy matters, Schumpeter warned, "Stay out of politics or your goal as an economist will be jeopardized." Thinking of Keynes, Schumpeter also railed against schools. Shibata quotes Shigeto Tsuru as being advised by Schumpeter: "There is no school of thought in chemistry or physics; economics has been nurtured a long time in a feudalistic, castle-like setting breeding mutually exclusive clannish schools of thought."[23]

8

The Fourth of July 1937 found Schumpeter still in Cambridge with no plans for visiting Europe again. Although the continent remained at peace, Spain was aflame, each side supported by contending European forces. Mussolini met Schuschnigg and then talked to Hitler in Berlin. The purges in Moscow were underway. Two full years had passed since the cycles book's deadline, and its incompletion increasingly bothered Schumpeter. Although still hard at work, he was entangled in historical and statistical data and their interpretation. In August, he planned to attend a meeting of the Econometric Society in Colorado Springs and to take a vacation in the west at the same time.[24]

Another matter assumed greater urgency in the summer of 1937: Elizabeth was pressing him ever harder to marry her. For a while she worried, lest she be pregnant. Earlier diagnosed as having diabetes, she was warned not to have a child. It was a false alarm. Elizabeth wanted Joseph to get away from the Taussig household and under her constant care and attention, where she felt her ministrations could assuage his depression. By now, she was fully aware of his frequent depressed states and wanted to help. Perhaps as much as romantic love, she needed someone to take care of, and she had decided that Schumpeter was the one. She also believed that he needed someone to take care of him. In a series of letters from Taconic, followed by meetings there and in Cambridge, she tried to persuade him to marry her.[25] Joseph too wanted to get away from the Taussigs. But although powerfully attracted to Elizabeth, he did not feel the great passionate love he had had for Annie. He was unsure what effect marriage might have on his work and whether he wanted to make a monogamous commitment. Elizabeth and his occasional and meaningless affairs satisfied, at least in part, his sexual urges, and he was reluctant to give them up.

In late summer, 1937, Elizabeth wrote from Taconic,

> You mellow in my society and then you go away and think dark thoughts. I have been willing to try to draw you back again and again, because I love you and because it seems to me that almost any life would be preferable to the one you are living now with its concomitant state of mind.... If you go to Big Horn you will go back again into your lonely gloom and distrust about the future. This time I shall not be on hand when you return and I shall not be able to draw you out of it.[26]

Elizabeth made it clear that, if they married, she would help him in his work, not by participating in it but by lifting all nonscientific burdens and providing tranquil surroundings. She would not demand his time or energy. In more pleading letters from Taconic she tried to entice him to visit her there. Finally, the self-styled "greatest lover of Europe," now fifty-four, capitulated. Cancelling his trip to Colorado, he went instead to Taconic.

On 16 August 1937, Elizabeth and Joseph took the train to New York and checked into the Waldorf Astoria. The next day, just turned thirty-nine, Elizabeth Boody married Joseph Schumpeter at the Community Church in New York. Not one of their Cambridge friends attended, nor did any of them even know of the wedding until later. Swishy (Marian Severn), a Radcliffe school chum of Elizabeth's and a New York lawyer, was the only friend there. The newly married couple returned a few days later to Taconic, where they spent the rest of the summer. Throughout this period, Schumpeter was hard at work on his cycles book. During the week of his marriage he struggled with chapter 11, trying to sort out income, expenditures, and bank balances. His diary that week recorded his concern over the book but did not even mention his marriage.

Notes

1   The Schumpeter diary chronicles the mood swings and degree of depression Schumpeter suffered. In his first two years in the United States, his depression occupied him only modestly.

2   Schumpeter's views and Elizabeth's reaction are revealed in his diary and in her letters to him in this period. They are preserved in the Schumpeter papers at the Harvard University Archives.

3   Frisch related this story in "Some Personal Reminiscences on a Great Man."

4   This letter to Fisher is in the correspondence file of the Schumpeter papers in the Harvard University Archives.

5   This quotation is from a letter to Fisher in the correspondence file of the Schumpeter papers at the Harvard University Archives.

6   Holyoke House has subsequently been torn down and a large, high-rise office building, occupied primarily by Harvard University, has taken its place.

7   This sketch is based on the recollection of friends and colleagues, such as Edward Mason, Wassily Leontief and others.

8   Paul Samuelson, "Schumpeter as a Teacher and Economic Theorist," 48-53.

9   The comments regarding Schumpeter's lectures come from the recollections of his students.

10   Several boxes of the Schumpeter papers at the Harvard University Archives consist of class outlines and reading lists, as well as class notes. The notes are on half slips of paper. He never used these notes in class.

11   Schumpeter recorded grades on scraps of paper that he placed with the class notes.

12   In conversations with both Fritz Machlup and Paul Sweezy, both told me that they were disappointed in Schumpeter's explanations of his theories and felt that Schumpeter did not want to defend them.

13   No friend of Schumpeter's mentioned that he believed that Schumpeter was personally a religious man, and nearly all of them said that he was not a religious person. One of those who knew him best, Wolfgang Stolper, remarked to the effect that the religious side of Schumpeter explains partly some of the things he never understood about Schumpeter.

14   I learned of the importance of the Rockefeller fellows at Harvard in the 1930s from conversations with Fritz Machlup, who was himself a Rockefeller fellow.

15   This expression, often including the underlining, appears in Schumpeter's diary in many places.

16   *Explorations in Economics: Notes and Essays Contributed in Honor of F. W. Taussig* (Cambridge: Harvard University Press, 1926).

17   This letter is in the correspondence file of the Schumpeter papers in the Harvard University Archives.

18   The memo to President Conant is in the correspondence files of the Harvard University Archives. Edward Mason told me the anecdote about John Hicks.

19   The details of his trip, including the bill, is in the Harvard University Archives. He kept a special diary while he was there and wrote in it extensively.

20   The notebook of this class is in the Harvard University Archives. He attended class regularly and did the exercises assigned by the professor.

21   Edward Mason and others recall that Schumpeter seemed to be the intellectual spokesmen for the department for most of the visitors to Harvard in those years.

22   The details of the Shibata visit come from my correspondence with him and from translated excerpts from his autobiography.

23   This quotation appears in the translated excerpts of the Shibata autobiography given to me by Professor Shibata.

24   His diary records plans to give a paper on statistics and the business cycle at the

Econometric Society meeting.

25   Her handwritten letters to Schumpeter appears in the correspondence file of the Schumpeter papers at the Harvard University Archives.

26   This quotation appears in one of Elizabeth's letters in the correspondence file of the Schumpeter papers at the Harvard University Archives.

4

The Secret Life (1937-1938)

All those who write diaries in a sense are writing at least a part of their own autobiographies. Schumpeter's diary records his plans and his daily activities in many cases. But, more important, it reveals what he thought about many different subjects—subjects that received different treatment in his public life. He wrote on his many prejudices that in public he treated more cautiously. He wrote of his obsessions, for example, about death and health, about which he said very little to his friends and colleagues. He even wrote about "voluntary death." He wrote in his diary about politics, revealing a much more conservative vein than he did in his professional writings or in speeches and conversation. He revealed the details of his personal religion and his relationship to his dead wife and mother. Despite his extensive diary writings and revelations that differ from his public stance, his diary does not reveal a Schumpeter significantly at odds with the public Schumpeter. Rather, it rounds out the portrait and shows facets of his life and thinking he seldom revealed in public.

1

Joseph and Elizabeth moved into the house at 15 Ash Street in Cambridge, about six blocks from the Yard, in September 1937. In a twinkling, Schumpeter had changed from aging widower in a tiny apartment in a friend's home to master of two homes and dependent of a doting wife. While adjusting to a new domestic routine that fall, Squire Schumpeter taught three

51

courses in economic theory, a trying chore even for an experienced theory teacher. Still plugging away on his cycles book, his only published writing during this semester was the English-language preface to the Japanese translation of *Die Theorie der wirtschaftlichen Entwicklung*. This was partly because his research interests shifted for a time as a result of the heavy dose of teaching theory. His 1934 plan had called for finishing cycles, then revising and completing the money book, and then working on a theory book. But in late 1935 and 1936, he sidetracked to examine the evolution and future of capitalism, a problem that had long preoccupied him. Failing to complete that work, he resumed the cycles book without publishing anything.

In 1937, he digressed again, applying for a small grant for research assistance to work on "The Mathematical Apparatus of Economics," one of his code names for the new theory he hoped to develop. He also called it the "Theoretical Apparatus of Economics." It was the project next in line after he had finished money and cycles.[1] That he had long thought about this project is indicated by the fact that one of his Japanese lectures in 1931 had the same title. In the years following 1937, he would return again and again to this ephemeral project, mentioning it to friends and colleagues many times, often using it as an excuse for not doing something he did not want to do, putting it on his agenda when any unoccupied time threatened to appear. His interest in the theory project was serious, almost consuming, even in the absence of results.

Research in theory differs from other kinds of research. In most economic research, the economist uses an existing theoretical framework to analyze facts and circumstances that he has investigated. In his work on cycles, for instance, Schumpeter used his own theory as the basis for a historical and statistical examination of three economies—that of the United States, England, and Germany—over a long period of time. But now he was searching for a completely new theoretical framework. Since existing literature can help only to a limited extent in this kind of research, the economist must rely on intuition, accumulated knowledge, experience, insight, and inspiration, as well as luck, to produce new theories. In this process, other scholars' theories are the closest thing the theorist has to specific research material. Schumpeter's search for a new theory, which necessitated examining in detail all other theories, reignited his interest in the history of economic theory, a part of his "sacred decade" work.

This theoretical work intermingled with his cycles book, now edging toward completion. Hundreds of pages of manuscript had existed for some time, but Schumpeter did not consider it finished. Even so, the department secretary told visiting Professor Shibata of Japan in the spring of 1936 that Schumpeter had finished the manuscript many months earlier.[2] But he continued to rework and rewrite, as well as add to various parts of it. This procedure continued through the fall of 1937 and into 1938, as he hoped for a theoretical breakthrough that never came.

Meanwhile, historical minutiae held him in their thrall. At Harvard, subtle pressure mounted for him to publish the book. Having spent much of his time producing articles and elaborations on his earlier work, Schumpeter had not published a major study in twenty-five years. With his colleagues wondering, but of course never saying anything, whether the "big book" would ever see the light of day, he felt the urgency and necessity to finish the project. Moreover, he was aware of the intellectual presence of Keynes, and recognized that anything he did would be compared with Keynes's work. Still dissatisfied with his work, he held on to what he considered the incomplete manuscript.

2

With Schumpeter struggling to complete the cycles book, trying to develop a new economic theory, maintaining his heavy teaching schedule, and adjusting to married life again, no one would have guessed that he continued holding on to his private and secret life.[3] But the rituals of silent worship, dedication to the *Hasen*, and shutting himself away with his diary would be practiced until he died. In a sense, anyone who writes regularly in a diary leads a hidden life, since few tell even intimate friends the things that go into a diary. Schumpeter's diary was no exception, and it provides a helter-skelter record of what went on inside his head. Unfortunately, his personal diary before 3 August 1931, the fifth anniversary of Annie's death, was destroyed along with other documents when the warehouse storing them was burned in a U.S. bombing raid in July 1944. However, in 1932 he did carry to the United States, his first recopy of Annie's diary, done between 1926 and 1931, and that year resumed work on his own diary. Although Schumpeter did not make a determined effort to keep his diary a secret—everyone knew he made and kept elaborate notes on everything—none of his friends knew that he kept one until after his death.

He wrote in a combination of languages. As the 1930s proceeded, the amount of German declined as the amount of English increased until, by the late 1930s, he wrote mainly in English. Much of the diary is written in *Gabelsberger* shorthand, and a scattering of French, Italian, and even Greek also appears. Schumpeter switched back and forth between languages and between languages and shorthand without any clear pattern. For example, he might start a sentence in English, follow it with some shorthand, and end in German. The thought is continuous, but the language or shorthand expressing it jumps from one to another in the middle of a sentence or paragraph. The language he used when he wrote in *Gabelsberger* was usually German, but occasionally English. His use of all these languages was often sloppy and careless, often not in sentences and paragraphs, indicating that he paid no heed to rules of grammar since no one but himself would see it anyway. Although his diary and other daily records were private, he spent quite a lot of time with them, as much as an hour a day (or more) on some days, and usually in the morning. Since his schedule was so full, his use of all that time and effort suggests that the diary had a high priority. On some days, however, he wrote little, perhaps only a few words; at other times, days or even weeks would pass without any diary writing as part of his daily activities; on other occasions he would write something daily for weeks.

Nothing about Schumpeter's diary suggests that it had a utilitarian function. He recorded his plans and accomplishments more as thinking on paper than as a record of events. He seems to have never referred back or reread it, nor is there any indication that he ever destroyed parts of it. Schumpeter believed that writing something in his diary would impress it on his memory; he would not have to look at it again. The diary served as a natural part of his thinking process as he contemplated his problems and his performance in response to them.

3

Most of the personal material centered around the intellectual activities of life, with the amount of commentary on his personal relations with others being modest. Although he sometimes wrote his opinions of others, such as his colleagues, he seldom described anything involving his personal relations with them, not even with his wife and closest friends. Rarely did he relate conversations he had, though occasionally he quoted or cited a friend. People played a significant role in the diary, but most entries dealing with people were *about* those people, not about Schumpeter's relations with them. And he wrote as intimately concerning what Gladstone thought about Disraeli as he did about Slichter's comments on bureaucracy.

Focussing on ideas, he rarely commented about the mundane matters of daily living. For example, he seldom mentioned money and never remarked about matters related to household and personal management, such as clothes, food, and drink. Elizabeth took care of all those ordinary daily concerns. Before he was married, he handled his own money, but until 1935 any spare money went to paying debts or financing his summer trips to Europe. After he married Elizabeth, Joseph turned over all his money to her, and she paid the bills, managed their finances, and took care of the house, his clothes, and everything. She provided him with whatever cash he needed—a Japanese custom.

The diaries show Schumpeter as a chronic complainer about his health, a hypochondriac, an aspect of his manic-depressive disorder. Most of his colorful health comments were general: He was weak, tired, ill, and decrepit; his bones ached, his heart thumped; the blood rushed or flowed languidly; his arteries were brittle and his mind was going. Still, he made few specific health comments that a doctor could use in diagnosis. During the times he made these complaints, his outward demeanor, as seen by colleagues and students, coincided with the typical image of Schumpeter as cheery and outgoing. And, despite his many health worries, he seldom went to a medical doctor; and, in the few times he saw one in the 1930s, the doctors said nothing was wrong with him. Infuriated by this, Schumpeter complained bitterly to his friends, expressing his belief that doctors should tell him what his problem was. He took no medicine regularly and did not seem to have had any physical ailment in the 1930s—not common to any man over fifty who overworks.[4]

The diary also documents the degree to which Schumpeter suffered from periodic chronic depression. The intermittent but frequent bouts of severe depression had begun plaguing him at least by the time of his second wife's death, and perhaps before. In his diary, he was seldom completely free from it, though he didn't always use the word depression: Hopelessness, desperation, despair, despondency, sadness, dejection, melancholy, gloom, discouragement, and many other similar words he frequently used to express his outlook. Judging from his diary, Schumpeter was desperately unhappy and tortured much of the time, differing dramatically from his public image. Although his depression did not make him an overtly unhappy man whose life among people was obviously miserable and disconsolate, it did affect his day-to-day life and influenced his outlook, with the degree of depression at any given moment determining his behavior.

Intermittently, he held a pessimistic, dark, cynical, and gloomy outlook toward his own life and surroundings, including his profession, university, city, country, and world. His friends could sometimes easily observe this variable manifestation of his depression, but he often masked these inner sentiments with bright sayings, clever quips, and an outwardly confident and easy-going exterior. Ironically, for the one really serious health problem he had—chronic depression—Schumpeter never sought medical advice. To do so would have meant asking for psychological or psychoanalytic help. With Freud as his contemporary, he knew enough of such matters to realize that this kind of help would require divulging more about himself than he was willing to do. In his day, neither sufferers nor medical men regarded noncrippling depression as a promisingly treatable ailment, and the drugs that have become so important in latter days were only a dream of pharmaceutical executives.

Schumpeter's diary also reveals his obsession with death—partly a fear of death, partly just the devotion of thought to the subject. His retention and display of his wife's and child's death masks for years and his leaving her room untouched exemplified this attitude. His 30 September 1934 diary entry gives an example of his obsession.

> When I see a person, I ask myself, how would he look on his deathbed? When I see a house, I imagine that someone dies in it.... The day of death comes closer and when I am tired I often feel that I don't belong any more.... In the past I forbade myself to think about death. I shuddered before death.... It could be true ... that it was awful, incomprehensible. But now there is a change.... Death could approach me in a friendly way as a welcome visitor.

Throughout the diary he contemplated death, wondering what it is like, anticipating it, welcoming it, and fearing it by turns. Late in life, he even contemplated "voluntary death."

4

One of the most fascinating features of his diary was Schumpeter's recording of daily grades for his own work performance, judging himself on a scale of 0 to 1, with 1 as the highest mark. He began grading himself only after he had been in the United States several years, and usually did not record grades in his daily writing, but rather in weekly summaries. For example, he began one weekly review in his diary:

Camb Mo 5 VII - So 11 VII 37,

meaning Cambridge, Montag [Monday], July 5 to Sontag [Sunday] July 11, 1937. Then he recorded in three lines of mixed English and shorthand his daily expressions of gratitude and praise for the *Hasen*. He next related the social functions he attended and the part of the *Krisenwerk*—the cycles book—he was working on. Further down the page, he graded himself as follows for each day in the period:

1   1   1/2   1   5/6   1   1

He always started with Sunday and graded by sixths. After more remarks, he often concluded with the word "full," or sometimes the German word "voll." Those words indicate that it was a full, or busy, week. The second week of July 1937, was an unusually good week, with Schumpeter giving himself the highest grade on every day but Tuesday and Thursday. The marks he used were 1/6, 1/3, 1/2, 2/3, 5/6, 1, and several variations of zero. A zero with a horizontal slash meant some work, but only when combined with another day's grade. A zero with no slash meant no work of any significance and, with a vertical slash, absolutely no work. A grade of 1, meaning an excellent day, although appearing regularly, was not frequent. For someone who appeared so casual in public about his work, Schumpeter was unusually conscientious in recording his work performance. Because he often called his diary his *protokoll*, meaning in German a record or report, we have to wonder if this strange practice was a report to his *Hasen*.

Schumpeter never recorded the criteria he used to grade himself, but it is clear that they reflected more than just the number of hours devoted to work, reading or studying. The high grades seemed to be most often associated with writing, seldom with teaching or with giving talks and papers. He often graded a day zero even though he had taught or given a speech that day. If he wrote a lot and thought the result was good, then he scored himself high. If he had an idea he thought would be useful and related to his writing, then his score would also be high. But a day of only teaching, consultation hours, talking to colleagues, meetings, examinations, and correspondence rated a low grade.

In addition to grading, some of his weekly diary summaries gave details of exactly how many hours he worked and what he worked on. For example, on Monday, 5 July, he worked on chapters 4 and 5 of the cycles book from nine to twelve, two to three, four to six-thirty, and nine to one. The next day was the same, except he worked straight through from two to six in the afternoon. On Wednesday he tackled chapter 6 from nine to twelve, one to three, and eight to eleven. He continued work on chapter 6 during the rest of the week with a similar schedule: a three-hour morning stint, a three- to six-hour afternoon work period, and an evening period of two to five hours. That week of 5 July, when he graded himself so high, he worked seventy and one-half hours. Because he was revising, chapter after chapter, the manuscript of the cycles book during this summer of 1937, he put in similar hours throughout the period.

5

The diaries disclose some information and sentiments that differ from what people well acquainted with Schumpeter knew about him. Still, they hold no dark secrets, no terrible aberrations of character or personality, no startlingly different attitudes, no new profound ideas or insights. Most of the daily records reveal the private person and thinking to be much the same as the public. For example, no vulgarity, profanity, or obscenity appeared in his diaries, as there were none in his speech. The diaries do illuminate a side of Schumpeter that even his friends and colleagues knew about only vaguely, if at all, including the depths of his depressions, his hypochondria, his obsession with death, his devotion to the *Hasen*, some of his personal and political views, and his religious beliefs. Although some deviations from his public stance appear in the diary, nothing constitutes a radical change. He was more candid—perhaps unguarded—in his observations about colleagues at Harvard and elsewhere, and about some economic, social, and political ideas, but his private musings would not lead one to alter significantly an assessment of his professional and scientific life.

The diary expresses his political stance more explicitly than his discussions with colleagues and friends indicated. Very conservative and a strong elitist, Schumpeter intensely disliked the ideas and programs of Franklin Roosevelt and others who wanted to intervene in the economy or interfere with markets and private decision making. He held more strongly negative thoughts about some economists—such as Keynes, Cassel, Marshall, and others—than the published record ever showed. Being anti-British and anti-Russian, he was pro-German, even pro-Hitler in a special sense, and pro-Japanese prior to and to some extent even during the Second World War. He disapproved of U.S. prewar foreign policies, as well as of its domestic economic policies. Much of this was known, but only to a few, and even they did not know the strength of his feelings.

His daily records reveal that the most important discrepancy between Schumpeter's public and personal life was his religious outlook. Although nominally a Christian, in public Schumpeter was a nonreligious man, neither irreligious nor antireligious. Born and raised as a Catholic, all his life he had enormous respect for the Roman Catholic Church and its influence. But his friends got the impression that religion was not important to him, except when it, through the church, exercized a social influence in the world. Even then, he was interested in religion only as a social phenomenon, not as a personal matter. On 10 May 1938, for example, he confided in his diary, "How is it that I have come to look upon the Catholic hierarchy as the solution in Europe and even for the Jewish question? ... Jewish question—the most important and the most hopeless of our time." Elsewhere, in his published writings, he commented that the church might play an important economic role, including serving as promulgator of the economic and social order to succeed capitalism.[5]

In 1925, he became a Lutheran—nominally, for the purpose of marrying his second wife—and listed himself in *Who's Who* as a Lutheran. In the Austria of 1925, there were only two religions: Catholicism and Lutheranism. His marriage to Elizabeth in 1937 took place in a nondenominational Protestant church in New York. Schumpeter never attended any church for religious devotions, although he loved to visit and study cathedrals and old churches. He gave no indication in his speaking, writing, or among friends that he depended in any way on a Supreme Being or was much concerned with anything other than his material and intellectual life. In word, in deed, in life, Schumpeter indicated no interest in religious sentiments, leading his friends to believe that he would have disdained religion personally on grounds that it was for ordinary people, not for someone like himself.

Further evidence of his lack of public religious belief is his decision to study economics, a conspicuously unreligious discipline. Religion does not in any way enter into the study of economics; economic man has no religion, nor does religion influence him. Markets know no God and the national income has no Savior. Economists, as economists, seldom profess religion, nor do they indicate that religion plays any role in man's life or in their own. In this sense, Schumpeter, by being silent publicly on religion, was in step with his colleagues, many of whom may also have had a personal religion about which they did not speak.

But paradoxically, Schumpeter's daily records reveal him to be a truly religious man, although not in the sense of being interested in devotional or theological affairs or studies, church matters, or living in conformity with any particular group's edicts or codes of moral conduct. Instead, he was deeply religious in his strong dependency on a superior being. Entreating and praying to that power for aid and support, he looked to God for protection and assistance. His half-human, half-divine saints—his second wife and his mother—acted as his representatives and intercessors with that power. Although both Annie and his mother died in 1926, he metaphorically lighted candles daily to their memory for the rest of his life. The depth of his religious life emerged in two places: in his own diary material and in his recopied version of Annie's diary. Her diary, as he amended it, played a central role in his personal religious life, since he drew from it much of the material for his prayers and pleadings.

In copying the diary in 1926 and 1927, and in recopying it many times later, his additional entries became, in effect, a part of her diary. Taken together, his and her diaries comprise Schumpeter's book of confessions. His prefatory entries, added by him daily, begin each page of Annie's diary (and some pages of his own diary and weekly summaries), as he repeated the same words, "O Herrin und Mutter, o seid ueber mir!" (O Mistress and Mother, protect me!). The word translated as "Mistress" is the feminine of Herr or "master," and has religious overtones because it connotes one who oversees and controls. Following this general plea, were Schumpeter's special pleas for specific help or protection. Further beneath his prayers were his recollections of aspects of their lives together (see chapter 12). His prayers, addresses, and pleas were repeated so often that they take on a clearly ritualistic character. In the different annual copies, certain mottoes and sayings were used again and again, but remained the same for a given date.

For example, each year on the anniversary of the day he got the Bonn job (5 October), he wrote, "Grosse Freude-Bonn erobert" (Great joy-Bonn conquered). On another day, he consistently wrote, "Du bist nun mein erster und letzter Gedanke" (You are now my first and last thought), a phrase taken from one of Annie's letters. The entries also reveal a set of "holy" days, about twenty in all, commemorating special days in their lives. His ritualistic statements also included incantations of praise for his *Hasen*. After dating an entry, but before writing anything substantive, Schumpeter might insert one of the two following psalm-like statements: "O Mutter und Herrin und das Gluck und [die] Freude meines Lebens!" (O Mother and Mistress, happiness and joy of my life!) and "O Mutter und Herrin und das Gluck und [die] Freude, Sinn und Stolz!" (O Mother and Mistress-Happiness and Joy, Meaning, and Pride!).

6

What does Schumpeter's relation to his wife's diary reveal? About the substance of his work, little. About his professional life, that he was not completely the cold-blooded scientist, but one who deliberately put to one side a set of beliefs about man and God in examining economic and social phenomena. It establishes that he was both scientist and romantic, and that religion played a significant part in his romanticism. About the man, the diary reveals that he was a loving, caring husband and a profoundly religious person, albeit in an unorthodox way. He grieved at the death of his wife and mother far beyond normal grief. He so desperately wanted to continue contact with them after their deaths that he transformed them into holy figures. His worship of these figures was at the center of his interior life. On more than one occasion, he recorded that the "Hasen spoke to me." His recopying of the diary, the religious notations added to the recopies, and his daily contemplation of the *Hasen* provided Schumpeter with comfort and eased the tension of depression. In a hardened world, it is touching that a man, a contributor to the economic and social thought of his day, was so devoted to his wife and mother that he daily commemorated their lives, personally and privately, in this fashion. And in his own mind he found no insurmountable barrier between religious belief and his work as a social scientist. It is also necessary to realize that psychologists would probably call his behavior unusual, perhaps an obsession, and his way of coping with depression.

The diaries, reflecting his worship of his *Hasen*, stood at the core of his personal religion. It was by no means the formal religion of either the Lutheran or Catholic church, although most of the Catholic and Lutheran holy days are noted frequently in the diaries. Yet he forged a personal relationship with some unnamed diety through the *Hasen* and thereby recognized some Power beyond himself as he expressed daily the hope that his wife and mother would intercede for him with that Power. The connection between the *Hasen* and the Supreme Being is unclear in Schumpeter's personal writings; sometimes they seem the same and other times the *Hasen* are only saints. In these personal writings Schumpeter never used the word God in the 1930s, nor do Christ or Jesus or other words so important in the Christian religion appear. He also never referred to the Bible or biblical characters. But, in the 1940s, the word "Gott," not as an expletive, begins to appear in his diary, suggesting that, as he aged, his religion took on more formalized and traditional character.

Schumpeter's private devotions also appeared in places other than the diaries. By habit, he wrote at the beginning of lecture and speech notes, and often on other pages of notes and written work, the words Annerl or Mami or both. He seems to have been dedicating his work to his wife and mother, as well as reminding himself of his dependence on the *Hasen*, almost as if he could not work unless he summoned their presence. Students in European Catholic schools often begin their class recitation papers with "A.M.D.G." (Ad majoreus Dei gloriam), meaning "To the Greater Glory of God." These initials serve to dedicate to God the work that follows. In the United States, the initials "J.M.J." (Jesus, Mary, and Joseph) are also frequently used similarly by Catholics. Schumpeter did not use these expressions, but substituted instead the words Annerl or Mami, as well as the initials "J u H" (Johanna und Hasi) and "J u A" (Johanna und Annerl) at the beginning of his diary notebooks and sometimes at the top of the day's entry or on lectures notes.

Schumpeter's diary also reveals interests generally unknown to others. For example, in early May 1938, he wrote "Note: funny how this pleasure I suddenly take in detective novels—shows how the cycl-ms drained me of all energy." Thus began a practice, little known to his friends, that relaxed the tension and helped to lift the depression weighing upon him. He became a fan of detective novels—Agatha Christie, Rex Stout, Dorothy Sayers, Ellery Queen, and others. Usually in the evening, after an enervating day of pen in hand, Schumpeter sat in his easy chair and in his mind observed the antics of Archie Goodwin in the service of Nero Wolfe, marvelled at the innocent cunning of Miss Marple and the intellect of Lord Peter, enjoyed the mind teasers of Ellery Queen, or saw how Hercule Poirot solved all mysteries by using his little gray cells. He preferred the stories of intellectual content, avoiding those that gloried in violence.

7

Although his private interests and daily work of the *Hasen* occupied his time and attention, Schumpeter maintained his public life and work as if nothing were out of the ordinary. Still he plugged away at the cycles manuscript in 1937 and 1938. For a long time now, the work had been just a matter of revising, getting this or that piece of information confirmed, adjusting an idea, polishing one or another paragraph. He would not let it go until he was satisfied. In the summer of 1938, his first summer of married life with Elizabeth, he stayed in Taconic and worked on the manuscript. But, as always, he spared some time for thinking about economic theory as well as mathematics.

In the fall of 1938, he had a full teaching load. Now teaching only advanced economic theory, Schumpeter passed on the basic economic theory course to Professors Chamberlin and Leontief because he didn't enjoy teaching the basic course and was not especially good at it. He also taught the seminar in business cycles and economic forecasting and the seminar in selected problems in money and banking. Then, in the spring of 1939, having finished the cycles manuscript, he took a leave of absence.

He had continued meeting intermittently with the Seven Wise Men in 1937 and 1938, but since some members had dropped out, the group was not as stimulating as it had been earlier. He also continued giving public talks to groups, such as the Graduate Economics Club and the Boston Economics Club, and lectured in other cities, including Montreal and Cleveland. Although most of his writing time during this period was spent working on the cycles book, he continued to pursue other interests, as always dipping into economic theory and mathematics, and occasionally into topics on which he had written earlier.

In late 1938, he wrote a three-page paper, never published, on the significance of social classes in modern society, as a reminder of unfinished business of his "sacred decade." His diary reveals that he planned to take up his 1927 article on the development of classes, which was in turn based on research done between 1909 and 1913. The new abstract discussed the origin of social classes, relating their beginnings to the achievement of individuals.

For many years, Schumpeter had been active in the Econometric Society, serving as a Fellow and a member of the Council of Fellows, the governing body, since the society's formation. One of the chief functions of that group was to decide who would become fellows of the society, a small number of distinguished economists from around the world, and this task required an extensive correspondence with Fisher, Frisch, and others about potential candidates. Many times Schumpeter had been asked to serve as an officer, but he always recommended someone else. Finally, in 1938, the Council prevailed upon him to be vice-president at a time when A. L. Bowley of England was president. An almost purely honorary post, the vice-presidency often goes to the individual who is next in line for the presidency. Schumpeter continued as vice-president and member of the council until he became president of the society in 1940, serving two one-year terms.[6]

8

By this time in the 1930s, six years after Schumpeter's arrival, Harvard had assembled a new and distinguished group of economists, with Schumpeter as the star performer, even though his new book was lagging. The 1934 English translation of his 1911 book had brought him to the attention of all U.S. economists. Through his professional activities in the American Economic Association and the Econometric Society, plus his visits to many universities, he was as well known throughout the country as any economic theorist. In addition, his devotion of several years' work to *Business Cycles* suggested to important economists of the country that Schumpeter was working on a "big" book.

But, despite his reputation, Schumpeter was not the only economist of note at Harvard in the late 1930s. The 1930s were revolutionary times in economics, and Keynes's contribution was only one of several. Harvard became the center of two other intellectual upheavals that, unlike the Keynesian revolution, were solid scientific advances not closely related to public policy. Different from the Keynesian analytical contribution, these theoretical and empirical advances were quickly absorbed by economics, and have become permanent features of modern analysis. Schumpeter thought both revolutions important and helped to disseminate their ideas.

Wassily Leontief had joined Harvard, partly at Schumpeter's instigation, in 1931. During the next six years, Leontief established a solid reputation in statistical and mathematical work in a successful effort to design a grand scheme to describe and analyze the entire economy statistically and analytically in a large table. With his analysis rooted in the Walrasian general-equilibrium model, he built such a table—called an input-output table—and published his first results in 1936. From that point on, his work expanded under his direction and that of others—students and students of students—until his technique became one of the most important methods of present-day empirical economic analysis. Schumpeter played a role in disseminating these ideas.

After laboriously compiling the data on what each industry buys from and sells to each other industry, Leontief manipulated the information so that he could, for example, estimate numerically the changes in all industry's outputs when some changes are postulated, for example, in changes in technology, government, or export demand. Input-output analysis was, in Schumpeter's view, economic science at its best. Combining economic theory, statistics, and mathematics, it was not only quantitative but also numerical. Leontief helped to move economics from the simple-minded little mathematical models and geometric figures to the thousands of numbers and relations that represent a much closer representation of the real economy. Before adequate computer capability existed, he pushed the capacity of Mark I—an ancient binary relay computer at Harvard in the 1940s—to solve the equations embodying his numerical description of the U.S. economy. Schumpeter respected Leontief as a brilliant economist and kindred spirit, and the two were intimate friends despite their age difference (Schumpeter was twenty-two years older) and different political outlooks. If Schumpeter had idols among economists, Leontief, along with Norwegian Ragnar Frisch and Irving Fisher of Yale, would be among them. Leontief now directs the Institute of Economic Analysis of New York University.[7]

Edward Chamberlin, another illustrious economist, contributed the other important innovation that developed at Harvard when he wrote his thesis in 1927 on a kind of competition that lies between pure competition and monopoly and partakes of the attributes of both. One of the stalwarts teaching theory at Harvard, Chamberlin spent most of his life elaborating on monopolistic competition and product differentiation, expanding the techniques he introduced. His work evolved into a major redirection in the economic theory of how business enterprise functions and the consequences of firms facing many different types of competitive conditions. In Schumpeter's early days at Harvard, he and Chamberlin were closer than they were in later years since Chamberlin had been one of the coterie of young people surrounding Schumpeter when he first came to Harvard. But a rift arose between them when Schumpeter tried to walk a tightrope between Chamberlin's work and that of Joan Robinson, an English economist, who developed many of the same ideas as Chamberlin at about the same time. Schumpeter's catholic outlook, recognizing merit in both Chamberlin and Robinson, offended Chamberlin, who believed the breakthrough was his alone.

The work of Chamberlin and Robinson expanded and altered economists' conceptions of how firms operate, how markets function, and what results from productive activity. Instead of markets in which there are only a large number of small sellers, none of whom have influence over price, economists came to realize that sometimes producers of a given product are few in number, make goods unique to the firm, and produce under demand conditions that confer upon them a much broader range of decision making. New tools, new insights, new analytical consequences resulted. Because it recognized the gray area between monopoly and competition where prices are higher and output is lower, the microeconomic revolution produced more realistic results on the basis of propositions that resembled more closely what was actually happening in the industrial world.[8]

Harvard also had some new recruits in the 1930s. Alvin Hansen, a specialist in business cycles, with many ideas similar to those of Schumpeter, came from the University of Minnesota in 1937. In the mid-1930s, Hansen criticized Keynes and *The General Theory* harshly, but he later became Keynes's chief follower and spokesman among U.S. economists. Hansen also believed that the rate of technological change was slowing down, thereby leading to economic stagnation. Still, he and Schumpeter got along famously despite these serious differences in views. Gottfried Haberler, along with Leontief, was probably Schumpeter's closest friend during the 1930s and 1940s. A 1922 graduate of the University of Vienna, Haberler had first visited Harvard as a Rockefeller scholar in 1927, the same year he became acquainted with Schumpeter in Bonn. He then became a visiting professor at Harvard in 1931-32. Finally, he left the League of Nations in Geneva and came permanently to Harvard in 1936, becoming a full professor in 1939. Haberler is known for his famous books, *Prosperity and Depression* and *The Theory of International Trade*, the latter originally published in German in 1933 with its first English edition in 1936, as well as scores of scientific papers. Still a professor emeritus at Harvard, Haberler now works for the American Enterprise Institute in Washington.[9]

9

During the 1930s, Harvard was not immune to the political turmoil affecting the rest of the country. Also affected by the depression, the university under President Conant's penny-pinching leadership sometimes allowed politics to influence decisions regarding which staff members should be retained when cutbacks had to be made. In the Economics Department, two extremely able instructors, Alan Sweezy and Raymond Walsh, were forced out by the department and the administration when the department's funding was greatly reduced. Since both Sweezy and Walsh were reputed to be leftists, other liberal and leftist faculty members charged the administration and the department with political bias.[10] Even Schumpeter noted in his diary his anger over the loss of these two excellent economists. Although conservative, Schumpeter could have cared less about the political views of these men, or any other economist. He seldom permitted prejudice of any kind—national, ethnic, racial, political, gender, or religious—to interfere with his evaluation of the scientific merit and capabilities of his colleagues, or of economists in general. He held such prejudices, but he remained a scientific purist when it came time to appraise the scientific qualifications of people.

Paradoxically, however, Schumpeter could not claim to rise above using race in evaluating people as people. He never tried to hide his belief that Jews were different, exclusive, and cliquish. These ideas, having been a part of his cultural heritage, dated back to Třešt, Graz, Vienna, and his childhood. His attitude toward Jews was strange and abstract, even contradictory, as were many of his beliefs. No doubt he held antisemitic views. But he did not believe that Jews were inferior or members of a lesser race, claiming often that their superiority gave them an unfair advantage over others. According to Paul Samuelson, Schumpeter believed that Jews were "early bloomers who would unfairly receive more rewards than they deserve in free competition." But Samuelson further stated: "Again, let me hasten to add the usual qualification that these two men [Schumpeter and George Birkhoff, mathematician and dean at Harvard] were among my best friends and, I believe, both had a genuine high regard for my abilities and promise."[11]

Ironically, Schumpeter once told fellow Austrian Herbert Furth of the staff of the Federal Reserve,

> Of course, the Nazis have a point when they deny that all races are equal. The question is only: which are the master races? Now, what is the greatest achievement of our civilization? Modern capitalism! Which race has made perhaps the largest contribution to that achievement? The Jews! If only the Nazis had recognized that the Jews belong to the master race, they'd have been all right.[12]

Despite this belief, among friends Schumpeter told the usual stale racial jokes: A Jew in Vienna stubs his toe and all the Jews of Budapest say "ouch."

An important part of his attitude revolved around the supposed clannishness of Jews, an idea taught him at his mother's knee on the basis of Moravian Jews' reputed behavior. Jews supposedly stick together and promote one another's interests, above the interests of any other group or loyalty. Schumpeter's firm belief in the merit system led to his fear that Jews would violate that system in promoting their own interests first.

He sometimes referred to Jews collectively as Asians or Hebs and asserted that their attitude of clannishness and exclusivity made them the racists. In his diary, he wrote incautious sentiments. On 1 July 1938, for example, he wrote, "We must have either Hitler or else the Jews." On 14 June 1939, he confided that "My attitude toward Hitlerism is so astonishing.... Haven't I hated the Prussian and fat German pig face—hawk face ... and attacked everything that Hitler stands for.... But now I'm all but partisan and I am as antisemitic as Schmidt or some kind of rich German-American."

Schumpeter did identify the Jews as a special group and sometimes, in unguarded moments, made invidious comments about them as a group. These racial attitudes emerged only rarely in private conversation with friends, but did appear in his diary. He would have been the first to repudiate publicly anyone who tried to use race as a criterion for any kind of public policy, or as the measure of men for any scientific purpose. Based on their personal knowledge and experience, some of Schumpeter's Jewish friends to this date refuse to believe that he was antisemitic. But his diary and remarks to friends convict him of a form of antisemitism, although this belief would not lead him to discriminate against or injure Jews. In many ways, Schumpeter is representative of those who matured in turn-of-the-century Vienna, where antisemitism was an almost universal cultural trait, an unconscious outlook afflicting nearly all of society.

The only instance I could find when Schumpeter may have considered— but did not use—race as a criterion for a decision, and even this instance was ambiguous, concerned an important European Jewish economist under consideration as a fellow of the Econometric Society in the late 1930s. After writing at length to a fellow council member concerning the man's qualifications, Schumpeter said he favored the man's admission as a fellow of the society, but added that "if one gets in," they will all want in, and many will succeed. Schumpeter did not specify which group he was referring to, but his colleague, knowing that the man under consideration was Jewish, assumed Schumpeter had misgivings about the admission of Jews into the society's elite Fellowship ranks. He charged Schumpeter with racial prejudice. Schumpeter protested that he was concerned because the candidate was a socialist, not because he was a Jew, and denied fiercely that he would use race as a criterion for a fellowship. Still, his response indicates that he attributed the same kind of clannishness to both Jews and socialists. And, despite these misgivings, he had recommended that this Jewish socialist become a Fellow of the society.[13]

Schumpeter's attitude toward Jews convinced some of his friends that he was himself a Jew and his antisemitism was overcompensation. Schumpeter never displayed any sentiment to his friends or in his diary that he believed that he was Jewish, and several remarks indicate the reverse. But he knew little of his family history—only what his mother had told him, which apparently was little. The detailed history of his family indicates that he was not Jewish.[14]

Schumpeter in his fifties and sixties was an unbelievably complex and paradoxical man. Outwardly, he was the jovial and friendly scholar and teacher, interested only in his science, his research, and his students, but still not taking his work so seriously that it consumed him. Inwardly, he suffered often crippling depression and worshipped his personal religion at the altar of his wife and mother, now long dead. In his communion with himself in his personal writings, he revealed beliefs and prejudices at odds with his public stance. His attitude toward minority groups and other races was ambivalent, although his overarching sentiment was elitist and racist. He lived many different and segregated lives, illustrating the oft-cited dictum that Western man maintains his sanity only by compartmentalizing himself.

Notes

1   At this time the Rockefeller Foundation had given Harvard a grant for research in the social sciences. Members of the Department of Economics each year applied for a grant for research and secretarial assistance. The titles of Schumpeter's research come from these small grants, usually only a few thousand dollars. He used the money for secretarial assistance.

2   Professor Shibata wrote to me in 1983, revealing his relationship to Schumpeter in 1931 when Schumpeter visited Japan and later when Shibata visited Cambridge. He also included translated excerpts from his autobiography.

3   This and the following sections are based on Schumpeter's diary, a loose, disorganized, and unbound collection of daily observations on scraps of paper in the Harvard University Archives.

4   This observation is based on conversations with friends and colleagues who saw him regularly in this period.

5   In his last paper, which he was writing at the time of his death, Schumpeter wrote: "A reorganization of society on the lines of the encyclical *Quadragesimo anno*,... no doubt provides an alternative to socialism that would avoid the 'omnipotent state'." See Joseph Schumpeter, "The March into Socialism," in *Capitalism, Socialism and Democracy*, 3rd edition (New York: Harper and Row, 1950), 416.

6   Successive issues of *Econometrica* in this period indicate the fellows and officers and their precise positions.

7   Leonard Silk, *The Economists* (New York: Avon Books, 1976), 137-71 contains an essay on the life and work of Wassily Leontief. Most of Leontief's work has been in scientific articles and require some understanding of statistics and mathematics.

8   William Breit and Roger L. Ransom, *The Academic Scribblers* (New York: Holt, Rinehart, and Winston, 1971), 54-66 has an essay on Chamberlin and others who developed imperfect competition theory.

9   Hansen, who died in 1975, was the leading U.S. proponent of Keynesian ideas and wrote a dozen important books on national income, business cycles, and fiscal policy. One of the most influential was *A Guide to Keynes* (New York: McGraw-Hill, 1953). Gottfried Haberler came from the Austrian tradition, coming to the United States (Harvard) to stay in 1936. He is not flashy but is sound and scholarly. He has written extensively on business cycles, national economic conditions, and international trade and finance.

10   The Cambridge Union of University Teachers published in April 1937 a paper entitled "Harvard's Liberalism: Myth or Reality," a statement on the dismissal of J. Raymond Walsh and Alan R. Sweezy. Eventually the department and the university were exonerated on the charge of discrimination, but the university has been severely criticized for short-sighted educational policies.

11   Paul Samuelson, "Economics in a Golden Age: A Personal Memoir," in *Collected Scientific Papers IV* (Cambridge: MIT Press), chapter 278.

12   This quotation is from a letter to me in 1983 from Herbert Furth, a retired official

of the Federal Reserve Board of Governors and long-time friend of Schumpeter.

13 This correspondence is in the Harvard University Archives.

14 Dr. Fritz Machlup, for example, was absolutely convinced that Schumpeter was Jewish and told all who were interested that this was so. He knew Schumpeter well and during his time at Harvard as a Rockefeller fellow in the 1930s was particularly close to Schumpeter. Schumpeter's family history, as noted in chapter 2, established that Schumpeter was not Jewish.

5

Business Cycles: The Amplified Vision (1939)

Business Cycles was a follow-up to Schumpeter's *Theory of Economic Development,* and he hoped that it would demonstrate that his development theory was either right or at least consistent with the historical facts. He hoped, also, that this book would help to redirect the attention of economists to the study of the economy and an effort to understand the economic interrelationships theoretically, historically, and statistically, rather than to promote policies that might address the country's economic problems. But economists were not listening. They acknowledged the scholarship but, ignoring Schumpeter's plea, continued to follow the lead of John Maynard Keynes.

1

All during the summer and early fall of 1938, Schumpeter slaved on the cycles manuscript in Taconic and Cambridge. Finally, on Monday, 2 January 1939, after a crowded holiday while vacationing in Taconic and attending the association meetings, he wrote exultantly in his diary,

On dec. 9, [1938] I finished my Cycle ms! It transpired practically—a little of course I owe to the courses and here and there to an hour's reading.... Fact is that laying aside Money in the summer 1934, I hoped to get the business cycle done in another year and that I planned accordingly. That may have been foolish to hope, yet I am now, with ref. to that program, late by (academically counting) 3 1/2 years which otherwise would possibly have given me a chance, which now has passed

71

through the ivory gate. For this I shall never be able to make up—and the periodic misery, laziness, idiocy from which I suffer must be accepted as a fact.

Containing 1,095 pages, this "big book" extended far beyond what he had originally planned. The canvas on which Schumpeter painted in *Business Cycles* was immense—no less than a complete theory and evaluation of capitalism and its performance over three centuries. First, it presented the theory of how the capitalist economy functions in equilibrium; then it discussed the theory of how the economy changes in time. He next evaluated capitalism's performance according to its statistical record and concluded by examining more than 150 years of history through which capitalism has travelled. Covering such a huge amount of territory, *Business Cycles* was strictly an analytical and historical book, not a practical or policy-oriented one. Its author did not propose to resolve the problems faced by capitalism during the 1930s or to recommend economic policies.

The chance he referred to in the penultimate sentence of the above quotation was that of writing the book he wanted to write on economic theory, that is a refinement and amplification of his first two books, instead of *Business Cycles*. In the summer of 1934, when Schumpeter put the money project aside, he decided to concentrate on the cycle book, planning to resume work on the money book again a year later. Then, in mid-1936, he wanted to finish the money book and begin work on an economic theory book, for which he specified no deadline. But no part of this plan had worked out. Work on cycles took until the end of 1938, or mid-1939 counting time spent correcting proofs. Begun in 1933, his cycles book was finally published in two volumes by McGraw-Hill in 1939.

Schumpeter chose the title *Business Cycles* because, during the two or three years before finishing it, he always referred to it as his cycles book in English, or *Krisenwerk* in German. Grumbling that all the good titles had already been taken, he didn't like the title, nor did it serve him well because the book's contents were much broader than the title implies. His more descriptive subtitle—*A Theoretical, Historical and Statistical Analysis of the Capitalist Process*—expresses the contents of the book more fully than the title does. In fact, the last three words of the subtitle, *The Capitalist Process*, would have made a better title than the one he chose.

In the first part of the book, Schumpeter endeavored to bring his analysis of economic change closer to the statistical and historical evidence by setting down a series of approximations that were increasingly realistic models of the economy. In his first and crudest approximation, he discussed what would happen in the capitalist economy according to the pure theory of economic development. Applying the theory he had developed two decades earlier, Schumpeter presented the idea that the economy would behave in a predictable manner following a known innovation. His theory begins with a model of static economy in which time does not yield any change and the economy simply repeats itself endlessly. Schumpeter's first book, *Das Wesen und der Hauptinhalt de theoretischen Nationaloekonomie* (1908), had offered a detailed analysis of such a static economy.[1]

2

Into the ideal static economy, Schumpeter introduced change. The agent of change was the entrepreneur, and the instrument of change was his innovation. The effect of such an innovation, as described by Schumpeter in the 1939 *Business Cycles,* was much the same as that described in his 1911 *Entwicklung* book, which became *The Theory of Economic Development* in 1934. Seeking glory, profit, and the satisfaction of inner urges, the entrepreneur plans to acquire them by altering the economy's productive relationships. Schumpeter called the change implanted by the entrepreneur into the productive apparatus of the economy "a new combination."

By innovating, the entrepreneur initiates disequilibrium into the economy which appears first as a period of prosperity with rising production, prices, incomes, and consumption. As the economy moves away from the grip of the previous equilibrium because of the effect of the impulse of changed production relations, everything in the economy adjusts to the changed situation. As it spreads through the economy, the impact of innovation also moves away in time from the moment of its initiation and thereby weakens. The forces of competition and self-interest initiate a second period, a recession, as they bring the economy back into a new equilibrium, one in which prices are different and output is higher than at the beginning of the prosperity. If all the adjustments were smooth and frictionless and the economy without error, no cycle would necessarily appear. The economy would move in an endless series of bursts forward, of prosperities and recessions, from one equilibrium to another, tracing out a path through time of rising and then falling prices, and increasing income as the economy produces new products or the same products with new methods.[2]

Even if the effects of the innovation stimulated no further changes in the economy, the receding prosperity might not end at the exact equilibrium position. But eventually the new equilibrium would assert itself, if no other innovation or change occurred. But in fact the innovation ignites other agents of change in the economy. In *Business Cycles,* Schumpeter sought a closer approximation to statistical and historical reality than the impact of the innovation alone—the primary wave—provides. He therefore introduced the concept of the secondary wave, in which the prosperity initially generated by the innovation produces changes that also affect the economy. Even those who are not entrepreneurs come to believe that they can benefit from the expansion and heightened prosperity. By expanding their production, they push the economy ahead and for a time justify their expectations. Favorable expectations, not a genuine change in production relations, are the basis for the actions of these businessmen. The disappearance of favorable expectations and the subsequent loss of the buoyant effects associated with the expectations, along with the eventual appearance of unfavorable expectations, may alter the timing of the primary wave's turning point and also change the course of the economy's receding phase.

At the height of prosperity, the turning point occurs and the period of recession begins. The secondary prosperity, however, was based on two sets of signals: one of the innovation and the other resulting from changes in the economy in responding to the innovation. Some of the later signals may be in error or may be mistaken judgments, misreadings of the real facts by business enterprises, or the commission of errors. With the resulting inefficiency and waste building up in the economy, a change from favorable to unfavorable expectations occurs because these imperfections burden the economy and become apparent eventually even to those wearing the rose-colored glasses of prosperity. As the economy therefore misses the equilibrium and slides into a depression, the unfavorable expectations and recognition of error and waste accelerate the movement. The depression and recovery from the depression are periods unique to the secondary wave, as the primary wave has only prosperity and recession.

3

In moving into the depression, the economy bypasses the new equilibrium position that had reflected the advances resulting from innovation in an abstract economy devoid of waste, inefficiency, and the results of false expectations. Prices and production decline beyond that justified by the equilibrium position. During the depression, two vital things happen that affect the economy's health. One is the spread of the benefits of innovation because of reduced costs and prices, as well as the diffusion of new products among more and more users. The other is the elimination of waste and inefficiency. The fat, which had developed and enlarged because of economically unjustified expectations and the mistakes and the errors arising when the economy was in motion, will now be eliminated by competition. The depression therefore burns away the dross and integrates into the economy all the effects of the innovations that had originally initiated the prosperity. Contrary to common belief, Schumpeter argued that the depression is not an unwanted and unexpected disaster with wholly negative effects. Instead, the depression is a necessary part of the capitalist process where markets perform a purging and disciplinary function that is just as useful and positive for capitalism's health as is the prosperity.

The depression, which results not from the innovation but from the secondary wave, may contain harmful elements because the economy went beyond its justified expansion during the prosperity of the secondary wave. In the ensuing depression, the economy surpasses its justified decline in an attempt to correct for the errors of the preceding prosperity. During the depression, values of prices and outputs are far distant from the equilibrium. Wages and prices, as well as production and consumption, have fallen too far, as the economy is paying the penalty for the earlier mistakes and inefficiency of the preceding prosperity. Finally, the economy's recovery phase ends the depression, as the forces of equilibrium once again increase production and prices and the economy approaches full-capacity equilibrium operation.

The economy, however, usually does not have the opportunity to complete the restoration to the new equilibrium because, as it approaches it, another cluster of innovations intervenes. Entrepreneurs could not have introduced their new innovations earlier because the economy was operating below par, they could find no financing, and they feared their ideas would fail in the depression. Entrepreneurs will take a chance only when the economy is in equilibrium or close to it. Potential innovations are always in abundance, lying around begging for implementation, waiting for the right men and the right economic conditions. But, because of the risk of failure, Schumpeter argued strongly that objective conditions result in the clustering of innovations. The success of the first innovation encourages the second entrepreneur, the second encourages the third, and so on. The banking system similarly finds it increasingly comfortable to lend to second and third entrepreneurs.

Schumpeter's theory, with only limited assumptions and apparent historical reasonableness, thus demonstrated that innovations—impulses whose origins lie in entrepreneurs' desires to reap profits as well as psychological rewards—impart a cyclical movement to the economy. Although innovations are not cyclical, they are periodic, setting the economy in motion and moving it out of its static orbit. Prices and production then change, according to the nature and magnitude of the innovation and the characteristics of the economy it interacts with, until they are caught in the grip of new gravitational forces—another equilibrium. Eventually, the economy settles down into a new orbit with stable prices and production, where it remains in steady-state motion until another group of innovations impinges upon it.

The bare bones of Schumpeter's business cycle theory in *Business Cycles* is much the same as that in the cycles chapter of his earlier *The Theory of Economic Development*. In this new book, he elaborated upon, went into detail, illustrated, and filled in with subtleties to a greater extent than in the development book. He tried to be more realistic. One important move toward reality in *Business Cycles* came with Schumpeter's recognition of a vast array of other possible causes of cyclical behavior in the economy. One possibility is an external event—war, crop variations, gold production, disasters, and other events whose origins are unrelated to anything happening in the economy. These can easily produce the appearance of cycles. Similarly, random impulses can produce cyclical responses wherein the economy adjusts by oscillating. Several theories—that of Eugen Slutsky, for example—generate cycles purely from the economy's response mechanism.[3] Another possibility arises when all the capital goods in an important sector of the economy are introduced or must be replaced at the same time; the result would be a strong impulse capable of generating a replacement cycle. All these external events and the economy's response to them are part of the reality observable in the performance of the economy, even though they may not share in the basic explanation of the cycle.

4

One of the major contributions contained in *Business Cycles* lies in Schumpeter's suggestion and support of the idea that more than one cycle in economic activities is possible. Developing this idea more than any other economist, he wrote of three cycles. One, called the Kitchin cycle after Joseph Kitchin, who first observed it through the use of periodogram analysis, lasts an average of only forty months. Evident in the statistical series of bank clearings, wholesale prices, and interest rates, this very short cycle is most important in time series of business inventories. Schumpeter did not regard it as a fundamental cycle initiated by innovation, but rather as a part of the economy's internal response mechanism. The fundamental cycle, the only one required in Schumpeter's analysis, is the eight- to eleven-year Juglar cycle, in honor of Clement Juglar, a Frenchman who first analyzed this cycle statistically in the 1860s after observing that the economy periodically expanded and contracted in a rhythmic and regular manner. Before Juglar's time, economists thought the economy was subject to irregular crises, but they had not observed their cyclical nature. The Juglar cycle is what most analysts refer to as the business cycle.

Schumpeter also accepted the view that there may be long cycles of fifty to sixty years. He named these Kondratieff cycles, after Nikolai Kondratieff, a Russian economist who wrote on the long wave in the 1920s. According to Schumpeter (but not Kondratieff), the long cycle is also an innovation cycle but its innovations are in larger groups and on a grander scale. Schumpeter regarded the Industrial Revolution, with its innovations of the steam engine, the development of the textile and metallurgical industries, and the introduction of the factory system, as the first Kondratieff prosperity. It began in the last quarter of the eighteenth century in England, a bit later in the United States and Europe. The building of the railroads in the United States and Europe and the early industrialization of the mid-nineteenth century may have initiated the second Kondratieff cycle. This was followed by the period of the great U.S. industrialization in the first part of the twentieth century. Included in this third Kondratieff high were the innovations of electricity, motor cars, and chemicals. Although Schumpeter didn't know it at the time he wrote *Business Cycles*, the fourth Kondratieff recovery was the post-World War II period, leading to the peak in the early 1970s and the trough in about 1990.[4]

Schumpeter carefully nested the idealized Kitchin, Juglar, and Kondratieff cycles together graphically and statistically, and then observed the resulting idealized statistical time series of prices and production. Even without the disturbances of external events, random impulses, responses of the economy, secondary and tertiary cycles, and many other factors, these data do not have the appearance of the normal textbook business cycle that resembles a mathematical sine curve. In Schumpeter's composite cycle, there appears to be an upward trend for a long period, followed by a downward trend, but no simple cycle is in evidence. Schumpeter argued that actual time series more closely resemble his idealized multiple-cycle time series than a sinusoidal curve oscillating around a rising trend. The resemblance to real statistical data would be even more striking if some random impulses or external events were added to the multiple-cycle series.

Stating his position with respect to multiple cycles with great care, Schumpeter did not regard the existence of multiple cycles as fact, nor did he even present the three-cycle schema as a hypothesis. He explicitly upheld the single-cycle hypothesis that he had first presented in 1911 as the explanation of the capitalist process. Because the evidence in its favor was slim and unconvincing, Schumpeter viewed the three-cycle schema as merely an interesting and suggestive possibility. But even the suggestion that there might be three cycles, coupled with his naming of them, was sufficient to identify Schumpeter permanently with multiple cycles in the economic literature. He asserted that in fact he favored a five-cycle schema, for which even less evidence existed. His real point was that the economy naturally moves in cycles, whether one, three, five, or a dozen different types, and those cycles depict the effects of innovation and entrepreneurial behavior on the economy. Such cycles are normal and to be expected since they are the way capitalism moves; in fact, capitalism can proceed through time only in a cyclical fashion.

Despite his caution in presenting the case for three or multiple cycles, many economists now regard Schumpeter as the chief proponent of multiple-cycle theory, particularly the theory of the long wave. Many who have not read *Business Cycles* believe that this concept is the book's chief element, and they therefore consider Schumpeter as a long-wave disciple. But this is not true. Schumpeter wrote:

> There is a theoretically indefinite number of fluctuations present in our material at any time.... Nothing in this implies a hypothesis. All it has to do with hypotheses is that it implies the refusal to accept one, viz., the single-cycle hypothesis. Nor are we going to make another hypothesis to take the place of the latter.... By saying that in adopting a three-cycle schema we are not making any hypothesis which is to replace the single-cycle hypothesis, but only a decision ... the three-cycle schema does not follow from our model ... the three-cycle schema may be looked upon as a convenient descriptive schema.[5]

Believing that the only realities of the capitalist process lie in its cycles, Schumpeter argued that the economy does not move in accordance with a trend reflecting any permanent underlying economic force or reality. It would be possible to draw a line, fitted by the mathematical method of least squares, through the time series of price and production data, for example, but that line would have no economic meaning. No fundamental forces produced what Schumpeter called a "result" trend because such a trend simply summarizes the economy's average performance over a period of time; it says nothing about the causes underlying the performance as reflected in the time series. Lest anyone think that the trend line represents some fundamental force, such as population growth or a trend of capital investment, Schumpeter undermined the argument by asserting that neither population growth nor capital accumulation are economic "forces." Rather they are results caused by activities of entrepreneurs and their innovations.

With the theory and history in *Business Cycles* carefully interwoven, Schumpeter displayed a grasp of scholarship that few historians could imitate. The years of reading, going back to his university days in Vienna, yielded little-known facts, improved interpretation of old facts, and allowed him to juxtapose propositions, present historical insights, and draw interconnections. This combination makes *Business Cycles* a rare book. Schumpeter presented the theoretical material in the first 219 pages of *Business Cycles*. The remaining 876 pages tell the historical story—the economic history of business cycles. He used the three-cycle schema as the temporal framework for discussing the economic development of the United States, England, and Germany. In a short space he analyzed fully the first Kondratieff, from 1787 to 1842. The second Kondratieff—1843 to 1897—he dispatched in eighty pages, about the same amount of space devoted to just the beginning of the third Kondratieff, 1898 to 1913.

The second volume of the book retraced many of the steps of the first, especially with respect to the specific time series. It also went back for many of its time series to the middle of the nineteenth century. For example, price and output series, both aggregate and for individual products, received detailed attention, as did series on unemployment, income, wages, measures of bank activity, interest rates, stock exchange measures, and many other time series. In the last third of the second volume, Schumpeter covered in great detail what happened between 1914 and 1935. The decade of the twenties necessitated more than 200 pages, and chapter 15 alone, dealing with just six years, 1930-35, is nearly 150 pages. While discussing this period of the Great Depression, Schumpeter included an analysis of U.S. recovery policy and what he called the "disappointing Juglar"—the failed recovery that should have returned the economy to prosperity in the mid-1930s.[6]

The purpose of this historical account was to confront theory and history in order to determine whether the theory provided a possible explanation. Schumpeter's method could not prove the theory correct, but he reasoned that, if he could find nothing in the historical account to contradict directly his theoretical scenario, then at least the theory is a possible explanation and might be a satisfactory explanation for what happened. In his attempt to interweave theory and history, he devoted greater attention to more recent times because they provided more factual and statistical data against which to compare the theory. He realized that, although a historical test of his theory or any theory would not satisfy scientific testing requirements, since the historical path might be explained by other theories, he believed his historical scholarship was sufficiently deep and probing to justify the belief that his theory was the best explanation yet.

5

Business Cycles was a one-man show. Despite the help of research assistants, including Edgar (Bum) Hoover in the early stages and Alice Bourneuf and others in the later stages, Schumpeter had to do the reading, the interpretation and analysis, and the writing, all of it on yellow foolscap.[7] As with his other work, he seldom sought the advice or ideas of his colleagues, choosing to tell them only in a general way what he was working on, and occasionally grousing about how hard he worked and how intractable the material was. His colleagues and students knew that he was working on a big book; they did not know how broad the subject or how deep the probe would be. Schumpeter complained now and then that the book was not going well, but only to those closest to him, such as Leontief and Haberler.

The basic problem Schumpeter had that prevented him from presenting a popular and path-breaking book, such as that of Keynes, was his unwillingness to state his theory in a simplified model and then draw policy conclusions from it—the same elements that delayed and finally killed his money book. He refused to propose a policy and then produce a theory supposedly to justify that policy. Only by making strong assumptions about some parts of the economy could he eliminate those parts from consideration. So long as he stuck with an evolutionary model in which prices, quantities, incomes, production and institutional structures, and financial measures all move, he would face insuperable problems. He was frequently unhappy that the pieces did not fit together well or that some elusive piece of evidence had yet to be chased down.

In his late 1930s diaries, he frequently complained that such things as "periodic misery, laziness, and idiocy from which I suffer" were the reasons for the delay in *Business Cycles*, but this was a common Schumpeterian pose. Accepting personal responsibility, he often attributed delays in the cycles book, as he did with his effort to develop a new theory, to his own indolence and depression. But the major obstacles lay even more in the nature of the difficult, perhaps impossible, problems on which he was working. A lesser but perhaps more clever scholar would never have undertaken such a task, or if he had incautiously started, he would have quickly abandoned it. Schumpeter never dreamed in 1934, when he contemplated writing the book in a year, that the result would be a work of over a thousand pages and would deal with the whole panorama of the theory, statistics, and history of business cycles. But the project itself assumed control, and his scholarly conscience would not allow him to stop work on it until he had, in his view, exhausted the subject.

All during the first half of 1939, Schumpeter complained of the endless hours spent reading galleys and page proofs, though the task was made less onerous by Elizabeth's help. When he told his friends that he had become a galley slave, he was only half joking. That work chewed up his leave of absence from the university during the spring term of 1939, and he had to cancel a planned trip to Japan. When *Business Cycles* finally appeared, he was disappointed. From the beginning, it was clear that the impact of the book would be much less than Schumpeter had hoped, largely because of Keynes's work. Once again, as in the study of money, Keynes had stolen the march on him. Published more than three years earlier, Keynes's ideas had steadily gained ground until they became the center of a major intellectual debate. *The General Theory of Employment Interest and Money* provided what *Business Cycles* did not: a simple model that seemed realistic at the moment and a solution to the problem of the depression. Policies of interest to everyone occupied the central position in Keynes, but they were absent in Schumpeter.

Keynes had treated the depression of the 1930s as something new and different, an unemployment equilibrium, and called on the government to apply bold new policies of deficit spending in order to confront the new situation. In contrast, Schumpeter explained that the situation of the 1930s was a correction for the errors of the 1920s and before, resulting from the economy's failure to adjust quickly and from inadequate and incorrect government policies. While Schumpeter continued to work within the framework of existing economic assumptions, Keynes intended to revolutionize economics by changing the assumptions. In the scholarly popularity contest between Schumpeter and Keynes, Keynes won. Schumpeter's model was too complex and difficult, and could not yield simple geometrical and mathematical results or come up with a simple policy, as Keynes's did. Schumpeter didn't provide plain and simple answers to difficult and complex questions, as Keynes seemed to, nor did he attack Keynes or other economists or indicate the weakness of the Keynesian model. While Schumpeter wrote what he thought was a high-minded scientific treatise, Keynes made a slashing assault on everyone who didn't agree with him. Keynes's work was a policy tract for the times, telling people what he thought was the new truth in economics, that the trouble was in the system and not in themselves, and that the government could straighten it out. Opposing this, Schumpeter said, "I recommend no policy and propose no plan," which was not what economists or the public wanted to hear in 1939.[8] Schumpeter's book, however, was not anti-Keynesian; it was non-Keynesian and pre-Keynesian. The world had just experienced a devastating depression, and people wanted a way out and a plan for avoiding another one. Economists wanted solutions and an analysis to support policy recommendations. Schumpeter did not satisfy their desires, nor even make the attempt.

If Keynes were wrong, the economists wanted to know why; they also wanted proof that his policy recommendations were wrong-headed. But Schumpeter wanted to give the world something else, arguing that:

> What our time needs most is the understanding of the process which people are passionately resolved to control. To supply this understanding ... is the only service the scientific worker is, as such, qualified to render.[9]

The world, however, was not much interested in what the scientific worker as such had to say. Desperately seeking answers, the world suffered—and still does—from policy-itis and short-run-itis. As a result, economists and others interested in economic matters examined the 1,100-page *Business Cycles* in a cursory fashion determined it to be pre-Keynesian, called it a classic, and put it on the shelf.

6

The reviews of *Business Cycles* in the press as well as in academic journals, began coming out at once. Many were favorable and even those not favorable were generous and tolerant. The *New York Times* reviewed it on 27 July 1939, followed by *The Saturday Review of Literature* on 5 August. A dozen other popular periodicals discussed it in the next few months. These reviews were favorable, but they also made it clear that, although impressed with the scholarship, they were not buying Schumpeter's long-run evolutionary analysis. They regarded the theory as imaginative, important, interesting, and useful, but not fully convincing. Mainly, they lamented the lack of a prescription for making things better, something people desired more than hearing about theory and history. The economic history overwhelmed many readers, but again most were not convinced that the history confirmed the theory. Schumpeter had never claimed that history confirmed his theory, but only that history was consistent with it. Yet, even if the theory were confirmed, so what? Neither the theory nor the history could tell them what to do.

The academic reviews were slower to appear. Simon Kuznets, later the 1971 Nobel Prize winner from Harvard but at the time at the University of Pennsylvania, praised the book in perhaps the most important and thoughtful review. Stating that all the analyses "contribute to an impression of a well integrated intellectual structure,"[10] Kuznets then questioned many of the fundamental elements of Schumpeter's work. Economists have long regarded one of the weak points of Schumpeter's economic development theory to be the periodic clustering or bunching of innovations. Many wondered why they should not be spread evenly in time or why they should not come irregularly and without any pattern.

Although Schumpeter constructed a strong argument in favor of bunching and periodic outbursts of innovations, Kuznets rejected his reasoning. Schumpeter had based his analysis on his reading of the facts. But Kuznets, an experienced economic historian, read them differently. Others, including Oskar Lange, supported Schumpeter on this question.[11] Kuznets went on to attack other points, especially unconvinced by the idea of the four-phase cycle. Like most cycle theorists, Schumpeter believed the cycle—in its secondary wave—went through prosperity, recession, depression, and recovery phases, but Kuznets argued that some of these phases may not represent meaningful periods of times. Questioning Schumpeter's explanation of the turning points, he also would not concede that Schumpeter's trend was a result trend only. Further, he would not admit the validity of the multiple-cycle thesis, even though Kuznets himself was working at the time to define and analyze yet another cycle.

When all is said, what did Kuznets, reflecting the opinion of many economists, think? In summing up, he wrote:

The [Kuznets] summary and critical discussion above necessarily fail to show the achievements of the treatise in providing illuminating interpretations of historical developments; incisive comments on the analysis of cyclical fluctuations in various aspects of economic activity; revealing references to an extraordinarily wide variety of publications in directly and indirectly related fields; thought-provoking judgments concerning the general course of capitalist evolution. It is difficult to convey the flavor of the book except by saying that in many of its parts it reads like an intellectual diary, a record of Professor Schumpeter's journey through the realm of business cycles and capitalist evolution.... And Professor Schumpeter is a widely experienced traveller, whose comments reveal insight combined with a sense of reality; of wide background against which to judge the intellectual conduct of men and the vagaries of a changing social order.[12]

Most reviewers correctly regarded *Business Cycles* as what it was: an updated and not critically changed restatement of Schumpeter's theory of economic development, and a perceptive economic history of business cycles. The book endeavored to integrate the two so as to produce a historically consistent theory and a theoretically enlightened history, an effort to use economic statistics and history to test, that is, refute, the theory. Although heady with scholarship, it provided no new theory, uncovered no new theorems, identified no new techniques of theoretical or empirical analysis, and established no new relationships or facts. It drew no new conclusions and made no policy recommendations. And its great bulk had the effect of turning off most economists.

On 13 October 1939, Schumpeter received a comforting letter from his friend Ragnar Frisch:

Please accept my warmest congratulations on the completion of your magnum opus ... you have given us something formidable. Every page is packed with meat. I have hardly ever seen a great work that is so free from from water. Your admirable combination of historical knowledge, theoretical depth, and the mathematical slant. The connoisseur will understand how penetrating your remarks are. And both he and the laymen must admire the brilliancy of your style. And last but not least, everybody must respect the 100% academic manner in which you treat other scientists and other theories. Let me tell you that I have never met a person with your ability to understand the other fellow's point of view and do him justice.[13]

8

Despite these uplifting words, few of Schumpeter's students or colleagues even read *Business Cycles*. Not considered a complete commercial failure, it still made little money for author or publisher, selling only 1,075 copies in the first eighteen months. Only one professor at Harvard (not Schumpeter) and one at Duke University used it as a textbook, and then for only one year.[14] In 1940, Schumpeter's students, in an effort to honor him, held a seminar to discuss the work. Some of those who attended later said that the only time they ever saw Schumpeter truly angry was at that seminar. Infected by the Keynesian virus, most students looked at everything through Keynesian-colored glasses and were determined to read what they considered antiquated analysis and policy recommendations into Schumpeter's book. When they tried to compare it with Keynes and discuss its policy and practical relevance at the moment, Schumpeter quickly realized that most of them had not really read the book or understood what he had attempted to do. In one outburst at the seminar, Schumpeter asserted that, considering the time he had spent working on the book, he expected serious economists to spend about 150 hours studying it. Yet they hadn't spent even fifteen hours. Still, they taunted him with questions like, "Have you not really assumed full employment?" Bitter and disappointed, he jestingly replied, "How could anyone be so unfashionable these days as to make that assumption?"[15]

Because of this kind of Keynesian mentality among students as well as his colleagues, *Business Cycles* went nowhere, stimulating no further research on the subject and inspiring no other scholars to pick up the ideas and expand upon them. The book just slipped down the ways and sank beneath the waters. Its timing could hardly have been worse. Economists were still absorbing Keynes's book, which seemed to offer something new, unlike Schumpeter's book. To make matters worse, shortly after Schumpeter's work appeared, war erupted. With economists entering the military and going to Washington, their attention no longer included such notions as the circular flow, innovations, or what happened in the second Kondratieff. The problem of the depression was finally in the past.

When professors and students began to return to campus in 1945, they faced a whole new set of problems. By that time, many professors believed they had found the key to economics in *The General Theory*. Many also believed, as my own professors told me shortly after the war, that the study of business cycles was a matter for the history of economic thought. Schumpeter's two-volume analysis of business cycles, most of which was history, therefore did not appear on the priority reading list of professors anywhere. Only a few students, impressed with Schumpeter and interested in history and cycles, bought it. For most, it was an unread "classic," a book to read when the crush of examinations and the dissertation were over. When that time came, other pressing matters claimed priority.

In 1964, McGraw-Hill tried to rejuvenate the book. Professor Rendigs Fels of Vanderbilt University, a student of both business cycles and Schumpeter, cut the book by more than one-half, hoping to make it more accessible. But that version also failed to attract attention. Summing up the poor timing of the original work, Professor Fels stated in his introduction:

> Schumpeter had bad luck with *Business Cycles.…* The publication date of *Business Cycles* proved singularly unfortunate. Had it appeared three years before Keynes's *General Theory* sent economists scurrying off in other directions instead of three years' afterwards, it would have gained from the enormous interest everyone had in business cycles in 1933 and might have been accorded a reception second only to that later received by the *General Theory* itself. Instead, it appeared just as the outbreak of World War II raised economic problems to which Keynes's tools, but not Schumpeter's, could be readily adapted.[16]

At present, although the original book is still in print, and although many respect it as a classic, it has only limited influence. The time of *Business Cycles* has passed or has not yet come.

Notes

1 There are no significant differences in Schumpeter's analysis of the static economy as it appeared in 1908, 1911, and 1939. Stylistic and explanatory differences exist, but the basic static economic theory of 1939 was the same as the static theory of 1908.

2 The analysis of the effects of innovation in *Business Cycles* is substantially the same as in *Entwicklung*. The 1911 book even had a business cycle chapter that sought to demonstrate how the effects of innovation produced cyclical movement. But that earlier analysis was less complete with more limited discussion of secondary and tertiary effects, and no discussion of multiple of cycles compared to *Business Cycles*.

3 "Sulla theoria del bilancio del consumatore," *Giorgnale degli economisti* July 1915.

4 The Kondratieff cycle, or long wave, has proved a hardy idea and keeps cropping up. Most economics textbooks mentioned it, including Paul Samuelson's *Economics*, 11th edition (New York: McGraw-Hill, 1980), 241, where he couples Schumpeter and the Kondratieff.

5 *Business Cycles* (New York: McGraw-Hill, 1939), 168-70.

6 Ibid., 1011-45.

7 Professor Hoover was a long-time professor at the University of Michigan; Professor Bourneuf was at Boston College for many years before her recent death.

8 *Business Cycles*, vi.

9 Ibid.

10 *American Economic Review* 30 (June 1940): 257-71.

11 *Review of Economic Statistics* 23, no. 5 (November 1941): 190-3.

12 *American Economic Review* 30 (June 1940): 270-1.

13 This letter is in the correspondence file of the Schumpeter papers in the Harvard University Archives.

14   This information appears in reports of McGraw-Hill to Schumpeter in the Harvard University Archives.
15   I talked to several who were at the seminar, including Dudley Dillard of the University of Maryland and Rendigs Fels of Vanderbilt University.
16   Joseph A. Schumpeter, *Business Cycles*, ed. Rendigs Fels. abridged (New York: McGraw-Hill, 1964).

6

Alienation and Isolation (1939-1942)

On his fifty-sixth birthday (8 February 1939), Schumpeter wrote in his diary,

To me it seems like 56 years of missed opportunities; possibly not true however—many opportunities there were, but some—and probably all that I had it in me to exploit—were rather promptly caught. And many opportunities to founder were miraculously avoided—the gran rifiuto [great waste] was [19]19-25, *moral* failure leading to failure in what might have been another career of some usefulness ... what looks like missed opportunities presumably was no more but a disequilibrated physical and moral setup, which made things impossible which at the same time looked quite within reach. This is so even in the scientific field.

Perceptive it was of Schumpeter to divide his life into the periods before and after the interval from 1919 to 1925. That troubled time, the "great waste," separated the two parts of his more successful academic and scientific career—from 1906 to 1919 and from 1925 to 1950. Written on his birthday, a time for analyzing and summing up his life, the diary entry presents a courageous insight in that, instead of blaming others or the circumstances (both of which figured significantly in his problems), he attributed his downfall to moral failure on his part . These remarks served as the confession of a sad man, an unhappy man, but a strong and honest one.

1

At the age of fifty-six, Schumpeter remained in good health, although he complained a good bit about being tired and ill and working too hard. With 156 pounds on his 5-foot, 8-inch frame, he was now a little thick set but not fat. His tennis playing, walks to and from his new office in Littauer Center, and his wanderings in Taconic kept him in reasonably fit condition, even if he did not think so.[1] Yet he was at loose ends intellectually. With *Business Cycles* having been sent to the publisher in early 1939, Schumpeter's scientific life stalled for a while as he tried to sort out what to do next. At Christmas 1938, he had resumed work on the money book set aside earlier, hoping now to finish it within a few months. But because the *Geldbuch*—the version he had written in the late 1920s and early 1930s was in German, he would have to translate and revise at the same time. Although he had a nearly complete manuscript and many pages of revisions, work did not go well because his concentration was weak.[2]

He complained of only nibbling at work during a period when he should have had more time available. On sabbatical leave in the winter of the spring term of 1939, Schumpeter dabbled with his money book. He was on leave but stayed in Cambridge because Taconic was too cold and difficult. The theory book was also on his mind, but it did not become a focussed research and writing project, absorbing his undivided efforts for any significant span of time. During this winter, he also began toying with essays on the evolution of capitalism and the nature of socialism, hoping to amplify the seminars he had given in Washington in the mid-1930s. By early spring, galleys and page proofs of *Business Cycles* began to inundate him, leaving him, hour after hour, with the dull and uncreative task of reading proof, a penalty people pay for writing books. Although Elizabeth helped him, the work was painfully slow because of the book's length.

With the page proofs behind him, Schumpeter's plans became more focussed. Back in Taconic by June 1939, he recorded his plan for a book of six essays.

1. Marxian Economics.
2. Can cap. survive.
3. Can Soc work.
4. Democracy and Soc.
5. Soc. pol.
6. Planning (and Control?).

This outline would evolve into *Capitalism, Socialism and Democracy*, completed less than three years later. The main differences between this initial outline and the book itself are the ambiguity of number 5, which turned out to be a historical sketch of socialist parties, and the absence in the book of number 6, the planning section, which, in fact, ended up as being included in number 3.

When this book was in gestation, Schumpeter mildly deprecated it, calling it his little book of essays. He had designed it as an interim project, a spare-time project, one almost of relaxation to be done while he tooled up for the next major task, either his money or his theory book. He worked steadily on the project, but it was not the hard grueling work that haunted him with the cycles book. He thought he could write much of it from his experiences and accumulated reading, foregoing difficult and time-consuming research. Some of the book had already been written, bits and pieces of the manuscript cluttered his studies, and he incorporated his seminars given at the Department of Agriculture in November 1935.

At this same time, he also began to plan for yet another book. Over the years, many publishers had been after him to authorize an English translation of *Epochen der Dogmen- und Methodengeschichte*, published originally in 1914 as an article in an important German encyclopedia. Later published as a monograph, this short and pithy survey of the history of economics had added luster to his reputation. But, because it was in German, it was inaccessible to most American and English colleagues and students who wanted to read it. Lionel Robbins of the London School of Economics, whom Schumpeter visited each year until 1935, had offered to take responsibility for a translation and for arranging its subsequent publication. In response to Robbins's offer, Schumpeter, on 10 January 1935, replied "when I wrote the Dogmen.... I did it with the intention of writing a preliminary sketch of what I planned to work out in detail later on."[3]

But, in 1939, he realized he could kill two birds with one stone. When the department asked him to teach a course called The History of Economic Literature since 1776, Schumpeter's interest in the history of economic analysis had been recharged. Reading his little book and other literature on the subject, he believed he could revise and translate it at the same time, as he also planned to do with the money book. But the money book was an economic theory book, requiring creativity; *Epochen* was a book about economic theory, requiring only scholarship. Because he had already done much of the research, he thought he could do the history of economics more easily and quickly.

Schumpeter now had two book projects that he expected would take little time or effort, as well as the money book, which required only translation and revision. But, as usual with his writing projects, things didn't work out as planned. By the spring of 1940, the little book of essays on capitalism and socialism had gotten its hooks into him. Always the determined scholar, he was not satisfied just to write something off the top of his head. He had to look things up, reread books he had studied years before, make notes, write, and rewrite. As a result, the essays didn't jell nearly as quickly as he thought they would. Even though he knew what he wanted to say, the researcher in him required that he dress the work in the appropriate scholarly garb.

2

Another subject occupied much of Schumpeter's attention during 1939: the impending war. When he and Elizabeth discussed plans for the summer early in the year, they considered travelling abroad. Elizabeth especially wanted to go to Japan, and they also debated going to Europe, either in combination with the Japanese trip or separately. But three problems arose. One was money. Elizabeth, who kept track of such matters, worried that their finances could not support summer trips. She tended to be conservative about money, unwilling to use capital or go into debt. Another problem was time. Joseph felt he had to get some work done—on money, theory, the little book of essays, anything but something—before going on a trip.

But the most important obstacle was the ominous looming of war, which gave the world a bad case of the jitters in mid-1939. Germany then occupied Bohemia and Moravia, Schumpeter's birthplace, and held Slovakia under "protection." Having renounced the nonaggression pact with Poland, Germany then signed one with the Soviet Union and entered an alliance with Italy. Europe just seemed to be waiting for someone to throw the first brick. The Schumpeters finally decided that the summer of 1939 was not the time to visit Europe, especially for a new U.S. citizen, formerly a German one.

On 3 April 1939, Schumpeter had taken the subway to the Post Office and Federal building in downtown Boston where he and a group of others swore allegiance to the United States and its Constitution. The next day, he wrote in his diary: "What a sorry crowd. No doubt though that Uncle Sam would be better off, at least eugenically, without us!" Ironically, he signed the certificate granting citizenship Joseph Aloys Schumpeter while the form has Joseph Alois Schumpeter typed on it. It also records his former citizenship as Czech, although his passport on entering the country was German and he never lived in Czechoslovakia.

Although a new U.S. citizen, Schumpeter's attitude toward the impending conflict did not reflect a new patriotism. Before the war's outbreak on 1 September 1939, he made clear to his friends and colleagues his belief that war should be avoided at all costs. Even if concessions to Hitler were necessary, they would be preferable to an all-out war that could destroy the European economy and, even more important, its culture. Not only did

Schumpeter fear the physical destruction of cities and the loss of many lives, he also dreaded the idea that European civilization itself might receive a blow from which it could not recover. Imagining yet another threat, he felt that capitalism could not survive a war. His alarm was not based on a fear of socialism, because he believed it would result from the natural evolution of capitalist society anyway, but he did fear fascism, state-controlled capitalism, and circumscribed personal liberties. He reasoned that a war would so change Europe that fettered and state-dominated capitalism in the hands of totalitarian regimes would become permanent features of European states. And, as he would say later, even the United States might share the same fate.

He realized that Germany was already becoming a fascist state, and he had no sympathy with the economic arrangements that the Nazis were installing. Believing that Hitler and the Nazis were temporary and would be thrown out by the German people in due course, Schumpeter hoped the worst features of fascism in the economy would then vanish. But, in the interim, Hitler stood as the one great European bulwark against Russia, which represented coercive socialism. Schumpeter felt it wiser to let Hitler achieve some of his aspirations in Europe, in return for saving Europe from Russia and totalitarian socialism. After all, the German people would eventually dispose of Hitler and his regime. Bolstered by this reasoning, Schumpeter began to oppose England's opposition to the increased German power that held the Russians at bay. Fearing that if England had its way, Germany would be crippled and unable to perform its historic function of containing the Slavs, Schumpeter grew increasingly out of sympathy with the British government—but not the English people. He also feared British influence on U.S. policy.[4]

Schumpeter made no secret of his prewar views, nor did he conceal his opposition to his country's economic and diplomatic pressure on Japan. Many of his listeners, as well as his colleagues, naturally interpreted Schumpeter's remarks on the war as pro-German and pro-Japanese. Some even went so far as to read support for Hitler into his comments. His public stance was ambiguous, but, among friends, he was less ambiguous. And with the *Hasen*, that is, in his diary, he was not ambiguous at all. As his diary shows, he was pro-German and to some degree even pro-Hitler in a very specific and limited sense. He favored the German stand against Russia and was attracted by the lip service paid to bourgeois virtues by the Nazis. But, above all, Schumpeter was staunchly antiwar as well as politically naive. He could not view the world situation through English or German or American or Japanese eyes. Despite his new U.S. citizenship, Schumpeter was a world citizen; he feared the consequences of war for all the world more than he feared German hegemony in Europe and Japanese advances in Asia.

While partially supporting Germany's aims, Schumpeter continued his opposition to the policies of Great Britain and the United States. On 30

August 1939, he wrote in his diary of his fear that Roosevelt was leading the country into war. In the same entry, he also expressed his dislike of English war policies, writing "World tumbling toward war." Clearly disheartened and depressed when the war broke out two days later, he wrote, lapsing into French as he did when feeling strong emotions:

> Nouvelles funestes [deadly news].... What is my first reaction? Sorrow, of course, but for the rest it's as always in the great catastrophes I have experienced or lived through—there is no reaction, my jardin secret is dumb, the birds are still; that old stunned feeling ... funny I don't feel that it is world war.

Schumpeter's naivete and desire for peace at any cost often led him to appeal for concessions to Germany. Somewhat awed by the might of the German war machine, he felt the odds of winning were on its side. On 24 September 1939, not long after war broke out and while the German army seemed on the road to an early military success, he wrote:

> *War:* as soon as, quite foolishly, Germany was driven into the arms of Russia, the chance for Germany to succeed became considerable. Yes there may be mistakes, mismanagement on West Front etc; attack on neutral and so a world war (which it is not yet); also Italy and Japan may possibly be won over—but in the normal course of things the war is really being decided in Germany's favor and even U.S. would not necessarily change the result.

> But the comfort is: if Germany wins in the sense of warding off the attack and securing what she can get in the East, there will be (?) a much more stable state of things—the structure of Europe better balanced and strains removed and more hope for peace than for a long time past. What about Hitlerism? Well history should have taught us that it is no good fighting a religion—that's why nobody would think of fighting bolshevism—: if it is to stay it will stay. But even so it is not unlikely that it will settle down—precisely after success—whereas I don't see what is to be done if Germany is *beaten*: I see nothing but another mutable structure.

A few months later, he continued with a religious analogy to express his waning sympathy for Hitler.

> It is religion that is needed—only religion can fight Hitlerism on its own ground. For people accept Hitlerian religion because (a) it is *this* religion they want and (b) it is *a* religion they want.

3

Since Schumpeter did not confine his political views to his diary, at the war's beginning he started to alienate some of his colleagues. On 19 October 1939, during a speech to Cambridge's Rotary Club on war and peace, he outlined a plan of negotiations and concessions that amounted to acceptance of most German demands. The *Boston Herald* reported these unpopular views, indicating that the Harvard professor preferred a German Europe to a continuation of war.[5] For obvious reasons, this kind of publicity did not sit well at the university, and Schumpeter felt increasingly estranged from his colleagues. While he was alienating others, he was also feeling a growing hostility toward and discontent with Harvard.[6]

It is at this point that the Federal Bureau of Investigation began to take an interest in the Schumpeters. Both Joseph and Elizabeth, the latter because of her interest in Japan and especially because of her editing of a book on Japan and Manchuria, were investigated intermittently throughout the Second World War. Indeed, the FBI's interest in Elizabeth was greater than its interest in Joseph.

Under the Freedom of Information Act, I obtained the Schumpeter files from the FBI. They do not contain any information of relevance, consisting mainly of correspondence concerning either Joseph or Elizabeth in connection with a possible charge of their having acted as propagandists or agents for either the Germans or the Japanese. Some of the information is wrong. The FBI reported "Joseph Alois Schumpeter, husband of Elizabeth Boody Schumpeter, former Austrian finance minister, reportedly escaped to the U.S. with considerable sum of money."[7]

The Washington FBI pressed its Boston office to produce information on which to base a charge of being a propaganda agent, particularly against Elizabeth. But, after several interviews of Elizabeth, and after reviewing her writings, the Bureau dropped the matter. In the war, the FBI reported:

Joseph Alois Schumpeter considered sympathetic towards Germans by one informant but otherwise a loyal American. No evidence of espionage. Elizabeth Boody Schumpeter has written books praising Japan and previous to Pearl Harbor in favor of Japanese over Chinese.[8]

On several occasions, J. Edgar Hoover impressed on his minions in the Boston office the need to find evidence on which to base criminal charges against the Schumpeters. At one time, the Schumpeter file was submitted to the Criminal Division of the Justice Department, but Tom Clark replied that the information did not support any charge.

After his return from the American Economic Association meeting in Philadelphia, Schumpeter was criticized in a January 1940, department meeting. The reason for the criticism is unknown, but he took it seriously, complaining in his diary of the "unpleasantness and mortification and humiliation and ... eating humble pie in my old age and all that ... to have worked a lifetime in order to have that Department to decide what I may or may not do." It is possible that the department criticized Schumpeter for his habit of giving irregular and nonexistent grades and for treating the grading process in a cavalier fashion. It is known that the department did criticize him for his grading, and it may have been at this meeting. But Schumpeter's response in his diary seems greater than the seriousness of the problem justified.

Another event increased his discontent. The university had created two important new professorships: the Thomas Lamont and the Lucian Littauer Chairs for the Department of Economics. Schumpeter naturally felt that one of these professorships should go to him. Although he already had the George Baker Chair, the new ones carried a bit more money and prestige, as well as a secretary. The university gave the Littauer Chair to Alvin Hansen and the Lamont Chair to Sumner Slichter, neither of whom, Schumpeter felt, had his stature.

Expressing his mounting criticism of Harvard and its Economics Department, he wrote the following note to himself:

> The atmosphere is languid and has no go. Not once has it happened within the writer's observation that at a meeting of the "full professors" a scientific question has forced itself into conversation, let alone being passionately canvassed. Work lacks intellectual ardor.

Believing his colleagues failed to engage in scientific work, Schumpeter complained that he had no one to talk to. His groups of young people had moved on to other universities or had become associate and full professors at Harvard, with little time or interest left for Schumpeter's seminars. With these groups gone, he felt he no longer had any influence at Harvard.

Still another event in the spring of 1940 added to his disenchantment. Paul Samuelson, the star student of the Harvard Economics Department in the mid- and late 1930s, and a favorite of Schumpeter, was completing his term as a university junior fellow. (He was the student to whom Schumpeter once gave an A++.) In the normal course of events, Samuelson would have become an assistant professor and, in a short time, worked his way to the top at Harvard. But Samuelson had a disability: He was brilliant and he knew it. On occasion, he lacked patience with those less talented and less hard working than he, even his former professors. When the time came to appoint him to the Harvard faculty, his less-than-brilliant colleagues did not seem enthusiastic about having a daily reminder of their inadequacy. Samuelson intimidated them too much. He also had another disability: He was a Jew, and Harvard was not noted for its racial tolerance. Instead of offering him the professorship he desired, the Economics Department offered Samuelson an instructorship.

Even though Samuelson wanted to stay in Cambridge, he had no intention of starting below the bottom rung of the academic ladder. The Massachusetts Institute of Technology had offered him a professorship; if Harvard wanted to keep him, they would have to match the MIT offer.

When the vote on matching the MIT offer was taken, Samuelson received a majority. But, by custom of the department, unless a candidate had unanimous or near-unanimous support, the department would not offer the position.[9] Schumpeter was infuriated by this action, feeling that it only confirmed his low opinion of his colleagues. In a strong letter to President Conant, Schumpeter protested the department's action, "I could understand it if they had voted against him because he was a Jew. But they voted against him because he was smarter than they are."[10] Although Samuelson went to MIT, he always remained on good terms with the best at Harvard, including Schumpeter.

Because of these events and Schumpeter's growing unrest, when Yale offered him the opportunity to teach in New Haven in the spring of the 1940-41 academic year, Schumpeter accepted. In his discussions with Yale, he indicated some of his dissatisfaction with Harvard. Yale did not hesitate; the department and administration began discussions with Schumpeter about the possibility of a permanent Yale appointment, where he would occupy the place of prominence held by Irving Fisher, who had retired four years earlier. Yale offered Schumpeter a Sterling Professorship—their most illustrious chair—and a salary matching that at Harvard. He could teach or not, as he pleased, and do whatever research, if any, he felt inclined to do. In addition, the Yale graduate economics program would be in his charge, not administratively but intellectually, meaning that he would have a strong voice over hiring and retention and thus over the quality of scholarship at Yale. So unhappy was Schumpeter at Harvard that he decided to take the job.[11]

In June 1940, he notified Harvard of his intent to resign. He explained his reasons in a note to himself:

Is it not one of the obvious shortcomings of university life that higher ranks in a faculty are *frozen* ... there they are, the fulls, and there they remain for say on the average 20 years.... So if I go, do I not liven up both Harvard *and* Yale?

In addition to his dissatisfaction with the intellectual climate, he was annoyed that Harvard had not hired Samuelson.

Aware that his resignation would stir up a fuss, he still could not have predicted the strong reaction at Harvard. He received letters imploring him to stay from every member of the department and professors in other departments, including those who were not his great admirers. But the most telling letter came from his students, most of whom have since become distinguished economists:[12]

June 3, 1940

Dear Professor Schumpeter.

We have heard that you are considering leaving Harvard. To us who have been closely associated with you as students for many years this news is most disturbing.

Each one of us has been stimulated by the breadth and vision of your thought. As no one else, you have always shown intense interest in our problems regardless of the field; and we have always had reason to be extremely grateful for your willingness to give us your time and energy. Our research has been greatly aided by your helpful criticism and generous encouragement. You have implanted in us a belief in the importance of a more exact and objective economic science and a desire to contribute to its development. Above all, you have been more than a teacher to us; we have always been proud to think of you as a true friend. We feel that your departure would be an irreplaceable loss to us and to future Harvard students.

Rightly Harvard has been regarded as a world center of research and teaching in the fields of theory and business cycles, and in large measure this has been your own achievement. We know that these branches would suffer without you. You have been a nucleus around which economic discussion and personal fellowship have taken form. We fear that this esprit de corps would not survive your departure.

We may not have conveyed well the loss to us and to the University which your leaving would mean, but we trust that you will sense the sincerity of our spontaneous expression. We beg you to consider these views in forming your decision.

Your devoted pupils,

Paul A. Samuelson	Maxine Yaple Sweezy	Sidney Alexander
Wolfgang F. Stolper	John T. Dunlop	Benjamin Higgins
Abram Bergson	Richard A. Musgrave	Shigeto Tsuru
Robert L. Bishop	James Tobin	Laughlin McHugh
John D. Wilson	Daniel Vandermeulen	Herbert Wooley

Marion C. Samuelson	R. M. Goodwin	William Salant
Richard E. Slitor	Russell A. Nixon	Wendell Hance
Heinrich Heuser	Lloyd Metzler	P.D. Bradley
Paul M. Sweezy	Julian Holley	

The barrage of support surprised Schumpeter, and the sincerity of both students and colleagues had a strong impact on him. Finally, Edward Mason took Schumpeter to visit with President Conant, who heaped words of praise on Schumpeter and assured him that Harvard valued his many contributions. On 21 June 1940, Elizabeth, then in Cambridge, received a letter from her husband, who was in Taconic. He wrote, "I am resigning myself to declining the Yale offer." Having preferred to stay at Harvard all along, Elizabeth was happy that Schumpeter had been wooed back into the Harvard fold by the outpouring of admiration.

4

Harvard has many idiosyncrasies, including the belief that its degrees are better than those from other universities. But on occasion, as in the case of Schumpeter, Harvard hires someone without a Harvard degree. University authorities, however, did not want to hear the accusation that some of their faculty didn't even have a Harvard diploma. To rectify this situation, at the June 1942 commencement, the most illustrious full professors without a Harvard degree, including Schumpeter, were given honorary M.A.'s.[13] This brought to four the number of degrees that Schumpeter held, one earned (the habilitation at Vienna in 1909 was not a separate degree) and three honorary. On 28 December 1938, the University of Sofia in Bulgaria had awarded him an honorary Doctor of Philosophy degree. All the details of this honor have vanished, destroyed during the Second World War. The University of Sofia no longer has specific information concerning the degree, nor does any information exist in Schumpeter's papers. The degree probably honored Schumpeter for his work in *Business Cycles*. The University of Sofia, in a letter to me dated 19 February 1982, confirmed that, by decision of its Academic Council on 28 December 1938, it had bestowed an honorary D.Phil. on Joseph Schumpeter, probably the result of efforts by a former Schumpeter colleague or student at Graz or Bonn. Oskar Anderson, a statistician of some repute who had known Schumpeter at Graz, was at Sofia in 1939.[14]

In the midst of the war's outbreak in Europe and Schumpeter's discontent with Harvard, his academic and scholarly activities continued on as usual, full of teaching and professional obligations. In the fall term, shortly after war started in September 1939, Schumpeter taught four courses, including his theory course (now called Trends in Economic Theory), a seminar in selected problems in money and banking, and a seminar in selected problems in business cycles and economic fluctuations, team taught with Gottfried Haberler. Finally, Schumpeter taught the history and literature of economic theory.[15]

During this same semester, Schumpeter became part of a new informal seminar that evolved into a serious discussion of the meaning of rationality in the social sciences. This group, consisting of Schumpeter, Talcott Parsons, D. V. McGranahan, Abram Bergson, Wassily Leontief, Gottfried Haberler, Paul Sweezy, and others, met in Emerson Hall from time to time, usually in the afternoon, to discuss papers that several of the seminar's members were writing. Schumpeter contributed an essay entitled "Rationality in Economics," later revised and expanded in the spring of 1940 and resubmitted for discussion. His paper was only one of many to emerge from this group. Talcott Parsons, for example, wrote a paper on "The Role of Rationality in Social Activities."[16]

Despite his active schedule, Schumpeter complained a lot about his health in the last half of 1939. Typically, his complaints were vague, but, in August, he lost his voice for a while. Fortunately, he had no speaking engagements scheduled and classes were not in session. Later, in October, Elizabeth wrote a letter to someone who was being a nuisance near their house and explained that her husband's health was delicate and he needed absolute quiet and rest. But Schumpeter rarely had time for rest if he was to keep pace with his commitments. He taught full time in the fall. On 17 November, he addressed the Exchange Club in Detroit. In December, he attended, as usual, the meetings of the American Economic Association, this year in Philadelphia, where he presented two papers, one at the Economic Association meeting and one at the Econometric Society meeting held at the same time. While in Philadelphia, Elizabeth gave a successful cocktail party for their many friends.[17]

Schumpeter found these annual meetings hectic but pleasant occasions. He was, as always, highly visible, stalking the corridors of the headquarters hotel, buttonholing anyone who seemed interesting to talk to, conversing with friends, introducing himself to strangers, and commenting on papers in the discussion periods. At the Econometric Society meeting, Schumpeter was elected president of the organization he had helped to found and of which he had been vice-president for two years.[18] He served through the 1940 and 1941 terms in that capacity. The main chore of the president is to organize the meetings of the society, a task involving a great deal of correspondence.

In late February and early March 1940, Schumpeter was again on the road, travelling to Champaign-Urbana to lecture at the University of Illinois. On 12 March, he talked to the Harvard Club of Boston about capitalism's survival.

On 26 March, he was in New York, speaking to the Harvard Club there on the subject of peace, and to the Political Economy Club at Columbia on protective tariffs. He made trips to Milwaukee, Chicago, and Detroit in April. Despite all this travel, Schumpeter managed to carry the usual teaching load of theory, money, and cycles in the spring of 1940. He also taught a course, never before offered, on the economics of war, a nonstandard course requiring a great deal of work on war finance, allocation problems, and other topics. In addition to teaching four courses, he also attended the mathematical economics class of E. B. Wilson, as he had in 1937, filling notebooks with mathematics. As if he weren't busy enough, in May he made notes and wrote some dialogue for a novel, though he never pursued the project beyond a few paragraphs.

Perhaps to counteract the hectic nature of his teaching and speaking load, in March 1940, Schumpeter began working in the Kress Economics Library, a place which became a retreat for him during the war. A remarkable place, the Kress Library is part of the George Baker Library of the School of Business Administration, just across the Larz Anderson bridge at the foot of Boylston Street (now John F. Kennedy Street). Located inside the Baker Library, the collection houses more than a million volumes dealing exclusively with economic matters. Its reading room is more like an elegantly appointed living room and study than a library, making it an ideal place for a scholar to work. Schumpeter began to spend all his spare moments there, reading the great classics of economics and pursuing his various research projects. Because of his newfound refuge, he optimistically noted in his diary on 25 March, that he would write "a little book every year; a paper every term." But Schumpeter never came close to this goal. In 1940, he published only one article ("The Influence of Protective Tariffs on the Industrial Development of the United States"); of no great import, it was his first in four years. [19]

5

He continued plugging away at his "little book of essays" on socialism, which had become his major scientific project in 1940, and work progressed steadily early in the year, convincing Schumpeter that the book was nearing completion. But he had, as usual, underestimated the length of time necessary to finish the project. Clearly tiring out from his tough schedule, on 4 September 1940, shortly before returning to Cambridge for the new academic year, he wrote in his diary:

I was going to write under the heading: Waking up to the situation—and to complain about not having achieved anything and not enjoying my little paradise here [in Taconic] that looks so exquisite at times; not even lectures prepared, tired and thwarted, with the prospect of a mess before me in the acad. year, with Yale and the Lowell lectures, and New Orleans.

Yet I am not going to write like this.... After all I have pushed hard on that socialism book and the situation simply teaches me once again that any achievement, however small, requires desperate concentration and neglect of all other plans. I could not have done more. It would not have been wise to try and the consequences must be accepted. Why, almost every morning I wanted to go into the garden to enjoy the morning air—have not done so more often than two or three times, almost always check myself and sat down at my desk. I have struggled and suffered. God what suffering "writing" means!—and made myself honestly tired. What, after all, can I ask more than this. And if the result is bad it is certainly all I could do.

This passage shows Schumpeter to be more forgiving of himself than he typically was. With his nearly impossible teaching, lecture, and meeting schedule, it's a wonder he got any research done at all. Yet, he almost daily devoted time to his research and writing. This independent scholarly work was the driving force of his existence, the activity he would not give up, no matter how slowly it progressed or how busy he was.

Though he felt "tired and thwarted," Schumpeter would not give himself a break and ease up. The "mess" referred to in the above diary entry was his plan to teach at both Harvard and Yale in the fall of 1940. For nearly four months, he travelled to New Haven each week, either from Taconic or Cambridge. At Yale, he taught his standard business cycles course, but he also prepared for a new course in international economics, a subject he had never taught before. At Harvard, he taught only advanced economic theory, his regular theory course. When this burdensome semester was over, Schumpeter still did not rest. In December 1940, the American Economic Association and the Econometric Society both met in New Orleans. As president of the society, Schumpeter had put together the meetings, a job that called for deciding on the topics to be discussed, inviting scholars to give papers, arranging for discussants of the papers, selecting chairmen, and hundreds of little details.

6

Even though Schumpeter was a busy and productive member of Harvard's Economics Department and his loss to Yale would have damaged the department, he was not always personally popular with most of the faculty. His opinions on the war were not welcomed, but they also were not well understood. During a cocktail party at Edward Mason's house just before the 1940 presidential election, for example, Schumpeter startled the group by announcing that as an alternative to Roosevelt and Wallace, he proposed a ticket headed by Adolph Hitler with Josef Stalin as vice-president. He said they could do no worse than the Democratic ticket had for eight years. The others at the party were shocked, not knowing if he was joking or had had too much to drink; they could not believe he was serious. Later, he mentioned to Mason that he could not understand why the people at the party were surprised and offended. Because of people's response to some of his ideas, Schumpeter began to drop out, losing interest in day-to-day events and avoiding his colleagues, whose political views differed dramatically from his own.[20]

From the beginning of the war in 1939 until America's entry near the end of 1941, Schumpeter felt that the United States should play the role of peacemaker in Europe and not take sides with England. Believing there was room for compromise between the English and the Germans, he hoped the war in Western Europe could end through negotiations. But the scenario he envisioned would have left the Germans in control of the European mainland—an essentially German solution. Schumpeter could not understand why England and the United States could not accept such a solution since their territorial integrity would remain unchallenged, nor did he understand why the United States did not use its influence to mediate rather than throw in with the British. He regarded the Slavs, primarily the Soviet Union, as the natural enemy not only of Germany but also of Western Europe and even of the United States. When Germany finally invaded the Soviet Union, Schumpeter maintained that Germany was serving the interests of the Allies, as well as its own. He could not understand why the United States would not recognize that the Soviet Union was the real threat in Europe, not Germany.[21]

When the war became reality in 1939, Schumpeter hoped it would end soon. At first the military victories of the Third Reich suggested that a short war might be possible. But, by the spring of 1941, even before the German attack on the Soviet Union, Schumpeter worried that the war would drag on, making a U.S. entry more probable. Yet, he still preferred a quick German victory so as to limit the war and prevent it from spreading worldwide, especially hoping that the United States could remain uninvolved.

According to Schumpeter, the precarious situation for the United States had two roots. One was England, as Churchill desperately tried to entangle the United States in the European war. Schumpeter feared U.S. assistance to England, correctly speculating that cooperation with the English would involve the United States in the war. The other root, entwined with the first, was Franklin Roosevelt. Not only did Schumpeter believe that Roosevelt was an Anglophile, he also distrusted Roosevelt's motives, fearing that he wanted war so he could establish a fascist state in the United States. On 13 September 1940, Schumpeter remarked:

> Talk to [Professor] X on War: Surprise! this clearheaded fellow perfectly sees that this [American] defence is aggression, that this country drifts into imperialist adventure and into fascism—and it is all right with him. This is how he rationalizes the acceptance of the English standpoint—Does that reflect the opinion of the Washington bureaucracy?

The degree of Schumpeter's own "ideological vitiation" on U.S. foreign policy was so great at this time that the accuracy of his interpretation of X's remarks must be questioned. The quotation more accurately expresses Schumpeter's pronounced anti-English and anti-Roosevelt views than any view of his friend.[22]

The ostracism of Schumpeter by his colleagues soon encompassed Elizabeth as well. She had long ago established her credentials as an economic historian, at first specializing in the history of English foreign trade. In the late 1930s, she worked as a research associate for the Bureau of International Studies, a joint Harvard-Radcliffe enterprise. In that task, she edited and wrote part of a study entitled *The Industrialization of Japan, Korea, and Manchuria, 1936-1940*, published in 1940.[23] Elizabeth's work convinced her that the Japanese economy was stronger than most economists believed. She had developed some sympathy for that eastern country, partly because she had studied its culture and language, as well as its economy. On her own, she had visited the University of Virginia in Charlottesville in 1938 to speak on the topic "How Strong Is Japan?" In 1939, 1940, 1941, and 1942, she wrote a number of short papers for the journal of the Institute of Pacific Relations. Although she did not deal exclusively with Japan, the articles did take up the broad economic problems of the Far East. Expressing other Eastern sympathies, in January 1939, she had written a paper on the question, "Is There an Open Door to China?" In 1940, Elizabeth wrote four articles dealing with the Yen bloc, the Far Eastern crisis, the problem of sanctions, and the possibility of a durable peace in the Far East. In 1941, she wrote five more papers, most of which dealt with Japan. Her paper published in the Institute of Pacific Relations journal in December 1941, was entitled "How Strong Is Japan?" The world found out quickly.[24]

Nearly all the professors at Harvard were pro-British, anti-Japanese, and anti-German. Although they did not favor war, many felt that Germany and Japan were on warlike courses that would eventually force the United States to go to war. Schumpeter never understood how they could be so blind. On social occasions, at meetings, and in the corridor, he did not withhold or temper his views in opposition to the war and to U. S. foreign policy. His outspoken attitude offended many of his colleagues, some of whom felt Schumpeter's views verged on the disloyal. As they shunned him, the easy camaraderie of earlier days disappeared. Now left isolated, he and Elizabeth were invited only to obligatory social events.

All through the fall of 1941, the war rumblings moved closer to the United States. With the United States now heavily committed to the Allies in Europe and to restraining Japanese expansion in the Pacific, most no longer questioned whether it would enter the war, but when and under what circumstances. Opposition to war received little more than lip service, as the vast majority of Americans favored England's war aims. U.S. policy in the Far East also had widespread approval. Only a few, such as the Schumpeters, opposed U.S. policy on all fronts. But they were uncomfortable with their bedfellows, since Schumpeter could not support or align himself with the American Firsters, the German-American Bund, or other antiwar groups. He was as unsympathetic and as disgusted with them as he was with U.S. policy. Nor did he fully understand why he believed the way he did. On 5 September 1941, he puzzled over his pro-German sentiments as he wrote in his diary, "Why am I so pro-German? ... I look fearfully at the headlines, whether in Russia disaster is growing ... and this hate against Russia, where is it coming from?"

After the United States entered the war in December 1941, Schumpeter moderated only slightly his pro-German stance. With his hopes for a quick end to the war now dashed, a black pessimism consumed him. He feared the ruin of European civilization and the destruction of Japan. He stopped writing in his diary or speaking in conversation against the U.S. war effort, but he would not tone down his opposition to Roosevelt's policies or his misgivings about the war.[25] Less interested in whether or not the United States would win the war, Schumpeter still hoped it could be ended by negotiations. But the United States, fearing a repetition of the First World War. wherein Germany could claim its army was undefeated, announced a policy of unconditional surrender. Schumpeter strongly opposed that policy, since it precluded negotiations and would stiffen Germany and Japan, thus prolonging the war.[26]

His discouragement about the world situation combined with his depression to isolate Schumpeter further from his colleagues, and forced him to withdraw more and more into himself. Fewer young men ambled through the Yard, and the halls of Littauer fell silent as students no longer came to discuss economics with Schumpeter during consultation hours. Even Cambridge, usually bustling with young people, stood almost deserted. The young men, even the faculty, began to disappear. And some professors barely spoke to Schumpeter, so hostile were they toward his war opinions.

7

Against a background of war drums sounding nearer, most Americans went about their business as usual. Schumpeter was no different. His nonpolitical views were still in demand. While he worked on his book of essays about socialism, he was invited to deliver a series of lectures at the Lowell Institute in March 1941. Because that educational foundation had such high prestige in Cambridge and Boston, it was a signal honor to be asked to deliver the series of eight lectures. In many cases, the results of such a series were published by the Harvard University Press. In the fall and early winter of 1940, Schumpeter began to prepare his Lowell lectures, hoping they would be compiled into a book that would serve as a companion to the socialism book. But the book never came to pass, although both Joseph and Elizabeth made many later references to this possibility in correspondence and in diary entries.[27]

He devoted a great deal of time to the Lowell lectures, laboriously preparing the longhand notes he would never refer to. He gave the eight lectures on Tuesdays and Fridays between 4 March and 28 March 1941, while at the same time teaching at Harvard and Yale. The Lowell lectures constituted a broad economic, political, and social study of U.S. recent development, presented in an historical setting. The study began in 1870 and ended with a look into the future, although Schumpeter carefully avoided making predictions. Still, unrelieved pessimism permeated the lectures: The war may destroy Europe; U.S. participation in the war is a strong possibility; destructive inflation may attend its participation; the U.S. economic and political systems are in danger. Regardless of the war's outcome, Schumpeter feared that the political fabric of the United States, even the Constitution itself, could crumble under the stress. Capitalism, if it survived the war, might bear the burden of heavy government intervention that would negate capitalism's benefits.[28]

In the first lecture, Schumpeter brushed in with broad strokes the time frame before the First World War. He argued that the country's economic structure was inherently unstable because it evolved from unfettered capitalism into decaying fettered capitalism. But the reason for the instability was not economic. Rather, it was social and political. As Schumpeter stated his familiar theme, he said:

> There cannot be any doubt ... that the very success of the capitalist economy tended to destroy the institutions that were essential to its working, private property, free contract and individual responsibility in particular.[29]

Business leadership had proved inept at political leadership, creating a situation wherein the country was increasingly run by a noncapitalist elitist leadership. Moreover, aggressive nationalism, increasing protection, activist foreign policies, and the loss of an ideal, parsimonious fiscal policy added more instability. Therefore, Schumpeter argued that, even by the time the First World War had arrived, U.S. and European capitalism stood on shifting sand.

In the second lecture, dealing with the decade between the end of the First World War and the beginning of the depression, Schumpeter found ominous developments. The international political settlements imposed on Germany by the United States, England, and France, he argued, could not last unless enforced by continued use of military power, which those nations were unwilling to supply. European economic development depended on continued U.S. lending, yet the war had stimulated industrialization in the United States, making it less interested in trade. The European nations, therefore, had to initiate their economic reconstruction themselves and along capitalist lines. Despite the presence of strong socialist political movements, Europe, with the exception of Russia, resumed its capitalist direction on its own. But the motor of capitalism—entrepreneurship—bowed beneath crushing taxation in most countries, while taxes soaked up savings, the fuel of capitalism.

Schumpeter devoted the next five lectures to the Great Depression of the 1930s. The third treated the impact of the crisis of 1929-33; the fourth examined investment, unemployment, and planning during the 1930s; and the fifth dealt with the role of monetary and fiscal policies. The sixth treated falling birth rates in the United States, and the seventh lecture explored international relations. In this core of the lecture series, he observed that the depression began as a normal depression, not unknown to capitalism. In the United States, government policy responded by asserting itself on three fronts: relief, recovery, and reform. Schumpeter argued that actions designed to relieve human suffering justified themselves, but efforts to reform capitalism only delayed recovery and permanently damaged capitalism's ability to produce further economic progress. Instead of leading to recovery, the measures that constituted the reform of capitalism—the New Deal—discouraged investment and weakened further the already debilitated engine of capitalism. Investors and businessmen, under attack, drew in their horns to wait out the siege, just as entrepreneurs refused to innovate. Schumpeter's evaluation of the 1930s emphasized disastrous outcomes arising from government intervention.[30]

In the final lecture, Schumpeter tried to estimate the effects of the war and its consequences. If the war ended quickly, the direct effect on the United States would be negligible. But a prolonged war, or a war in which the United States became a belligerent, promised to undermine U.S. prosperity, he argued. Above all, Schumpeter feared inflation as the war's aftermath. He also worried about further government encroachment on the economy, including the takeover of complete control over industry and the investment process. Viewing government encroachment as a threat to the present political system, he believed it could develop into "a militarized and centralized economy and civilization, a new social world that, for good or ill, may fundamentally differ from what is meant by the American way of life."[31]

Those attending the lectures agreed that Schumpeter's analysis of the past reflected a preference for conservative policy measures, but he still would not voice specific policy recommendations. Listeners also observed that Schumpeter was unbelievably pessimistic about the future, displaying his belief that the intervention and inflation occasioned by the war would weaken, destroy, or alter significantly the economic and political system of the United States. In both the Lowell lectures and in his diaries, Schumpeter repeatedly expressed his fear that the U.S. economic and political system could not stand up to the pressures of approaching war and was too easily influenced by other countries, especially the British, and by domestic special interests which would benefit from intervention.

For some time after delivering the Lowell series in March 1941, Schumpeter planned to ready the lectures for publication, but he had to set this project aside in order to complete the socialism book. By the time his "little book of essays" emerged as *Capitalism, Socialism and Democracy* in the spring of 1942, the United States had entered the war under circumstances that elicited maximum support from the people. Perhaps feeling that Americans would not want to hear his dispassionate analysis of the U.S. position, and recognizing that huge changes would result from U.S. participation in the war, Schumpeter dropped the idea of publishing the lectures for the time being because they would require a thorough reworking. These lectures are now being published in a volume edited by Richard Swedberg of the University of Stockholm.

8

During the time he prepared the Lowell lectures, another dolesome chore arose. In the early months of 1941, Schumpeter had to write the obituary of Frank William Taussig, his friend and mentor who had died 11 November 1940 at the age of eighty-one. In the last years, he had not seen as much of Taussig as he had earlier, but Schumpeter had remained very fond of him personally and had had great respect for him professionally. The obituary of Harvard's great man of economics was full of praise.

Like [Alfred] Marshall, whose path was different but fundamentally parallel, he [and Marshall] ... succeeded in building an organon of analysis that was classic....

Both made the organon serve a great historical vision and an ardent desire to solve the burning questions of the day. He was one of the first to realize that economic theory ... [is] but a tool with which to analyze the economic patterns of real life. Hence the teacher's task consists in imparting a certain way of looking at facts, a habit of mind, an art of formulating questions which we are to address to the facts.... It is not enough to say that students loved him ... he succeeded in impressing something of his breadth of spirit and his high sense of public duty upon everyone who came near him.[32]

On invitation of the *American Economic Review*, Schumpeter also contributed an evaluation of Alfred Marshall in celebration of the fiftieth anniversary of his *Principles of Economics*.[33] Schumpeter still had some misgivings about Marshall, especially his unwillingness to embrace general-equilibrium analysis and his failure to make overt use of mathematics. But he recognized the greatness both within the book and the man. He would sometimes refer to Marshall as one of the four greatest economists of all time, and the only Englishman. The others were all French: François Quesnay, Augustin Cournot, and Léon Walras.

When the Lowell lectures and the writing tasks regarding Taussig and Marshall were completed, Schumpeter took off for Detroit on 13 April 1941 to present a lecture to the Economics Club there. In his talk on "The Future of Gold" (later converted to a manuscript but never published), Schumpeter rejected the theory underlying the gold standard—the commodity or metallic theory of money. He outlined his dual reasons for opposing the gold standard: It was scientifically unsound, and economists must avoid advocating policy. Still, traces of Schumpeter's long-standing views favoring the gold standard crept into his speech, though not for economic reasons. The gold standard was an automatic mechanism designed to bring about equilibrium without political intervention. He supported its use because it prevented politicians, whom Schumpeter deeply distrusted, from tinkering with the monetary standard to make it serve their ends.[34]

While in Detroit, Schumpeter also talked to the Harvard Club and met various local notables who took him to visit the Plymouth Assembly plant, the tank plant at Grosse Point, and the Country Club. When he returned to Boston, he spoke before the Boston Economics Club, on a radio program, and at Yale on the history of science.

By June 1941, still pushing to complete the socialism book, commuting between Harvard and Yale for the semester, working up the Lowell lectures, and bouncing around the country for speeches and meetings, Schumpeter was exhausted. All of this, added to the kind of stress a world at war causes, took its toll. That month, he wrote to Herbert Zassenhaus, a former Bonn student, to say:

I have had a laborious academic year. I am trying to finish my book on socialism. As soon as I am rid of that I want to return full steam on economic theory and forget as much as possible the times in which we live.

Although he had hoped to finish the socialism book in June, when June came he was telling Trygve Haavelmo, a promising young student of his friend Ragnar Frisch, that the socialism book still wasn't completed. Since he was still working seventy-hour weeks, it is difficult to see how he found time to work on the book at all. But, instead of recognizing and appreciating all that he had accomplished, as usual he chastised himself for not accomplishing more. At about this time, he received the last letter he had from Klaere Tisch, one of his favorite Bonn students. Then in Wupperthal, Germany, her next and last residence would be a Jewish concentration camp.

9

Schumpeter rested in Taconic during the summer of 1941, but it was a troubled rest. The failure of *Business Cycles* (which sold only 1,500 copies at $10 each by the end of the year, meaning that Schumpeter earned only about $2,000 for five year's work), the war, and his general weariness led him to write in June 1941, "Not much point in coming down here [to Taconic]. funny this winding up of an activity—an element of dying in it." (He was referring to finishing his teaching at Yale, where he had also taught the preceding year.) With his depression deepening on 28 June 1941, he complained of being "tired and ill ... bones ache ... physically I can hardly play tennis any more." His frequently recurring obsession with his health soon became linked with his preoccupation with old age and death as he wrote on 12 July 1941, "the truth is that the will to live is dying within me." But somehow Schumpeter managed to revitalize himself because, by 5 September 1941, he was writing, "In some respects, though not in others, old age comes smiling kindly." The sentiment echoes, but also contradicts, a diary entry from earlier in the war: "I have no time for growing old. I have my work to do." Schumpeter was still the paradoxical man.[35]

As he always did when depressed, he called upon the *Hasen* for help, just as he thanked them when things went well. But, by 1941, Schumpeter's relationship with Annie and his mother had changed subtly. Before, he had seemed closer to them personally and appeared to be carrying on a dialogue with them, writing as if he were composing personal letters and hearing back from his *Hasen*. By the beginning of the war, his writing tended to be more of a monologue, with his addressing the *Hasen* more prayerfully and distantly. Annie and his mother had become more remote, more holy. Continuing to mention the *Hasen* in his own diary, as well as in his additions to Annie's diary, which he continued to recopy, in 1941 Schumpeter also began writing the large letters "JSA" on his diary's cover in an ornate, almost drawn, script. The three initials seem to mean "Joseph selig Annie," a dedicatory phrase to his late blessed wife. The prayers preceding his entries in his wife's diary became more like real prayers for help rather than just expressions of gratitude. Cries for assistance in health and work matters were frequent. For example, he might write, "Ich vertrottle ja," meaning "I am becoming stupid," or, in an English passage, "My bones boil." As he became more conscious of his advancing years and worried about what he believed to be precarious health, his pleas for help with death also became more frequent. But his feelings about death were contradictory; he sometimes wrote as though dreading it and sometimes as though to welcome it.

By 1941, the captions introducing the entries in Annie's diary had also changed, becoming more ritualistic. He now repeated them mechanically, as though reciting a formula. Still, they carried more meaning because they had evolved into themes related to subjects of great concern to Schumpeter's inner life. For example, on 5 November 1941, the sixteenth wedding anniversary (to Annie), he wrote on the flyleaf of the recopy of Annie's diary, "Mon Dieu, un enfant comme ça" (My God, a child like that). This expression came from one of Annie's diary entries in early 1923: "Je voudrais un enfant comme François" (I want a child like François [referring to a child in the family where she was a servant in France]).

Schumpeter's remembrance of this remark and his subsequent repetition of this theme shows his intense desire for children. No one remembers his ever saying aloud that he wanted a family, but he expressed that same sentiment through his fondness for children and his willingness to spend hours playing with those of his colleagues. Beginning in 1941, Schumpeter repeated these words or a variations on them many times, suggesting that his failure to have children galled him more and more as he grew older. Yet he had agreed with Elizabeth back in 1937 that they would not have a family, an agreement probably reflecting their concern over her age—thirty-nine—when married and her diabetes.

Elizabeth knew her husband labored over his former wife's diary. But, since they never discussed it, she did not know the substance of these personal writings. She was aware of his obsession with his dead wife and mother, but that obsession seemed not to interfere with their relationship. She knew more about Joseph's concerns over health and death, since he talked about these things, yet she did not know all the details because she had not read his diary. Although Joseph kept a picture of Annie on his bedside table in his own bedroom, Elizabeth was tolerant and understanding. She was aware of his attitude toward his second wife from the beginning. She therefore never objected to his sending money, 200 marks a month by 1941, to Annie's family in Vienna.

Elizabeth was clearly devoted to Joseph and loved him deeply. But, even though she had the ability to help with his professional work, her role seems to have been largely one of a caretaker. Elizabeth and Joseph were not always at the same residence at the same time. Sometimes he stayed in Taconic while she did chores in Cambridge, or he taught in Cambridge while she went to Taconic. But when this happened, Elizabeth left nothing to chance, not trusting Joseph to do the simplest things around the house. She wrote notes, telling him what to do and when to do it. She prepared huge piles of roast beef and other food, leaving it in the refrigerator with detailed instructions on its door. She even left large pitchers of Manhattans or martinis for her inept husband's before-roast-beef relaxation.[36] As a result of their arrangement, both Schumpeters seemed to get what they wanted: Elizabeth had a great man to take care of, and Joseph had the caretaker he needed.

10

After his summer of rest in Taconic, Schumpeter returned full time to Harvard, teaching his regular courses in the fall of 1941: advanced economic theory, business cycles and economic forecasting (shared partly with Haberler), and the history and literature of economics. Rare for Schumpeter, he and Haberler also taught an undergraduate course in business cycles. In the spring of 1942, he added a half-course seminar in selected problems in money and banking and a course at Radcliffe. Although unrelated to his teaching of five courses in that spring term, Schumpeter received a salary increase to $12,000. He may have been unpopular in the department because of his political and war views, but Schumpeter was one of the busiest professors in the classroom, most productive in published scholarship, and most prestigious. The university rewarded him accordingly.[37]

Despite the country's recent entry into the war, the American Economic Association met in December 1941 in New York. Schumpeter, as usual, was there, much in evidence, especially delighting in introducing his students to anyone within earshot. He introduced Paul Samuelson and Lloyd Metzler as two of the most promising young horses in his stable. At the meeting, Schumpeter chaired a roundtable called Cost and Demand Functions of Individual Firms, a discussion including Hans Staehle, Joel Dean, Gerhard Tintner, Oskar Lange, Arthur Smithies, and Lloyd Metzler—all students of Schumpeter.[38]

Even though Schumpeter taught more than usual during the 1941-42 academic year, he managed to complete *Capitalism, Socialism and*

Democracy in March, more than two and one-half years after he had begun. With this project complete, his scientific life again became unfocussed. The question of whether he should spend all his time on one project, or spread out his time and effort in many directions, always bothered Schumpeter. In June 1942, he addressed this question, listing in his diary the seven activities that prevented his single-minded pursuit of scientific matters:

1. Women
2. Art [and architecture]
3. Sport [and horses]
4. Sciences (and Philosophy)
5. Politics (Public Career)
6. Travel
7. Money (Business)

Repeatedly, he remarked in his diary that, in order to get anything done, he had to concentrate all his efforts on one project and ignore the seven activities that had always distracted him. Crediting his successes to concentration and his failures to pursuit of the seven-fold agenda, still, he wrote, "I did not do so badly." With another book under his belt, Schumpeter was again the scientist in search of a subject worthy of his study.

He had made several efforts to formulate a new theory as he resumed work in 1942 on *The Theoretical Apparatus of Economics*, his proposed new theory book, assaulting the subject again and again, but without success. On that vast canvas he would paint for a while and then smudge over what he had just done. Now he decided the canvas was too big. Instead of trying to carry the main canvas to completion, he invented a new project that would only sketch in the basic outlines of his great painting. "P.V." or "Prel. Vol.," meaning preliminary volume, now became a standard notation that cropped up frequently in his diary and agenda as his code word for this new preliminary theory book. Still, to produce even a sketch, the nearly complete theory must be in hand—perhaps not the final and full-blown theory, but at least its framework. One reason for working on theory at this time was his desire to pursue some project far removed from the realities of the world.

Yet, during the summer of 1942, spent in Taconic, Schumpeter flitted from one project to another, unable to settle down and dig in on any one. He played around with mathematics, enjoyed reading Greek classics, and even studied the language a bit. He read some detective stories and took long morning walks along the shores of Taconic's twin lakes. When he finished proofreading *Capitalism, Socialism and Democracy* for Harper and Row, he tried to resume work on his Lowell lecture notes, still thinking he might turn them into a book. The book on money had receded to the background.

Although he now had many projects, he had no deadlines, and his summer's work lacked direction.

In late 1942, Schumpeter finally decided to proceed with the revision of his earlier study on the history of economics. He had already done some writing on the subject, especially the early period. To him, the history of economics was the history of economic theory. By reading the theories of the past, he might learn something to help him formulate the theory of the future. Thus, even while focussing on the history of economics, he also kept in touch with theory, his other main interest. Hidden away in the Kress Library, Schumpeter concentrated his research on the economic writings of the Greeks and Romans, the Scholastic doctors, and the natural-law philosophers, topics not fully covered in his earlier book. He had, in effect, begun work on another "big book." But, even as he did, his little book of essays, now *Capitalism, Socialism and Democracy*, was making a significant splash not only in the academic community but among serious readers everywhere.

Notes

1   Schumpeter's height and weight (and brown eyes) are given on the certificate granting him U.S. citizenship, in his papers in the Harvard University Archives. His diary in this period records relatively few health complaints.

2   He kept the manuscript of the money book in a small trunk. His papers in the Harvard University Archives do not include the German and English translation of the book as published in 1970, since Schumpeter's widow gave the manuscript to Arthur Marget. A part of the manuscript, in German and with lengthy notes in German, English, and shorthand appended to each page remain in the Archives.

3   This letter is among those in the correspondence file of the Schumpeter papers in the Harvard University Archives.

4   Schumpeter discussed all these matters of war and peace in his diary, not in the form of essays, but usually in isolated sentences, epigrams, and disconnected remarks.

5   *Boston Herald* 20 October 1939.

6   His diary records many derogatory remarks about Harvard, and his friends, including Gottfried Haberler, Edward Mason, and Wassily Leontief, remember his growing disenchantment with Harvard.

7   This quotation is from the material supplied by the FBI under the Freedom of Information Act. It is dated 25 July 1941.

8   FBI Freedom of Information Act report, based on report of 23 July 1942.

9   Information concerning the Samuelson appointment comes from colleagues such as Edward Mason as well as Paul Samuelson. Those who supported Samuelson were the research-oriented professors such as Hansen and Schumpeter. The opposition came from some of the older institution-oriented professors.

10 The letter is lost or perhaps was never sent. The quotation was given to me by Professor Mason, with whom Schumpeter discussed the matter.

11 The letters from Yale, including the offer at Yale, are in the Harvard University Archives, but Schumpeter's letters in connection with the Yale offer are missing.

He probably wrote by hand and kept no copies.

12   This letter is in the correspondence file of the Schumpeter papers in the Harvard University Archives.

13   If Schumpeter received a diploma, it was lost. The Harvard University catalog records the granting of the degree.

14   In response to my inquiry, the University of Sofia provided the information given in the text. Wolfgang Stolper suggested that Anderson may have been the one who recommended Schumpeter's name. The Harvard University Archives do not disclose the degree or any correspondence concerning the degree.

15   Schumpeter's teaching in this year, as well as others, is recorded in the catalogs of Harvard University, a record which may contain some errors since some changes may have been made after the teaching plans had been printed in the catalog.

16   An edited version of Schumpeter's paper was published in *Zeitschrift fuer die gesamte Staatswissenschaft* 140, no. 4 (December 1984): 577-93. I gave the paper I found in the Schumpeter papers to Wolfgang Stolper, and he, along with Rudolf Richter, editor of the journal, edited it for publication.

17   Schumpeter wrote of the meetings that year and about the party that Elizabeth gave in his diary. He was very pleased with the party and with Elizabeth's handling of it.

18   Some writers have reported that Schumpeter was president for four years. The back issues of *Econometrica* indicate that he was vice-president for two years and then president for two years.

19   *Proceedings of the Academy of Political Science* 19 (May 1940): 2-7.

20   Schumpeter's diary indicates that his contacts with colleagues became more and more limited as war approached and became a reality. His colleagues, such as Edward Mason and Gottfried Haberler, also recall that Schumpeter tended to stay more to himself.

21   Schumpeter recorded in his diary his dismay that his colleagues could not see what to him was an obvious fact that what he called the Slavs—the Soviet Union—was the real enemy and that Germany was in reality doing England and the United States a favor by confronting the Soviet Union.

22   The term "ideological vitiation" was a favorite of Schumpeter's and expressed the influence of ideology on one's views, often even though the individual is unaware that ideology is blurring facts and logic.

23   The book was published by MacMillan and Company of New York. Elizabeth was the editor and wrote a small part of the book. The book implied that Japan had built a stronger industrial base than was generally recognized. Much of the FBI file made available to me under the Freedom of Information Act concerns this book and the possibility that it was propaganda. After an extensive "propaganda analysis," the FBI decided that perhaps 10 percent of it could be construed as propaganda, maybe.

24   According to information revealed in the FBI files on Elizabeth, the FBI believed that Elizabeth was a propagandist for the Japanese. They were especially interested in her having contacted the Japanese consulate in New York while preparing the book and the fact that the consulate bought multiple copies of it. At one point during the war, J. Edgar Hoover indicated that he wanted her indicted as a Japanese propagandist, but the Criminal Division, under Tom Clark, reported that no basis for an indictment existed.

25   There is nothing in his diary, and colleagues do not recall any remarks, that indicate disloyalty to the United States during the war. Nor did the FBI before and during the war find any evidence that indicated a preference for Germany or Japan over the United States. Still, he did not sympathize with U.S. military war aims.

26   He feared that the unconditional surrender policy would stiffen the Germans and Japanese and make them fight to a bitter and destructive end.

27   Most of the Lowell lectures were taken down in shorthand and typed after the lecture. These typed manuscripts, along with the detailed notes of the first lecture, which was not taken down in shorthand, are preserved in the Schumpeter papers in the Harvard University Archives. These typescripts have some notes and corrections in Schumpeter's handwriting on them.

28   Although many of the predictions—regulation of the economy and fascist assault on democracy—were correct, their implications were not. Schumpeter greatly underestimated the strength of U.S. political institutions, although the postwar period did suffer from fascist attacks. Schumpeter feared that the regulated economy would slow down and stagnate, but the U.S. economy, even with greater regulation, grew rapidly.

29   Typescript of the Lowell lectures, Harvard University Archives.

30   Although couched in cautious language, Schumpeter did not hide his hostility to the economic policies of Roosevelt and the New Deal, which he interpreted as an effort on the part of the government to control the economy.

31   Typescript of the Lowell lectures, Harvard University Archives.

32   *Quarterly Journal of Economics* 55, no. 3 (May 1941): 337-63, written in collaboration with A. H. Cole and E. S. Mason.

33   In "Alfred Marshall's Principles: A Semi-Centennial Appraisal," published in the *American Economic Review* 31 (June 1941): 236-48.

34   This talk was never published, but a mimeographed summary of his remarks was circulated. Schumpeter had little use for the theory underlying the gold standard or for the proponents of the gold standard. What attracted him to it was the fact that as an automatic mechanism the gold standard prevented politicians from manipulating the money supply.

35   Much of this section is based on the Schumpeter diaries and on remarks by his friends.

36   Elizabeth's efforts to have everything arranged for her husband comes from friends who visited Schumpeter while Elizabeth was away.

37   Schumpeter was one of the dozen highest paid professors at Harvard, all of whom received that amount.

38   The group's discussion was later published in the *American Economic Review* 32 (March 1942).

7

Capitalism's Fate (1942)

Schumpeter conceived of *Capitalism, Socialism and Democracy* as a book of essays, and he worked on it as such between late 1939 and early 1942. Drafts of the chapter on the history of European socialist parties had been written in the 1920s, while a version of another chapter—"Can Capitalism Survive?"—had been given as a speech to the U.S. Department of Agriculture in 1935. Even the basic ideas underlying the book go back to the 1920s or even earlier. Schumpeter outlined the critical idea of capitalism's political instability in some detail in an article for the *Economic Journal* in 1928. The book's main thesis—the replacement of capitalism by socialism—appears in elementary form in *Die Krise des Steuerstaates* in 1918, but he may have arrived at this proposition as early as his university days. Capitalism's doom and replacement by socialism had been a favorite thesis among fin-de-siècle Viennese intellectuals, often representing wishful thinking by the socialists and decadent pessimism by proponents of capitalism. When Schumpeter worked on *Capitalism, Socialism and Democracy* then, he was drawing on material long ago placed on his "sacred decade" agenda, material that finally reached fruition when he was nearly sixty years old.

1

Schumpeter recognized his own long-standing interest in capitalism and socialism in the book's preface when he said that the work "is the result of an effort to weld into readable form the bulk of almost forty years' thought, observation and research on the subject of socialism."[1] Given its date of publication, one might expect the experience of the Great Depression and perhaps even the beginning of the Second World War to play an important role in the book's argument. In fact, however, they play only a small role, and none in the central thesis. To Schumpeter, capitalism had been doomed long before the depression, and for reasons unrelated to the economy's ups and downs. The depression and war may have deepened the pessimism of the book, but they added nothing to its overall scenario.

Schumpeter's consuming interest in Karl Marx, displayed in the first four chapters of *Capitalism, Socialism and Democracy*, originated in the paradox between Marx's close identification with socialism and the fact that his work was exclusively an analysis of capitalism. Marx, the proponent of socialism, made no contribution to the theory of socialism or to the resolution of problems that socialism might face when replacing capitalism. Schumpeter was also less interested in socialism than in the process by which capitalism mutated to become socialism—that is, the capitalist process. Like Marx, he was a theorist of capitalism, not of socialism. Still, Schumpeter, the supporter of capitalism, paradoxically went much further than did Marx in examining the economics of socialism, as well as in addressing the implications of its introduction.

The element drawing Schumpeter and Marx together is not socialism but rather their competing theories of capitalism, both of which rely on a grand vision of the capitalist process. Both attempt to show how capitalism works and evolves over a long period of time. Even more, both of their theories indicate that capitalism ends in the same place: socialism. But the similarity of vision and analysis of the process, evolution, and culmination of capitalism ends here.

Marx did not attract Schumpeter because he felt the Marxian vision was right. Schumpeter did not believe that Marx had described the capitalist process correctly, did not think that the Marxian evolutionary path was accurate, and disagreed that capitalism would end for the reasons Marx gave. No, in nearly all the particulars, Schumpeter felt Marx was wrong. He gave Marx the highest marks only for his approach. For his theories, Schumpeter flunked him, refusing to accept his theory of social classes, the economic interpretation of history, the analysis of the economic process, or his thoughts on the activities and performance of capitalism's economic actors. Perhaps the most important reason for Schumpeter's absorption with Marx was that their theories are competitive because so similar, not in substance or in process, but in method. Both are evolutionary; both trace capitalism's historical course; and both point to capitalism's demise. Stressing their similarities and differences, Martin Bronfenbrenner, professor emeritus of

Duke University, has often called Schumpeter the rich man's Karl Marx.[2] Both Marx and Schumpeter envisioned an explanation, though each saw a different one, of the development of mature capitalism—its path through time. Marx's path emphasized misery and conflict despite greater production to the end of capitalism; Schumpeter focussed on progress and plenty until the denouement.

The genesis of Schumpeter's own theory of economic development may have come from his consideration of Marx's theory, but not in the sense of borrowing from Marx. Finding Marx's theory unacceptable, Schumpeter was seeking an alternative explanation of how capitalism evolved when he stumbled onto his own theory in the years leading up to 1906-1910, perhaps some of it even during university days. In the introduction to the Japanese edition of the *Theory of Economic Development*, printed separately in English in 1937, Schumpeter said:

> It was not clear to me at the outset what to the reader will perhaps be obvious at once, namely that this idea and this aim [the explanation of the capitalist process] are exactly the same as the idea and aim which underlie the teachings of Karl Marx. In fact, what distinguishes him from the economists of his own time and those who preceded him, was precisely a vision of economic evolution as a distinct process generated by the economic system itself.[3]

Schumpeter's great admiration of Marx shines through despite his jaundiced view of the fundamental meaning of Marxism, as well as harsh criticism of nearly every detail of Marx's work. Expressing both admiration and reserve, Schumpeter called Marxism "a religion," with Marx as the founder and prophet. This new religion became so widely embraced because it supplied ultimate ends, including the meaning of life and standards for judging actions and wants. As a guide to those ends, Marxism showed the plan of salvation and the nature of the devil, promising paradise before the grave. More than anything else, Schumpeter believed that its religious component explained the success of Marxism and its many revivals.

But Schumpeter also felt that Marx's scientific efforts, despite some merit, failed. Slogans, invective, and emotion-laden prose can go only so far in the social sciences. Beyond them, only prophecy, wrapped in science and framed in scalding words, coupled with the personal force of Marx, can explain why his ideas live on. Judging Marx purely as an economist and social scientist, Schumpeter slipped him into a small niche in the English classical school, a disciple of Ricardo. Although Marx may have imagined the yearning of the worker and presented a false religion, to his credit he did not delude himself by idealizing the worker or pandering to him. He was a social scientist with a vision of what was, is, and will be. He saw the immense productive power of capitalism and its historical necessity. But Marx also saw that, by its own logic, capitalism would fail, inexorably, and be succeeded by socialism.

Marx's economic interpretation of history asserted that conditions of production have a logic of their own that determines social structures. Schumpeter called this analysis a great achievement in sociology and a valuable working hypothesis. But, although Marx presented an important insight, Schumpeter did not believe it to be an unqualified or universal truth.

Contrary to the Marxian position, Schumpeter argued that, although men make economic choices within a framework determined by the conditions of production, the social structure may reflect more than one productive system since conditions long past linger in society. Marx went on to define the history of society as the history of social classes, and he based his definition of social classes on an economic criterion: ownership of capital. Those who own capital are capitalists; those who do not are workers. Everyone is in one of the two classes since no other classes—tradesmen, professionals, etc—can persist. Yet, these two classes remain locked in perpetual antagonism even though sweet harmony reigns within each class.

Schumpeter maintained that, in developing this theory, Marx had selected a scenario that would lead to a predetermined conclusion; Marx needed a classless socialism. Because antagonism was inevitably present with two classes, Marx had to remove antagonism by eliminating one of the classes, leaving only one class under socialism. The property-owning class would cease to exist as a class once its property was expropriated by the socialist state. This would leave only the nonpropertied class, which Marx defined as workers. Only this theory of social classes would produce the results Marx wanted, and only this scenario would prove Marx's theory correct.

2

Despite some misgivings about Marx's analysis of history, Schumpeter believed that Marx shone resplendently as an economist, even if wrong. He was learned and familiar with the writings of all the economic theories of his time, and he had borrowed many of their ideas, though he often bit the hands that fed him. Marx especially respected David Ricardo, calling him the last great representative of classical political economy, and he drew heavily on the Ricardian theory of value, which maintained that the value of a good was proportional to the quantity of socially necessary labor it embodied in competitive equilibrium. But, according to Schumpeter, much of the failure of Marxian economic analysis stemmed from the weakness of this Ricardian theory.

Marx, aware of other theories of worker exploitation proposed by socialists, rejected them because force, bargaining power, or special circumstances undergirded them. In his theory, Marx needed systemic exploitation based on the normal operation of the economy, not exploitation that depended on evil men, politics, or weak positions. But how could he build a theory to attain this ideal circumstance?

In a master stroke, he applied the labor theory of value to labor itself, arguing that a worker's value is what it takes to produce and maintain him. This includes food, clothing, shelter, and other expenditures necessary to raise him from childhood and then to maintain him as a worker. But when the worker labors, he creates and imparts to the commodities he produces a greater value than the value that he embodies as a worker. The capitalist then sells the commodities for the value of the labor embodied in them, not the value embodied in the worker, and pays the worker the equivalent of his embodied labor. Because commodity's labor value is larger than worker's labor value, the capitalist pockets the difference, called by Marx the surplus value. Even though the capitalist profits, he is not the one who exploits the worker. The system—capitalism and the way it works—exploits the worker.

Schumpeter found this application of the labor theory of value to be untenable. Among the theories of wages based on subsistence that were circulating in Marx's time, Schumpeter preferred many others to Marx's theory because he believed that workers do not result from rational cost calculations. But Marx could not accept any other theory since he needed one in which the system exploited labor automatically and unconsciously. Schumpeter was further disturbed by the failure of Marx's theory to explain why firms, all benefitting from exploitation, did not expand, driving wages up and thereby in equilibrium eliminating the exploitation. This aberration did not disturb Marx, for he viewed capitalism as constantly changing and never reaching an equilibrium in which exploitation might vanish.

In his theory of concentration, Marx maintained that the capitalist uses the surplus value taken from the worker to build additional capital goods, necessary because of competition from other firms. If firms did not grow and become more capital-laden, they would lose out in the competitive struggle. But, instead of increasing, the profit rate tends to decline as fixed capital enlarges its share of total capital at the expense of wage capital, the only real source of surplus value. With firms becoming larger and larger, the pressure on wages heightens. Unemployment also rises as capital substitutes for labor.

Schumpeter regarded Marx's theory of concentration as a brilliant insight, but he viewed his theory of immiseration of workers, resulting from concentration, as flawed. Marx argued that the real wage rate and the standard of living of workers would fall, but Schumpeter showed that this has not happened in history. Marx applied the theory of surplus value as integral to his argument because it, as well as the theories of concentration and immiseration, result in the creation of the industrial reserve army, as well as the disaffection of the proletariat, and ultimately the breakdown of capitalism. To Schumpeter, the Marxian prophecy of the demise of capitalism was an accurate prediction, but he regarded Marx's analysis of the breakdown as a non sequitur.

Summing up Marx as an economist, Schumpeter wrote:

> In the court that sits on theoretical technique, the verdict must be adverse. Adherence to an analytic apparatus that always had been inadequate and was in Marx's own day rapidly becoming obsolete; a long list of conclusions that do not follow or are downright wrong; mistakes which if corrected change essential inferences, sometimes into their opposites—all this can be rightfully charged against Marx, the theoretical technician.[4]

Yet, even with all these deficiencies, Schumpeter still argues that Marx was the first economist of top rank to see and to teach systematically how economic theory may be turned into historical analysis and how the historical narrative may be turned into *histoire raisonée*.

Schumpeter looked on Marx as a giant for having cut the path and notched the trees into the methodological wilderness of the analysis of capitalist evolution. But Marx then got lost in the forest, wandered around, and failed to find the sunlit clearing of understanding how capitalism functions, changes, and evolves into socialism, finding instead a weed patch of poisonous plants. Still, Marx must receive the highest marks for having realized that there was a wilderness, that a path could be hewn, and that a bright green meadow of understanding existed, even if he hadn't found it. Although he did not say it in this or any other book, Schumpeter believed that he, born the year the Marx died, had explored the same sylvan space, discovered the secret path to its center, and revealed its mystery.

3

At the beginning of the second essay, the centerpiece of the *Capitalism, Socialism and Democracy*, Schumpeter asked "Can capitalism survive?" He answered, "No. I do not think it can."[5] Although this was his prophecy, he argued that the prophecy itself was unimportant. What mattered were his reasons for believing it. Since the social sciences cannot make reliable scientific predictions of this type, Schumpeter merely suggested that present evidence and observable trends of capitalism indicated that it would not survive. Much could happen that would change the trend, resulting either in its immediate collapse or prolongation, and Schumpeter was careful not to give a timetable. At the same time, he carefully pointed out that his belief in the replacement of capitalism by socialism must not be read as an indication that he favored either capitalism or socialism. He was simply presenting an analysis leading to a hypothesis.

Before assessing capitalism, Schumpeter examined how the capitalist economy had performed. Despite many measurement problems, evidence suggested that, between 1870 and 1930, the U.S. economy had grown at a rate of 3.7 percent per year. How, then, might the economy perform in the future? Since the depression, he argued, did not represent a real break in the trend, growth might continue as it had in the past. Making an allowance for a higher rate of growth of goods for investment purposes, Schumpeter felt that a 2 percent growth rate would be a very conservative estimate. He thus believed that capitalism by 1978 "would do away with anything that according to present standards could be called poverty."[6] The economy in fact has performed better than Schumpeter estimated, but. ironically, society's definition of poverty has outpaced the growth of the economy.

In *Capitalism, Socialism and Democracy*, Schumpeter returned to his thesis that the economy moves in waves of economic change that periodically restructure the productive processes. These waves, initiated by innovations, have resulted in avalanches of consumer goods, articles of mass consumption. Once the economy provided silk stockings only for the Queen. By the time Schumpeter was writing in 1942, it supplied silk stockings to factory girls. The reduction of the work week and the elimination of child labor demonstrated the economy's ability to handle problems while providing the means for social legislation. Although these measures cannot eliminate unemployment and hardship, they can help keep economic disaster from the door of the unemployed. Capitalism can also provide for its aged and infirm and educate its people. The incentive system of capitalism rewards with success and punishes with failure. More important, success for business is success for everyone in the economy. By rewarding those who supply the goods efficiently and at the lowest price, the profit motive also rewards the population as a whole. Because it provides the incentive to work, capitalism yields full and effective employment and thus the largest income for its people.

In this section of *Capitalism, Socialism and Democracy* Schumpeter penned a phrase that has since entered the language: "This process of Creative Destruction is the essential fact about capitalism. It is what capitalism consists in and what every capitalist enterprise has got to live in."[7] Capitalism most of all rewards the innovator, those who introduce new goods and processes into the economy. But this creative and profitable act by innovators also destroys by eliminating old products and processes and the capital and jobs that supported them. Schumpeter is probably better remembered for that phrase, often misunderstood, than any other single formulation he ever made. While it is far from an adequate summary, it does encapsulate, when properly interpreted, his theory of development.

Part of that development theory rests on the idea that the economy's evolution produces large and strong enterprises and occasional temporary monopolies. Usually, these monopolies are unable to abuse their positions because remaining competition and yet more innovations will undermine them. But, without the prospect for profits (the reward to entrepreneurs for innovation), entrepreneurs would be slow to innovate. Although they will try to protect entrepreneurial profits behind monopolistic barricades, they seldom succeed. Schumpeter maintained that pure competition—competition in which there are so many producers offering a product for sale that no producer can exercise any influence over price or product characteristics—is not only rare, but also that economists have vastly overstated its virtues.

Schumpeter disagreed with most of his colleagues about the desirability of pure competition because, in those sectors where it has prevailed, such as agriculture and retail trade, innovation was absent. Pure competition tended to reduce and eliminate profits and, by doing so, stifle economic change. The change that has occurred in purely competitive sectors has resulted from innovations by suppliers—agricultural implement makers and manufactured goods, for example—and not because of innovations by competitors. Many economists have touted highly the fact that goods produced in pure competition could not be produced more cheaply. But Schumpeter felt that this idea rested on an unproved assumption that cost conditions of pure competition would be the same as cost conditions of imperfect competition and monopoly. Monopolistic and oligopolistic firms, he believed, often have a cost advantage because size and entrepreneurial advantage often yield lower unit costs for them in comparison with the costs of the small, purely competitive firms.

Many economists have taken exception to Schumpeter's display of tolerance toward monopoly. Even though he asserted that monopolistic abuse was rare, he still did not favor exploitation by monopolies or any breaking of the law. Nor did profits bother him, because he was convinced that most were entrepreneurial profits, the temporary profits attending innovation. While entrepreneurial profits are similar to monopoly profits, competition, however imperfect, usually wrings most profits from the innovating enterprise in a short time. This belief led him to fear that too much competition by not permitting profits would stifle innovation, the well-spring of economic progress.

According to Schumpeter, capitalism has created the economic progress of the last two centuries. To test this idea, he suggested five other potential sources of growth: government actions, gold discoveries, increasing population, new lands, and technological progress. Government action, he felt, cannot claim the credit. If anything, it has added encumbrances to capitalism that slow it down. Neither can the gold plethora after 1890 explain the growth that began two decades or more earlier; thus, neither gold nor other monetary arrangements could take credit for the performance of capitalism. Population increases are an external factor, operative under any system, but, since this is a positive factor, it may have increased output beyond that attributable to capitalism. New lands by themselves have no meaning aside from the opportunities provided by an economic system to use the land. Without an evolving capitalist order to exploit the land, new lands could not contribute economic growth. The same reasoning applies to technology, which depends upon capitalism if it is to appear and contribute to economic progress. Thus, past growth must be attributed to the capitalistic economic order and not to other factors.

Having outlined how capitalism created great economic progress, Schumpeter then asked, Has capitalism now shot its bolt and outlived its usefulness? Has it so changed that it can no longer perform in the future as it did in the past? Schumpeter answered the first question "not necessarily," but "yes" to the second. He did not accept, however, the reasoning of most economists. The length and severity of the Great Depression caused many to believe that capitalism was malfunctioning. And the stagnation thesis, which became popular during the Great Depression and was most assiduously promoted by Schumpeter's colleague Alvin Hansen, also asserted that opportunities to invest were disappearing because of saturation. If innovations stopped, then private investment could no longer continue. If private investment inevitably declined, then capitalism's prospects would be dim. But Schumpeter argued that, although unfettered capitalism could continue to produce progress, it would also produce conditions hostile to it and induce chilling intervention that eventually would result in its replacement by socialism.

4

To understand capitalism and its fate, Schumpeter looked to the nature of its social system and civilization. Fifty thousand years ago, prerational, collectivist and conformist thinking predominated. The continual failure of nonrationality drove people eventually to rational actions that, once tried and repeated, became habitual. Economic necessity therefore forced independent and rational thought processes on individuals, even though rationality, such as the search for profit and self-interest, is independent of the economy's organization. Still, capitalism differs from other systems since it heightens and amplifies rationality. Capitalism exalts the monetary unit, which becomes the easy-to-understand tool for calculating costs, profits, and incomes. The monetary unit thus represents the measure of success.

Science, building on similar quantitative measures, produced the ultimate rationality—logic. Rationality produced not only the scientific attitude but also the people and the resources to initiate and continue progress. Science then uses rationality as the tool for expanding knowledge. While Schumpeter explained that rationality lies at the root of economic progress, he also asserted that rationality will undo capitalism. "Capitalism ... has after all been the propelling force of the rationalization of human behavior."[8] Not only production and physical capital, not only technology and organization, but all features and achievements of civilization are products of capitalism. The growth of science, new products, institutions, medicine, education, art, manner of living, and individualistic democracy all bear capitalism's imprint. It has also made possible social legislation, providing both the resources and the will to focus on utilitarian ideas for mankind's betterment and the elimination of class rights. Although capitalism is only an economic mechanism, it exercises a powerful influence on all human activities through its influence on the human mind. It is rationalistic and antiheroic.

But while it has delivered the goods and produced a unique culture and civilization, capitalism cannot be said to have made people better or happier. Its culture and civilization can be called good only by adding a value judgment. Men need not, however, choose between capitalism and something else since capitalism arose and will decline, to be followed by something else, independent of men's will. Because economic and social arrangements move along by their own momentum and internal forces, capitalist performance in a given period is irrelevant to its prognosis. Most economic and social orders fall before they fulfill their promise.

Schumpeter believed that, in 1942, the walls of capitalism were already crumbling. This trend would continue, largely because one of its main pillars, the entrepreneur, would cease to function as an innovator, as innovation became routine due to mechanized progress. When the entrepreneur lapses into desuetude, the economy settles down to steady growth—probably slower growth—instead of the explosive growth occasioned by innovations. The entrepreneur's function—to revolutionize the structure of production—becomes more and more the task of specialist teams. But these specialists change the structure of production by small predictable increments, not revolutionary innovation. They routinely produce growth, but not real change. In contrast, the entrepreneur produces novelty, but not routine growth. When change becomes automatic, only management remains.

The disappearance of the entrepreneur affects the bourgeois class because, when progress halts or becomes automatic, this economic mainstay of the business class is reduced to hired hands. Since capitalist enterprises tend to make progress routine, capitalism itself renders capitalism superfluous. The coffeehouse conspirators and agitators will not be the precursors of socialism. Rather, the Vanderbilts and Rockefellers, by making capitalism a success and progress routine, have undermined capitalism and prepared the way for socialism. Capitalism earlier destroyed the institutional arrangements of feudalism. The manor, the village, and the craft guild could not stand against the productive structure of emerging capitalism. King, court, and clergy—the remnants of feudalism—long protected capitalism from its own rationality, as had happened in Schumpeter's beloved dual monarchy. The symbiosis between capitalism and these lingering political forms lasted until the First World War. But, ultimately, capitalism's rationality destroyed the political forms that had supported it. Subsequently, the bourgeoisie tried to govern itself, but failed.

Because capitalism is rational and antiheroic, it has no internal magnetism, enlists no loyalties, and projects no personal appeal. When capitalism eliminated the nonrational holdovers of past political systems, it exposed itself to the full force of its own rationality in governance. But, by doing so, capitalism began eating away at its own institutional structure. To be rational, large firms must dominate production, causing the small producers, the mainstay of capitalism, to give way before unpopular but efficient large enterprises. The cry of monopoly and declining competition rises in the wake of this domination. Property itself and free contracting lose meaning. No longer does anyone feel a sense of proprietorship. Owners do not behave as owners and managers serve their own interests as bureaucrats.

Hostility toward capitalism grows. In turning against property and its own values, capitalism opens itself to attack from all sides. Its performance carries no weight, and rational argument cannot quiet discontent and criticism. Since capitalism spreads its rewards unevenly in time and place and among individuals, grumbling by the people about the consequences of capitalism becomes commonplace. The case in favor of capitalism is complex, requiring analysis and long-run thinking beyond the ability of most people, even economists. The hostility toward capitalism by the people, although heightened by the intellectual, is more important than the hostility of the intellectual. Educated, well meaning, and having a way with words, the intellectuals formulate and express the views of others. The labor movement, although not created by intellectuals, is manipulated by them; and politicians and bureaucrats, having lost allegiance to capitalism, repeat their slogans. Even the businessman, now without his own sense of property and ignorant of capitalism's logic, turns against his own kind.

Entrepreneurs cease to innovate. In large corporations, no one need function as entrepreneur since any innovation that takes place is deliberate and planned. The disintegration of the family also removes support from capitalism, and people question the value of children, the traditional home, the family, dynasty, and name. The time horizon shrinks to the short run, giving rise to an antisavings attitude. But without savings, capitalism cannot survive. In the midst of this scenario, no one sees himself as capitalism's defender. Because the system no longer makes sense to the capitalists, they are meek in the face of attack and won't fight. Capitalism thus destroys itself. According to Schumpeter, everything then points to the succession of socialism. Capitalism itself has created the institutions and conditions, such as mammoth corporations, that can be easily transformed into a new system. In this sense, then, Marx was right: Capitalism gives way to socialism. But Schumpeter did not believe that socialism would triumph because of the failure that Marx saw inherent in capitalism. Rather, capitalism would give way to socialism because of its success. It would have done its job too well. Only the future can tell when, how, and in what form socialism will take over.

5

In the third essay of *Capitalism, Socialism and Democracy* Schumpeter asked "Can socialism work?" He answered, "Of course, it can."[9] There would be transition problems preceded by an advanced stage of capitalism, but socialism could work.

Schumpeter defined socialism as a system requiring a central authority to control the means of production and the production process. He also argued that the socialist economic blueprint does contain a core of logic. Based upon the data, interrelationships, rules of economic and societal behavior, and rules laid down by socialist authority, it would be possible to determine prices and amounts of production, as well as distribute the goods. Socialism then, could be as determinate an economic system as is capitalism.

Other economists held varied opinions on the viability of socialism, and Schumpeter took issue with them in this third essay. Ludwig von Mises, strong proponent of capitalism, had expressed doubts, believing that without markets there would be no way to solve the millions of equations that constitute the economy. Schumpeter, an equally strong supporter of capitalism, paradoxically had long argued that socialism was a logical system, pointing to the proof of Enrico Barone in 1908.[10] And in 1942, he could also use the work of his own Bonn students, Klaere Tisch (1932) and Herbert Zassenhaus (1934), as well as Fred Taylor and Oskar Lange, especially the latter, who fully resolved the question in *On the Economic Theory of Socialism* (1938).[11] They outlined the mechanism by which a central planning authority could imitate the operations of markets. Socialism's central planning board would impose behavior rules on producers, rules that would have the same result as capitalism's search for profits. If each producer determines the amount of his output by equating the addition to revenue to the addition to cost, then all producers together will make no profits. The productive part of the socialist economy, observing the rules, would function exactly as fetterless capitalism did.

Socialism could separate the distribution method for what the economy produces from the production process, choosing the distribution system it pleases. It could opt for complete equality of income distribution or any degree or kind of inequality it deems appropriate. Each individual would receive a part of total production, as determined by the central board, and would then be free to spend his allotment as he chooses. The board, setting prices on the basis of the history of prices and production of all products, would by trial and error choose market-clearing prices for all products. If a surplus appeared in a market, the board would lower the price. If a deficit appeared, the board would raise the price. If a surplus or deficit persisted after a price change, another price change in the same direction would follow. The Board could determine whether surpluses or deficits occurred by watching inventories. Inventory accumulation would mean producers are offering more than consumers want to buy at that price, while depletion of inventories would imply that consumers are willing to buy more of the product than producers want to sell at that price.

The enterprise, the socialist producer, need only follow simple rules. It would produce the amount—no more, no less—at which the price of the product (set by the central board) exactly equals its marginal cost of production.

The marginal cost is the extra cost incurred by producing the next unit of production, that is, the cost attributable only to the production of that single next unit. If the total cost of producing ten units is $1.20 and the total cost of eleven units is $1.30, then the marginal cost of the eleventh unit is ten cents.

The producer under capitalism, in order to maximize profits, produces up to the point where its marginal cost equals the price set by the market. If marginal cost exceeds price or is less than price, the producer can improve profits by producing less in the first case and more in the second. The socialist manager would behave in the same way, not to maximize profits, but because having the price equal marginal cost is his standard operating instructions.

As recipient of the ownership of the output of all enterprises, the central board would then distribute claims to shares of this output among people, according to whatever distribution scheme it chooses. The choice of distribution system represents the critical difference between capitalism and socialism. Under capitalism, the claims to production are distributed according to the productivity of those responsible for production through wage and other payments. Under socialism, distribution would be a political or bureaucratic decision, not an economic one. Except for having a distribution system that would not mesh directly into the productive system, socialism would replicate capitalism. Individuals under socialism would be free to spend their claims as they choose.

Producers would produce and sell according to costs. Least-cost decisions by enterprises and the rule that price equal marginal costs would guide production and assure efficiency. Socialism could accommodate to economic change and accept new products and methods that resulted from whatever motivation impelled innovators. New techniques and new products would yield "profits" to the enterprise and signal an expansion that would eventually raise costs and eliminate the "profits."

Schumpeter strongly asserted that socialism could be more efficient than the capitalism it would replace. Although some excess capacity may continue,

socialization means a stride beyond big business on the way that has been chalked out by it, or ... that socialist management may conceivably prove as superior to big-business capitalism as big-business capitalism has proved to be to the kind of competitive capitalism of which the English industry of a hundred years ago was the prototype.[12]

Part of the reason socialism might prove to be the superior economic system is that capitalism cannot avoid involuntary unemployment, although it can mitigate its worst consequences. But socialism could avoid such unemployment by directing labor where it chooses. Socialism could also spread technological change more quickly and efficiently because of centralized direction. No friction would exist between the public and private sectors since no private economy would exist. Neither would taxes, since the board would distribute to the government what the government wanted. The legal profession would languish or, as Schumpeter put it, be forced to do useful work, just as the state would concentrate on the positive task of operating the economy, not on the costly chores of taxing, regulating, and repairing its inadequacies.

In his detailed discussion of the merits of socialism and capitalism, Schumpeter did not explicitly recognize a severe limitation of some of his analysis. He often compared a capitalist system, warts and all, that exists with a model of socialism that does not exist. No one knows how the socialism envisioned by Schumpeter as the successor to capitalism might work; it is a path not taken, yet. In practice it may have many inadequacies that cannot be known until it becomes a reality. When comparing a model to a reality, the model nearly always wins, as it did in Schumpeter's case. And it took but a few sentences for Schumpeter to dispose of the comparison between Soviet socialist reality and capitalist reality. In that case, capitalism won, mainly because the Russians did not follow anything even remotely resembling Schumpeter's blueprint of socialism.

6

Until Russia tried socialism, no one seriously questioned the compatibility of socialism and democracy. Socialist theory of the nineteenth and early twentieth centuries indeed equated capitalist control of the instruments of production with exploitation and dictatorship by capitalists. Socialists inferred from this that true democracy could exist only when socialism has ended the tyranny of capitalism. The vagueness of what people meant by democracy forced Schumpeter in the fourth essay of *Capitalism, Socialism and Democracy* to develop a theory of democracy and to define its characteristics.

To Schumpeter, democracy is simply a method. Not an end or a goal, it is only a means, a bloodless and virtueless technique. Because democracy is a *way* of making decisions, it has nothing to do with the substance, nature, quality, and merit (or lack thereof) of political decisions or any other kind of decision. Democracy is a device for rule by people, and people comprise the group designated by society to participate in the decision making process. When society decides who the players are, democracy is the method for reconciling the conflicting interests among them. Democracy is neither good nor bad; it just is.

The eighteenth-century philosophy of democracy said that the achievement of the common good was the beacon light of policy. Representatives exist only to carry out the will of the people by achieving this common good. But, according to Schumpeter the common good is a phantom, carrying a different meaning for different individuals and groups at different times. Actions undertaken by a government, even in pursuit of what it thinks is the common good, will benefit some and damage others. To those damaged—those who pay taxes, for example, to support unemployment relief—the action is hardly the pursuit of the common good. Those benefitted by the same action—the unemployed—might consider it the common good, but it is in fact only a special good for them. The task of government, then, should be to reconcile values and interests, not to seek the common good. Since what is good for one group and its will contradicts the good and will of another group, the combined public will and common good have no rational unity or sanction. According to Schumpeter, the public will is the illegitimate creation of a political or economic group that seeks to promote its own good by claiming that government actions serve its own selfish definition of the public will. But such actions may damage the interests even of the actual majority.

Despite the durability of the classical doctrine, which still survives in the popular mind and in political rhetoric, Schumpeter proposed a theory of democracy that he believed better fitted the facts. This theory emphasized competition for political leadership. Two or more leaders present themselves as capable of representing the conflicting interests of groups and then reconciling those differences. The people select one leader. Schumpeter believed that, in reality, the role of people in a democracy is to produce a working government, not to aspire to some lofty ideal of common good: "The democratic method is that institutional arrangement for arriving at political decisions in which individuals acquire the power to decide by means of a competitive struggle for the people's vote."[13]

When Schumpeter asked whether democracy and socialism can coexist, he answered in the affirmative.[14] There would be neither a necessary affinity between democracy and socialism, nor a necessary incompatibility. But conceptual compatibility is one thing, and living side by side in the real world is another. In order for democracy to continue under socialism, possible but improbable conditions must prevail, with the practices of democracy fitting the requirements of socialism. The strongest qualification for the coexistence of socialism and democracy would be placing limitations on the range of decisions made by the political leadership. If the effective range of political decisions were too wide, encompassing too many details of economic and technical matters, then socialism would be so interrupted and mangled by political interference that it could not function properly. Technical matters, therefore, must be left to a well trained and professional bureaucracy, free from political influence.

Politicians must show uncharacteristic heroic restraint, as must the people, or else self-seeking will undermine any socialist plan. People would elect politicians who give general guidance to the bureaucracy running the socialist system. If people dislike the results, they elect another group of politicians to establish another set of general guidelines. The bureaucracy would continue to run the system, but with the new guidelines and new political leadership. Direct participation by either the people or the politicians, or insistence on guidelines that are too specific, would destroy the socialist process. The language Schumpeter used makes it clear that, although he thought it possible, he did not fully believe democracy and socialism would coexist when the latter arrived. As the creation of capitalism, democracy may not survive in a hostile socialist environment. The only hope for democracy in socialism lies in the fact that the ideology of socialism also springs from capitalism.

Following Schumpeter's standard practice of seeking historical confirmation of his analytical propositions, the last section of *Capitalism, Socialism and Democracy* is an historical essay. He examined the development of European socialist parties, in and out of government, from about 1870 until the beginning of the Second World War. As history, the essay is interesting and stimulating, but deep and detailed history is impossible to present in seventy pages. This section rounds out the book, but adds nothing to Schumpeter's thesis or to the evidence in its favor. Nor do most of his later additions—the chapter added in 1947, the evaluation of English socialism in 1949, or his final scholarly paper—accomplish more than to reiterate the proposition and to review the evidence. The only exception to this statement was Schumpeter's later addition that socialism would probably show fascist features.

7

Capitalism, Socialism and Democracy was widely and favorably reviewed, and nearly all the reviewers were impressed. But not many were convinced. Some reacted as did Clarence E. Ayres, a leader in the institutionalist camp of economics and a professor at the University of Texas. He wrote:

> His prodigious erudition, his mastery of forensic strategy and tactics, and his amazing command of English idiom and literary skill in the larger sense, together produce an effect that is no doubt wholly unintended. The reader is not so much convinced as overwhelmed. However, this stylistic over-compensation, as it might be called, would be much less noticeable in a writer whose intellectual position was different. By a singular coincidence it happens that Professor Schumpeter's opinions differ from those of his various groups of readers in such a way as to convey an impression of consciously sophisticated superiority by which those of other ways of thinking are seemingly identified as credulous fools and dupes of vulgar superstition; and strange to say this is equally true of the partisans of capitalism, of socialism, and of democracy.[15]

Joan Robinson, Schumpeter's old English friend, wrote, "The reader is swept along by the freshness, the dash, the impetuosity of Professor Schumpeter's stream of argument." She tempered her praise, however, with the caution that we must pause and consider that Schumpeter compares a socialist blueprint with a capitalist reality, not a socialist one. Robinson added that, if socialism does come, it will come as a complex and messy reality, not as a neat blueprint. Still, she concluded, "But no matter whether it convinces or not, this book is worth the whole parrot-house of contemporary orthodoxies, right, left, or centre."[16]

Fritz Machlup, the friend with whom Schumpeter lunched several days a week during the summer of 1936, wrote a long review for the *American Economic Review*. He characterized the book's style as "humorous-ironic" and called Schumpeter a "cynic." Commenting on the relationship between socialism and democracy, Machlup pointed out that Schumpeter shows that a socialist system built according to his blueprint might use the democratic process as he defines it. Might use—but will it? This Schumpeter does not believe himself; personally he thinks that socialism will more likely mean dictatorship. Too bad that he spent seventy pages to prove what may be possible, but only a few lines to state what is more probable.[17]

Although he outlined and commented on the book part by part, Machlup refused to make an evaluation as a whole. Clearly, he too was unconvinced in detail. He suggested to the reader instead:

Read it yourself and even if you, in places, may dislike what Schumpeter says, you will always like the way he says it. Schumpeter's literary style is grandiose; for it distracts the reader, slows him down and makes him pause—for applause, so to speak.

The quality and controversial nature of *Capitalism, Socialism and Democracy* can be seen in the fact that its ideas are still alive and well today. In 1978, Harper and Row published part 2, the section entitled "Can Capitalism Survive?" as a separate book with an introductory essay by Robert Lekachman. He observed:

If Nobel Prizes were posthumously awarded, Joseph Alois Schumpeter would certainly merit the honor, preferably with an oak leaf cluster. More than a generation after his death in 1950, he is universally esteemed as a great economist.[18]

Schumpeter would blush at but accept such a review, but he would probably refuse the Nobel Prize if it were awarded for *Capitalism, Socialism and Democracy*. He knew it was a vague, nonscientific book, containing mainly conjecture and games of *histoire raisonnée*. But he would also be secretly pleased and thankful that he had produced thoughts worth considering.

In 1981, Arnold Heertje edited a volume in which nine economists, most of whom had known Schumpeter well, presented their evaluations of the 1942 book.[19] Among the contributors were Paul Samuelson, Arthur Smithies, Gottfried Haberler, and Herbert Zassenhaus. They unanimously agreed that Schumpeter's estimate of socialism replacing capitalism was wrong. They evinced many reasons, most of them relying on data not available to Schumpeter. Presenting their own ideas, some argued that capitalism would struggle on, while others asserted that something other than socialism would replace capitalism. A few wrote that Schumpeter might yet be right. But they all agreed that right or wrong, Schumpeter was brilliant, provocative, and suggestive.

Yet another recent book evaluated Schumpeter's analysis in *Capitalism and Socialism: Schumpeter Revisited*, edited by Richard D. Coe and Charles K. Wilber.[20] In his essay, Warren Samuels of Michigan State University argued that a corporate state could just as easily evolve from Schumpeter's analysis. As in other evaluations, the authors—including the editors, Warren Samuels, Gary Becker, and Samuel Bowles—recognized Schumpeter's brilliance and the book's erudition, but they accepted little of the analysis. Today, the book remains widely respected and is still capable of stirring up arguments, but most economists reject Schumpeter's thesis that socialism will inevitably and naturally replace capitalism. In a sense, then, Schumpeter to most economists stands respected, not accepted, but studied, right next to Marx, the man Schumpeter so admired and disagreed with in his "little book of essays."

8

Schumpeter always made a great pretense of disdaining *Capitalism, Socialism and Democracy*, often calling it a "potboiler." He wrote it not for his colleagues but for the general reader, so in a sense it was a "popular" book. He let people believe that he had tossed it off during a few weekends at Taconic, while he was also engaged in serious things. This attitude belies the travail and suffering that went into writing it. Yet he feigned scorn because it was not the economic theory book that he so badly wanted to write. He wanted the capstone to his career to be his PV, *The Theoretical Apparatus of Economics*, a preliminary volume of the theory book that remained his goal during the last quarter of his life. By comparison with that never-completed work, he viewed *Capitalism, Socialism and Democracy* as a weekend book. He wanted to be known as a scientist, not a social commentator, no matter how wise.

As time passed in the 1940s, Schumpeter gradually expressed more respect for his book among his most intimate friends. He realized that he had accomplished what he set out to do at the beginning: to weld into readable form forty years of thought, observation, and research. And he came to believe that a senior scientist is entitled to, and indeed should, write down these kinds of thoughts because they would be important for the future course of capitalism and economic theory. Others, especially the young, could write economic theory, but only Schumpeter could have written this book. The propositions he emphasized were unknown to many people and were being systematically ignored by most political leaders and economists, as they often still are.

Schumpeter wanted to be known primarily as the great economic theorist, and he would be displeased if he knew that much of his reputation today, among noneconomists and economists alike, comes from *Capitalism, Socialism and Democracy*. He feared, as is the case, that the book would be taken too seriously, when he never meant it to be a serious prediction or prophecy. He was not playing Marx's game of predicting an inexorable socialist wave of the future. Rather, *Capitalism, Socialism and Democracy* presented an elaborate hypothesis, a suggestion, a possibility. He was prepared to abandon any or all of his comments on presentation of convincing contrary evidence. His generalizations were intended to titillate readers, to make them think, perhaps even to make them do some work to disprove a proposition. It was Schumpeter opening minds again.

An important fact to remember about Schumpeter is that he was a scientist. In his analytical work, he sought to know how things worked, be it a market, the process of capitalist development, how people change their thinking under the barrage of goods capitalism makes available, or the potential efficiency of socialism. As a scientist, he did not "believe" in much of anything. He fully accepted no theories, not even his own. To Schumpeter, everything was tentative, subject to change.

Readers should approach *Capitalism, Socialism and Democracy* with a similar attitude. The book is a complex and detailed working hypothesis—serious, playful, and provocative, as well as suggestive, perhaps even useful, but not to be taken seriously as a finished piece of scientific or scholarly work. As a potpourri of economic theory, sociological speculation, historical interpretation, and political and economic analysis, it was designed to stimulate thought, not settle issues.

Any satisfaction Schumpeter may have gleaned from the book and the response to it by his colleagues and social scientists throughout the world, was dashed by the harsh realities of war. By the time the book had been published in the summer of 1942, the ranks of professors remaining in Cambridge were thinning. Nearly all the instructors were gone. Some young professors, such as Chamberlin and Sweezy, had entered the military. Others, Mason among them, moved to Washington. The daily stories of battles and casualties muted social life. The war even threatened to take Taconic away from Schumpeter, since his castle and place of refuge required a long drive at a time when gasoline and rubber were scarce. Made distraught by world events, Schumpeter did not conceal his antiwar sentiment, an attitude that did nothing to endear him to the Cambridge community, wholeheartedly in support of the war.

Notes

1   *Capitalism, Socialism and Democracy*, 3rd edition (New York: Harper and Brothers, 1950), xiii. (Earlier editions were published in 1942 and 1947.)

2   This is an expression Bronfenbrenner used in several discussions I had with him and in his writings.

3   Author's Preface (in English) to the Japanese Edition of *Die Theorie der wirtschaftlichen Entwicklung* (Kanda, Japan: Iwanami-Shoten, 1937), 3

4   *Capitalism, Socialism, and Democracy*, 43.

5   Ibid., 61.

6   Ibid., 66.

7   Ibid., 83.

8   Ibid., 125.

9   Ibid., 167.

10   Enrico Barone, "The Ministry of Production in the Collective State," in F. A. Hayek, editor, *Collectivist Economic Planning, 1935* (London: George Rutledge, 1935). Originally published in *Giorgnale degli Economisti* October 1908).

11   B. Lippincott, editor, *On the Economic Theory of Socialism* (Minneapolis: University of Minnesota Press, 1938). Lange was a Rockefeller foundation fellow at Harvard and discussed the matter with Schumpeter when he wrote the central essay "On the Economic Theory of Socialism" in *Review of Economic Studies* in 1937. These essays are published in the Lippincott volume.

12   *Capitalism, Socialism and Democracy*, 195-6.

13   Ibid., 269.

14   Ibid., 296-302.

15   *Southern Economic Journal* 9, no. 4 (April 1943): 293-301.

16   *Economic Journal* 43 (December 1943): 381-383.

17   *American Economic Review* 33, no. 2 (June 1943): 301-320.

18   Joseph A. Schumpeter, *Can Capitalism Survive?* introduction by Robert Lekachman (New York: Harper and Row, 1978), vii.

19   Arnold Heertje, ed., *Schumpeter's Vision: Capitalism, Socialism and Democracy after 40 Years.*

20   (South Bend, Ind.: University of Notre Dame Press, 1984).

8

Toil and Turmoil (1942-1945)

The war years for Schumpeter were dreary. The war made his depression more severe. Most of the students and many of the faculty left Cambridge, leaving Schumpeter and a few other older professors to do the teaching. Despite the fact that the university operated at half-steam, Schumpeter worked very hard, one term teaching five courses and regularly teaching more than full professors ordinarily teach. But gone were the young admirers and most of the graduate students. He felt isolated and alienated from Harvard.

With few students, limited social life, and disenchantment with his environment, Schumpeter spent most of his time working. He had two major projects: his book on economic theory and his book on the history of economics. He made the unhappy discovery that he had scant success in theorizing, a task that requires creativity as well as scholarship. So he spent much of his time on the history of economics, whose principal requirement was reading, memory, and scholarship, all of which he had in abundance. Still, his depression, his discomfort, his unhappiness left Schumpeter in constant mental turmoil.

1

In late 1942, the tide of battle in the European war began to turn, at first only tentatively, as U.S. troops, 400,000 strong, stormed ashore in North Africa, and Rommel, in full retreat, lost Tobruk and Benghazi. Desert warfare enthroned the tank in 1942 and 1943. Although many battles were still to be fought, German power in Africa had passed its zenith. After Patton and Montgomery invaded Sicily in 1943, Italy surrendered two months later, leaving only Germany to fight on in Italy. The long hard battle up the Italian boot began. At the same time, the Royal Air Force started bombing Berlin, beginning the revenge for London. In 1943, the Allied powers began the trek back that would end with their penetration into the heart of the German and Japanese empires. In central Europe, the holocaust was underway, with the ovens for human beings working overtime. Guadalcanal had fallen to the Americans in a bloody encounter, and the island hopping that characterized the reconquest of the Pacific began. The Pacific theater campaign became a question of who had the most and the largest ships and the greatest firepower. The war in Europe increasingly took to the skies as the Allies bombed Germany around the clock. Although the casualties on both sides mounted daily, Americans, never in doubt about the war's final outcome, began to sense the coming victory.

In early 1943, Schumpeter was still publicly voicing his belief that Germany would not be defeated, reflecting his hope that the Allies would grow weary and, unable to breach Fortress Europe, would negotiate the end of the war. But he was not so confident in his private diary writings.[1] On 22 November 1942, for example, he had written: "Why am I so horribly unhappy about the war's turning as it seems." He then mentioned the Temples of Nikko and the palaces of Kyoto, obviously fearing for their survival under bombardment. Much of Schumpeter's antiwar sentiment stemmed from his despair over the war's destructiveness. Back in June,1942, he had written: "infamous war—in which mankind and genius wither and mass production prevails.... The outcome of the war depends on whether or not fliers and bombers can be made foolproof." Although some economists have praised a war's ability to stimulate the economy, Schumpeter privately envisioned nothing but destruction. He also despaired over what he saw as the stupidity of war and its probable outcome, writing on 9 November 1942: "If I assume that with the successful landing in North Africa and with the defeat of Rommel, the fate of Germany and Hitlerism is sealed." He continued, "And should this world really be ruled by the English ideas and Russian Jews and chipmunks?" (He was referring to Roosevelt's prominent teeth.)

Still hoping for a negotiated peace that would save Germany and Japan from ignominious and destructive surrender, Schumpeter worried when it became increasingly apparent that his desired scenario would not occur. Although he did not follow the war news closely, largely because he didn't want to hear it and therefore deliberately avoided it, his diary shows his continuing interest in the subject. More importantly, it shows his continuing confusion as well. He vacillated in support of one side and then the other, not always certain of what he believed. Nor did he always understand why he believed what he did, and he still demonstrated confusion over his feelings in support of Germany. In a diary entry dated November 1943, he mused, "I cannot understand at all this revirement [reversal] of my sympathies [for Germany] since 1916." Having been staunchly anti-German during the First World War, perhaps because Germany represented a threat to his beloved Austro-Hungarian monarchy, Schumpeter wondered why he favored the Germans now. Possibly he feared that the war threatened all of German culture. He never really resolved this question, and the overriding result was that he remained depressed much of the time throughout the war. He feared the destruction of civilization and the seeming madness war produced. Finding himself in such a lonely minority in Cambridge, where nearly everyone was avidly in favor of U.S. policy, Schumpeter could do little more than retreat further into isolation and sink into deeper sadness.

Let it be clearly understood that, despite his opposition to much U.S. policy, some sympathy for Germany and Japan, and a desire for an early and negotiated end to the war, with no winners, Schumpeter in no way was disloyal to the United States and said and did nothing to give aid or comfort to his country's enemies. His strongest opinions were confined to his diary. Some of his closest colleagues had an inkling of his views, but Schumpeter made no effort to influence them or anyone else. He made no speeches or public statements during the war that could be regarded as prejudicial to the United States. Nor was he in contact with any agents of Germany or Japan. Despite considerable effort, the FBI was unable to find any evidence that Schumpeter said or did anything harmful to the United States.[2]

2

Schumpeter's persistent depression as well as despair because of the war spilled over into other aspects of his life. His diary entries from 1942 to 1945 consistently reveal a man in turmoil, one generally filled with doubt and foreboding. By the fall of 1942, Schumpeter was again thoroughly unhappy at Harvard. After an unidentified incident at a dinner meeting of the department, he wrote:

And with all the fuss about nothing—instead of observing, with quiet humor, Burbies busybodiness and Blacks stodginess (feet on dining-room table), Crums goosestepping, "laws of the department"—but pleading he does not know what is its official announcements, and the Department—capital!—directing this or that— well, instead of being amused by the cunning antics in the professorial monkey cage I was so irritated that I could not work at all and I felt so defeated, so defeated! so frustrated and weak and old—so lost in this stifling atmosphere of Harvard is more like a brewery ... stifling atmosphere.

Despite this unhappiness with Harvard, he attended nearly all the department and Executive Committee meetings, a task which must have been painful since some of his colleagues extended at most only minimal courtesy and otherwise shunned him because of his views on the war.[3]

Though disenchanted, Schumpeter had a busy 1942-43 academic year. He taught his usual advanced economic theory and history and literature of economics, a course that by now had become a part of his regular repertoire. In addition, he and John Williams taught the principles of money and banking, while he and Gottfried Haberler taught the seminar in business cycles and economic forecasting. In the spring 1943 term, Schumpeter taught another course at Radcliffe, bringing his total to five for that term.[4] But, with the war hovering over everyone's head, teaching lacked the luster it usually held for him since most of the regular students and faculty had left Cambridge to assist the war effort.

During this period, Schumpeter became more introspective and even more self-critical than usual. Summing up his life, he scolded himself for his failures, particularly with respect to leadership. On 20 October 1942, he wrote, "I singularly lack the quality of leadership—with a fraction of my ideas a new economics could have been founded." On 23 November, he continued with the same theme:

> Funny how I survey my life and my present situation—quite apart from the fact that subjectively I was unhappy most of the time, it was a failure. And the reason is quite clear—even in my scientific activity and in spite of an *"oeurve"* a fraction of which could have been enough for "fame" I do not carry weight: for I am typically "unleaderly"—in fact I am a man without an aura (and without an antennae).

As this entry shows, Schumpeter was sometimes unhappy with who he was; he wanted to be someone else—a leader, a scholar to be sure, but a leader of scholars, like Ricardo or Keynes. From what he wrote in his diary, he was never jealous of Keynes's economic analysis because he felt it was inadequate, but he did envy Keynes's ability to rally people to his views. Despite all of Schumpeter's ranting about the danger and perniciousness of schools in economics, there were times—and the war years were one such period—when having a school or at least a scholarly following might have pleased him.

His personal feelings momentarily overcame his sense of scientific purity. He was human enough to enjoy and crave the attention of people he respected; thus, in the loneliness of the war years, his sense of inadequacy, especially with regard to his failure as a leader, preoccupied him. He felt, correctly, that his colleagues had rejected him and his ideas, not only in matters of economics and economic policy, but also in national and world affairs. Incorrectly, however, he attributed this repudiation not to his ideas but exclusively to his lack of leadership. His eclectic nature also fed his feelings of inadequacy. He perceived that his failure to hold firm convictions played a part in his lack of leadership and influence. After a cocktail party he had attended in 1942, he wrote of his student and friend, Paul M. Sweezy, a dedicated Marxist, "what I mind in him and at the same time love is that he cannot throw it [his ideological and political outlook] off—ever: he talks at an intimate party as he would to a mass meeting." He then lamented his own lack of belief in anything, adding: "Now I have no garb which I could not throw off. Relativism is in my blood."

His unhappiness and sense of hopelessness emerges time and again in his war years' diary. In late 1942 he confided, "This is no longer my world. I am a stranger to the mortals and their doings, to the shadows and their marionette drama." Viewing the war as "the suicide of civilization," he seems to have felt abandoned by a world he could no longer fit into or understand. His diary from this period projects a deep pessimism along the lines of an October 1942 entry: "I think the most interesting fact about life is death ... to me now life feels like a pageant on which I looked without much interest and which now recedes from me." Echoing these sentiments, he soon after wrote: "Why do I worry and fuss? ... What do I care what happens—earth belongs to the living.... God has the kindness to show me that I don't lose much in dying. It is *some* comfort!" Even the beauty of Taconic, where he wrote this entry, could not soothe the deep sadness haunting Schumpeter during the war years.

The company of friends might have helped relieve some of his feelings of alienation, but his social life now limped along. Since the young had gone to war and the middle aged and old were working overtime, Cambridge society was muted. Harvard was becoming a war factory, working year round training military personnel. His colleagues and their wives, for the most part, were uncritical in their acceptance of the government's war and foreign policies, while Schumpeter was unsparing in his criticism of Roosevelt, the British government, the policy of unconditional surrender, and many other facets, big and small, of wartime policies. His blunt remarks did not endear him to his associates and further enhanced his isolation. On the few occasions when he did venture out, he would not hold his tongue. As colleagues tired of this, some hosts and hostesses forgot to invite the Schumpeters to their parties.[5]

3

Seldom reading newspapers or listening to the radio, Schumpeter tried to hide from the war, burying himself in subjects totally unrelated to what was happening in the world. Much of his time was spent in the Kress Collection of

Baker Library, where he surrounded himself with economic theory, past and present, in order to avoid thinking about the world outside. For several years now, Schumpeter had been banging his head against the blank wall of economic theory. He also studied a great deal of mathematics, hoping to find a method that would permit him to formulate his development theory. He was trying desperately to produce a determinate general-equilibrium development theory in which a set of equations related all the principal variables to one another. Such a theory would integrally involve time, permitting him to trace the time path of the variables. But he wanted more than just equations; he wanted relations that embodied the social and economic fabric of society and depicted its changes.

Walras, his hero in pure economic theory, had earlier developed a general-equilibrium theory stated in an appropriate mathematical formulation. But his analysis had been static and changeless, failing to include time in any way in any of the equations. Schumpeter saw that his new theory must involve time, and he believed this was possible if he used either of two different types of mathematical equations. Differential equations would involve a variable, for example y, which might stand for income, as well as another variable, dy/dt, the rate of change of income with respect to time. Another method, difference equations, would relate the variable y at a specific time t, $y(t)$, and y in another time period, such as $y(t-1)$, that is, income in the previous time period.

In order to obtain a result using difference and differential equations, it would be necessary to specify in advance the values of all the parameters and the initial conditions (the situation at $t = 0$). When these are specified, the mathematical solution would trace out all values of the variables for each time period from t = minus infinity to t = plus infinity, without permitting any change in the parameters or initial conditions. This method did not satisfy Schumpeter since he still wanted an evolutionary model, similar to the one used in his 1911 book wherein the position of the variables in time $t = 5$, for example, depended on what had happened in $t = 4$ and other intermediate times in addition to their initial position and the values of the parameters at that time.

Schumpeter toiled over mathematical tomes almost daily in search of the understanding that would show him how to formulate his economic model with the appropriate mathematical tools. At the same time, he studied economic theory, looking for the understanding that would permit him to perceive a model that could be subjected to those tools. But he failed, again and again, to find the tools necessary to produce a determinate economic model. He could, as he had in his 1911 theory, achieve partial determinacy, the determinacy of the static economy at the initial time period before change begins, as well as at the final time period when the economy had struggled back to equilibrium and the change's full effects had worked themselves out. Still, the models he developed had an indeterminate evolutionary path for all the time periods in between and an indeterminate point in time when the innovation occurs. Discouragement over this failure matched his disillusionment over the war, adding to the unhappiness he suffered during this period.[6]

4

Because of the time spent working on the development of a new theory, Schumpeter's published writing in 1942 and 1943 was limited. In December 1941, he had chaired the Roundtable on Cost and Demand Functions of Individual Firms at the American Economic Association meetings. The *American Economic Review* published his note in 1942.[7] In 1943, Seymour Harris edited and published a volume entitled *Postwar Economic Problems*, which included an essay on "Capitalism in the Postwar World" by Schumpeter.[8] Harris also suggested that he write a book on money, leading him to dig out the old money manuscript he had promised to work on when he finished *Business Cycles*. But he did little more than fuss with it now and again. Originally written in German, Schumpeter had scribbled the revisions on the manuscript in English, German, and shorthand. He now wrote more notes on half-sheets of paper that he attached to the page he intended to revise, but he made no real progress. His diary shows that he again contemplated turning his Lowell lecture series into the planned book, but he soon abandoned this project as well.[9]

Other published writing in 1943 consisted of an introduction to *Interest and Usury*, a revision of the Ph.D. thesis written under Schumpeter by Father Bernard Dempsey, later of St. Louis University.[10] Earlier, Schumpeter had reviewed a book entitled *The Theory of Price*, written by University of Chicago Professor George Stigler, who would later win the 1982 Nobel Prize.[11]

At about this time, Schumpeter wrote in his diary that some of his colleagues had noted the absence of dedications in his books. Most of his professor friends usually dedicated their work to their wives, parents, children, professors, or colleagues. Schumpeter had dedicated his 1908 book to his mother, but *Die Theorie der wirtschaftlichen Entwicklung*, *Business Cycles*, and *Capitalism, Socialism and Democracy* carried no dedication. Schumpeter wrote that he had more cause than Sweezy and Beckerath, both of whom had just published, to dedicate his books to his wife than they, but he added "I forgot completely—Egoism or self-centered."

Instead of writing for publication during the war years, Schumpeter spent most of his time either wrestling with theory or increasingly writing on what he called the history of theory. In 1942, he wrote some of the early chapters for the book that became the *History of Economic Analysis*, including a chapter entitled "The Beginnings" (which dealt with Graeco-Roman economic thinking) and chapters on the scholastic doctors, the philosophers of natural law, the consultant administrators, and the pamphleteers. He also wrote an essay on historical method that later became a part of the book. Schumpeter typically retreated to the history of economic theory when he made no progress with his own theoretical work. But his attempt to write theory at the age of sixty defied his own dictum that a scholar's original contribution would be made in that all-important third decade when the mind is powerful, fresh, and uncluttered with doubt and superfluous knowledge. Yet, paradoxically, here he was, starting his sixties, trying to do something original.

The creative juices, however, had abandoned him. He could no longer produce new and original theories. The alternative to creativity and original contribution is scholarship. At age sixty, Schumpeter knew he was on solid ground with scholarship; he could make a contribution to the history of economics, a subject in which profound knowledge, a prodigious memory, wide reading, literary skill, and analytical ability counted more than invention and inspiration. Possessing all of these qualities in abundance, he tired of failure in attempting to theorize; thus, he began spending more and more time reading and writing on the history of economics. In January and February 1943, he wrote a long analysis of equilibrium, as well as an early version of wages, unemployment, and poverty theories. On 19 March 1943, he informed Trygve Haavelmo of Norway, a student of Ragnar Frisch, that he was writing the history of economic theory, not the history of economic thought.[12] This was the first time Schumpeter drew the sharp line that became one of the principal methodological stances he took in his book, the distinction between writing the history of economics as a science and the broader topic of the history of economic thinking. His direction was becoming more focussed once again.[13]

As had been the case with *Business Cycles* and *Capitalism, Socialism and Democracy*, Schumpeter was highly optimistic about when he could complete the history of economics book. In early 1943, he thought he would finish the project six months later; as each year passed by, he planned to complete it later that year, or during the next at the latest. But, the more he studied, the more there was to study. The more he wrote, the more there was to write. Late May 1943 found him in Taconic, "enjoying lake and flowers," and still plugging away on the history of economics. He revised the chapters on consultant administrators and the pamphleteers and wrote a section on population and increasing and decreasing returns. He also wrote a section on mercantilist literature. But he was not satisfied with his progress, and pessimism and depression soon overtook him; in July he confided, "history practically at a standstill." For days on end he struggled with his history of economics, but by the end of summer he had produced mostly notes, little real manuscript. Again expressing his frustration, he wrote in August: "I am stuck. History is not what I bargained for when I thought I would finish by the end of June. But this is not all—the truth is that I am failing, no exercise. I hardly ever leave the grounds."

At the end of the spring term of 1943, Schumpeter, having taught five courses, was exhausted. As one of the few regular professors still around, he felt he had to carry a heavy load or little would be taught. On April 25, he admitted,

> Ostersontag [Easter Sunday]. Here I am, lecture term over gestern [yesterday] and it left me exhausted as EB had said it would ... five courses were too much ... fumbling and fussing.... Yes, I am old, but less crestfallen than I thought I should be. But why, why do I grieve so much about this war and its obvious infamy.

He continually worried about the war, politics, and the approach of old age, writing in March 1943: "... but I struggle on in deepening despair. Like everybody else I do believe that Germany and Japan are lost—why do I grieve so much I'd like to know ... the work and lack of exercise, but all at once I am an old man!" Reaching the age of sixty bothered Schumpeter because he dreaded being forced into retirement by Harvard at the age of sixty-five.

Only one event brightened his outlook for a while during the spring. A group of colleagues and former students, now professors, arranged for an issue of the *Review of Economic Statistics*, one of Harvard's illustrious in-house journals, to be dedicated to Schumpeter in honor of his sixtieth birthday, 8 February 1943.[14] Fourteen articles, written by Abram Bergson, Richard Goodwin, Trygve Haavelmo, Paul Samuelson, Fritz Machlup, Jacob Marschak, Lloyd Metzler, Arthur Smithies, Hans Staehle, Wolfgang Stolper, Paul Sweezy, E. B. Wilson, and Jane Worcester, discussed the importance and the relevance of different aspects of his work.

But despite this honor, his mood remained subdued and sad during the summer of 1943. Although worn out from his heavy teaching schedule, he again tried to work on theory—the PV project. Still struggling with the history of economics at the same time, he also continued his study of mathematics and Greek, most nights reading the classic Greek plays in bed the last thing before lights out. He played around with a novel to be entitled *The Honest Hunter*, scribbling notes about a ruthless, able, and strong protagonist. But this novel idea, like the others, was abandoned. Returning to his now recurring theme of aging, in late August he wrote, "I feel so often dead tired ... doze off in the evening ... fact is I am alive in force only three hours of the day."

Schumpeter began a new practice in his diary during that summer of 1943 of recording sayings and aphorisms. He even started a section in his diary headed "Aphorisms" or usually just "Aph." Most do not possess profound meaning and all are not original, but they do comprise a record of the things going through his mind at the time. Many expressed bitterness and cynicism, and some occasionally found their way into his published writing. Some of his colleagues and students remember having heard Schumpeter say them. Following is a small sample:

> Common sense is a method to arrive at workable conclusions from false premises by nonsensical reasoning.

> Men can never recognize a truth except by making nonsense of it.

> Why form a party when he can form a pressure group? (Slichter in his quiet humor told me that). Oh profound saying that sums up the politics of this nation.

> To live is to love but also to hate. To live is to fight and also to die.

> It is our mind that looks for simplicity, not nature.

> Whatever you do in Germany after having conquered [her] do not forget to learn from her.

> Humanity does not really care for freedom; the man of the people quickly realize that they are not up to it.

> Equality is the ideal of the subnormal but even the subnormal do not really desire equality, but only that there be nobody better.

> A statesman is the animal who works with phrases instead of with the burglar's jimmy.

> Masses do not want freedom, still less responsibility ... they crave and need to be led and ruled.

> Two kinds of people I distrust: architects who profess to build cheaply, economists who profess to give simple answers.

5

Joseph loved Taconic and commented frequently on how much he enjoyed the flowers, the sunshine, the changing of the seasons, the walks between Twin Lakes, and the peace he found away from the grime of Cambridge and the annoyance of his Harvard colleagues. To be there usually brightened his spirits. In 1942 and 1943, he and Elizabeth tried but failed to resettle a Japanese-American to Taconic, offering their spare house at Windy Hill in return for work on the property and assistance with the nursery. For a while, gas and rubber rationing during the war threatened their frequent trips to Taconic, but somehow he and Elizabeth managed to have enough to go by car most of the time. On occasion, however, it was necessary to take the train, a long and circuitous route. He tried to arrange his teaching and examinations so that he could stay at Windy Hill for longer periods of time, if less frequently. This may have been because even his pessimism and depression seemed less pronounced there. All through the diaries he sang the praises of Taconic; every season of the year, even the gray November days and the white blankets of December and January snow, drew applause from his pen. He always felt more content working in Taconic. After viewing the lovely winter scene surrounding him, for example, he wrote in late 1944, "I feel happy and Xmasy and not as I should in Cambridge."

The war, political differences with colleagues and friends, the lack of sympathy with the foreign and domestic policies of the government, and the ostracism by and alienation from their friends and acquaintances combined to produce one good result for the Schumpeters: It strengthened their marriage and brought them closer together. Joseph's interest in other women and his occasional philandering, which was never serious and amounted to only a few peccadillos, declined as age and lack of opportunity took their toll. Elizabeth probably knew of his few indiscretions, but she took no notice and they never threatened their marriage. As Joseph aged, home, preferably Taconic, became his fortress, and Elizabeth his guardian and champion.

In the summer of 1944, the Schumpeters found a new friend when they decided to get a dog. On the day the new puppy was delivered in Taconic, the Haberlers had come out from Cambridge for a visit. When the dog arrived, Elizabeth and Friedl Haberler were upstairs at Windy Hill, while Gottfried and Joseph were downstairs. Elizabeth asked Friedl, "Can we trust an Austrian gentleman to determine the sex of a dog?" They decided they could, and Elizabeth called down to inquire about the sex of the puppy. After a brief bit of empirical research, Joseph called back, "It's a boy dog." Without hesitation, Elizabeth decided to name the dog Peter. This beautiful Irish setter became a great pet and comfort to them both, perhaps helping to fill the void left by the loss of so many friends. She went everywhere with Elizabeth, and her name remained Peter to the end of her days.[15]

6

Schumpeter's teaching in the fall of 1943 continued much as it had in the past, even though most of the regular students had gone off to war. The soldiers and sailors who replaced them studied mathematics, engineering, and similar technical subjects. Because of this, many economics classes were small and less demanding, and the students weren't as good as before the war. Schumpeter taught his theory course, a part of the money and banking course, and his usual history and literature of economics. With Wassily Leontief, he also taught a new course, entitled Programs of Social and Economic Reconstruction, dealing with the many national and international plans suggested for implementation at war's end. All through the war, the department functioned at half-steam because not only the students but also the faculty had joined the war effort in various capacities. As a result, the graduate program in economics dwindled. In 1941, Harvard had granted seventeen Ph.D.s in economics, the largest number up to that time. Degrees granted included those to Paul Samuelson, Joe Bain, Abram Bergson, Father Dempsey, Russell Nixon, Shigeto Tsuru, and David McCord Wright, among others, all of whom went on to illustrious careers. In 1942, the number of Ph.D.s declined to fifteen. But during the deep war years, 1943 and 1944, the numbers were only eight and seven. In 1945, ten doctorates in economics were granted by Harvard.[16] The smaller number of graduate students did not reduce the work of those professors like Schumpeter who remained; instead, their load increased because they had to cover whatever was left undone by those faculty members who were no longer around. Harvard itself was bustling. Although in 1944 only 611 College students were civilians, the university enrolled 45,000 officers and officer candidates in all its programs.[17]

During this semester, Schumpeter continued his work on the history of economics, but slow progress still plagued him. In September, he wrote to his colleague, Edward Chamberlin, then in the Office of Strategic Services overseas,

I shall take this winter off, and hope that I will finish my lagging history of economic thought, or to complete the piece of what is really responsible for the lagging of the history, namely, a volume on economic theory which is to present the gist I want to elaborate in a more comprehensive work that I hardly hope to live to finish.[18]

With the war occupying the attention of nearly everyone, Schumpeter buried himself in work, feigning lack of interest in the world's turmoil. He explained in a letter to Arthur Smithies, then in Washington, that he was working on the history of economics because "It is simply the subject, among all those at hand, that is furthest removed from current events."[19] During the fall, he wrote an early version of the Scope and Method chapter, which eventually became part 1 of *History of Economic Analysis*. He also wrote a section on the political and intellectual scenery in the period of the classical economists, another section on senior's four postulates, and an essay on *Sozialpolitik* and the historical school. By 1943, the amount of material written on the history of economics totalled more than 500 pages, some 250,000 to 300,000 words of the published edition of *History of Economic Analysis*. Still, his output represented less than half of that book, and Schumpeter realized that he had a lot of work left to do.[20]

At the January 1944, American Economic Association meeting held in Washington, Schumpeter chaired the Honorary Member Committee, the group responsible for recommending select foreigners for honorary membership in the Association. That year, the Committee recommended mainly Englishmen—Lord Beveridge, John Hicks, Lionel Robbins, Joan Robinson, Friedrich von Hayek, and others. But it also nominated Gunnar Myrdal and Bertil Ohlin of Sweden, Ragnar Frisch of Norway, and William Rappard of Switzerland. Joan Robinson's recommendation resulted largely from Schumpeter's influence. In his committee report to the association, he wrote:

I know I shall be considered out of order if in this anti-feminist country, I suggest honoring a woman, but Mrs. Joan Robinson of Cambridge had a well-earned international success with her book on the *Economics of Imperfect Competition* in 1933. By virtue of it she holds a leading position in one of the most popular lines of advance [of economic theory].[21]

A new course called The Economics of Socialism became a part of Schumpeter's repertoire beginning in the spring term of 1944. Despite his distaste for teaching undergraduates, he learned that a course in socialism was popular among them. Previously taught by Paul Sweezy, who had left for the war, this course in Schumpeter's hands contained many of the ideas presented in *Capitalism, Socialism and Democracy* but with a heavier dose of the economics of capitalism and socialism. Thereafter, Schumpeter taught it nearly every year for several years.

But most of his work during 1944 focussed on the history of economics. He devoted much of his time to writing the section on the theories of value and money before 1790, as well as the chapter on the scholastics and their successors. Later in the spring, he revised the scholastics chapter and made extensive notes for other chapters. In early summer, he told his friend Irving Fisher that he was about three-fourths done with the book and that he had made considerable progress in the spring and early summer. Still, he felt overwhelmed by the amount of work lying ahead. He explained the reason in a mid-1944 letter to Henry Spiegel of Catholic University, a specialist in the history of economics, when he wrote: "My history of economics has developed into an entirely new thing that has cost me an incredible amount of time. It should be ready for the press by September [1944]"[22] But 12 February 1945 found him telling his diary:

> How *did* I get into this mess with History? which can never repay the trouble and which was so much nicer in the short sketch. But the question is what to do *now*? Only move I see—finish as quickly as possible with reasonable care!

This entry was written five years before Schumpeter died, leaving the work still unfinished. As usual, he had vastly underestimated the time necessary to complete it. Also as usual, the amount of time spent on the book prevented him from writing much else for publication.

In 1944, he did manage to review Harold Laski's *Reflections on the Revolution of Our Time*.[23] He also finished an article entitled "Capitalism" for the *Encyclopedia Brittanica*, but it was not published until 1946.[24] In 1944, on the basis of *Capitalism, Socialism and Democracy*, Schumpeter was made a member of the Eugene Field Society of St. Louis (an honorary literary society).[25]

Because he had finally been granted a leave from Harvard, the Schumpeters rented their Cambridge house in the fall term 1944 and then spent most of the time in Taconic. Occasionally, he had to return to Cambridge to give examinations or to get research material; when there, he stayed at the Continental Hotel. Then he would hurry back to Taconic to be with Elizabeth and to work on the history of economics, as well as to spend some time with PV, his theory project. As always, he also tried to work daily with mathematics and Greek. Windy Hill was organized around Schumpeter. His main study was a converted upstairs bedroom with a fireplace; the small downstairs study had been a pantry. But his work sprawled out all over the house—in the bookcases in the living rooms and on tables and shelves.

During that fall mostly spent in Taconic, Schumpeter also struggled through Paul Samuelson's *Foundations of Economic Analysis,* his doctoral dissertation, which would win the David Wells Prize. Harvard University Press, on Schumpeter's and others' recommendation, published the book in 1947. Only with difficulty could Schumpeter follow some of the mathematics of Samuelson's work, but he recognized the study as a major step forward because it dramatically showed the power of using mathematics in theory. Rather than envy Samuelson, Schumpeter felt proud of his former student, but he was angry at himself for not having produced his own theory. His failure was not for lack of trying. In November, he recorded in his diary that he was starting to write PV and he spent quite a bit of time on the subject that winter.[26] No manuscript resulted, however. His work later ceased, as he was caught up in other projects, none of which became publications. During this time, he fussed with his money book some more, looked at the Lowell lectures again, and spent time with a statistics book that his colleague Leonard Crum was writing. He lamented in his diary that he was too busy even for his detective stories anymore.

The time in Taconic in the fall of 1944 was also a busy time for Elizabeth and her research. For a while during the war, she served as editor of the *Quarterly Journal of Economics*, even though she had stopped writing for publication. But her interest in Japan and the Far East continued. She read a great deal about the country, continued her study of the Japanese language, and prepared material for a book on Japan's economy. In October, she submitted a formal proposal, including some manuscript, to McGraw-Hill. When they replied that they were not interested in publishing a book on the Japanese economy at that time, Elizabeth was crushed, seeing several years' work swept down the drain. Although she did not completely abandon scholarly work and Japan, she made no further move after that toward producing a book of her own on Japan or anything else.

7

As he had done in 1942 and 1943, Schumpeter continued his introspective examination in 1944 and 1945. His depression also continued, impeding his work and coloring his attitude toward life. His mood in January 1944 was not helped by a bout with the flu that knocked him out for eight days and left him weak for longer. A diary entry from this time reads: "What is this interval between two sleeps? What is a day and what is a life? A blank of marble that God gives you to make a work of art." Then he noted an idea for a novel: "On lives that are successes studded with failures and on lives that are failures studded with successes." A few weeks later, he again returned to the subject of success and failure. "Really, I don't quite regret any of my errors and failures—every one of them taught me something about myself and life that uniform success would have hidden."

This success and failure theme recurs often in his writing and thinking of the period, reflecting his adopted habit of introspection—a practice not uncommon in people who are conscious of aging. On 4 November 1944, for example, a reporter for the *Harvard Crimson* quoted Schumpeter as saying:

> Early in Life, I formed an idea of a rich and full life to include economics, politics, science, art, and love. All of my failures are due to the observance of this program and my successes to the neglect of it; concentration is necessary for success in any field.[27]

Once in a while Schumpeter engaged in an elaborate and balanced self-appraisal, trying to evaluate objectively his past and come to terms with it. On 21 January 1945, one such appraisal was entered in his diary:

> Looking back on these months here [at Taconic] and on the weeks that are still left, and looking back on my life in the process, three things stand out:
>
> 1) always the same mistakes committed and the same type of strength and weakness displayed.
>
> 2) the story might be written in terms of lost opportunities (though of course that stands out in retrospect; there were those that were seized and used promptly enough.)
>
> 3) yet there is no regret—if I had used everyone of those opportunities I should not have done a better job of it all—perhaps even the contrary, for success up to the hilt with any one of them would have stuck me on the particular line—and not only narrowed me but landed me in uncomfortable situations ... if I had stayed in Cairo, if I had got the job in Berlin or before in Vienna, if my ministry had been a success or Biedermann, the situation would been much the same, being what I am. It would be nice to have money to retire, yet, who knows? ... it is all well. Thank you, you Hasen.
>
> ease me gently into my grave.
> Never grudge the time
>
> a) to think
>
> b) for a bit of math

Then, at the bottom of that page, he noted yet another idea for a novel: "story of a careerist and seiner Mutter [his mother]." These reportings of introspective reflection capture some of the paradox within Schumpeter's internal life and between that private life and his public one, illustrating the mood swings between misery and acceptance, depression and hail-fellow, well-met. Chafing under his isolation in the fall of 1944, he wrote: "Laune! [a

German word meaning spirit]. This is just what I have not got ... misery, disgust and sick of it all!" This was written while he was at comfortable Taconic. At about this time, he even admitted in his diary that he was a cynic, but a few months later he swung the opposite way. As usual, he used his birthday as an occasion for summing up, cheerfully writing on 8 February 1945, his sixty-second birthday:

> Good morning friend. how does it feel to be 62? and definitely old and definitely to feel old. One thing to be recorded is humble thanks to the U.S. No repining, no sterile regrets, no sorrow about the state of things: acceptance rather and a feeling: could be worse! ... Thank you, Hasen, and ease me gently into my grave! No joy of course ... but peace ...

In another few months, at Easter time, he would be writing of the "unrelieved gloom" pervading him and his work, and comment on being "so terribly depressed." He was still working on his history of economics project and on economic theory.

Schumpeter returned to Harvard for the spring term of 1945, the last one of the war period, and he taught the undergraduate course in principles of economics with Leontief. Schumpeter and Leontief teaching elementary economics—that must have been a rare experience for those few freshmen and sophomores that semester. He again offered his socialism course and, with Hansen and Williams, taught the undergraduate money and banking course. Reflecting the absence of professors, he also taught his advanced theory course and the history and literature of economics. In early 1945, he did some general reading, praising Van Wyck Brook's book, *New England's Indian Summer*, and commenting on George Bernard Shaw's latest book:

> Yes, he shocks his readers, in the way and within the limits they expect to be shocked and like it; but not beyond. He lets people's blood "curdle" or something at the idea of love and marriage between brother and sister—for the country would have been shocked, really and unpleasantly.

Through the early part of that year he gave himself good marks, with many "voll" weeks and high daily ratings—5/6 and 1—indicating progress in his writing.

For his work on the history of economics book, he read English history to prime himself on the period leading up to classical economics. Then, in the spring and summer of 1945, he wrote the final drafts of several chapters, including those on Graeco-Roman economics and the scholastic doctors and philosophers of natural law. He also resumed work on the economic theory project, developing another plan for what he called his theoretical handbook, or PV, at Easter. Although Burbank, the department chairman, kept him in Cambridge for the spring reading period (usually three weeks at the end of the lecture period), Schumpeter hurried to Taconic in June to spend the summer. Again, week after week, he recorded "voll," as his work, primarily in the history of economics, went well. His only real complaint was about his health, as he noted: "heart bumps in a way it did not even a few months ago," possibly the result of having gained some weight. In 1945, he weighed nearly 180, about fifteen to twenty pounds more than his normal weight.

As late as 1944, Schumpeter told his friends that Germany and Japan might yet not lose the war.[28] But, by this time, nearly all Americans and their political leadership were convinced the Allies would win, probably in 1945 or 1946. The economic and financial planning for the postwar period then began, particularly its international aspect. Many of Schumpeter's colleagues and students participated in this postwar planning for the U.S. side. Alvin Hansen, by that time a spokesman for the Keynesian viewpoint, became a technical advisor to the 1944 Bretton Woods meeting in New Hampshire. That meeting sought to establish the institutional framework and operating procedures for international trade and finance. Arthur Smithies, Schumpeter's great friend, was the technical secretary. Many other Schumpeter students were also on hand, including Edward Bernstein, who had received his doctorate in 1931 and met Schumpeter when he visited Harvard in 1927-28 and 1930. Bernstein and Emilio Collado, a State Department official with a Harvard doctorate in economics, were influential in the planning.[29]

Harry D. White, another Harvard Ph.D. in economics, wrote the principal planning document that became the basis of the International Monetary Fund and the International Bank for Reconstruction and Development. Other Schumpeter students involved included Eleanor Dulles, Andreas Papandreou (until recently prime minister of Greece), and Schumpeter's old friend, Redvers Opie. Despite the adoption of the U.S. (White) proposal at Bretton Woods, Schumpeter in late 1944 thought the victory belonged to England: "English politicians must speak of Bretton Woods with cool indifference— must not do to say: having most auspicious beginning of reconquest of America." Even so, he expected the English to ask for more concessions, which they did later: the $4 billion U.S. loan to England and the Marshall Plan.

As one of America's leading economists, why was Schumpeter not an important figure in these talks? He had, by his personal and professional attitude and interests, ruled himself out of any discussion of the postwar economy, just as he had stood apart from economic policy during the depression, except for the private Butler-Columbia book. Even if he had been asked, his antipathy to Roosevelt would have prevented his cooperation with the government. But he wasn't asked because his attitude was well known to the government through his colleagues and students with connections in Washington. He also had made no secret of his anti-British sentiments, yet the British were one of the principal participants at the meeting. To further insure his exclusion, he was not in sympathy with the Keynesian and proplanning attitude that both England and the United States brought to the discussions, where Keynes was the chief British spokesman. Since long before he had come to the United States in 1932, Schumpeter looked askance at policy advocacy by economists, never tiring of trying to convince economists that they were scientists and should therefore eschew policy matters. It would not do, then, for Schumpeter to interest himself publicly in postwar economic policies. He again sat on the sidelines, absent from another major economic debate of his time.

Thinking of Great Britain and Bretton Woods, as well as of what he considered would be an inevitable conflict with Russia, Schumpeter confided in his diary, "U.S. can defend herself against a world of enemies, but who is going to protect her from her allies?" He feared harmful events at the war's end, and wondered what would happen now that "We have produced what we feared—the military power that rules Europe and Asia; much more, too, than, in their wildest dreams the Germanophobes can ever have believed, Germany would. We have set up the very thing we went out to fight." The end of the war came as Schumpeter was busy in his study, just as he had been all through July and August 1945. On 14 August, he thought of the two atomic bombs dropped on Japan and summed up much of his antiwar attitude when he wrote: "It is a stupid bestiality or a bestial stupidity."

Notes

1   Many of the statements concerning Schumpeter's feelings and sentiments in this and the following sections are based on his diary material as well as on conversations with his friends and colleagues, especially Edward Mason, Gottfried Haberler, Wassily Leontief, Wolfgang Stolper, and others.
2   The hundreds of pages of correspondence and reports on Joseph and Elizabeth Schumpeter made available to me under the Freedom of Information Act by the FBI show a significant effort on its part to uncover evidence for criminal proceedings against one or both of them.
3   The Full Professor's Committee of the Department of Economics had become the Executive Committee with substantially the same functions.
4   Harvard University catalog and Schumpeter's diary.
5   During the war, of course, all social life was muted, but colleagues recall that the Schumpeter's had a very low profile, attending few parties.
6   Schumpeter's diligence in studying theory and mathematics shows up dramatically in his entries in his little "agendas"—little vest pocket appointment books in which he recorded, in color-coded fashion, using key abbreviations,

initials, or words, what he was working on, day by day. The agendas for all his Harvard years and for several years before are in the Harvard University Archives.

7 *American Economic Review* 32 (May 1942): 349-350.
8 Seymour Harris, ed., *Postwar Economic Problems* (New York: McGraw-Hill, 1943), 113-26.
9 His diary contains entries about his plans and alternative plans, and discussions sometimes of the pros and cons of one project or another.
10 Preface to Bernard W. Dempsey, *Interest and Usury* (Washington, D.C.: American Council on Public Affairs, 1943).
11 *American Economic Review* 32 (December 1942), 844-7.
12 This letter is in the correspondence file of the Schumpeter papers in the Harvard University Archives.
13 The order and timing of his writing of the various parts of what became the *History of Economic Analysis* appear in his diaries as well as in the Editor's Note, written by Elizabeth Schumpeter, of *History of Economic Analysis*.
14 *Review of Economic Statistics* 25, no. 1 (February 1943): 2-100.
15 This anecdote was told to me by Professor and Mrs. Gottfried Haberler.
16 The Harvard University catalogs, year by year, record the degrees, subjects, theses,and recipients awarded by the university.
17 *Harvard Magazine* September-October 1986.
18 This letter is in the correspondence file of the Schumpeter papers in the Harvard University Archives.
19 Arthur Smithies gave to the Harvard University Archives a group of letters, nearly all handwritten, that he had received from Schumpeter. They are kept with the Schumpeter papers in the Archives.
20 The entire manuscript, including several versions of what Schumpeter wrote, are in twenty-five boxes in the Harvard University Archives.
21 A copy of Schumpeter's report is in the Harvard University Archives.
22 This letter is in the correspondence file of the Schumpeter papers in the Harvard University Archives.
23 *American Economic Review* 34 (March 1944): 161-4.
24 *Encyclopedia Brittanica*, 14th edition (Chicago: Encyclopedia Brittanica, 1946), 4:801-807.
25 The membership notice is on file in the Harvard University Archives.
26 No manuscript of this book can be identified in his papers. There is some handwritten manuscript—about twenty-five pages long—that carries no identification but deals with consumer and producer attitudes, along with notes on the same subject, which could possibly be the beginning of such writing.
27 *Harvard Crimson* 4 November 1944: 1.
28 Several colleagues related to me Schumpeter's attitude toward the war. His 1944 belief that Germany might win was told to me by Paul Samuelson.
29 *Harvard Magazine* September-October 1986.

Elizabeth Boody Firuski, economist with a green thumb, whom
Schumpeter was courting and in 1937 married, when she was thirty-
seven and he was fifty-four (1935). *Courtesy of the Harvard
University Archives.*

Schumpeter on the way to class in Harvard Yard with Memorial Chapel in the background (1947). *Courtesy of the Harvard University Archives.*

Schumpeter relaxes atop Mt. Riga near Taconic, Connecticut (1948). *Courtesy of the Harvard University Archives.*

Schumpeter talking to Professor Gottfried Haberler of Harvard (1948). *Courtesy of the Harvard University Archives.*

Schumpeter at sixty-five; though he was at retirement age, he was still teaching and writing (1948). *Courtesy of the Harvard University Archives.*

9

A New and Uncomfortable World (1945-1947)

Schumpeter did not care much for the new world that emerged at war's end. Harvard had changed, he thought, for the worse. The young men, anxious to get on with their careers, did not surround him. They were more interested in political economy, in telling the government what to do. Schumpeter still felt that, with few exceptions, Harvard did not value pure scholarship. Despite his disgruntlement, he carried on. Always the educator, he helped write a textbook in mathematical economics and began to write more papers.

His differences with the international, economic, political, and military policy of most of his colleagues mattered little after the war. But, after all those years of isolation, Schumpeter could not fully rejoin the community that he had found so pleasurable in the 1930s. He remained on the outside, critical of Harvard, his colleagues, economics, and a world that moved ever further from his vision of how the world ought to be. His depression continued, augmented now by the belief that he had not and would not make the contribution to economics that he wanted. He ground away on the history of economics, interspersed with work in economic theory. In 1946, he, along with many others, evaluated the work of Keynes, who died that year. These early postwar years were years he endured but did not enjoy.

1

The war was over, a great victory for the United States, but for Schumpeter it signalled yet another defeat. His newly adopted countrymen had defeated and now occupied three countries he loved—Germany, Austria, and Japan. While the victors had divided Germany into parts governed by each, a U.S. general dictated to the emperor of Japan and his people. Russian troops, to Schumpeter the hated Slavs and tyrannical communists, occupied Austria. His homeland was once again under the nominal leadership of his old chief, Dr. Karl Renner, chancellor of Austria in 1919 when Schumpeter was state secretary of finance. Austria faced problems akin to those he had confronted, but they did not concern him now. As he had predicted, both Austria and Germany became pawns in a game of world power. Facing a new world, Schumpeter found it an unappetizing place. He feared that the United States would squander its largess on the English and knuckle under to the Slavs, forcing the seeds of conflict to sprout in a Europe divided.

Even the environment of Harvard University had changed, and, with the Keynesian intellectual victory, economics had almost ceased to be his beloved science, changing instead into a politicoeconomic game he felt would surely backfire. Despite his own successes in economics, including the acclaim of his most recent book, *Capitalism, Socialism and Democracy*, he believed he had failed as a contributor to his science. Nothing that he or like-minded scientists had done had prevented what they considered the Keynesian corruption of economics. Having long since recovered from the failure of his theory of economic development to gain general acceptance, he was still smarting from the fact that *Business Cycles* had silently slipped into obscurity just as it was published. The reviewers had been generous but reserved, and the book stirred no one. Although professors and students gave it lip service as a classic, they ignored its content and no one rallied to its flag.

Schumpeter had spent the war years almost as a monk, holed up in the Kress Library, searching economic theory for some useful truths. His task had been two-fold, but it remained unfulfilled. He was optimistic on many occasions that he had nearly completed his objective of writing a new history of economics, but at war's end he was still only halfway around the track. The second task was to find a new theory among the old. He desperately wanted to turn his theory of economic development into a rigorous, determinate, and operational one. Because he felt this required almost daily study of nearly all types of mathematics, he chastised himself when he missed a day or two or more, convinced that his new theory would be mathematical. Constantly on his mind, his search guided his reading of all the great economists and his ventures into related fields, such as ergonomics and the theory of rationality. But even with this great effort, he had failed to move beyond square one in formulating a new theory, no matter how hard he tried. Writing something now and again that resulted in nothing useful, he still refused to give up. When he reached an impasse in theory, he switched over to working on the history of economics with the idea of later returning to theory again.

His efforts and failures stood in sharp contrast to the resounding success enjoyed by John Maynard Keynes in convincing economists, especially the young, of his work's merit. Schumpeter seethed within at the growth of the Keynesian school—the "new economics." Schumpeter's outlook compelled him to regard his own work as simply that of another scientist engaged in the huge enterprise of economic science. His purpose was to move economics ahead a bit, and he viewed others who had established schools as corrupters of the subject he loved. If Schumpeter felt he had some special place in economics, it was as one with the duty to remind economists of their science's nature and their responsibilities to it, a Jeremiah who tried to keep economists on the straight and narrow path of scientific endeavor. Because of his antischool attitude, he resented those who did build schools, or who used their analysis to support policy. David Ricardo's advocacy of free trade had diminished Schumpeter's regard for that eminent English economist, just as his esteem for Adam Smith had dimmed because of Smith's support of laissez faire.[1] His annoyance with Keynes was especially patent, although he acknowledged and respected Keynes's contributions to analysis. Others who built schools, or tried to, such as Gustav Cassel, did not earn great respect from Schumpeter. His scientific idols were Léon Walras, Irving Fisher, John Bates Clark, Knut Wicksell, Eugen von Boehm-Bawerk, and others whose work had become embodied in the corpus of economics but who left no following or school.

With a well-endowed ego, however, Schumpeter was bothered because his work did not receive more recognition. He wrote in his diary during this period, "The misery is that I see everywhere and on every page of my lecture reading Keynes ... and myself, where?" He did not fully admit it, even to himself, but he sometimes would have liked to have a kind of school, or at least recognition. Enjoying the times when he was surrounded by young and promising scholars, he soaked up their attention and loved to bask in their deference, devoting great effort to stimulating them in their work. He would have been pleased if these young people agreed with his general approach to economics and his scientific outlook. It would have pleased him even more if his students followed in his footsteps and carried on his work.

But Schumpeter was unwilling to pay the price of presenting his ideas so that he and others could simplify and popularize them, and he refused to indoctrinate potential "followers" with his views and analysis. His periodic denunciation of schools, and those who form them, precluded the possibility of a Schumpeter school. Still, the idea of having a group of followers attracted him. In the 1940s, for example, he confided in his diary, "Why do I have only so few and characteristically useless followers—from [X] to [Y] to [Z]? Why not the splendid praetorians of Keynes?" Yet even those he mentioned were not followers in the sense of accepting and promulgating his views; they were merely students and admirers who thought highly of Schumpeter's ideas, while not necessarily fully accepting or promoting them.

One of the many paradoxes of Schumpeter's character was the cold comfort he gave to those who wanted to agree with him. Appearing throughout his writings and even in his speech, this attitude was most obvious in *Capitalism, Socialism and Democracy*. In that book, he presented capitalism as a most remarkable instrument of economic progress. But, instead of giving a prognosis for a long and happy life, Schumpeter paradoxically predicted that capitalism was even then dying. It would succumb not because it failed, but rather because its admirers, those people who benefit from it (among them, his readers) had turned on capitalism and undermined it. He theorized that it would be followed by socialism—not a system that capitalism's admirers greatly prized. Schumpeter then went to great lengths to establish that not only would socialism work, but it could also be efficient.

Even more, he tried to prove that socialism would be consistent with democracy, the preferred political system of those who esteem capitalism. His "proof," of which he made much, failed to convince except in the abstract and did not square with his own conviction that the twain shall never really meet. One can admire the scientific objectivity that permitted him to pursue his analysis to such conclusions. But the effort provided no rallying cry either to the capitalist system that he clearly favored or to the analysis that produced results so repugnant to him and many others.

The result of what he saw as rejection of his science caused unhappiness and self-criticism to burn within Schumpeter. On the outside, he remained the cool, amused and amusing, cheerful and pleasant Austrian gentleman of aristocratic bearing. If he was no longer as ebullient, it was because, at war's end, he was sixty-two, mature, dignified—even a bit pompous. Always courteous in speech and overly polite in manner, he was most respectful of the person and the ideas of everyone. Despite his secret and often gloomy meetings with his own and his second wife's diaries, where he recorded his misery and pleaded with his *Hasen*, on the outside he exuded confidence, cordiality, and commitment to science, but always tinged with cynicism. To some of his colleagues and students, he had confided at least an inkling of his darker thoughts. But they could only guess at his internal struggles, his bitterness, the strength of his convictions, his sense of inadequacy, and the torture to which he subjected himself.

2

After the war ended, Schumpeter tried to repair the ruptured professional and social relations it had disturbed. To some limited extent, the war had taught him to curb his tongue, which led him back into the good graces of his colleagues at Harvard, even though some animosities remained. But the war had permanently ruptured the old set of student and collegial relationships he had enjoyed. The flood of postwar students now washing through Harvard Yard did not re-establish the old camaraderie Schumpeter had had with students in the 1930s, nor did the junior faculty rally round him as they had earlier. The Seven Wise Men did not revive, and there were no more special seminars. Schumpeter worked alone and was lonely. With more students in the enlarged classes, teaching became more difficult and time consuming; more examinations, more theses, more papers to grade, and more students to see crowded his schedule. Harvard's golden years of intellectual stimulation continued, both for students and faculty alike, but they were also years of hard work.

Schumpeter was as active as ever in promoting the interests of students, scheduling his consultations and talking to students whenever he could, but Harvard was becoming almost a Ph.D. factory. Because of this, Schumpeter remained unhappy with most of his colleagues and with Harvard. The faculty roster had not changed significantly in the first half of the 1940s. Some, such as Professor Chamberlin in the Office of Strategic Services and Professor Mason in Washington, did not return immediately to Cambridge in 1945, and others were often away on government chores. There were no additions to the senior staff, nor had any promotions been given in wartime. Since the promotion of Gottfried Haberler in 1939, no one was promoted to full professor until Wassily Leontief and Seymour Harris belatedly became full professors in 1946 and Edwin Frickey in 1947.

The professors and students were just beginning to dribble back to Cambridge as the 1945-46 academic year began shortly after the war's end. Most of the students couldn't enroll before the fall term, which was fine with the department because it remained short-staffed. Schumpeter taught his standard fare. He gave his course in advanced economic theory both terms. In the fall, he also taught a new course, an experimental course offered only once, on the theory and policy of European central banking. In the spring of 1946, he taught his regular history and literature of economics, as well as his undergraduate course on the economics of socialism.[2]

Because so many students had spent the war years in the military and missed the opportunity to attend graduate school, the Harvard Department of Economics decided to admit more students than usual in the immediate postwar years. The depression and the war had so enhanced the reputation of economics as a profession that the department did not have to reduce admission requirements or standards of performance in order to obtain more students. But the increase of students did mean that Schumpeter and others had to teach courses filled with thirty to fifty students, sometimes even more, rather than the usual ten or so. It also imposed a heavier burden of general and special examinations, both of which were oral, conducted by a board of professors. The increased amount of advising necessary to the greater number of Ph.D. dissertations also bore down on those professors who were accessible to students, as was Schumpeter.

During the 1930s and until the U.S. entry into the war, Harvard's Department of Economics had granted an average of fourteen Ph.D.s each year—with a low of five in 1935-36 and a high of twenty-two in 1938-39. But, during the four war years, the number of degrees dropped to an average of only seven and one-half per year. The result was a bumper crop of Ph.D.s in economics in the decade's second half, consisting of the increased number of students admitted beginning in 1945 and 1946, as well as the backlog of people who had not finished their degrees during the war. Concerned lest the quality deteriorate and the curriculum stagnate, Schumpeter participated in a departmental committee in December 1945, for which he wrote a memo on graduate study urging maintenance of departmental standards. With the war's end, the burden on faculty members had thus shifted from an increased numbers of classes to an increased numbers of students.

3

In spite of the heavy student load immediately following the war, Schumpeter, as usual, found time for research, writing, and lecturing as he picked up the pace and the travelling to match that of prewar years. In 1938, Leonard Crum had written a brief paper for the *Quarterly Journal of Economics* on mathematical techniques useful to economists. In 1945, Schumpeter and Crum decided to convert the article into a little book for instructional purposes. Mathematical techniques were becoming increasingly important in economics, and even those with no intention of specializing in economic theory or in topics requiring some knowledge of mathematics needed an elementary understanding of some mathematical methods, especially the calculus. While also working on the English classical tradition in his history of economics project during the last half of 1945, Schumpeter fiddled with the book on rudimentary mathematics, not an especially uplifting task since the level of both mathematics and economics was so elementary. It was to be a teaching aid, not even a textbook.

Still, Schumpeter felt strongly that students needed such a book. and none existed on the market at the time. Unknown to him, R. G. D. Allen, an

English economist, was at that moment preparing a much better and more complete book on the same subject. When Schumpeter complained that the writing of this book was not the appropriate work of a scholar, he was right; yet its publication did fill a genuine need. Published in 1946 by McGraw-Hill, *Rudimentary Mathematics for Economists and Statisticians* turned out to be a slender little volume—only 183 pages. It was more elementary than Allen's book and served only students unprepared to tackle any real mathematics. Schumpeter admitted how elementary it was in remarking to colleagues that it would take students "from the creeping to the crawling stage" of their mathematical preparation.[3] In his review of the book R. T. Bowman said,

> The volume under review ... does much to fill a pressing need of economists for help in understanding mathematical ideas useful to them.... It is an excellent presentation of the salient mathematical ideas and techniques useful to economists.[4]

In the last forty years, economists have made phenomenal progress in their mastery of mathematics and in applying it to economic analysis. Even though his little book is now obsolete, some credit for this progress must go to Schumpeter for his efforts to promote the use of mathematics.

After the completion of the mathematics book, Schumpeter again hit the road to deliver some important lectures. In November 1945, he travelled to Montreal at the request of a former student, Emile Bouvier, who had become a professor at the University of Quebec. There, Schumpeter spoke informally at the university and then delivered a speech on 19 November to a group of Quebec businessmen and engineers, the first convention of L'Association Professionelle des Industriels. Speaking in French, Schumpeter addressed the topic "L'Avenir de l'Entreprise Privée devant les Tendances Socialistes Modernes" (The Future of Private Enterprise confronting Modern Socialist Tendencies).[5] This speech contained the first public suggestion of an idea he had earlier raised in his diary: that the Catholic Church might provide an alternative to socialism. In *Capitalism, Socialism and Democracy*, Schumpeter held that only socialism could succeed capitalism, but in this speech he backed off a bit, allowing for the possibility that the Pope's 1931 Encyclical, the *Quadragesimo Anno*, might provide the basis for a social, economic, and moral order to succeed capitalism.

Although Schumpeter had created his own personal religion, and never expressed much interest in any formal, church-related religion, he still maintained high respect for the Roman Catholic Church. Regarding the church as a part of society's cement and an institution commanding near universal esteem, he believed it could influence the economic order. True, he looked upon the church as a remnant of feudalism, and, as such, prerational;

but even though feudalistic, it had played an equally important role in the success of capitalism. In 1945, Schumpeter began to think the church could play an important role as capitalism fades. Some of this attitude derived from his respect for the governance system of the Austro-Hungarian monarchy. wherein the church had occupied a critical place, just as some stemmed from his belief that the values of the church were an appropriate guide to behavior. Although recognizing that self-interest was a powerful force and had served capitalism well, Schumpeter did not want to accept it as the basis for a future economic and social order.

Soon after his speech in Montreal, Schumpeter attended the first postwar meeting of the American Economic Association, held in Cleveland 24-27 January, 1946, where he wore his usual mask of affability and good humor. Many remember meeting him at this and other postwar meetings at a bar or a social hour sponsored by a publisher or university. Commanding the center of attention, he was welcome at all parties. If a mutual friend did not introduce him to people, Schumpeter would stick out his chin and his hand, saying "Hello, I'm Joe Schumpeter," and then proceed to carry on an animated conversation about a paper someone gave that afternoon, the state of economics, or the need for more research on this or that topic. At the Cleveland meeting, Schumpeter delivered a paper summing up "The Decade of the 1920s" in which he said:

No decade in the history of politics, religion, technology, painting, poetry, and whatnot ever contains its own explanation ... towards the end of the nineteenth century and in the first decade of the twentieth a number of industrial events occurred that were bound to change the world's economic structure fundamentally, but partly owing to the "first" world war, did not take full effect until the twenties.... The following facts constitute adequate explanation of the "disaster" [the Depression] in the United States ... the first fact is the speculative mania of 1927-1929.... The second fact was the weakness of the United States banking system.... Third in importance was the mortgage situation, both urban and rural ... entirely due to reckless borrowing and lending.[6]

Thus, although he argued that the depression itself was a natural and necessary economic event, the debacle and misery of the Great Depression resulted from man's follies and not the malperformance of the economy.

4

Despite his willingness to declaim publicly on anything from Adam Smith's private life to the causes of the Great Depression, most of Schumpeter's work in 1945 and 1946 was private and unknown to colleagues, students, or the public, as he continued researching and writing on his history of economics. During this period he revised the section on Greek and Roman economics, as well as his chapters on the scholastics and natural law philosophers in part 2 of the book. He also wrote drafts of many chapters contained in part 3, including most of the material related to the period from 1790 to 1870—the period of the English classical school.

Although the history of economics commanded most of his writing time, Schumpeter hauled out his money book but did little real work on it. Seymour Harris had again asked him about writing a money book, this time for a series Harris was editing for McGraw-Hill. In late 1945 and early 1946, he also made an effort to work on economic theory—his PV project. On top of this, he helped his colleague Arthur H. Cole, who by that time was a professor in the School of Business Administration, do the preliminary work that led later to setting up a new history research center. Schumpeter's interest in promoting the study of the entrepreneur from a historical standpoint was revived as a result of his association with Cole. This subject would produce several academic papers by Schumpeter starting in 1947.

The late winter and spring of 1946 were uneventful. With the war over, Schumpeter was no longer a controversial figure, and he rejoined the local lecture circuit, giving speeches at university functions and around town. On 27 February, for example, he talked to the Boston Economics Club on the "Savings Scramble." During this spring semester, he also audited Crum's course in national income statistics, a topic fast becoming increasingly important. The attendance of a professor at another professor's classes was certainly uncommon, though not unheard of; yet Schumpeter was a dedicated student, attending even during the blizzard that hit New England that semester.[7]

Although no longer an outcast, Schumpeter's mental attitude had still not improved, and his diary shows his continuing depression and hypochondria. In his secret mental alcove, he convinced himself that his health was terrible, that his "brain may be going," and that he was on his way to the grave, a reflection of his deep depression. He did work very hard and was certainly tired and unhappy, but he was not ill. His dark thoughts stemmed instead from his seeing futility on all sides. In January 1946, for example, he confided, "Makes no sense to preserve my life. Why not make the protest through a means to eliminate me?" He continued by displaying an unusual disgust for economics, "My science is nothing but a silly medley of slogans for the day.... Is it the end? Time is killing not only ability to work but also the wish to work." Students from those days remember Schumpeter remarking:

If we had any sense at all, at the age of 40 we would all commit suicide. Either we have accomplished whatever is in us to accomplish by that time and thus need live no longer, or by that time it is clear that we are not going to accomplish anything and therefore need live no longer.[8]

Students took this as a flip remark exemplifying his puckish sense of humor. But in reality, it was only partly that. Yet, paradoxically, he continued to work long hours on his many projects, grousing in his diary as he did. A few months later he would record his plans to write four books.

Schumpeter's disgruntlement with U.S. policies also continued. He strongly opposed, in his diary and among close friends, the war crimes trials, believing that legitimate criminal acts by individuals in the enemy camp should be prosecuted, but civilized societies should not use retroactive criminal laws. To Schumpeter, redefining war as a crime and charging people with crimes for activities never before so regarded was a legal monstrosity. In his diary he remarked, "It is not the legal and moral aspects that beat me, it is the stupidity." In this matter, time proved him right. Time also proved him right in other pessimistic political views. While many lived in the mistaken euphoria of a new peaceful relationship with the Soviet Union, Schumpeter wrote in March, "And Stalin having declared that so long as capitalism exists in the world, there must be war—which foreshadows armaments which can only be directed against U.S. We go on supplying him with goods and training." Along with everyone else he deplored the holocaust and made no effort to defend those responsible for its inhumanity. But, unlike most, he related it in some mysterious way to the German prosecution of the war. He also did not believe the Nazis had killed 6 million Jews, and his thinking that only 2 million had died seemed to make some kind of difference to him.

Such vestiges of unpopular war sentiments meant that his sense of isolation did not completely disappear with the war's end. To be sure, much of the contention with his colleagues dissipated, but Schumpeter still felt somewhat estranged. He now recognized, however, that much of his isolation was his own fault. On 3 April 1946, he wrote in his diary:

> Well, I have declined invitation of [James Washington] Bell to attend Amec-Ass's [American Economic Association's] Princeton spring meeting—dont be sort of nettled at being left "out of it" so far as Ass is concerned in the future. There is no doubt [much] to be said for keeping to myself, going my way, retiring from the world—but it must then be accepted that I don't count.

Schumpeter had trouble accepting the idea that he didn't count, and his decision to retire from the world was only temporary. Still, he sought an escape from the pain of his situation, recording in May 1946:

What beats me is not the bestiality but stupidity of our time.... Man in the mass is always brutal and stupid.... The economists difficulty in speaking of practical measures is that he talks to—if he is not himself—a vicious child that screams and kicks and never wants the means when it wants an end.

5

Retreating to Taconic, Schumpeter noted in his diary that the summer of 1946 "did not begin auspiciously." But he soon undertook the significant task of writing the obituary of John Maynard Keynes, who had died in April, and other related pieces. Even though it depressed him to write about Keynes, because doing so reminded him of his own mortality, the orgy of evaluation necessarily began when Keynes died, with Harvard and Schumpeter playing an important role in estimating his importance. Seymour Harris edited a collection of essays by dozens of economists on special aspects of Keynes's work. For this book, *The New Economics: Keynes' Influence on Theory and Public Policy* (1947), Schumpeter wrote the essay on "Keynes the Economist."[9] Meanwhile, a Harvard house journal, the *Review of Economic Statistics*, devoted an issue to Keynes's career in November 1946. Schumpeter wrote the article on "Keynes the Statistician."[10] These two works were in addition to the obituary that appeared as the lead article in the September 1946 issue of the *American Economic Review*.[11]

To say that Schumpeter and Keynes did not agree is an understatement. Although they were not personally estranged, neither were they in communication with one another. Basically, their relationship can be summarized by saying that Keynes largely ignored Schumpeter, but, to the extent of his limited knowledge of his work, regarded him highly as an old-fashioned Austrian economist of an era long gone, and Schumpeter belittled Keynes's theoretical contribution, did not accept his income theory as valid theorizing, disagreed with the policies he advocated, and resented Keynes's coupling of theory and policy. In earlier years—during the 1920s through 1935—Schumpeter's frequent visits to England allowed the two to meet with some regularity every year, and they occasionally had lunch. In those days they even corresponded a bit, but never about substantive issues or serious economic questions. They were never close, never collaborated, and never established a mutual admiration society as Schumpeter had with many other economists, such as Ragnar Frisch, Irving Fisher, Lionel Robbins, Wesley Mitchell, Joan Robinson, and others with whom he both agreed and disagreed. A part of the reason for this mutual aloofness may be that each considered himself to be the chief representative of economics from his own cultural tradition—Keynes from the English tradition and Schumpeter from the Austrian and Continental tradition. Keynes's pretension was the greater, since he did not accept the thought that any but the English tradition existed. Perhaps both were prima donnas and each recognized the other as a rival.

So much separated the two men that they had little in common. They differed in the substance of the economics they accepted and taught, and they differed in the method and approach of their science in relation to economic problems and policies. They differed in their vision of what capitalism was, how it operated, and its future. They differed also on the policies they preferred to see implemented. And they differed in human terms, possessing diverse backgrounds, characters, and personal attributes. Given these differences, it is not at all surprising that Keynes and Schumpeter would live and die worlds apart.

Keynes and Schumpeter had two sharply different visions of the economy. Keynes's concern in his analysis was for the short run, for a period of time during which production techniques remain the same. In his economy, rigidities persisted so that market equilibrium was not the norm; wages and prices therefore would not adjust and perform their function. His narrowing of the economy's ability to adjust led to his belief that unemployment would persist, a situation Keynes described as an underemployment equilibrium. But clearly, the economy whose equilibrium-adjustment mechanisms didn't work could not be in equilibrium, meaning that the income adjustment resulted in a false equilibrium.

In contrast, an economy in equilibrium served as the base for Schumpeter's vision. He saw development through recurring cycles whose essence consisted of equilibrium, impulse, change, response, equilibrium, and then repeat. The economy was an equilibrium system that worked, even though it was constantly changing its productive structure under the impulse of innovation. But even when production was changing, the economy was struggling toward the next equilibrium. The short run held no interest for Schumpeter because it represented a special position of the economy in an uninteresting state that was sure to change and therefore could reveal nothing general about the economy. Schumpeter often said that the only thing wrong with Keynes's *General Theory* was its being a special theory.

Another key difference between Schumpeter and Keynes was their attitude toward savings. To Keynes, savings was the source of economic problems because people saved rather than spent, leading to an excess of savings in relation to investment. Excessive savings results in a decline in income to the point where people want to save exactly that which investors want to invest. To Schumpeter, this interpretation was a terrible and unjustified indictment of savings. He saw savings as the source of economic development, the wherewithal for introducing new goods and new processes that are the essence of capitalism. Anything that would reduce savings, as Schumpeter feared Keynesian notions might, would undermine capitalism.

A basic methodological gulf also separated Keynes and Schumpeter. Schumpeter believed economics was a science; as such, the study of its theories, its techniques, and its methods could be justified as the pursuit of knowledge. Keynes, however, wanted to hitch his economic analysis to policy conclusions, as he sought solutions to the deplorable state of the world, especially England. Building an analytical system that would yield a resolution to the problem of mass unemployment, he wanted a theoretical analysis designed to justify the policy. To Schumpeter, this methodological approach was anathema. Economic policy advocacy was for politicians, not for economists, and, above all, the economist must not rig his economics to achieve a result that implies the policy favored from the start.

Beyond these differences, human differences also separated the two men. Both were aristocrats, conscious of their place and aware of their intellectual superiority. But Keynes was from a country with its empire still intact around the world, while Schumpeter's world had collapsed and his empire evaporated. Even if Schumpeter felt that Keynes misused his position, he could not help but envy Keynes's leadership among economists, his access to politicians and the press, and his standing at the center of things. Although believing himself to be the world's greatest economist, Schumpeter was aware that the world had given that place to Keynes, making him the undisputed leader among professional economists after 1935 and practically a household name among those who followed economic news. Keynes achieved this while Schumpeter's name remained unknown outside a small circle of economists and social scientists. Doubly galling to Schumpeter was his belief that the world's esteem of Keynes rested not on his ability as an economist, but on his being a leader, politician, and propagandist.

One other human element undoubtedly influenced Schumpeter: his knowledge that Keynes was homosexual and later bisexual. To a man who regarded himself as a great lover and took pride in his sexual prowess and attractiveness to women, Keynes's homosexuality was an offense. Keynes was also known for being often foul-mouthed and inconsiderate of others, whereas Schumpeter almost never used unseemly language, not even in his diary, and was usually the ultimate gentleman in his dealings with others. These attributes would not have colored Schumpeter's views of Keynes's ideas, but they would have influenced his attitude toward Keynes personally and his relationship with him.[12]

6

On a much smaller scale, conflict of another sort surrounded Schumpeter in the winter of 1946-47. A letter written by the Socialist Party of Boston to the Harvard Economics Department asked for a debate on capitalism and socialism. When the department turned the letter over to Schumpeter, he responded that the classroom was an inappropriate place for such a debate, but he would arrange for the Graduate Student Club to sponsor the event.[13] Schumpeter was greatly chagrined when the Graduate Student Club timidly declined to touch it. After much discussion, the debate finally was held, without a sponsor. The debaters were Schumpeter and Paul Sweezy, his former student and then assistant professor of economics at Harvard. When Sweezy, a well-trained economist and even then a leading Marxist, had earlier worked as Schumpeter's assistant, the two had become true friends. Many years later, in *Newsweek*, Paul Samuelson described the event:

Let me set the stage. Schumpeter was a scion of the aristocracy of Franz Josef's Austria. It was Schumpeter who had confessed to three wishes in life, to be the greatest lover in Vienna, the best horseman in Europe, and the greatest economist in the world. "But unfortunately," as he used to say modestly, "the seat I inherited was never of the topmost caliber."

Opposed to the foxy Merlin was young Sir Galahad. Son of an executive of J. P. Morgan's bank, Paul Sweezy was the best that Exeter and Harvard could produce. Tiring of the "gentlemen's C" and of the good life at Locke-Ober's with Lucius Beebe, Sweezy had early established himself as among the most promising of economists of his generation. But tiring of the conventional wisdom of his age, and spurred on by the events of the Great Depression, Sweezy became one of America's few Marxists.

Great debaters deserve great moderators, and that night Leontief was in fine form. "The patient is capitalism. What is to be his fate? Our speakers are in fact agreed that the patient is inevitably dying. But the bases of their diagnosis could not be more different. On the one hand there is Sweezy who utilizes the analysis of Marx and of Lenin to deduce that the patient is dying of a malignant cancer. Absolutely no operation can help. The end is foreordained.

On the other hand, there is Schumpeter. He, too, and rather cheerfully, admits that the patient is dying.... But to Schumpeter, the patient is dying of a psychosomatic ailment. Not cancer but neurosis is his complaint. Filled with self-hate, he has lost his will to live. In this view, capitalism is an unlovable system, and what is unlovable will not be loved. Paul Sweezy himself is a talisman and omen of that alienation which will seal the system's doom."[14]

The audience overflowed Littauer Center Auditorium, and even Elizabeth, who by that time did not normally attend such functions, was present. During the discussion period, she jousted with Sweezy. In response to a question from her, Sweezy facetiously complained that it was unfair of Schumpeter to bring "the big guns" of his family into the debate. The house roared and enjoyed the evening immensely. But Schumpeter "lost" the debate. Samuelson's romanticized version of the debate does not reveal Schumpeter's usual discomfort in propounding and defending his views. Failing to present an adequate statement of his theory of development, he allowed Sweezy to seize and maintain the initiative; on the defensive, Schumpeter then did not counterattack or perform well.[15]

The story related by Samuelson regarding Schumpeter's three ambitions is probably the best-known anecdote about him, and many vaguely familiar with Schumpeter take it as the summary assessment of the man. Although many variations on the story exist, one of which ends enigmatically with Schumpeter stating only that he did not achieve one of the ambitions, the Samuelson version is the most nearly authentic. In response to the story's repetition in the *Economist* in 1983, Professor Theodore Morgan of the University of Wisconsin, who received his doctorate at Harvard in 1941, reported: "Several of us young instructors invited him, in the late winter of 1943, to be our guest at a lunch to celebrate his sixtieth birthday. I asked whether the story of his three ambitions was correct. Actually, he said, he had five: He wanted to be an accomplished connoisseur of art, and to be successful in politics."[16] Schumpeter's diary of the 1930s had also mentioned success with money and the desire to travel as goals. No one can judge whether he was the greatest lover in Vienna, but he failed to accomplish the other ambitions. He continually strove to meet all of them, however, so his failures did not result from lack of effort. His failure to be accounted by the world as its greatest economist galled him most of all in his later years. Perhaps, more than any other failure, this one haunted him most of all.

7

Despite his ongoing depression and discouragement over what he perceived as a lack of sufficient progress in his research, Schumpeter continued to present the public visage of a sprightly and happy teacher. In a sense, he was. He enjoyed teaching immensely and knew that he excelled at it, although he knew also he was not a good systematic teacher of the basics of economics. For this reason, he taught only advanced economic theory, a variation on the seminar he had taught back in the 1920s, leaving the basic courses to Professors Leontief, Chamberlin, and others. But even with this weakness, Schumpeter was superb at his avocation as "teacher." The breadth and depth of his knowledge, and his genuine and manifest interest in students, provided the ammunition needed to stimulate and inspire them, to get them to achieve more than they thought possible, and to persuade them to think and study. Because of this, he was not the ideal teacher for the average student. Most former graduate students have a short list of those professors from whom they learned the most and who had the most influence on their careers. Such a mental list doesn't usually coalesce until some years later. In those golden years at Harvard from the early 1930s to the early 1950s, Schumpeter would probably be on most students' list of the top three.

Throughout his teaching career, Schumpeter never abandoned his little idiosyncrasies. At any moment he would whip out a piece a paper, write something down, and then continue talking as if nothing had happened. Even when he was well past sixty, no class notes were ever in evidence, yet there was never a hesitation in his lectures that flowed like easy conversation. But neither did his German accent improve with time. One student, perhaps not too attentive, confessed at the end of a lecture his belief that Schumpeter was talking about an Italian economist named Inventorio when in fact he was discussing the inventory cycle. Always Schumpeter made heavy demands on his students, assuming often that they knew a lot more than they did and thereby forcing them to spend extra hours doing basic reading so that they could follow him. He sometimes asked questions of his students, often rhetorical questions, but incorrect or irrelevant answers did not disturb him. He was most gracious in answering student queries, even the stupid ones. His consultation hours had become famous, and few were the students who did not avail themselves of his help.

He did not officially direct many doctoral dissertations because his interests—pure economic theory, the history of economics, and business cycles—did not attract many students. Still, Schumpeter advised many writing their theses even though he was not a member of the student's dissertation committee or his official advisor. Typically, when a student ran across a difficult theoretical problem, off he went to Schumpeter's consultation for advice and help; and typically he received it. On returning by train to Cambridge after a meeting of the American Economic Association, for example, a not-very-illustrious student spotted Schumpeter conversing with several of his Harvard colleagues. When the student broke in and asked to speak privately to his professor, Schumpeter obliged. After finding other seats, the two spent the next seven hours going over the student's thesis outline, his methods and procedures, and each step necessary for researching and writing the thesis. The entire car listened while Schumpeter did all of the student's creative and intellectual work. By the time the train arrived in

Boston's South Station, the student had only the empirical and calculating work left to do.[17]

Even though the best and brightest students respected Schumpeter enormously, the camaraderie of the 1930s no longer prevailed among the young people in the postwar years. Students, having lost time in the war, were anxious to finish their course work and get their degrees. Schumpeter's popularity among the young therefore waned. Those whose enthusiasm for the "new economics" outdistanced their knowledge and maturity regarded him as the quaint old Austrian—many thought German—professor, old-fashioned and languishing in the backwater of economics. Still, Schumpeter never lost his interest in the students. He spoke to the Graduate Economics Student's Club more frequently than did any other professor—once a year at least—and met with groups of students interested in special topics. Because of his availability, he also let students know he was concerned not only with their academic problems but also with their personal ones as well.

On his walks from Littauer Center to his home at 7 Acacia Street, Schumpeter frequently met students and asked them to accompany him. Their conversations ranged from the theoretical niceties of Walras to the stupidities of "that wild beast, the politician," to the state of economics. Once, when Dallas Steinthorsen, the Canadian student who later became a high United Nations official in Geneva, asked for Schumpeter's views about the state of economics, Schumpeter replied with a paradox: "Economics is getting better and better, but economists are getting worse and worse."[18]

While visiting Dallas Steinthorsen (whose rooms were at the front of the house just across the street from Schumpeter's home on Acacia Street), I witnessed the fact that Schumpeter's note-taking was not an affectation. One Saturday about noon, he came strolling down Acacia, returning from Littauer or perhaps Widener Library. A woman from the neighborhood was walking toward him and they met just in front of his house. No one else was in sight. We two graduate students watched them from a window across the street. After Schumpeter displayed his old-world courtesy by removing his hat and bowing, he and his neighbor stopped to chat for a moment. When the short conversation ended, the lady walked on and Schumpeter strode up the sidewalk to his porch. Just as he reached the porch steps he stopped suddenly, took out a piece of paper, wrote something on it, put it back in his pocket, and disappeared into his house. Across the street, two graduate students erupted into laughter and spent the next half hour wondering what Schumpeter had so urgently written on that piece of paper.

In some ways, Schumpeter was something of an oddity at Harvard after the war, and many postwar graduate students did not like what they considered to be his old-fashioned views and manners. But most regarded him as the one whose knowledge was deep and broad, and whose interest in students was high. A decade and a half earlier, in Bonn, Schumpeter had referred to his goal of being one who "opens doors, never closing them." Whether they recognized it or not, even these students who found him odd were helped to enter one intellectual room after another because of his efforts.

Reflecting this, his emphasis on pure scholarship remained his single criterion in personnel matters in the Department of Economics. When Harvard discussed retaining Paul Sweezy, then an assistant professor, Schumpeter strongly favored him. Even though Sweezy was a Marxist, and therefore separated from Schumpeter by a great ideological gulf, Schumpeter felt that he should be allowed to compete in the Harvard intellectual marketplace because he was above all a scholar. Partly because the president was still in a stingy mood, permitting only one of several promising young men to be hired, a man with more practical interests was chosen. When Sweezy left in 1947, Schumpeter was bitter, once again accusing Harvard of displaying a lack of interest in serious scholarship.

8

By the 1946-47 academic year, the rising tide of students had turned into a flood as the GI Bill of Rights permitted many academically qualified but financially disabled students to attend Harvard. Faced with the influx of new students, all faculty members were unusually busy. Schumpeter once again taught courses in theory, history of economics, and socialism. He also taught business cycles and economic forecasting, a course he had worked on for more than a decade. When not teaching, he spent most of his Cambridge time working at the Kress Collection.

That Thanksgiving, Joseph and Elizabeth escaped to Taconic, as usual, where he drank too much and, having long since graduated from Moselle wines to Manhattans, suffered a terrible hangover that continued even on Monday. He made a joke of it in class that day, eliciting laughter and sympathy from his students.[19] Although Schumpeter was not a heavy drinker, he did drink nearly every day, usually having one or two or three before supper. Occasionally, he didn't stop with two or three. His doctor discouraged his drinking, but didn't forbid it. Schumpeter was far from being an alcoholic, but the before-dinner drinking did not encourage effective after-dinner writing. To avoid work, he sometimes indulged in his detective stories or in other light reading—history and biography—before going to bed.

The first part of 1947 progressed routinely, filled with a heavy teaching load, public speaking, and what seemed to be never-ending research. In January 1947, Schumpeter attended the American Economic Association meetings in Atlantic City, where he engaged in his usual rounds of socializing and scientific discussions. Back in Cambridge in late winter, he spoke to several groups, including the Boston Economics Club and the Graduate Economics Club on Appian Way. He regarded the maintenance of close contact with graduate students as part of his professorial duties, and he nearly always attended the parties sponsored by the club. With the war over and his political isolation now a part of the past, he began to have lunch with his colleagues more regularly, especially Leontief and Haberler. He enjoyed these opportunities for social and scientific discussions again available to him because they made him feel connected to his colleagues as friends and to Harvard's intellectual life. Increasingly, he was impressed with Leontief's work, and exclaimed of him in his diary "what a genius." When Leontief later became discouraged at Harvard and received an offer from the University of California-Berkeley, he seriously considered taking it. Schumpeter was instrumental in persuading him to stay at Harvard.

But Schumpeter did lose a friend and respected colleague when Irving Fisher of Yale died at the age of eighty in April 1947. Despite the fact that no two people could be less alike, their friendship dated back to Schumpeter's first visit to the United States in 1913. In addition to his stature as one of America's great economists, perhaps the most able and illustrious that the United States had ever produced, Fisher was opinionated about economic policy and a million other things. He was also a crusader in such things as eugenics, the temperance movement, hygiene, world peace, and other worthy causes. Always a health nut, Fisher did not indulge any of the minor vices and was stern, humorless, and authoritarian—almost the exact opposite of Schumpeter. Schumpeter enjoyed all the minor vices, wore his policy garments ever so loosely, and seemed the height of gaiety and spontaneity when compared to Fisher. But, putting these surface differences aside, the two recognized in one another a common devotion to economic science.

Trained as a mathematician, Fisher applied mathematical and statistical techniques to economics. His Ph.D. thesis at Yale, published in 1892 as *Mathematical Investigations in the Theory of Value and Price*, became one of the great pioneering books of economics. Yet it was only the beginning; he went on to write thirty books, eighteen in economics, and made many important contributions. One major contribution was Fisher's role in the founding of the Econometric Society in 1930. Serving as the U.S. anchor in the society's early organization, he soon became its mentor and first president. Schumpeter had visited Fisher many times in New Haven, and it was partly Fisher's influence that almost persuaded Schumpeter to accept a position at Yale in 1940. Later, in a very unHarvard-like act, Schumpeter sponsored a 1942 party in honor of Fisher on his seventy-fifth birthday. Schumpeter even invited a couple of other Yale men to come to Cambridge for the gathering. To a man, the Harvard Department of Economics toasted Fisher and then sat around drinking and telling stories until Fisher was the only sober man present.[20] In great sorrow, Schumpeter wrote one of the obituaries about Fisher. His moving article assessed Fisher's contribution to technical economics and praised him as a theorist and the pioneer of econometrics. Summing up, Schumpeter wrote, "I venture to predict that his name will stand in history principally as the name of this country's greatest economist."[21]

The fact that several of Schumpeter's colleagues and contemporaries—both friends and foes—were now dying in the postwar period did not help Schumpeter's obsession with death. In February 1947, Alvin Hansen hosted a party in honor of the visiting Ragnar Frisch. At this social occasion, Schumpeter told Frisch that he was "staggering toward his grave."[22] Still, Schumpeter wore his jovial mask, and Frisch noted that he seemed well and happy. Yet his 1947 diary contains numerous references to health problems, including "weakness, pressure in head, tiredness, low spirits … paralysis, breakdown feeling … puffing and spasms." In April 1947, he complained of dizziness and wondered if he had had a stroke. Perhaps it was a TIA—transient ischemic attack—forerunner of a stroke and not even identified nor named in his day. We can't know what actually happened but, based on the strength of his response, the experience certainly jarred him:

> Does that alter anything in my life and work? I do not think so—do not care to put order into my little things for I want the end to be the end, not even for biography, etc.… Never had such a dying *look* such a dying feeling. So that's probably the real thing … lingering as a piece of human wreckage … it is not my world any more.

Soon after writing this, Schumpeter learned about the death of another person who had been important in his life. The war had interrupted his correspondence with Mia, which had already slackened in the late 1930s as they went about their separate lives. After the war, Schumpeter heard rumors from European friends that Mia and her husband, who had joined the underground, had been caught and shot by the Nazi secret police in Yugoslavia, where her husband had been a government official before the war. He refused to accept this news, believing that, when things were sorted out, Mia would turn up. But on 1 May 1947, the rumor was verified by a letter from Mia's father. Representing another deep loss, Mia's death served as a further blow to his mental stability.

As usual, much of his lingering depression during this period centered around his unhappiness with his work. The renewed interest in the history of entrepreneurship, spurred in part by Arthur Cole, helped some, but Schumpeter still made no real headway on his theory work. Though work did progress on the history of economics, it seemed as though the more he did, the more needed to be done. A 14 June 1947 letter to Arthur Smithies summed up his frustration with the project: "I am worried to death by work and my damned History—grind, grind, grind *every* day—dog tired and grouchy." With so many irons in the fire, none of which were really starting to blaze, Schumpeter regularly listed in his diary the tasks he hoped to accomplish in an effort to keep himself organized. He noted such things as the parts and chapters of the history of economics book he planned to work on, the lectures he must prepare, and ideas for other papers and tasks cluttering his desk. He regularly listed math, Grk (Greek), brush (meaning review), spiel [play], PV (meaning that he must study mathematics, differential equations in particular), Greek plays, review and revise manuscripts and lectures, and play around with theory—the preliminary volume.

Every few pages in his journal, he listed his projects and plans, but his goals were unrealistic much of the time, too massive for any one person to complete successfully. In a sense, Schumpeter set himself up only to take a fall. If he had been less demanding of himself, perhaps he would have felt less frustrated, less like a failure. But, instead, he kept planning to accomplish the impossible and refused to give himself a break when it proved to be unattainable.

Still he kept plugging away, writing an introductory chapter entitled "Some Questions of Principles" for the book that would become *History of Economic Analysis.* He later wrote four chapters that served as the book's final introduction. The original introductory chapter was not published until 1987.[23] He also worked on several of the chapters dealing with economic theory from 1870 to 1914, the neoclassical revolution. But, despite this progress, he complained constantly about the book. Schumpeter also wrote a new chapter and an additional preface for the second edition of *Capitalism, Socialism and Democracy* that was published in 1947. The new preface answered some of the criticisms raised in response to the first edition, especially the one charging him with defeatism for arguing that socialism was inevitable. This he hotly contested,

> I deny entirely that this term is applicable to a piece of analysis.... Facts in themselves and inferences from them can never be defeatist.... The report that a given ship is sinking is not defeatist. Only the spirit in which this report is received can be defeatist: The crew can sit down and drink. But it can also rush to the pumps. If the men merely deny the report though it be carefully substantiated, then they are escapists.[24]

The new chapter in the book dealt with the consequences of the Second World War, focussing chiefly on the tendencies toward socialism in England, the problems of Russian imperialism, and U.S. postwar prospects. He rejected the stagnation thesis—the proposition that investment opportunities were vanishing—an idea identified with Keynes. Yet he argued that the fettering of U.S. capitalism by high redistributive taxation, regulation, and social and political disapproval of entrepreneurship may discourage innovations. Such an economic and social malaise would then encourage the government to control the economy even more, and eventually persuade the people to accept socialism. Thus, Schumpeter saw nothing in the war or in the immediate postwar situation to lead him to modify the book's conclusions. If anything, postwar conditions reinforced them. The world had changed, becoming new and uncomfortable for Schumpeter. But his analysis remained the same. He had sacrificed much in his life, but never his science. An economic truth was simply an economic truth, not to be tampered with because the analyst doesn't like it.

Notes

1   Schumpeter in the classroom and in his writings compared Keynes with Ricardo, arguing that both used economic analysis to promote a favorite economic policy.
2   Schumpeter's teaching load, semester by semester, is recorded in the Harvard University catalogs.
3   This remark comes from a paper entitled "Schumpeter: The Man I Knew," by R. M. Goodwin (1982), typescript, given to me by its author, a former colleague and student of Schumpeter.
4   *American Economic Review* 36, no. 5 (December 1946): 925-927.
5   Published in the proceedings of the convention, Comment Sauvegarder l'Entreprise Privée (Montreal, 1946). A copy of this paper is in the Harvard University Archives. A variant of this paper was published in the *History of Political Economy* 7, no. 3 (1975): 293-8.
6   *American Economic Review* 36, no. 6 (May 1946): 1-10.
7   Joseph P. McKenna of the University of Missouri-St. Louis, attended this course also and was one of the few to brave the elements during the snowstorm.
8   Joseph McKenna gave me this quotation, saying that he heard Schumpeter say this in class.
9   Ed. Seymour Harris (New York: A. A. Knopf, 1947), 73-101.
10   *Review of Economic Statistics* 28 (November 1946): 194-6.
11   *American Economic Review* 36 (September 1946): 495-518.
12   Arthur Smithies, "Schumpeter and Keynes," *Review of Economics and Statistics* 33 (1951): 163-9 as well as Charles Hession, *The Life of John Maynard Keynes* (New York: MacMillan, 1984).
13   This correspondence is on file in the Schumpeter papers in the Harvard University Archives.
14   *Newsweek* 13 April 1970.
15   Paul Sweezy of New York and Wilton, New Hampshire told me of the Schumpeter-Sweezy debate.
16   *Economist of London* 17 December 1983.
17   Harris told this story in his introduction to Seymour Harris, editor, *Joseph Schumpeter, Social Scientist.*

18 Dallas Steinthorsen related this story to me.

19 I was auditing a part of that course and attended that class.

20 Paul Samuelson, "Irving Fisher and the Theory of Capital," *Ten Economic Studies in the Tradition of Irving Fisher* (New York: John Wiley, 1967), 37.

21 *Econometrica* 16 (July 1948): 219-31.

22 Frisch reported this in his essay, "Some Personal Reminiscences of a Great Man."

23 Warren Samuels, editor, *Essays in the History of Economic Thought* (New York: JAI Press, 1987).

24 *Capitalism, Socialism and Democracy*, 3rd edition (New York: Harper and Row, 1950), xi.

10

Effort Rewarded, Contradictions, and Solace (1947-1948)

By 1947, the war was definitely in the past and Schumpeter was hard at work on the two projects that consumed him during the last years of his life: a new theory of development, which continued to frustrate him, and his history of economics, which used a large amount of time and which he just could not bring to an end. Often he reported to his diary that at such and such a time, it would end. But, when that time arrived, it required more work. He also became more interested in economic history and in the role of the entrepreneur as an historical figure.

In 1948, he achieved the reward that comes to the outstanding in U.S. economics. He was elected president of the American Economic Association. After the association meeting at which he was elected, he and Elizabeth took a working holiday in Mexico, the second of two foreign trips since 1935. During most of 1948, he worked to prepare for the association meetings. In those days, the president arranged the sessions in addition to giving a major address. Schumpeter worked hard on his address, a plea for methodological purity. But also during these late years, Schumpeter devoted much thought to the personal religion he had constructed over the years. Although it was uniquely his, in the last years of his life his closet devotions came to resemble more orthodox religions, with explicit recognition of prayer and God.

1

In his heart of hearts, the romantic in Schumpeter probably believed capitalism in its unfettered state to be the best of all possible economic arrangements. He also believed that those who supported any dilution of its purity were wrong. Paul Samuelson, one of Schumpeter's students during the 1930s, illustrated this attitude when he related the story of meeting Schumpeter at a cocktail party in the late 1940s. There, Schumpeter remarked to Samuelson, "I'd expect a socialist like you to believe that," referring to some interventionist economic policy. Samuelson protested, asking, "Do you really take me to be a socialist, Joe? After all, I was brought up by the Chicago School under Frank Knight and Henry Simons.... By what single criterion would you, after knowing me those many years, define me as a socialist?" Schumpeter squirmed, obviously uncomfortable at the confrontation. He was a polite and gentle man and political truth-telling is seldom appropriate on social occasions. But he finally blurted out, "My dear Paul, I was merely making reference to what you will not deny, that you lack respect for the pietistic verities of capitalism."[1]

Schumpeter in his romantic soul did not lack such respect or piety. Capitalism, indeed, was one of the few things he did believe in, although he was not always prepared to confess even that. As he grew older, he also grew increasingly cynical, perhaps the result of a lifetime of frustration, loss, and failure (both real and imagined). During the fall semester of 1947, Schumpeter was on sabbatical and spent much of his time in Taconic. Because he had more free time, he made more entries in his diary. But, even though he was usually less depressed when in Taconic, his late-1947 diary reveals several cynical remarks, among them: "An economist who is not unpopular like hell is not worth his salt," "You may cry over the ruins of civilization, but Harvard is but a laugh," "To lead men you must say certain lies," and "Economics deals only with surface forms." With this attitude, it is sometimes difficult to imagine how and why Schumpeter kept up his high level of production and activities. He was frequently so distressed with his job, his science, and mankind in general that one wonders why he bothered to continue giving all he could to a subject and a world when he sometimes seemed to receive so little pleasure and sense of achievement from them in return: another Schumpeterian paradox.

But he kept plugging away, researching, writing, and pursuing a new economic theory. In September 1947, Joseph and Elizabeth went to New Haven for the seventh annual meeting of the Economic History Association. During the summer, he had written a paper on the theory of economic growth for presentation at this meeting. Although he had hoped to say something new in the paper, he soon realized (and lamented) that he was relying on his same old theory of economic development. He and Simon Kuznets, a noted economic historian, presented the major speeches at this meeting; Schumpeter's was later published as "Theoretical Problems of Economic Growth" in the association's journal.[2] During this period, Schumpeter, at the suggestion of Arthur H. Cole, also wrote another paper for the the same journal entitled "The Creative Response in Economic History."[3]

Schumpeter was helping Cole define the activities of what became the Research Center on Entrepreneurship in the fall of 1947 (His comments on the idea are still on file at Widener Library).[4] Through case studies and other research, the center would seek to understand the role of the entrepreneur in the historical economic process. Schumpeter consented to serve on the center's board and to help persuade the Rockefeller Foundation to fund it. Other senior members included Cole, who was the director, as well as Thomas Cochran of New York University and Leland Jenke of Wellesley. The center later initiated a journal and sponsored many studies of entrepreneurship, the origin and background of entrepreneurs and the consequences of their work. Schumpeter's association with the center reinforced, toward the end of his life, his long-standing sentiment that history was important as a tool for understanding the economy.[5]

But here arises yet another paradox. To be sure, Schumpeter's entrepreneur was a historical figure. But, in his theory of development, Schumpeter described the entrepreneur as an abstraction, hardly a human being but rather a function—the activity of introducing a novelty into the economy. No person was an entrepreneur; some few persons performed entrepreneurial functions for a brief period in their lives. Such people can be identified historically, but most of their lives had little to do with their act of Schumpeterian entrepreneurship. Yet here was Schumpeter, encouraging and sponsoring historical studies of people called entrepreneurs.

His failure to produce a new theory of development, and his inability to turn the many hours of studying mathematics to his advantage convinced him more and more that history might provide the key to a more penetrating understanding of the mystery of how the economy worked and developed. Although most young economists were by that time enamored of mathematics, they and their new techniques were contributing only modestly to the study of economic change. Schumpeter, always the paradox, even the reverse chameleon, now sought the answer in history. Still, he never gave up his feeling for mathematics.

2

In December 1947, Schumpeter finally received partial reward for his many years of hard work. He was elected president of the American

Economic Association, an honor long overdue. The presidency signalled that the one chosen had made a major contribution to economics in the United States and earned the highest esteem of his colleagues. Each year, an elected nominating committee selects an outstanding economist who is then obligingly elected by the membership. Schumpeter had been considered for this post many times since he had joined the association in 1929 while still a German at the University of Bonn. But year after year the association rewarded good men for work whose merit did not exceed that of Schumpeter.

Many reasons explain why Schumpeter's turn seemed never to come. Until 1939, he was not a citizen of the United States, and the association had never elected a noncitizen. And, until 1939, he had not written a major work in the United States, never mind in English. By that time, U.S. sentiments were clearly anti-German while, coming from German-speaking Europe, Schumpeter was considered a German in the eyes of many, and he had been pro-German politically and to some degree even pro-Hitler, making little effort to conceal his attitude or his displeasure with U.S. policy in Europe and the Far East. Other reasons for the reluctance to elect him as president were his foreign education and the fact that he did not have a Ph.D. in economics, although his doctorate and habilitation from Vienna were the equivalent of the Ph.D. The association had never elected anyone who had these three strikes against him. After all, it was a U.S. association. Still, Schumpeter's name came up periodically and, in the postwar period, it became increasingly difficult to deny his stature in economics or the fact that he was a U.S. economist. At the sixtieth meeting of the American Economic Association in Chicago, his election was announced. Schumpeter was pleased, even though his diary entry was subdued: "to assume Presidency ... quite pleasant ... but I am too tired to give a vivid picture."

Part of the reason for not saying more about his election may have been because he had just learned that his old friend from Vienna and Bonn days, Gustav Stolper, was dead in New York. A great patriot of a democratic Germany, Stolper had stood by Schumpeter and assiduously promoted his interests, even though the two men had drifted apart after both moved to the United States. The diary contained a note reminding Schumpeter to write an essay about Stolper, but he never got around to it.

The president-elect of the American Economic Association had little to do immediately upon his election. But, during the ensuing year, Schumpeter had many chores, two of which demanded much time and energy. He was to give the presidential address at the association's meeting at the end of his term—which would mean late December 1948. This speech, seldom a technical analysis, usually represents the outgoing president's mature thoughts on economics. For many presidents, this address is the most important and thoughtful public statement they ever make. The second chore was to organize the association's annual meeting, a laborious job that chewed up many hours in correspondence, telegrams, and telephone calls. The task included defining the topics and sometimes even the particular papers for the sessions and inviting the chairmen and people to give papers. Arm twisting and calling in all outstanding debts of many colleagues to get them to participate is the usual method for eliciting cooperation. Then it becomes necessary to put off many others with vague half-promises in order to deny participation to those unsuited by talent or subject. Schumpeter met with his executive committee not only at the 1947 and 1948 association meetings, in Chicago and Cleveland, but also on 9 and 10 April 1948 in Princeton, New Jersey.

3

Still basking in the warmth of his election to the presidency of the American Economic Association, Schumpeter and Elizabeth took off for Mexico on 7 January 1948. In November 1947, Schumpeter had received an invitation from the Escuela de Economía of the Universidad Autónoma de Mexico to come and lecture. Dr. Gilberto Loyo, dean of the Escuela, would be the host. The Schumpeters decided they would go together, not only so that Joseph could give the lectures, but also so that both of them could make a holiday of it. They flew to Mexico City via Dallas on one of the few flights, and the longest, Schumpeter ever took. He had no U.S. passport, but he did have the necessary visitor's card; more importantly, he had the impressive Harvard "passport." Addressed to Harvard men of all climes and signed by the president, dean, and head of the Alumni Association, it introduced Schumpeter to all the Harvard worthies in Mexico City.[6]

Staying at the Hotel Emporio, Joseph and Elizabeth made the rounds of the sights, sounds, and smells of Mexico City. They saw the Diego de Riviera murals at the university and visited nearby towns such as Cuernavaca and Taxco. In Mexico City, they rode up and down the Avenida de la Reforma and took in the Anthropological Museum, the National Museum, and other sights around the city. They dined and had their pictures taken at Ciro's. As always, Schumpeter was interested in the architecture, so different from that of France and Germany, and he visited many churches and public buildings, making detailed notes that expressed less than enthusiasm for their structure and aesthetic appeal. He and Elizabeth even made the trip to the Mayan pyramid near Mérida in Yucatan, far from Mexico City, as well as Oaxaca and other cities. His journal is full of notes concerning Mexican history and culture. Joseph and Elizabeth were having a great time.

Regretting his inability to give his lectures in Spanish, Schumpeter did write much of the material in his journal in Spanish, although he complained,

"But I paid the penalty, once more, of not following my own insight: I *knew* it would not do without brushing up my Spanish!" Schumpeter had never studied Spanish systematically, but his knowledge of Latin and Italian was so intimate that he could read Spanish without difficulty, even though he couldn't speak it. In English, Schumpeter presented two series of lectures at the university. One consisted of five lectures entitled "The Progress of Theoretical Economics during the Last Twenty-Five Years." For these lectures, Schumpeter had made detailed narrative notes that were later included in the last part of the *History of Economic Analysis*. While preparing the manuscript for publication, Elizabeth found the notes, recognized that they fit well, and used them.

He then gave another series of five lectures entitled "Wage and Tax Policy in Transitional States of Society." In these lectures he examined a society— he was thinking of the United States—that had lost cohesiveness because major discrepancies had divided formerly compatible class interests.

> The business class has lost the power it used to have, but not entirely. Organized labor has risen to power but not completely. Labor and a government allied to the unions can indeed paralyze the business mechanism. But it cannot replace it by another mechanism. Hence we have a situation in which no class interest or viewpoint can work out the policy congenial to its social system and everybody checkmates everybody else.[7]

He then examined wage and tax policies, often contradictory, that will result from this stalemate. To do so, he discussed how these policies appear first in laissez-faire liberalism, then under centralist socialism, and finally in modern society. He concluded:

> We still rely in the United States upon the motives and mechanisms of the private-property economy. But we tax it in a way that will not allow it to function properly. We still retain the principle that wages are fixed by private contract, which means that they should vary according to the business conditions that prevail. But we do not allow them to do so. The consequences of this could be much mitigated if these contradictions were frankly realized instead of being hidden in clouds of political phrases.

4

On 30 January 1948, after almost three weeks in Mexico, the Schumpeter's arrived back in Taconic, tired but happy with their trip. Relaxed after his classroom sabbatical absence, he plunged back into the Cambridge routine upon his return, teaching his socialism course, the history and literature of economics, and his usual advanced economic theory, which

Haberler had taught while Schumpeter was on leave. Along with his teaching, Schumpeter juggled half a dozen projects all through 1948. Always, his history of economics, his theory, and his money books hovered over his head. Of the three, most of his time went into the history project, but other smaller projects also assumed importance, including the Fisher obituary. In late March and early April, he squeezed in a visit to Buffalo, New York, where he lectured on business cycles to the Chamber of Commerce and visited the University of Buffalo and Fritz Machlup, his summer colleague of the 1930s. In the spring, he also wrote a statement on the choosing of textbooks, published later in the *American Economic Review*.[8]

In addition, Schumpeter worked on an inflation article for *Nation's Business* magazine. This springtime project was a bit of popular writing that did not require a great deal of research, but it did demand careful exposition. At one point, he thought he had finished it, but then he wrote in his diary "Ouch! Setback! Inflation paper not yet in order." The occasion for the paper was the continued postwar inflationary pressure, still running strong in 1948. Drawing not only on his knowledge of contemporary economic affairs, but also on his personal experience as citizen, professor, and secretary of finance in postwar Austria, Schumpeter wrote a devastating attack on the policies that kept inflation bubbling, arguing that inflation was not an economic problem but rather a political one. The article, entitled "There Is Still Time to Stop Inflation" judicially stated Schumpeter's policy position, a revelation not new to associates but still the first such public statement since his Bonn days. After writing that "It is not possible to stop inflation in its track, without creating a depression," he asserted that inflationary pressure could be eased by credit restrictions, reductions of government expenditures, and a prosavings fiscal policy. The policy conclusion represented the standard Schumpeterian stance.[9]

Added to these projects were Schumpeter's continuing study of mathematics and Greek, along with several speaking engagements. After speaking to the Young Republicans and a Social Relations Colloquy in March, he travelled to Colby College to present a seminar. In April, he gave talks at the MIT Graduate Students Club, the Boston Economic Club, and Leverett House, in addition to conducting the Princeton planning meetings of the American Economic Association. As if this weren't enough, Schumpeter also made notes for another novel inspired by an incident from his youth. He remembered the story of a student who, disappointed at having failed an examination, shot the professor, an event that amused Schumpeter greatly. The thought that anyone could take an examination so seriously as to harm a professor struck him almost as funny as the proposition that being a professor was a dangerous occupation.[10]

On top of all this activity were the ever-present preparations for the December meeting of the American Economic Association. A great deal of

Schumpeter's time throughout 1948 went into working out the program details. Although an honorific position, the president of the association makes a real difference for that one year. By determining the topic and even inviting the individual papers, the president emphasizes what he thinks is important for the rest of the profession. For one year, the agenda of U.S. economists is his agenda.

Schumpeter's program design reflected his interests, and he called on the economists he knew best and trusted. One part of the program would deal with business cycles, not only current research but also its international variations. Reflecting his judgment that Wassily Leontief's work was important, Schumpeter also included sessions on input-output analysis, giving that subject added impetus. Another part of the program would examine the history of economics, Schumpeter's principal research topic, while yet another session on entrepreneurship catered to both his theoretical and historical interest in the author of innovation.[11] Throughout the year, Schumpeter also worked from time to time on the speech he would deliver at the meeting, hoping to make it a memorable statement. This association activity delayed his research program, but he was so pleased with his election that he didn't seem to mind.

Finally, in recognition of his responsibilities as president of the American Economic Association, the department gave Schumpeter a light teaching load for the fall of 1948. He taught only his advanced theory course, but this light load did not begin to make up for the many times he had voluntarily taught a heavy one. The department also provided him with a part-time secretary to help with the heavy correspondence concerning the association's meetings. For most of his sixteen years at Harvard, Schumpeter had had no secretarial assistance. Although the department secretary helped him on occasion, she was also the chairman's secretary and handled many of the department's administrative details. Forced to write most of his letters by hand, Schumpeter kept no systematic file of outgoing letters. Most of the letters he received were torn into quarters and used for scratch paper for his note-taking. When he needed to have manuscripts for books and articles typed, he usually hired the wives of graduate students, paying them out of his own pocket or from small grants from the Harvard Social Science Project, funded by the Rockefeller Foundation.

With teaching, many research irons in the fire, various speaking and professional engagements, and the association meeting preparations, the first half of 1948 saw the partial return of the prewar Schumpeter after the long wartime hiatus and isolation. His diary shows that he seemed to be enjoying life more, his pessimism was less profound, and some of his colleagues struck him as a bit more interesting. Schumpeter, along with a few other senior professors in the university, received a raise in February 1948, bringing their salaries to $14,000 a year, the highest salary Harvard was paying at the time. When he was busy and involved in many different activities, Schumpeter complained less in his diary. If his health bothered him in 1948, he wrote little about it, and fewer morbid comments on death and dying appeared, except during a time when Elizabeth's health was threatened. Even his acerbic political comments seemed to be more rare. His diary consisted primarily of comments regarding his activities and plans. Sometimes, for a given week he outlined a "Plan A" and "Plan B," the only difference being the order of the things he wanted to accomplish. His most frequent comments were complaints about lack of time.

Although his professional activity level was as high as it had been in the prewar years, the Schumpeters were still not as socially active as they had been in the late 1930s. In a letter to a colleague, Schumpeter wrote that all he did was work, having no time to go out, see friends, or answer—even open— mail. Among his collected papers are several letters from colleagues at other universities that to this day remain unopened but that carry postmarks dating in the late 1940s. Although Schumpeter did attend an occasional party in Cambridge or visit with neighbors in Taconic, his social life was limited in the late 1940s.

5

Returning to Taconic for the summer of 1948, Schumpeter stopped the running around and speech making, although he still worked on numerous writing projects and always that "blasted History." That summer, as he had for several past summers, he did enjoy several concerts at nearby Tanglewood. He and Elizabeth fixed up the apartment over the garage at Windy Hill and sometimes invited friends to stay overnight when they all went to the concert. He played with the idea of amplifying his Mexico City lectures into a book, but nothing came of it. Most of his time was spent "ruminating on AEA speech and on next steps in history." With less frenetic activity and more time alone, Schumpeter's depression returned, and he expressed several cynical sentiments about the sorry state of economics, the university, the nation, and the world. Pessimistic about all of them, he wrote, "Govt of fools for the fools by the fools" and "We all of us like a sparkling error better than a trivial truth." The entry for 2 August begins with the word "Despair" written in large letters covering the upper third of the page. At one point during the summer, he even considered the possibility of retirement, for which he was now eligible. But it was a solitary mention, a passing thought. Yet, he did decide that he needed a rest and planned eight weeks of relaxation. Then he proceeded to list all the things he would do on his vacation: mathematics, Homer, PV, reading, scanning some history, work on parts 2, 3, and 4 of the history of economics, and so on.[12]

By looking at his journal and small appointment book, the degree of his work in mathematics becomes apparent. Believing the subject to be critical to economics, he studied mathematics on most days for more than fifteen years, a degree of involvement unknown to his colleagues or students. Paradoxically, considering this massive effort, he rarely used mathematics in his writing or his teaching. One reason may have been the realization that, despite his great effort, he did not have a mathematical mind; as he told a student in another context, "It is one thing to be able to read German. It is quite another thing to write German poetry."[13] In 1948, he identified one of the basic reasons why mathematics did not serve him well when he wrote, "Evolutionary math?" There is no such thing as evolutionary mathematics. Yet the absence of this method resulted in his continued failure to formulate a better, more rigorous, and satisfactory theory. Hoping against hope that he could find a path, Schumpeter still made the effort.

His 1948 diary reveals another reason for his dogged study of mathematics. During this period, almost every entry indicates mathematics as one of his projects, partly because "Whatever other advantages math may have, it is certainly the purest of human pleasures." He genuinely enjoyed studying mathematics and did it for fun, as a pleasant pastime, something interesting to do when not writing. He preferred it to listening to the radio or going to the movies, activities in which he seldom indulged. He had but few pleasures. Although he still read detective stories in the evening, he guiltily criticized himself for that habit. He also still read himself to sleep with Greek, another of his human pleasures.

His diary, along with comments to colleagues, also reveals the mature Schumpeter's opinion of his fellow man. Many are the epithets that people hurl at scholars like Schumpeter: elitist, racist, antisemitic, eugenicist, fascist, arrogant, and others. Based on his remarks, writings, or comments in his diary, all these terms could be applied to Schumpeter. But then there are also contradictory remarks and behavior that belie them. Yet, by no means did he have a great love for all mankind nor believe that all people were alike. He spoke of the "subnormals" frequently and was concerned lest subnormal human beings gain and increase their control over public policy to the detriment of continued economic progress and capitalism. The following remarks, written in his diary during the last few years of his life, expressed such sentiments:

The enemy is the sub-standard.

Equality of men is the most stupid of all credos.

There is not only one enemy of humanity—the sub-normal—there is another, the idealist.

Equality is the ideal of the sub-normal, but even sub-normals do not really desire equality, but only that there be nobody better.

The true problem is the problem of the sub-normal, but instead of solving it, we take them into consideration.

What a country, not of mediocrities, but for mediocrities.

The genius of the country—it has created a world for mediocrities.

These remarks, as well as other statements, illustrate Schumpeter's belief that humanity was not homogeneous, men were not equal, and they could never be so. A few people were supernormal, and some were close to the average, but, statistically speaking, the average was a fiction representing no significant numbers of the population. That meant that most of the population, as he saw it, was subnormal. It fell to the supernormal to propel society forward, economically, politically, and culturally. The subnormal, the average, and the poor went along for a free ride.

One then has to ask whether Schumpeter believed that society consisted of races having enduring characteristics and whether he singled out the Jewish race as special in some way. To the first part of the question, Schumpeter would probably answer yes, but nowhere in his private or personal writings or in his remarks to friends is there any indication of racial or Jewish hatred or fear of Jews. Nor is there any evidence that he believed Jews were inferior or should be punished or discriminated against, economically or politically; he opposed violence to or discrimination against any group because of race or creed. Indeed, he commented on many occasions about the superiority of the Jewish race.

That which seemed to bother him most about Jews was what he perceived as their clannishness and attitude of racial superiority. In his diary: "I don't like Jewish philosophers for theirs is a Jewish philosophy. Racial creed is the Jewish creed." In effect, he accused Jews of racism and believed they stuck together, thinking and acting alike for racial reasons. For example, he commented on the political influence of the "New York Jews" as though they were a homogeneous entity, attributing to them a degree of power as a group far beyond that which they possessed. Such remarks suggest that he believed that Jews, as a race, were far removed from him and his world. Still, the Jews he knew personally did not seem to be members of that distant, homogeneous group. The ones he knew, of course, were fellow scholars and students. He felt that, if anything, economists who happened to be Jews were often superior economists; but paradoxically they were not Jewish economists, only economists who happened to be Jews.

Despite his disparaging comments about the racism of Jews, Schumpeter—the eternal paradox—also had a sense of his own race and its uniqueness. It is not, however, clear what he believed his race to be. Whatever it was, he believed in its integrity and in eugenics; he was convinced that the entire human stock could and should be improved by maintaining and improving racial stocks through selective breeding. He wrote in his diary that men and women, as parents, have a duty to improve the stock, and some of his remarks are remarkably similar to those heard in Germany in the late 1930s and early 1940s: "The essential character of a society is how it treats its inheritance—the token of its stock" or "We could solve all the problems of this country if we limited citizenship to people whose parents were born here. Even better, whose grandparents were born here." Despite the racially loaded comments in his diary, he sometimes equivocated, wondering, for example, "Am I losing my faith in race?"

Because of comments such as those above, Schumpeter is often suspected or even accused of fascism—a term so vague that it is difficult to be sure what a fascist is. But Schumpeter's political sympathies were not fascist. He was always a monarchist and a limited democrat, meaning that he did not make a virtue or fetish of majority rule. He had constrained faith in the intelligence of a broad electorate. As he said many times, he favored tory democracy. In a debate with Seymour Harris concerning the 1948 presidential campaign, Schumpeter took the Republican side "because we don't have a monarchist party in the United States." While Harris supported the standard Democratic-Keynesian position, Schumpeter, on the other hand, argued that higher taxes for middle income earners (who spend everything they make) and reduced taxes for the rich (who save much of their income) would fight inflation and provide resources for private investment to perk up the economy. This statement was not really tongue in cheek.

Schumpeter did not have unbounded confidence in the ability of democracy to yield, in the long run, the greatest economic, social, political, and cultural benefits to a society. Favoring a monarchy restricted by a constitution and restrained by a parliament, he often expressed his admiration for the English political system, although during and after the war he opposed many of the policies of the English government. His early support of some of Hitler's policies was certainly not for his political system. At first, he sympathized with the bourgeois attitudes Hitler seemed to express—for example, the Nazi emphasis on the importance of the family and of savings. Later, Schumpeter favored what he thought would be a stable European geopolitical arrangement in which Germany acted as bulwark against bolshevism. Never did he support Hitler's fascism and the repression and violence it gave rise to. Still, he feared majority-rule democracy, believing that the subnormals—the vast majority—might someday control it and use it for their short-term benefit. If this happened, they would destroy the machine—capitalism—that yields the benefits. Favoring instead maximum personal, civil, and economic liberties for individuals, Schumpeter never hesitated to point out that democracy could trample such freedoms through slavish adherence to majority rule.

6

Many of Schumpeter's opinions and attitudes did not change markedly over the years, though they became more refined. His personal appearance, however, did change. In these postwar years, he had grown somewhat heavier. Now almost completely bald, his face appeared more round in contrast to the more oval shape of the 1930s. But his jutting chin was as prominent as ever. His brown eyes sometimes seemed almost oriental, and the bags underneath them, which had appeared many years earlier, became more pronounced. He never wore glasses. His vests had to be altered because he had developed a paunch, giving the impression of a more rotund figure. Still, he continued to dress impeccably, mostly in expensive, tailor-made suits from English cloth, purchased at the shop of Mr. Vesper, a tailor in Harvard Square. His dress was more conservative than it had been when he was younger, usually consisting of three-piece suits, except on those social occasions when Elizabeth permitted perhaps a dressy sport coat and a velvet vest.

Students, seeing their professors regularly, come to know a teacher's habits of dress as well as the items of apparel. To his students, Schumpeter presented a sartorial challenge. It often seemed that he never wore the same clothes twice, so large was his wardrobe and so skillful was Elizabeth in mixing and matching the clothes she laid out for him every day. She used a complex rotation system to create the illusion that he wore no outfit more than one time in any given semester and seldom repeated in any given academic year. By the late 1940s, Schumpeter, now in his sixties, did begin to show some evidence that modernity had caught up with him. A wristwatch often replaced the vest-encased pocket watch of earlier days, and he wore a simple gold band on the third finger of his right hand, denoting his married state. On days when he did not go to his office and had no classes and no appointments, he wore around the house in Cambridge, slacks, a dress sport jacket, and a tie. To Schumpeter, an open collar was akin to nudity. Almost always present, the sport jacket, usually buttoned, and shirt, tie, and comfortable slacks were his typical attire in Taconic.

7

Until his death, Schumpeter's interest in his students and their welfare remained as strong as ever. The late Harry Johnson, of the University of Chicago and the London School of Economics, related an incident that illustrates Schumpeter's commitment to those he taught. Johnson, a Harvard graduate student in the late 1940s, had found an incorrectly inverted ratio, never noted before, in one of the numerical examples used by David Ricardo in his classic 1817 book. Even though Johnson was still only a graduate student, Schumpeter urged him to write a short article about his discovery. After several discussions with Schumpeter, Johnson submitted an article to the Harvard house organ, of which Schumpeter was an editor. The *Quarterly Journal of Economics* published it in 1948. Johnson remarked that professors at the other Cambridge, where he had also studied, would never have treated him the way Schumpeter did, as a colleague, and given him such encouragement.[14]

But despite his good relations with students, Schumpeter still was unhappy with Harvard, retaining respect for only a few of his colleagues and none at all for the institution, not even his own department. He once expressed the view that, of the senior professors, only Leontief and Haberler were doing any useful research work in economics. Edward Mason, whom he also greatly admired, spent a lot of his time in administrative work as a dean. Schumpeter's opinion of Harvard can be seen in a letter to his prewar Japanese student, Shigeto Tsuru. Until the winter of 1941-42, the two had worked together, and Tsuru, who was repatriated, even lived for a time with the Schumpeters in Taconic. By 1948, Tsuru had taken a post at Hitotsubashi University, successor to the Tokyo University of Commerce where Schumpeter had lectured in 1931. When Tsuru wrote to inquire about coming back to Harvard to brush up on his studies, Schumpeter responded in September 1948:

> It is with particular pleasure that I welcome you back to academic activities which as in the 5th century in Rome, are perhaps the least distasteful to indulge in, in the world as it is.... Of course, distance always beautifies but I who am near enough to Harvard cannot say that I experience very much stimulus from my surroundings.... Fundamental ideas, methods and approaches you know, and original achievement can be built upon this [study in mathematics and statistics] in Tokyo as well as in Boston.[15]

Schumpeter was busy in the fall of 1948, taking care of the details related to the upcoming association meeting, polishing his speech, and working on other projects. He hosted a visit to Harvard by Tjalling Koopmans and spoke on fiscal policy at Dunster House. Although the history of economics was temporarily abandoned because of lack of time, he worked on an article that reviewed several books dealing with the postwar English economy.[16] To test his thinking, Schumpeter gave a talk on this subject to the Graduate Economics Students' Club in early November 1948. As a senior staff member, he also spent some time at the new Research Center in Entrepreneurial History, then operating with the Rockefeller money that Schumpeter had helped acquire.

But the high spirits of the trip to Mexico and springtime had faded and Schumpeter returned to his frequent complaining. In late 1948, he confided, "your blood bumps through brittle arteries and you are no more of it ... but I am old and mude [weary] ... unrelieved misery." To compound his sadness, Schumpeter learned that Wesley Clair Mitchell of Columbia University and the National Bureau of Economic Research had died on 29 October 1948. He and Schumpeter had been close colleagues and associates since 1913, when the two met at Columbia and instantly recognized the greatness in the other. They kept in touch all through the years. Often they did not think alike on economics, since Mitchell had serious reservations about most kinds of abstract economic theory. Knowing a great deal about theory but questioning its value, Mitchell spent much of his life trying to study the business cycle from a statistical viewpoint. Along with Edwin Gay, the Harvard economic historian, he founded and then directed the National Bureau of Economic Research for many years. During Mitchell's tenure, the Bureau produced massive statistical tomes about the cycle, always promising that when the statistical work was completed, the theory would emerge. It never did. But the differences between Mitchell and Schumpeter did not in any way mar their mutual respect.

Schumpeter went to New York in early December 1948, to deliver the eulogy at Mitchell's memorial service. Despite Mitchell's rejection of theory, Schumpeter praised him as the great pioneer in the empirical study of business cycles. He also undertook the task of writing Mitchell's obituary for the *Quarterly Journal of Economics*, but he neglected this task for nearly a year because he had so much other work to do. He finally completed it two weeks before his own death. In this obituary that Schumpeter never saw in print, he wrote:

If Mitchell had been able to complete his unfinished manuscript, this also would have been no more than a beginning.... Here was a man who had the courage to say, unlike the rest of us, that he had not all the answers; who went about his task without either haste or rest; who was full of sympathy with mankind's fate, yet kept aloof from the market place; who taught us, by example and not by phrase, what a scholar should be.[17]

He could have been writing his own obituary.

8

Although Schumpeter worked on many and varied projects in the fall of 1948, the focus of his attention was the American Economic Association meeting and especially the speech he would present. The presidential address is one of the highlights of the association meetings, even more so in 1948 because Schumpeter's reputation had preceded him. At the meeting, held 27-30 December, he finally had his moment in the limelight when he spoke before the packed ballroom at the Cleveland hotel. But having reached the moment he had planned for all year, Schumpeter did two paradoxical things. He did not dress formally; he even wore a blue shirt rather than the customary white. This act annoyed some people, who felt that Schumpeter was thereby downgrading the importance of the association and the honor it had bestowed on him. He may have done it to please the photographers. Also uncharacteristically, Schumpeter brought notes to the lectern when he gave his speech, something he almost never did. But he had no need to be nervous because he was in fine form that evening, speaking impeccably and with verve.

Despite the two atypical acts accompanying his speech, he had, characteristically, turned from the substance of economics to its methodology for his topic. Early in the speech, entitled "Science and Ideology," he set forth his primary thesis:

There exist in our minds preconceptions about the economic process that are much more dangerous to the cumulative growth of our knowledge and the scientific character of our analytic endeavors because they seem beyond control in a sense in which value judgments and special pleadings are not ... [these are] Ideologies.[18]

Schumpeter went on to explain that the basis of any economist's work is his vision. He necessarily envisions what an economy is, what its ingredients are, how in general it functions, what it does, and how it does it. All this precedes any analysis. The vision represents an intellectual commitment concerning the nature of the subject, and it may indeed contain unconscious elements of the individual's ideology—the set of ideas that embody the values, needs, interests, and aspirations of his group or class. Conscious or not, the analyst may bring to an economic problem ideas that may introduce ideological bias and vitiate the results of analysis.

Most economists develop their vision from pre-existing concepts of what the economy is, how it operates, what its elements are, and what it implies. The economist studies prices, allocation of resources, decisions of producers and consumers, distribution of income, and growth because these elements, as well as the notion of how the economy functions, are parts of the economist's vision of the reality he thinks he sees when approaching problems. The vision itself is not an analytical result. It is, as Schumpeter called it, a preanalytic cognitive act, a composite of the subjective ideas, value judgments, and interests, often fused with analysis but always more than analysis. In this way the vision embodied in the preanalytic phase is, through analysis, introduced into the results of analysis.

The vision tells economists what problems are to be addressed, what the variables are, and sometimes even the relations that may or may not exist. Visions may be ideologically vitiated because the economist may define the problem, establish relations, or choose assumptions in order to produce an analytical result that favors some economic interest or justifies that interest. Schumpeter implied that economics is not and cannot be a pure science. Through the vision, the opinionated, value-laden human element inevitably enters analytical results surreptitiously. If the economist's beginning—his vision—has elements of bias that contaminate his results, then the value of economics as pure science is limited.

This conclusion had always greatly troubled Schumpeter because he wanted to regard economics as a pure science, independent of all value judgments, special pleadings, and ideology. But, in his speech to the American Economic Association, he reluctantly concluded that this cannot be. He mentioned that all science can be threatened by ideological vitiation— a favorite expression of Schumpeter's in his mature years—but that economics is more vulnerable than most. With this conclusion, he resurrected, at least in part, the bugaboo that philosophy and politics interfere, albeit in a more sophisticated way than before, with scientific results. But, although he sensed the danger, he did not believe the risk to be great.

To extricate himself from his own uncomfortable conclusion, Schumpeter noted that, of course, ideological bias is always a possibility and has often arisen in economics. Since such bias must be regarded as inexorable, must economists also conclude that economics is inevitably and fatally flawed? Schumpeter answered no. Economics as a science can still hold up its head for two basic reasons. The techniques of economic analysis—developed over the centuries, honed, amplified and restricted, qualified, rejected, and supplemented—are barriers to ideology because they are neutral and have no ideological component. Bringing the theory (pure logic) and techniques to bear upon facts and circumstances eliminates the ideological bias that the analyst may have. The methods of economics therefore force the economist to shed his ideology whether he likes it or not. Should some element of ideology still slip through the technical and methodological safeguards of economics, another safeguard exists to protect economics as a science: competition. Should Economist Green produce an analysis afflicted with ideological bias, Economist Brown will hasten to point this out and, even if Brown is afflicted with the opposite bias, Economists Black and White are always ready to point out the error of both. Thus, the interactions among economists tends to stamp out bias and assure scientific neutrality.

But still the nagging question remains: Can economics be fully independent of ideological bias? Schumpeter answered no. If ideological bias means nonscientific influences representing interests and attitudes of people and groups, then, according to Schumpeter, economics, the neutral scientific superstructure, necessarily rests on an ideological base and may contain value elements and interest-laden propositions. Even though only one reality exists in the world of phenomena, there are many perceptions of that reality. The scientist, in his vision, accepts one of them. He could not resist citing the case of Keynes as an example when he stated: "Keynes's vision ... of mature and arteriosclerotic capitalist society that tries to save more than its declining opportunities can absorb" determined first his policy conclusion that government deficit spending is necessary and then the theoretical framework in which the government behaves as surrogate investor to save capitalism from itself.[19]

Schumpeter thus stopped short of arguing that economics can be completely neutral and wholly independent of ideology. Although economics must keep its guard up constantly against the likes of Ricardo and Keynes, it cannot view ideology as a wholly undesirable element:

> That prescientific cognitive act which is the source of our ideologies is also the prerequisite of our scientific work. No new departure in any science is possible without it. Through it we acquire new material for our scientific endeavors and something to formulate, to defend, to attack. Our stock of facts and tools grows and rejuvenates itself in the process. And so—though we proceed slowly because of our ideologies, we might not proceed at all without them.[20]

When he spoke those final words on that night in Cleveland, the usually staid membership of the American Economic Association uncharacteristically rose to give Schumpeter a standing ovation. Afterwards, friends and well-wishers crowded around to compliment him. Immensely pleased, he even recorded this gratifying response in his diary and thanked his *Hasen*.

9

In the last two or three years of his life, Schumpeter's diary and personal communion with Annie and his mother took on a new intensity and importance to him. He continued working with his dead wife's diary, but his entries became more intermittent in the late 1940s. Still, he filled several bound notebooks, heading each entry with a prayer and including a saying or motto in remembrance of their lives together. His own diary assumed a more prominent position as his work with Annie's diary declined. But his memory of her did not decrease; instead, the *Hasen* became more solidified as figures for personal worship. Schumpeter never referred to his diary as a diary or a journal. It was his *protokoll* (protocol), his report, statement, or record. His entries continued to be reports to the *Hasen* as he expressed thankfulness and pleaded for help and protection, especially in matters of health. Usually writing to the *Hasen* in shorthand, he still used the initials "H s D," meaning *Hasen sei Dank* (Thank you, *Hasen*). As the years passed, Schumpeter's diary transformed into a more traditional religious forum for his private worship. Back in the 1930s, he had used his *Hasen* as intercessors for an unnamed and shadowy God whose presence was more implied than expressed. By the late 1940s, that God had become Gott im Himmel. Although God is often mentioned in connection with the *Hasen*, Schumpeter began addressing some of his prayers explicitly to God.[21]

The line of distinction between God and the *Hasen*, however, was somewhat blurred. In most of the diary entries, the words for his "beloved *Hasen*" appear. He continued to attribute all good events to the intervention of the *Hasen*, who possessed great power, including the power to answer his prayers, protect him, and promote his interests. "The might of the Hasen stood out gloriously," which he wrote after his presidential address, is a characteristic remark of the late 1940s. And, whenever anything bad happened, he appealed to the *Hasen* for help, protection, and support.

But, while the *Hasen* remained a guiding force in his life, his personal religion was expanding to include a more traditional concept of God—a figure who is also worshipped. He initiated what he called a program of morning prayer, and later added an evening prayer as well. "What about this program: To conclude every day with a prayer and a request for concentration," he wrote. He also began observing—privately—many religious holidays, celebrating with personal devotions such holy days as Good Friday, Easter, and Ascension. To him, such days carried some mystical, personal meaning. Although he never mentioned Christ or Christian theological propositions, on those holy days he seemed more at peace with himself and expressed fewer complaints and less cynicism.

Schumpeter's deeply felt religious sentiments and his relationship to both the *Hasen* and God remained unknown to his friends, who never suspected that he had any personal concern with religion. His inability to confide in friends about his religious sentiments, coupled with his ability to report in protocols to the *Hasen* with complete honesty, suggests that Schumpeter did not believe his colleagues would understand, whereas the *Hasen* would. His public posture as a scientist, an unbiased seeker of truth, may also have inhibited him. Scientists, including many of his colleagues, do not typically have religious sentiments because they believe that acceptance of religion requires taking things on faith and relying on nonobservable and nonverifiable propositions. Many social scientists, even more so than natural scientists, have asserted that the gulf between their science and religion is so great that rejection of all things religious offers the only course of action.

One might ask, then, why did religion, albeit private, consume so much of Schumpeter's attention in his later life? One can never be absolutely certain. In part, it appealed to and confirmed the strong romantic side of his personality. The intensity of the conflict between his romantic outlook and his intellectual scientific background and stance may be partly responsible for his continuing unhappiness and depression. In order to do his work, he had to summon a high degree of concentration that excluded everything except what he was working on. Yet, other matters, especially nonscientific matters, continually intruded, making him miserable and convincing him that he was a failure. Schumpeter's religion seems to have helped smooth over this contradiction, acting as an antidote to the poisonous effects of depression. In short, I think he needed his religious beliefs for the maintenance of his mental health. Had he not had his *Hasen*, his belief in their power, and the ability to communicate with them, depression would have overwhelmed and undone him. His religion was the solace that made his continued work possible.

Notes

1   Paul A. Samuelson, "The World Economy at Century's End," a paper given at the World Economic Conference, Mexico City, Mexico, 1980, 20-21.

2   *Journal of Economic History* 7 (1947): Supplement, 1-9.

3   *Journal of Economic History* 7 (November 1947): 149-59.

4   "Comments on a Plan for the Study of Entrepreneurship," Widener Library, HUH 775 (13 January 1947).

5   The center lasted several years at Harvard, and published a journal and several books dealing with entrepreneurship. See R. P. Adrien Taymans, "Le Research Center in Entrepreneurial History," *Economie Appliquee* 3 (1950): 615-35. Research in entrepreneurship and entrepreneurial history continues in the School of Business Administration at Harvard University, a legacy of Cole and Schumpeter.

6   The invitation from Mexico City and the elaborate Harvard passport are in the

Schumpeter papers in the Harvard University Archives.

7   The notes and some typescript of "Wage and Tax Policies in Transitional Societies" are in the Schumpeter papers in the Harvard University Archives.

8   *American Economic Review* 38 (September 1948): 626.

9   *Nation's Business* 36 (1948):33-35, 88-91.

10   Schumpeter told this story to many of his friends and it also appears in diary.

11   Schumpeter's program appears in the *American Economic Review* 39 (May 1949): vii-ix, which reported the 61st meeting of the association over which Schumpeter presided.

12   Much of this section is based on Schumpeter's diary and reports of his friends and colleagues.

13   This quotation comes from a personal communication with Joseph P. McKenna, University of Missouri-St. Louis.

14   Personal conversation with Professor Johnson, who was a graduate student in Cambridge at the same time I was there.

15   This letter is in the correspondence file of the Schumpeter papers at the Harvard University Archives. More correspondence is on file for 1948 and 1949 when Schumpeter had secretarial assistance.

16   This was published as "English Economists and the State-Managed Economy," *Journal of Political Economy* 57 (October 1949): 371-82.

17   *Quarterly Journal of Economics* 64 (February 1949): 139-55.

18   *American Economic Review* 39, no. 2 (March 1949): 345-59).

19   Ibid., 355.

20   Ibid., 359.

21   This section is based primarily on Schumpeter's diary.

11

Reviewing the Troops (1942-1949)

Schumpeter will long be remembered as an historian of the science of economics. His reputation in this subject competes with his stature in economic theory, economic history, methodology, sociology, and as a prophet of capitalism. The basis of that reputation primarily rests on his *History of Economic Analysis*, the book on which he worked for much of the last nine years of his life. Unfinished at his death, Elizabeth edited the manuscript and Oxford University Press published it in 1954.

1

Schumpeter did not regard the history of economics as a special field within either economics or history, or as a discipline in itself. To him, the history of economics was just a facet of the study of economic theory. His interest and willingness to devote so much effort to it—not only late in life but also earlier, dating back to university days—did not stem from his interest in the history of economics for its own sake. Economic science—past, present, and future—fired his soul. The history of economics exemplified, and for him proved, his interpretation and approach to that science.

The fundamental fact about economics for Schumpeter was that it is a science, an exact and even numerical science. His notion of what constitutes science would pass muster among other methodologists, such as John Neville Keynes, Lionel Lord Robbins, and Fritz Machlup in economics, as well as Imre Lakatos and Sir Karl Popper among philosophers. Still, methodology is a controversial area of study, uninteresting to most economists, and even today, universal agreement has not emerged.

Facts and logic are the basis of economic theory. Theory is a collection of tools and techniques with which to analyze economic relations, circumstances, events, problems, and policies. The history of those techniques and tools is a part of economic theory, a record of how the science has developed and progressed, and, according to Schumpeter, a necessary part of the knowledge of the economic scientist. With this outlook, it is not surprising that he had a lifelong love affair with the history of economics. His first lectures on the subject were given at Czernowitz just three years after his graduation from the university when he was twenty-six. Those lectures later became the monograph *Vergangenheit und Zukunft der Sozialwissenschaft* (The Past and Future of Social Science), published in 1915.[1] A year earlier, in 1914, his brief study *Epochen der Dogmen- und Methodengeschichte,* translated by R. Aris as *Economic Doctrine and Method* (1954), was first published.[2] Part of the stimulation for *Epochen* was the 1913 class meetings of the course on economic theory types taught by Wesley Clair Mitchell in New York that Schumpeter had attended. After class, he and Mitchell often had lunch and discussed economic theory and its history.

But by far Schumpeter's most important historical work was the *History of Economic Analysis.*[3] He had begun work on it in 1942, or earlier, and was still at work on it until a few days before he died. Shortly after his death, Elizabeth began finding parts of the manuscript scattered everywhere. She had not read any of it before Schumpeter died because he wanted to get further along and present her with a nearly completed manuscript.

Schumpeter worked in four locations. One was his office, M-5 Littauer Center, but most of the work done there related to teaching and correspondence. Even so, Elizabeth found parts of the manuscript at the office, some stuffed in drawers, some on its way to the typist and some returning. A second place of work was the house on Acacia Street in Cambridge, where she found manuscript scattered around in various places. In Taconic at Windy Hill, he had two studies. His preferred work place was his study with the fireplace upstairs, but he sometimes worked in the small study downstairs. In different states of progress, the material was discovered in, on, and under desks, in corners, in piles, in closets and in bookcases.

Part of the manuscript was little more than handwritten first draft, often revised with inserted and scratched out words and arrows pointing to where sentences and paragraphs were to be moved. Barely legible is a generous description of it. Other parts of the manuscript consisted of drafts that had come back from the typist. Some of the typescript he had revised extensively, and it was ready to go back to the typist as another draft. Other typescripts were cleaner, indicating only the beginning of revision, and some drafts, especially material written in 1949, had not been touched.[4] It took Elizabeth at least six months just to round up and put in order all the material. Another two years she spent getting it ready for the publisher. She lived long enough to begin reading galley proof on the book, a task completed by Professors Haberler and Leontief, two of Schumpeter's closest friends and colleagues, who saw the book through the final stages after Elizabeth died in mid-1953.

To bring *History of Economic Analysis* to publication, Elizabeth faced a formidable task. No outline of the book existed except for a paragraph indicating the five parts. Whole sections and chapters had no titles, and manuscripts for some parts were mixed in with other parts. Some paragraphs, sections, and chapters were missing altogether.

Schumpeter sometimes began but did not finish parts of the manuscript, trailing off into a shorthand that Elizabeth could not read. In other cases, more than one version of the same piece existed, forcing her to choose between them. For example, he wrote two versions of part 1. The published version consists of four short chapters. The unpublished version is a single chapter of thirty-eight typed pages entitled "Some Questions of Principle," which I found in his papers. It was recently published along with a detailed comparison of it with the four previously published chapters.[5] The recently published version contains some material not included in the *History of Economic Analysis.*

Elizabeth did yeoman service in putting the book together, and scholars owe her a deep debt of gratitude for her work. Her editorial experience with the *Quarterly Journal of Economics* in the 1930s and early 1940s, as well as her intimate familiarity with Schumpeter's thinking as well as his handwriting, were prerequisites. She, in turn, was indebted to the help of some of Schumpeter's colleagues, notably Arthur Marget, Paul Sweezy, Gottfried Haberler, Wassily Leontief, Arthur Smithies, Richard Goodwin, and others who worked with parts of the manuscript. But Elizabeth had the final word. Making it a rule not to change anything in the manuscript, she wrote in her editor's introduction, "I conceived my editorial task to be the simple one of presenting as complete and accurate a version of what J.A.S. actually wrote as possible but not to attempt to complete what he had not written."[6] She did write chapter, section, and topic headings, but, whenever she included such clarifying material, she put it in brackets. She added nothing of substance.

2

The theoretical framework of the book, as in Schumpeter's 1914 book, makes an issue of the content and scope of the history of economics. The title is the tip-off, saying Analysis instead of Thought or Doctrine or Ideas, the words used by most books and courses on the subject. Schumpeter might well have used The History of Economic Science as a title, or The History of Economics, or even, as he had planned earlier, The History of Economic Theory. Other scholars had written primarily about the development of theory or analysis, but no one before Schumpeter had made such a fuss about it. Nor had anyone argued so cogently and forcefully that this approach was not only legitimate but more appropriate and useful than the broader approach that included history, policy, and other nontheoretical thinking about economics.

Schumpeter's goal was to relate the development of man's ability to analyze the economy. The book begins with the words:

> By History of Economic Analysis I mean the history of the intellectual effort that men have made to *understand* economic phenomena or, which comes to the same thing, the history of the analytic and scientific aspects of economic thought.[7]

He proposed to give economic history, events, and circumstances short shrift. Economic policy and philosophy shared a similar fate. He also asserted that economists whose work deals with facts, history, events, conditions, and policies deserve scant attention in a history of science, although they may loom large in other contexts. Because of this, anyone who travels with Schumpeter will get a partial view of the history of economic thought, but not as narrow as Schumpeter intended, for he violated his own strictures.

Those who received most of his attention were the contributors to economic theory. The ones playing important roles not only in economic science, but also in economic policy commanded Schumpeter's interest according to their analytical contributions only. Smith and Ricardo, for example, overcame the waning mercantilists in policy, thereby becoming responsible in no small part for the conversion of public policy from mercantilism to free trade and laissez faire in Great Britain and the United States. And they are known as much for that contribution as for their theoretical ones. But only the analytical ideas of Smith and Ricardo merit Schumpeter's attention and appraisal. That Smith and the nineteenth-century English economists began to understand, however imperfectly, the nature of value, how price is established, how resources are allocated, how income is distributed, and how the economy functions was all important to Schumpeter. That they were giants in public policy was irrelevant.

The *History of Economic Analysis* has 1,260 pages in five parts, the first of which, a tiny forty-seven-page fraction of the book, deals with scope and method. The fifth part, no longer than the first, is a sketch of modern developments—the period from 1915 to 1940. This last part had received little of Schumpeter's attention and is therefore the least complete. The rest of the book—parts 2, 3, and 4—is divided into roughly equal sections. The second part discusses the history of economics from its beginnings with the

Greeks to about 1790. The third part covers from 1790 to 1870, the period of classical economics. The fourth part traces developments from 1870 to 1914, a period when economics underwent revolution and blossomed into neoclassical economics.

3

In part 1 of the *History of Economic Analysis,* Schumpeter outlined his views on economics, economists, and the history of economics. Although he said little that differed from his earlier published writings, he did elaborate, extend, and give a more thoughtful presentation of his ideas.

Note, for example, his reasons for studying the history of economics. First, such study provides meaning and direction to economic theory, without which the theory would be incomplete and difficult to understand. As he wrote, "The state of any science at any given time implies its past history and cannot be satisfactorily conveyed without making this implicit history explicit."[8] Second, Schumpeter argued that the history of science inspires students and guides tyros to scientific success. Only the sluggish mind fails to experience creative impulses from studying the record of past developments and achievements. Third, "the highest claim that can be made for the history of any science ... is that it teaches us much about the ways of the human mind."[9] In learning the history of science, we learn how the mind addresses, wrestles with, and solves problems. Without this lesson, we cripple ourselves in learning how to solve new problems.

In describing his goal in writing the book, he asserted that

> our main purpose [is] to describe what may be called the process of the Filiation of Scientific Ideas—the process by which men's efforts to understand economic phenomena produce, improve, and pull down analytical structures in an unending sequence.[10]

Schumpeter thus argued that economics is not only a science but that, as a science, it makes progress.

He then briefly offered multiple definitions of science: "any kind of knowledge that has been the object of conscious efforts to improve it," "any field of knowledge that has developed specialized techniques of fact-finding and of interpretation or inference (analysis)," "any field of knowledge in which there are people, so-called research workers or scientists or scholars, who engage in the task of improving upon the existing stock of facts and methods," "refined common sense," and "tooled knowledge."[11]

It mattered not to Schumpeter, nor to economics, whether a new or old theory was right or wrong, useless or useful. Instead, the business of science is to make mistakes, to be wrong, to cast up and cast off screwy ideas. That, along with the funerals of old professors, is how science progresses, as Schumpeter told his students.

Early economists had cramped views of what the economy does and how it does it. They lacked data and sometimes reasoned imperfectly, leading to frequent errors in their work. With improved information, with a broader view of what the economy includes and how it operates, and with mental tools and equipment to help in reasoning, later economists developed better theories.

Schumpeter's reasoning forces the conclusion that all present economic theory may eventually be found inadequate or unsuitable, to be replaced by better formulations. Men such as Smith, Walras, Marshall, Fisher, Schumpeter, Knight, Leontief, Hicks, and Samuelson will populate our future as they have our past and present. With them will come new ideas, improvements resulting from the accumulation of knowledge and the passage of time. Science does not necessarily progress evenly, as with the fabled drip, drip, drip of small scientific contributions. Occasionally, and especially with young sciences like economics, a contributor lays down a large and important foundation stone all at once. As time passes, other scientists assimilate and improve upon that new knowledge. Later, yet another major contribution appears, to be followed by another period of elaboration and refinement. Through this process, science progresses.

The contributor to economic science need not have set out deliberately to advance the science. Many contributions are made by accident, while the scientist is looking for something else; in the act of merely observing the economy, an economist may hit on a fruitful method of analysis. Nor are all contributors seeking knowledge. Someone may be looking for a way to improve the position of his own or his country's treasury or balance of trade, or trying to help a bank or enterprise. A new scientific idea may also arise from idle curiosity. It does not matter how, when, whence, or by whom a contribution to analysis appears. What matters is that when it does, the growing arsenal of science expands.

In another part of the first chapters, Schumpeter raised the problem of ideology and continued addressing it throughout his work. Fundamentally, Schumpeter regarded ideology as a major obstacle to the purity of economic science. His most complete treatment of this problem appeared not in the *History of Economic Analysis* but rather in his 1948 presidential address to the American Economic Association, where he discussed how an economist's politics, philosophy, and vision of the economy can influence his science.[12] If they penetrate and govern economics, then the value of economics is limited and scientific progress in economics is meaningless. Again taking up this problem in his book, Schumpeter argued that "the garb of philosophy is removable."[13] Economics has not been determined by the philosophical views held by economists, nor has it been held hostage to the politics and policies that economists have advocated. Philosophy and politics do not necessarily flow from economics.

But, since economists must begin somewhere, they tend to frame their analysis in terms of their vision of how the economic process operates. Unfortunately, the vision, including the ideology that forms its base, may contain elements of what the economist wants to see, subjecting the vision to nonanalytical and value-tainted beliefs whose origins transcend science. When this happens, science is corrupted by ideology. Schumpeter continued, "Our only comfort is in the fact that there is a large number of phenomena that fail to affect our emotions one way or the other, and that therefore look to one man very much as they do to another."[14] Thus, visions may be insensitive to different personal estimations and vested interests. Another even more important guard against the influence of ideology may assert itself as the rules of science combine to uproot unwitting ideological bias.

> But we also observe that the rules of procedure that we apply in our analytic work are almost as much exempt from ideological influence as vision is subject to it ... these rules, many of which, moreover, are imposed upon us by the scientific practice in fields that are little or not at all affected by ideology, are pretty effective in showing up their misuse ... they tend to crush out ideologically conditioned error from the visions from which we start.[15]

4

Having argued for the importance and relevance of the history of economic science, Schumpeter then turned to that history itself. The first major section of the *History of Economic Analysis*, part 2, marches resolutely from Plato to Adam Smith. Schumpeter did not follow an exact chronological scenario, but he generally went from Greeks to Romans, to the scholastic doctors and philosophers of natural law, to writers and administrators, and finally to the early econometricians, the physiocrats, Turgot, and other continental and English thinkers. The last three chapters of part 2 deal with particular theories, including population, returns to scale, wages and employment, value and money, and finally mercantilism. The degree of detail and attention to scholarship in this, as well as other parts, is awe-inspiring. The day after day of "grind, grind, grind" that Schumpeter complained of in his diary and letters, and the week upon week in the Kress Library, can be understood in light of the final product.

Page after page is half-filled (or more) with footnotes, plumbing highly specialized literature in many languages. He often examined the life and work of minor figures and outlined the ideas of hundreds of contributors, as well as those who commented on them. So detailed is the scrutiny in some instances that one suspects the professor just might be showing off a bit. Schumpeter undoubtedly read and pondered every author he mentioned and much more, but sometimes the scholarship seems a bit thick when a thinner coating would have been more than adequate.

Traditional scholarship usually attributes relatively modest scientific merit and progress to preclassical economic thought. To many, Adam Smith in 1776 was the pioneer or even the "founder" of economics because his book began systematic economic analysis. But Schumpeter denied this, as he must, given his outlook on what constitutes economic science. He credited the ancient Greeks, the schoolmen, and especially the philosophers and practical men of the seventeenth and eighteenth centuries with substantial progress in economics. So great was that progress that it included the analytical foundations upon which *Wealth of Nations* was built. Adam Smith had only to assemble and fit together the analytical parts. Schumpeter therefore demoted Smith's book from the position of pioneering analysis to one of great survey and synthesis.

He viewed the eighteenth-century threesome of Sir William Petty, Richard Cantillon, and François Quesnay as deserving of much of the credit for the development of scientific analysis in economics. Regarding Cantillon as the first to establish the reasoning process for economic analysis, Schumpeter attributed the discovery of the circular flow—the static repetitious economy—to him.

> Cantillon was the first to make this circular flow concrete and explicit, to give us a bird's-eye view of economic life. In other words, he was the first to draw a *tableau economique*. And barring differences that hardly affect essentials, this tableau is the same as Quesnay's, though Cantillon did not actually condense it into a table.[16]

The physiocrats—Quesnay and his disciples—with whom Smith studied in the years before writing *Wealth of Nations*, as well as Anne Robert Turgot, earned high honors from Schumpeter. Even though elements of what the physiocrats developed can also be found in earlier literature, they perceived the fundamental economic problems, including the determination of outputs and inputs in a rational economic process. With economics in an embryonic stage in the mid-eighteenth century, this French contribution in the third quarter gave the budding science an enormous push. Across the Channel and up the coast, Smith quietly inserted much of the analytical substance of the physiocrats into his own book, where it became a part of the English classical tradition.

This discussion in part 2 covered the period up until Adam Smith, the culmination of all that had gone on before. Smith was the synthesizer, the summarizer, and the capstone of all serious thinking about economics before 1776 by such worthies as Turgot, Quesnay, Sir Dudley North, David Hume, and many others. Smith signalled the change from inchoate bits and pieces at the hands of his predecessors to systematic presentation; while his own analytical contribution, which was minor according to Schumpeter, did not effect the change, his great book heralded a new day. In the last chapter of part 2, Schumpeter lavished praise on Sir Josiah Child, Isaac Gervaise, Cantillon, Hume, and others. But, in his evaluation of Smith, Schumpeter concluded: "In *Wealth of Nations*, Adam Smith did not advance beyond Hume but rather stayed below him."[17] It is paradoxical, and deplorable, that Schumpeter did not devote a section and more detailed analysis to Smith. Part 2 goes up to Smith and part 3 starts after him. Comments on Smith, of course, are scattered throughout the book, making him a dominating presence, but Schumpeter never felt it necessary to deal with him separately or to honor him with a systematic discussion. The closest Schumpeter came was the inclusion of an incomplete reader's guide to *Wealth of Nations*.[18]

Near the beginning of the nineteenth century, the English classical school began, initiated not by Smith but on the basis of his 1776 work. This school held sway until after John Stuart Mill made his definitive contribution in his 1848 book, *Principles of Political Economy*. Yet Schumpeter carried the period in part 3 on to 1870, the date of the marginal utility school's entry onto the lists, as well as of Karl Marx. The critical chapter is entitled "Review of the Troops," half of which Elizabeth arranged to have published separately in the *Quarterly Journal of Economics* before the publication of the *History of Economic Analysis*.[19]

In part 3, General Schumpeter marched up and down the ranks of anticipators, Ricardians, and also-rans in England, France, Germany, Italy, and the United States. Here and there he paused to scowl at scruffy shoes, a soiled uniform, a rusty musket, or an unshaven face. Occasionally, too, the general swelled with pride at a few well-turned and articulate troopers or men who showed great promise. He lavished praise on Antoine Augustin Cournot and Heinrich von Thuenen, for example, both well ahead of their times, both propelling economics forward. With the erudition again overwhelming, Schumpeter did not hide an attitude toward ordinary economists akin to what the Olympian gods might display toward mere mortals.

Schumpeter's lack of admiration for the English classical school shines through this section of the book. He regarded their scientific contribution as modest and quickly superseded, but, even more important, he was greatly disturbed by their enlisting primitive theories in their fight for free trade and laissez-faire policies. By doing so, they brought disrepute to economics, sullying the science and setting a pernicious pattern of mixing economics with policy and politics. Schumpeter was especially hard on Ricardo, the one who, with the greatest promise, brought the greatest disappointment.

> Ricardo was not the mind that is particularly interested in either fundamentals or wide generalizations. The comprehensive vision of the universal interdependence of all the elements of the economic system that haunted Thünen probably never cost Ricardo as much as an hour's sleep. His interest was in the clear-cut result of direct and practical significance ... he cut that general system to pieces, bundled up as large parts of it as possible, and put them in cold storage.... He then piled one simplifying assumption upon another until, having really settled everything by these assumptions, he was left with only a few aggregative variables ... so that, in the end, the desired results emerged almost as tautologies.[20]

This method Schumpeter dubbed "the Ricardian vice", an epithet that many others since Ricardo have earned because of their theorizing by assumption. Wassily Leontief called it "implicit theorizing" and tagged the Keynes of *The General Theory*, as well as others, with it. So did Schumpeter. On the same page where he coined the phrase "the Ricardian vice," he noted how, despite great differences in substance, Ricardo and Keynes amazingly resembled one another in method. Ricardo's great contribution had been his leadership, the attribute that Schumpeter often bitterly complained that he lacked. Economists flocked to Ricardo's banner because he espoused causes, such as free trade, that they wanted to believe in. They did not follow Ricardo because of the merit of his analysis but because he believed, and persuaded others to believe, that the analysis yielded policies that served the dominant interests of industrializing England. People accepted Ricardo's theories because those theories supported the policies they favored. But few understood either his theories, his method of theorizing, or the relation of his theories to his policies. Despite this, Ricardo set the tone for the entire group of political economy students in the first half of the nineteenth century. Other economists of the time, who played cameo roles in Schumpeter's review, made modest analytical advances.

With the pieces of the classical system on display, Schumpeter tried to divine the vision embraced by the classical economists. Although Smith was not an English classical economist, he assembled some of the theoretical scaffolding that that school later accepted and completed before nailing its banner to. Ricardo, whose *Principles of Political Economy and Taxation* was published in 1817. Ricardo and his followers contributed the basic theoretical outlook and the method of theorizing—a move beyond Smith. At the same time, Thomas Robert Malthus, differing from Ricardo, also made important contributions. It then remained only for John Stuart Mill in 1848 to produce the full flower of classicism.

On the basis of Mill's work, Schumpeter endeavored to compile the general picture of classical economics, weaving into it the contributions of all the others, including Nassau Senior, Jean-Baptiste Say, John Charles de Sismondi, Claude-Frederic Bastiat, Friedrich List, Johann Karl Rodbertus, and others. The vision of most of these economists centered on a future stationary state toward which the economy moves because of inexorable economic laws. The central element in this process is the circular flow, in which independent competitive markets, propelled by self-interest of participants, function. In constant motion, the economy simply repeats itself in each time period.

The classical school recognized the stationary state as a model, but it also believed that reality would eventually approach it. In the interim, the population increases, leading to increased demand and price for food products. As the demand for food increases, less and less fertile land must be used to produce it, which creates land rent paid to the owner on the more fertile land. As rent share of production increases, the amount of total production going to workers and capitalists declines. Although subsistence puts a limit on what workers receive, worker's incomes must increase because of higher food prices. With rents and wages rising inexorably, profits necessarily will fall. Falling profits ultimately halt savings, investment, and economic growth, culminating in a stationary state. Schumpeter criticized this analysis of the classical school harshly, especially its value theory—the labor theory of value—and the distribution theories that culminate in the stationary state.

5

Part 4, covering the period from 1870 to 1914, is the longest and the last of the three main parts of the *History of Economic Analysis*. Economics, according to Schumpeter, began to come of age as a science in the last quarter of the nineteenth century. With the fireworks ignited by William Stanley Jevons, Carl Menger, and Léon Walras near the end of the century's third quarter, economics jumped ahead and built a solid scientific foundation. In such men, economics found its theme, its methods, and its vision, resolving many, but by no means all, the pressing problems confronting analysis. Some of the chapters in this part, as well as some in part 3, are patchy, clearly indicating that Schumpeter intended further work.

Schumpeter began his discussion with the marginal utility school. Its three codiscoverers remade economics within only a few decades, although Schumpeter singled out Walras as "the greatest economist of all time" and his work as "the Magna Charta of economic theory."[21] But the coming of marginal utility and productivity was not without travail. Many long refused to accept the new ideas. Many more did not or could not understand them. The underlying mathematical structure of neoclassical economics, its reliance on calculus, its ahistorical nature, and the appearance of mechanical arrangement appealed to many. But it turned off and aroused animosity among others. Most of the European heel-draggers, however, were finally won over by the patient, synthesizing work of Alfred Marshall, in appearance nonmathematical but in reality just as mathematical in its own way as Walras's work. John Bates Clark and Irving Fisher created the neoclassical mainstream in the United States.

Much of the neoclassical vision was the same as that of classical and earlier economists. But it surpassed its predecessors by acquiring greater precision, generality, and accuracy. In detail, its theory of distribution, its theory of value and price, and its analysis of markets were neater and cleaner, requiring fewer special explanations. The neoclassical concept of change was much the same as in the science of mechanics. No stationary-state nirvana awaited the economy for the neoclassicists. Instead, economic progress could and would continue indefinitely. Many explanations of cycles came forth during this period, but none were fully satisfactory.

General Schumpeter once again reviewed the troops—a company of younger men from all nations. He inspected every country's garrison of economists and rendered judgment on their scientific stature, paying greatest attention to England's Alfred Marshall, Sweden's Knut Wicksell, and Austria's Eugen von Boehm-Bawerk. But the Americans—John Bates Clark, Irving Fisher, Frank Taussig, and others—also received full attention. Although the stopping point of part 4 is supposed to be 1914, Schumpeter, in order to present a coherent statement, continued beyond that date. Robbing the last part of the book, he dealt here with more recent contributors, especially in the discussion of general economics and equilibrium analysis. Be it noted that Schumpeter wrote nothing about that Austro-American theorist of economic change, Joseph Schumpeter. One problem with this section is that the dividing line in time between the origins and the full development of neoclassical economics is, at best, unclear, with Schumpeter moving it back and forth with each writer under discussion.

Another problem is the choppy and incomplete nature of many chapters. In those dealing with general economics, equilibrium analysis, money, cycles, and credit—some 250 pages—Schumpeter presented basic economic theory, giving us a textbook (old-fashioned by present standards) of economic analysis. Yet often when on the brink of an important disclosure, Schumpeter stopped. A note by Elizabeth then explains the manuscript ended at this point and the book proceeds to another topic. This incompleteness is sometimes annoying and frustrating. He had planned to finish the book in 1950 but, given his penchant for optimistic planning, it probably would not have been completed for several years.

Of all the sections, part 5 is the least complete and informative. It is short, partly a result of Schumpeter's having treated material belonging in this section in part 4. Still, he gave a brief overview, some of which consists of the detailed narrative outline of his five lectures given at the Universidad Autónoma de Mexico in January 1948. This section's brevity, like that of his discussion of consumer behavior and monopolistic competition, limits much of its value. Even his discussion of Keynes, which ends the book, is skimpy, less detailed than Schumpeter's review of *The General Theory*, his obituary of Keynes, and his 1947 articles. Schumpeter does note, highlighting again his own problem, that Keynes, like Ricardo, was a leader. He praised Keynes's leadership qualities and credited him with directing the attention of economists to problems of production and income, even though Schumpeter believed the analysis was wrongheaded.

6

The reviews of the *History of Economic Analysis* were many and generally favorable. Since they came five or six years after Schumpeter's death, many of them reviewed not only the book but also his career. Jacob Viner, in the flagship U.S. economics journal, the *American Economic Review,* reported that Schumpeter wrote, as "the last of the great polymaths, ... by a wide margin, the most constructive, the most original, the most learned, and the most brilliant contribution to the history of the analytical phases of our discipline which has ever been made."[22] Echoing this sentiment, Frank Knight, in the *Southern Economic Journal,* wrote that "this volume suggests the expletive, *c'est formidable!* ... practically every sentence will merit thoughtful attention ... learning and the penetrating reflections ... truly stupendous."[23]

George Stigler, in the *Journal of Political Economy,* said that "the quality of the performance is not rivalled by any other book."[24] Overton Taylor called it "a magnificent work."[25] Lionel Robbins, in the *Economic Journal,* reported it "without serious rival."[26] George Richardson, in an English journal, dubbed it "one of the most important books on economics to be published in the last half century."[27] In *The Canadian Journal of Economics and Political Science,* Vincent Bladen hailed it as "a very important book which no economist ... can afford to neglect."[28]

While recognizing Schumpeter's scholarship, Mark Blaug, a latter-day master of the history of economics and author of a recent standard work, also thinks that Schumpeter failed to sustain his argument for progress in economics.[29] Taking a different approach, Ronald Meek called the book "the great reinterpretation of the history of economic analysis."[30] Unlike most, Meek addressed Schumpeter's views on science, ideology, and scientific progress; he concluded that Schumpeter had failed to prove that science, or at least economics, progresses. Still, he wrote in his review that the book "will remain for many years to come the greatest single quarry of ideas."[31]

Most reviews did not fail to note the book's deficiencies: that it was long winded, filled with idiosyncrasies and prejudices, overambitious, arrogant, and pretentious. Despite Schumpeter's call for a pure history of economic analysis, the book is replete with politics, sociology, philosophy, and obiter dicta. Some argued that Schumpeter vastly underestimated Smith and the English classical school.

One question arises in view of the anti-English attitude that Schumpeter manifested in the late 1930s when he returned again to the subject of the history of economics. This outlook is especially noticeable in his diary, but close friends were also aware of it. In the *History of Economic Analysis,* Schumpeter evaluated Adam Smith, the English classical school, Alfred Marshall, and John Maynard Keynes rather more harshly than did the conventional wisdom of his day. One may therefore ask: Did his attitude toward the English in the war and postwar period influence that evaluation? The answer is no.

Schumpeter's evaluation of the great English economists predated the 1940s, with much of it going back to the second decade of the century, the World War I period, when Schumpeter was pro-British. His evaluation followed from his general scientific stance. If the question is rephrased to read "Did Schumpeter's Austrian and continental background influence his attitude toward some British economists?" then, the answer is yes. His economic *weltanschauung* was general-equilibrium analysis, utility theory of value, anti-utilitarianism, and purely scientific outlook, none of which were congenial to the English. They were pragmatic, utilitarian, favored partial equilibrium, cost-of-production value theory, and a policy-oriented climate. Still, he did rate high some Englishmen, such as Nassau Senior, William Stanley Jevons, and Francis Ysidro Edgeworth. And he recognized the genius and the leadership of Smith, Ricardo, Marshall, and Keynes even as he expressed doubts about their economics.

Although the reviewers of the *History of Economic Analysis* sometimes differed in their criticisms, seeing a variety of weaknesses, they all agreed on some fundamental points. All lamented that Schumpeter had not lived to finish the book, and all considered the work to be a great book and the product of genius. Schumpeter, from his Olympian heights in heaven, would have been pleased with the reviews but not entirely satisfied. The fact that the published book was unfinished would have annoyed him because it gave reviewers the opportunity to make condescending remarks like "had he finished it, he would have done thus and so ... it would be better had he lived to complete the work ... he would have revised this or that before sending it to the publisher." He would have been harsher on himself than any reviewer, unforgiving of even first- or second-draft inadequacies.

Despite the overwhelming accolades, the *History of Economic Analysis* did not convince the economics profession of its main contentions. In economic method, which he strongly emphasized, Schumpeter suffered the fate of being ignored. His evaluations of individual economists and groups of economists are universally respected and often noted, but not always agreed with. In other instances, Schumpeter only emphasized the increasingly accepted view. For example, the high position of Léon Walras was already established when he wrote *History of Economic Analysis*, in part because of his own earlier work. The *History of Economic Analysis* only solidified that position. His praise of Augustin Cournot, Heinrich von Thuenen, and William Stanley Jevons helped to rescue them from obscurity, but their reputations would still have been recognized without Schumpeter's help. Schumpeter's high regard for the Greeks, the scholastics, and the natural law philosophers similarly helped to secure their places, but again, not far from the positions they would have occupied in any case.

His more negative evaluation of Adam Smith, David Ricardo, and the English classical school, as well as of Alfred Marshall and Lord Keynes, has indeed forced a harder look at those men. Before Schumpeter's work, these men were the towering giants of economics, held in high esteem by almost everyone. Still, his analysis did not reduce them to the place that Schumpeter had consigned to them. Although they are now a bit less god-like to most economists, they remain among the greatest in the pantheon of economics. Where Schumpeter differed from the conventional wisdom in his evaluation of economists, he moved the conventional wisdom a bit, but his work did not cause a revolutionary shifting of positions in the firmament of the history of economics.

Yet, because of his work, many economists and social scientists today regard Schumpeter as the great and idiosyncratic historian of economics. His posthumous book continues to be a landmark in the field while his 1914 book, translated into English and still studied, is looked upon as the work of a prodigy. All authors of books in the history of economics published since 1954 have referred to the *History of Economic Analysis* and related their books to the work of Schumpeter. The book represents a degree and kind of scholarship to which all other writers on the subject aspire but have never matched.

Notes

1   Published as a part of *Schriften des sozialwissenschaftlichen akademischen Vereins en Czernowitz* (Writings of the Academic Social Science Club in Czernowitz) (Munich and Leipzig, Germany: Duncker and Humblot. 1915).
2   *Grundriss der Sozialwissenschaft* (Tuebingen, Germany: J.C.B Mohr [Paul Siebeck] 1914), 19-124. The English translation was published by Oxford University Press, New York, in 1954.
3   (New York: Oxford University Press, 1954). In 1987 it was still in print.
4   The entire manuscript, from handwritten foolscap of the very first draft through the clean copy sent to and edited by the publisher, is in twenty-five boxes in the Schumpeter papers in the Harvard University Archives.
5   Warren Samuels, editor, *Research in the History of Economic Thought and Methodology* (Greenwich, Conn.: JAI Press, 1987), 93-116.
6   *History of Economic Analysis*, ix.
7   Ibid., 3.
8   Ibid., 4.
9   Ibid., 5.
10   Ibid., 6.
11   Ibid., 7, all quotations.
12   "Science and Ideology," *American Economic Review* 40 (1949): 345-59.
13   *History of Economic Analysis*, 31.
14   Ibid., 43.
15   Ibid., 43.
16   Ibid., 222.
17   Ibid., 367.
18   Ibid., 186-93.
19   *Quarterly Journal of Economics* 65 (1951): 140-80.
20   *History of Economic Analysis*, 472-3.
21   Ibid., 827, 242.
22   *American Economic Review* 64 (1954): 895.
23   *Southern Economic Journal* 21 (1955): 261.
24   *Journal of Political Economy* 82 (1954): 344.
25   *Review of Economics and Statistics* 37 (1955): 12.
26   *Economic Journal* 69 (1955): 3.
27   *Oxford Economic Papers* ns. 7 (1955): 136.
28   *Canadian Journal of Economics and Political Science* 22 (1956): 103.
29   *Economic Theory in Retrospect*, 3rd. edition (Cambridge, England: Cambridge University Press, 1978).
30   *Economics and Ideology and Other Essays* (London: Chapman and Hall, 1967).
31   *Scottish Journal of Political Economy* 4 (1957): 17.

12

Reunion with the *Hasen* (1948-1950)

Disaster struck the Schumpeters in 1948 when Elizabeth learned she had breast cancer. A favorable prognosis followed surgery, but now the dread possibility of recurrence cast a shadow over a shaken Schumpeter. More forceful than the gradual aging, more pointed than reaching the age of retirement, this event reminded him of his own mortality and plunged him into depression, even wringing from him comments about "voluntary death." He seemed to have some premonition that the end was near even though he had no major ailment.

Despite his concern for Elizabeth and his own physical worries, Schumpeter continued to work hard, even accelerating his writing. He struggled with his book on the history of economics, and puzzlement over economic theory still occupied much of his time. But he was also writing papers, on entrepreneurial history, Vilfredo Pareto, the Communist Manifesto, the historical approach to business cycles, and the march toward socialism. He gave more seminars and lectures, committed himself to a European trip in 1950, made plans for more books and articles. Death came suddenly, unexpectedly, as he prepared to leave Taconic to go to Chicago for a lecture series.

1

In the early 1930's Elizabeth had developed diabetes, yet she managed to control its pernicious effects through the regular use of insulin so that it never became a disabling disease. But in the fall of 1948 she discovered she had

219

something far more dangerous: breast cancer. Her doctor, Clark Peterson of Lakeville, recommended radical mastectomy. Elizabeth entered the hospital in Sharon, Connecticut, only a few miles from Taconic, for the operation on 15 September 1948. Luckily, the surgery resulted in a satisfactory prognosis. For the moment, at least, she seemed to be out of danger, but the Damocles sword of malignancy now hung over her head, a sword that descended less than five years later.

The appearance of a life-threatening disease naturally created consternation in the Schumpeter household. Joseph was greatly disturbed, with the event causing him to evaluate seriously his relationship with Elizabeth, something he had avoided for years. He now realized how much he depended on her, used her, and had taken her for granted. She had served him, shielded him from the world, and lifted nearly all the ordinary burdens of daily living from him, sacrificing her own professional career on the altar of his personal convenience and his scholarship. Elizabeth had provided the order, the organization, and the framework of his life. He could barely survive without her since she handled all the details of everyday life that occupy most people, excusing him from everything except his intellectual labors. No housework or household tasks, no telephone, no shopping, no errands, no driving, no money problems, no concern with clothes, no community chores, and no interruptions distracted him. Even their limited social life was completely arranged by Elizabeth.

Now, confronted with her mortality, Joseph was shaken and even more depressed, forced once again to deal with the possible loss of a wife. Shortly after he learned of the diagnosis of cancer, he recorded in his diary the following remarks:

> The lightning from blue skies has struck me. Note that 1.) the sky was clear. 2.) I completely depend upon Elizabeth. And that my feelings were not felt and even those expressed were but a sham and a deception. That she gave me more than I her, and that I actually did not know it. 3.) still beneath this there is a deep attachment, the product of 11 years together. 4.) I could not go on without her. All that is only half whining. Now suddenly everything becomes serious. Since the end approaches anyhow and nothing enjoyable will happen between now and then, it is irrational to continue to live.

Elizabeth's illness clearly frightened Schumpeter. Despite his clandestine communion with his second wife and the spiritual succor she provided, he also needed the material ministrations of Elizabeth. And, in his own way, he loved and devoted himself to Elizabeth, with mutual trust and interests cementing their partnership. Now that her life was in jeopardy, he came as close as he could to feeling remorse for his lack of consideration for her over the years. Without her, he believed he could not survive. Friends and colleagues noted that Schumpeter was greatly distressed by his wife's illness and became uncommonly solicitous in all matters concerning her during his last year and a half.[1]

Joseph poured the depths of his feelings into his diary. typically seeing the bleakness of the situation. On 14 September 1948, he wrote:

> Tomorrow is the operation. In this book there is little about the whole matter and the bravery with which the courageous woman faces her ordeal. And this is the beginning of the end. I have no desire to philosophize and to write about it. It is just too serious. One does not philosophize on a sinking ship. And also there is not much to plan any more. Just the little papers and the necessary correspondence. And now what do you have? What do you want? What is so unbelievable is the emptiness and eeriness. Is death avoidable? If it is not, then it is clear that there is nothing. Why not go yourself? I will not feel sorry for Elizabeth when she has to depart. All good is done and past for her and for me.

He soon again lamented the problem of Elizabeth's health. Under the heading of "The Knock on the Nose," he wrote of "This poor child....[and her] failed [first] marriage ... [then] intellectual life ... Japan [book] failure." He described her joy when working in her nursery, but added next "And then that [cancer]... Poor child, and God and the ladies [Herrinen, his second wife and mother], Let me help her and not to fall and be a burden."

At the end of 1948 and beginning of 1949—the time near the end of his term as president of the American Economic Association—Schumpeter remained terribly depressed. He derived some consolation from the reception of his presidential address, but then his thoughts darkened, as he wrote:

> Thank you, Hasen, for supporting me and for one of the richest presents. Everyone rose for my presidential address. The whole of the Cleveland ballroom audience rose and gave me applause. That was not poor and that was not small. And yet so undeserved. Thank you, Hasen. O give me strength O Gott and Hasen. And let me slowly get accustomed to the idea of a voluntary death. Should I say, help me to a voluntary death? O Gott and Hasen, thank you. Bless 1949 if you want to. Not much more than a year can I expect.

The word suicide appears nowhere in his diaries, but it was certainly on his mind many times during this period under the guise of "voluntary death." In his musings about death he frequently commented on the uselessness of life. He also greatly feared the prospect of illness, of becoming a burden, and especially of being unable to work. Such an outlook was in keeping with his cultural heritage, partly arising from his experiences with some turn-of-the-century intellectual Europeans who escaped unbearable tensions through suicide. But, paradoxically, despite his obsession with death and dark hints of suicide, Schumpeter continued to work, to plan, and to look ahead.

All through 1949, he frantically struggled to complete the history of economics manuscript, which was still far from finished. Even though he had written that he could expect not much more than a year, an enigmatic statement, the meaning of which is not clear, Schumpeter took on additional chores that would require performance in 1950 and years beyond. He spoke to his more intimate friends, including Arthur Smithies, of even longer-term projects, including work in cultural, economic, and social history. In a deep sense, then, resignation and suicide were contrary to Schumpeter's basic nature. He remained dedicated to opening doors, a task that required his continued efforts. He was just not the type to give up or throw in the towel when things became difficult. This trait is nowhere more obvious than in his work—witnessed by his continual plugging away at his writing when the end results seemed so elusive. He exhibited this same kind of staying power in living his life which must have seemed an endless obstacle course of disappointment and despair.

2

Despite the contradictory thoughts of life and suicide, Schumpeter's last year was one of his busiest. His stint as president of the American Economic Association ended with his presidential address in late December 1948. But, instead of slowing down to deal with the personal problems beseiging him, he picked up the pace with regard to his research, publication activity, and his teaching. As always, his teaching was taxing, even though he taught no new courses. He offered the customary advanced economic theory course in the spring of 1949 and then the other half of the course in the fall. In the spring he also taught the history and literature of economics as well as the economics of socialism. In the fall term, he added business cycles and economic forecasting to his schedule. Along with these five courses, he kept up his usual heavy consultation and advising schedule.

In the midst of teaching, he found time to bring to fruition eight articles and one book review in 1948 and 1949. Yet they were not his principal research and writing projects. His main task, as always in that last decade, was his work on the history of economics. Still not even close to being finished, he was on the downhill side of it and had produced mountains of manuscript. Aside from the history of economics, other topics he worked on suggest that some of his thinking that last year also revolved around the future of capitalism. And, as always, he spent some time in the vain hope that his theoretical work, forever on his mind, would jell. He also devoted some casual thought to his money book, safely tucked away in a trunk awaiting his attention, nor did he neglect his speaking engagements. In the fall and early winter of 1949 especially, he worked on lectures that were scheduled for January 1950.[2].

One of his most important pieces from this period was his special preface for the third edition of *Capitalism, Socialism and Democracy*, published in 1949. The publisher, Harper and Brothers, prepared this volume specifically for England. Schumpeter's new preface dealt primarily with socialist developments in England, developments he regarded as confirming his analysis: "This situation [in England] seems to me to bear out my diagnosis of 1942 and to verify, so far as verification is possible in such matters, the arguments by which it was arrived at."[3] When the general third edition was published in 1950 in the United States, after Schumpeter's death, the new preface occupied the penultimate position, instead of being in the front with the others.

Further evidence that the future of capitalism greatly concerned him was his continued interest in Marx. In the University of Chicago economics journal, he wrote an article, entitled "The Communist Manifesto in Sociology and Economics," commemorating 100 years of that document.[4] Schumpeter was respectful of Marx in outlining succinctly the substance and content of the *Manifesto*, but he pointed out that Marx had not yet studied economics when he wrote it. Marx's economic training came later, while he was studying in the British Museum and in his tiny apartment in Dean Street. Thus, the full analysis of capitalism's fate and the reasons for it had to wait. Schumpeter, however, hailed the *Manifesto* as possessing the intuition, vision, and prelude that Marx later brought to the larger canvas he painted.

Still another piece, this one still unpublished, showed his concern with the broad outlines of capitalism. In Taconic, the Institute of World Affairs, a private educational organization directed by William Yandell Elliott of Harvard's Government Department, regularly invited scholars and students from around the country to attend its summer courses and seminars. For several years, Schumpeter had made the short walk to the institute, sometimes on several occasions, where he gave an impromptu or informal talk on whatever he happened to be thinking about, picking up cigarette money for his trouble. His 29 August 1949 lecture, given at the Hadden House Library, was entitled the "Policies of Laborism." His comments on English laborism reflected his unhappiness at the road England was travelling at the time. He worried not so much about England as about the possibility that England's course might point the way for capitalism around the world. In notes taken by Peter Oglobin, a Harvard student, Schumpeter is reported as saying:[5]

I advance the proposition that not imperialism, but *laborism* is the last stage of capitalism. Laborism signifies here that capitalist society in which the labor interest is dominant... In the laborist society, other interest groups count only insofar as they serve indirectly labor interests. Such a society is a dress rehearsal for socialism. Authorities level high incomes, control labor and capital markets, and focus spending on the support of the working class.

Rounding out his thinking about capitalism and socialism in 1949 was an article entitled "English Economists and the State-Managed Economy," also published in the Chicago journal.[6]. This article reviewed six recent books by English economists—A. S. J. Baster, Sir Oliver Frank, Roy Harrod, John Jewkes, James Edward Meade, and Lionel Robbins. Rather than reviewing them one at a time, Schumpeter discussed them as a group, concentrating more on their subjects than on the books as such. His point was not so much that these were bad books, but rather that they did not make the contribution needed. He concluded by saying:

> Much though I regret to have to say so regarding the work of fellow-economists... there seems to be hardly any writer who has built the analytic complement of all this or has made any comprehensive attempt to add to our analytical engine the new parts which it requires.[7]

Then, reflecting his immersion in the history of economics, he added in a footnote:

> This shows that analytic work is not... exclusively conditioned by the analyst's environment.... Leontief's work has been done in and for the United States, although, so far as practical application is concerned, there is more need and scope for it in England.

In addition to all this work, he wrote two articles dealing with the historical approach to economics. One, entitled "Economic Theory and Entrepreneurial History," was a chapter in the book *Change and the Entrepreneur,* the first fruit of the Harvard Research Center in Entrepreneurial History.[8] Schumpeter's chapter surveyed the history of the concept of the entrepreneur and treated some aspects of the history of enterprise; it also commented on the role of economic theory in entrepreneurial history:

> In the handling of old and new facts, the historian will gain from keeping in touch with theorists. Neither group should ever be distant from one another—but here the promise from collaboration is particularly great for both parties.[9]

The other piece was a paper, entitled "The Historical Approach to the Analysis of the Business Cycle," delivered at a meeting of the Universities-

National Bureau Conference on Business Cycle Research, 25-27 November 1949 in New York. In it, Schumpeter stressed at the outset that he was not recommending historical analysis in preference to theoretical and statistical work, but in addition to them. "Economic life is a unique process that goes on in historical time and in a disturbed environment," he said. He then argued that the "darkest hues of cyclical depression" were due to adventitious circumstances and that such circumstances and their consequences could be eliminated without disrupting the cyclical mechanism itself.[10]

Several other pieces round out the year's publications. His obituary of Wesley Mitchell for the *Quarterly Journal of Economics* did not appear until the year following.[11] His review of Elmer Bratt's business cycle textbook for the *Journal of the American Statistical Association* also did not appear until 1950.[12] Schumpeter also wrote a centennial piece about Vilfredo Pareto, the great Italian economist and sociologist.[13] Pareto and Walras were always closely related to one another in Schumpeter's mind. In the fall of 1949, he also promised an article to *Foreign Affairs* that would discuss the future of capitalism. The substance of that article would probably have reflected his lecture at the Institute of World Affairs in Taconic in August and his paper for the *Journal of Political Economy* in October.

3

In addition to his many articles, Schumpeter addressed several groups in 1949. In early March, he spoke to the Harvard Club of Philadelphia on the topic of "New Creeds and Old Facts." He talked to the Boston Economics Club about business cycles in mid-March, and then he addressed the Choate Club on the "Decay of Capitalism" a week later. Next, he spoke to the Yale Graduate Students Club in April. But he refused to testify before a congressional committee on behalf of the Economists National Committee on Monetary Policy, telling Walter Spahr that he would not be good at it because he feared that his statement would reflect a low regard for policitians. His audience, he knew, would soon suspect that he considered them to be morons.[14] Later in the year, on 30 November, he lectured on the "Inadequacy of Economics" to the Graduate Student's Club, six weeks after speaking at Radcliffe College.

During this time Schumpeter also continued to act as unofficial host to visiting foreign economists. A bumper crop of distinguished visitors graced Harvard that fall, and Schumpeter was in the thick of it. John R. Hicks, a leading English economist and the 1972 Nobel prize winner, presented a paper at Harvard in 1949. After taking Hicks to lunch, Schumpeter later introduced him at the seminar. In his introduction Schumpeter uncharacteristically expressed admiration for Hicks's older nonmathematical, but tightly reasoned, theory book, *The Theory of Wages* (1929), in preference to the new mathematical one, *Value and Capital* (1945). Hicks surprised Schumpeter by agreeing. Schumpeter also spent time with Sir Austin Robinson, secretary of the Royal Economic Society and another leading English economist, during his visit to Cambridge in September 1949. He also introduced Margaret Cole, widow of the eminent English historian, economist, and sociologist, at a Radcliffe event on 10 October. François Perroux, the illustrious French economist whom Schumpeter admired, also visited Harvard in November 1949.

November 1949, also saw a visit from Erich Schneider, then of Kiel University in Germany but formerly a student and colleague of Schumpeter's at Bonn. I remember meeting Dr. Schneider and watching him with Schumpeter in the seminars and casual gatherings around Littauer. Dr. Schneider, a leading German economist of the day, followed Schumpeter around like a little puppydog, in the fashion of European assistants to the master professor. Schneider tried to persuade Schumpeter to visit Germany in 1950, but he refused, giving Schneider the impression that he just didn't want to see the changes that he knew had occurred in Germany and Europe. Even so, Schumpeter was tentatively planning to return to Europe, but not Germany, in 1950. He would visit Paris in August for his installation as the first president of the newly organized International Economic Association.

Economists from around the world had founded the International Economic Association in the late 1940s. By 1949, it was 5,300-members strong. Gottfried Haberler represented the American Economic Association to this new group, which was temporarily headquartered in Paris in association with the United Nations Educational, Scientific, and Cultural Organization. In 1949, the IEA nominating committee named Schumpeter as president, Jacques Rueff of France as vice-president, and Roland Walker of Australia as second vice-president. Nomination in such groups is tantamount to election.[15] Another singular honor for Schumpeter, his selection signified he held the leading reputation among economists the world over.

4

Along with several articles, many speeches, and frequent hosting activities, Schumpeter, in the fall of 1949, mapped out an elaborate plan of work that would require years to complete. His many plans in his personal writings belie earlier diary comments, made in deep despair, about voluntary death. His immediate task was to finish the *History of Economic Analysis*. With a great deal of manuscript either at the typist, ready to go, or just returning, he expected to complete the book in 1950. But given his propensity to underestimate the time necessary to finish projects, this time table was wishful thinking and reflected more his desperate hurry to be done with it and get on with other projects. During 1949, he concentrated on the first and last parts of the book, the "Scope and Method" and the incomplete "Sketch of Modern Developments." He also wrote or revised much of the sections dealing with partial and general-equilibrium analysis and the production function. In that one year, he probably wrote manuscript that totalled about three hundred pages, nearly a quarter of the final book.

He also worked occasionally on his theory book in late 1949. Having accepted that he could not complete a book on theory in his lifetime, he continued to concentrate on at least producing a sketch of it—his PV, or preliminary volume. But even this sketch kept him buffaloed all during the 1940s. He would work on it for a week or a month, then abandon it for other projects. He sometimes thought he was making progress, but he always came up short. He described his work to Arthur Smithies in an undated letter in the mid-1940s:

> Two months were real work and spelled progress in what I described to interested publishers as a book that should do from my standpoint what Keynes' General Theory did from his (which Washington agency now prosecutes dishonest advertising?) But then I had to break off to invest the remaining two months in my History, damn and blast it, which just won't shape decently.[16]

Still, he kept at it. On 8 November 1949, he wrote Albert Hart to explain that his "preliminary volume" would require another year or two for completion; but when finished, it would "block out the essential ideas which I believe necessary to a scientific picture of the scientific process." Schumpeter mentioned no title in this letter, but he was obviously referring to the project that had haunted him for more than a decade, *The Theoretical Apparatus of Economics*. Paradoxically, when he wrote this statement to Hart, Schumpeter had written none of such a book, which was to be his summary of a new theory that he would not live to discover. Only scattered notes on theory, and no coherent manuscript, are in Schumpeter's papers.[17]

Even if he had lived, he would probably never have finished even a preliminary volume of a theory book. He was looking for something that probably does not exist (at least no one else has yet discovered it): a formal, at least partly determinate and mathematical model similar to that of Walras that would also be dynamic and evolutionary, close to reality but abstract, into which he would pour economic and social history and fact. He wanted much, too much, and his continued attempts to develop a theory that might never be found made him feel like a failure. Try as he might, he could not come up with what he had so long searched for.

In the history of economics, he was progressing well, despite his many negative comments, because this project entailed reading, remembering, and fitting pieces together. In teaching he also had no difficulty. But, in making an original contribution, that which he most wanted to do, he was failing. He continued to hope for a breakthrough—a burst of insight that would light up the entire topic, but that guiding light never switched on for him, nor has it done so for anyone else since. Part of the paradox surrounding Schumpeter is this failure to discover a nonexistent theory in a futile search that his own pronouncements about fertility of the "sacred decade" and noncreative nature of subsequent work had amply warned him. His continued effort, however, attests to the persistence and near masochism of a man who will not give up and repeatedly pounds his head against an enigmatic wall.

A week after writing to Albert Hart about progress on the theory book, Schumpeter wrote to his colleague Seymour Harris about yet another project—the long-contemplated money book. Harris had been pressing Schumpeter for such a book, hoping to publish it in the McGraw-Hill Economic Series. On 16 November 1949, Schumpeter wrote Harris to say he was working on a book called the *Theory of Money and Banking*, but he could not guarantee it would be suitable for the McGraw-Hill series. Schumpeter claimed his deadline for this book was the summer of 1951, which implied that he would write it during the winter and spring of 1950-51, a wildly optimistic judgment. There is no evidence that he had done any work on it other than that which he had written in the 1920s and revised in the early 1930s. He referred to his many other projects as the reason for not having finished the book earlier, telling Harris he had been "hunting several hares at the same time." In fact, he was nowhere near completing this project. He had some manuscript in German and extensive notes in German and shorthand dating back to the 1920s and 1930s. He had largely finished an inadequate theoretical monograph on money by the early 1930s and had been fussing with it ever since. But to complete a book, he would have to start from scratch in English. Complicating this task was the fact that his ideas on money were so complex and so subtle that it seems highly improbable he could have finished it in less than several years.

Schumpeter's letters to both Hart (on PV) and Harris (on money) contain a certain amount of bravado and a lot of wishful thinking. Still deeply immersed in his history of economics book, he could not possibly have written two more major works within the next two years. But, whatever his reasons for claiming he would do just that, these letters clearly indicate that his contemplation of "voluntary death" resulted from his deep depression, and that most of the time he continued with planning a busy and productive future.

Schumpeter had many other plans beyond the three books he was writing on. He wanted to do something with the two series of lectures given in 1948 in Mexico, but he never touched his notes after he came back. Elizabeth later incorporated some of them into the *History of Economic Analysis*, but other notes remain unpublished. Another major project still gathering dust was the book he planned to fashion from the shorthand notes and typescripts of his 1941 Lowell lectures. Other projected writings included many essays mentioned in his journal: "An essay on interest," "Essay: Education down... We breed ourselves down, We educate ourselves down, We plan for a world of idiots," and "Essay: The Justice Racket." His diary contains so many essay ideas, and so few of them ever came into being, that we can only regard them as flashes of thought, not serious intentions. On several occasions Schumpeter also mentioned writing an autobiography, even going so far as to include two pages of scattered notes in one diary notebook. To friends, he mentioned plans for other studies that he wanted to do, including a book on sociology to deal with the broad aspects of economic and social affairs, a cultural history, a book on banking, some other sociological studies of an historical nature— probably an extension of his analysis of imperialism and social classes—a book on the theory of aesthetics, and several novels.[18]

5

Another project undertaken shortly before his death was his agreement to deliver a series of six lectures in Chicago in January 1950. Invited by the Charles Walgreen Foundation at the University of Chicago, Schumpeter decided to discuss "American Institutions and Economic Progress." The University of Chicago Press asked him to send the manuscript he would lecture from so that it could initiate processing the book. Schumpeter replied that there would be no manuscript until after the lectures, but he agreed to let the press publish the speeches if he turned them into a book or if they were recorded by someone at the lecture and edited. The first lecture was to be given on 9 January 1950—the day after Schumpeter died. No manuscript of the speeches exists, but an inkling of what he planned to say is contained in a typescript that I found in the Harvard University Archives. These notes, a highly summarized view of his lecture plan, have since been published in a prominent German economic theory journal.[19] In the first lecture, he intended to discuss factors of economic change, followed by an examination of institutional change. The third lecture was to deal with the interaction between factors of economic and institutional change, while the fourth would treat the politics and policies of groups and classes. The fifth lecture would deal with the personal element and the elements of chance in which he would outline the principle of indeterminateness. The last lecture's title was "How Capitalism Created and Destroyed a Civilization."

Schumpeter's last actual writing is now included in the third edition of *Capitalism, Socialism and Democracy*. Originally presented as a paper on 30 December 1949 at the American Economic Association meeting in New York, "The March into Socialism" was first published in the *American Economic Review*.[20] Elizabeth later suggested its inclusion in the book, largely because its subject seemed so appropriate with the topics discussed in the book. The burden of his argument centered around the socialist impulse provided by inflation. After briefly restating his position that observable trends indicate the triumph of socialism because no one wishes to defend capitalism, he concluded:

> A state of perennial inflationary pressure will have, qualitatively, all the effects of weakening the social framework of society and of strengthening subversive tendencies (however carefully wrapped up in 'liberal' phrases) that every competent economist is in the habit of attributing to more spectacular inflations.[21]

At the end of the article, in paragraphs written by Elizabeth from her memory and his notes, Schumpeter, remaining convinced to the end that socialism, under whatever name, would replace capitalism, predicted:

> Perennial inflationary pressure can play an important part in the eventual conquest of the private-enterprise economy by the bureaucracy... A situation may well arise in which most people will consider complete planning as the smallest of possible evils. They will certainly not call it Socialism or Communism... under the circumstances, capitalism (the free-enterprise system) as a scheme of values, a way of life, and a civilization may not be worth bothering about.[22]

6

Based on the writings of his last few years, some scholars have called attention to Schumpeter's apparent tendency late in life to emphasize historical research and to downplay mathematics, stating that he displayed the common pattern of emphasizing mathematics in youth and history in maturity. One of his last papers, given in November 1949 at the National Bureau of Economic Research and entitled "The Historical Approach to the Analysis of Business Cycles," seemed to show that he viewed historical research as more promising than some mathematical models of the economy. Supporting this idea is the first version of the introductory chapter to his *History of Economic Analysis*, called "Some Questions of Principle," noted earlier, in which Schumpeter wrote:

I wish to testify to my belief that if for the training of an economist I had to choose one of the three fundamental fields to the exclusion of the other two, my choice would not be theory but economic history. Economic life is a unique and irreversible process in historic time. Familiarity not only with the great contours of past development but also an adequate complement of details is hence the first prerequisite for understanding the problems of our own time and for competence in economic matters in general. These contours and those details are pregnant with important truth about economic life which, though refractory to cut-and-dried formulation, may convey to us an intimate sense of organic necessities which we can never derive from mere theorems.[23]

Did Schumpeter change his mind about the importance and applicability of mathematics to economics? The above quotation would indicate that he did, but in fact he never rejected the importance of mathematics in economic analysis. For him, mathematics, history, and sociology all play essential roles in economics. When he began writing, he endeavored in his first paper to promote the use of mathematics in economics. But bear in mind the date— 1906. At that time, there were few mathematical economists, little interest in the subject, and either indifference or great opposition to the use of mathematics from the majority of people in the profession. In Austria and Germany especially, history and sociology were in vogue. Schumpeter was a voice in the wilderness, crying for more rigor in economic theory.

By the late 1940s, mathematics and statistics were beginning to convert the economics profession into a branch of applied mathematics. No longer did economists need to be convinced of the importance of rigorous theory. Econometrics, which Schumpeter had helped to launch in the 1920s and 1930s, was not only accepted but was capturing the profession. The growing acceptance of mathematics caused many to regard it as *the* answer, needing nothing else, and many students no longer thought of history as relevant. Schumpeter always believed that his American students especially knew little history and, more importantly, lacked a sense of history, which he saw as a cultural deficiency. The new breed of economists had all but read economic sociology and history out of the profession. Hence, the Schumpeter of the late 1940s, believing exactly what he had forty years earlier, raised the cry for history and sociology; this meant, paradoxically, that he seemed to play down mathematics. But, in fact, he was determined that no doors ever be closed, and he continued as the reverse chameleon of his early days. Evidence of his continuing interest in mathematics comes from his personal agenda of study. In his last years, his little appointment book and diary contain notations about what he was studying, virtually on a day-by-day basis. The most frequent entries, made almost daily, were math, brush, his, and PV. Grk also appeared frequently, and mat or matrices, a special form of mathematics, appeared occasionally.

Among the attitudes Schumpeter railed at most was the belief of many students and colleagues that some single element—technique, insight, theory, fact, institutional arrangement—was *the* answer. Neat, simple, determinate mathematical models, devoid of empirical and historical content, annoyed him: he viewed them as toys, not science. Science knows no simple answers. He referred to Harvard's Keynesian teaching as the "Keynesian nursery" in which the new economics could be learned in a fortnight.[24] In reality, his opposition to simple mathematical models was not opposition to mathematics or even mathematical models, but rather opposition to their abuse and misuse. He viewed mathematics in economics as a tool, a device to enhance insight and productivity, not a plaything to impress journal editors, puzzle colleagues, dazzle students, or justify a pet policy.

In some minor economic topics, Schumpeter did shift his position slightly late in life. He came to recognize that large-scale enterprise could innovate, whereas earlier he had regarded the innovating entrepreneur as a special kind of free-wheeling person, never a corporate bureaucrat. Accumulating evidence to the contrary convinced him of his error. He also saw that the existence of innovating corporations implied that capitalism might be able to progress and survive longer. If modern corporations could continue to produce the new products and new methods that comprise the lifeblood of economic change, they could delay, but not change, the fate of capitalism. Despite this shift, Schumpeter never really changed his mind about the future of capitalism; he still maintained that socialism would replace it at some future time. It would appear after capitalism had trustified, slowed down by high taxation, regulations, and government intervention, requiring, as Schumpeter said, "an oxygen tent" to keep it alive. His belief was supported by the fact that capitalism following the First World War was increasingly trustified and government intervention had risen during the century.

In a sense, however, Schumpeter waffled on the precise nature of capitalism's replacement. In addition to centralized socialism, he suggested the possibility that some countries might develop a system along the lines of the papal encyclical, *Quadragesimo Anno*, while in other countries some kind of corporate state might inherit the mantle of capitalism. At some point in capitalism's evolution, he believed that control and decision making would change from private to public hands. Although most people might continue to call this different system capitalism, guided capitalism, mixed capitalism, or whatever, it was really no longer a capitalist economic system. Schumpeter called it socialism. But mostly, he regarded all this as quibbling and semantics. In "The March into Socialism," his last paper, he argued that a situation in which public planning dominated would eventually emerge. Although perhaps not called socialism, it would represent control of the economy by the public sector.

7

With his professional life proceeding at full tilt in 1949, and filled with a myriad of prospective plans for the future, Schumpeter's interior life still showed no real change in his final year. He continued to depend heavily on his *Hasen*, although he more frequently mentioned God in his prayers, entreaties, and expressions of gratitude in 1949. While many statements were open avowals of dependence, trust, and faith, still his devotions remained in the closet. He seemed to be even more devoted to his mother in 1949 than in previous years, mentioning her more often in diary entries and remembering her birthday, namesday, and death day. His worship of the *Hasen* also continued to entail work with his second wife's diary. One of the extra comments he frequently entered in his recopy of Annie's diary was the motto "Und sie ist mein Weib und wir gehoren zusammen" (And she is my wife and we belong together). But on 29 April 1949, he followed it with the phrase "und vielleicht auch im Grabe" (and perhaps even in the grave). After that date, he copied these two phrases combined in her diary until his trip to the National Bureau Conference in New York in late November, 1949, six weeks before he died. He never resumed work on her diary after that trip, but a gap of several months in his recopying task was common in his last years. Clearly, to the end Schumpeter remained obsessed with his mother and second wife in a way that transcended filial and conjugal devotion.

He acted on this devotion in 1949 after hearing from Annie's brother, Willy Reisinger, who had been a German soldier during the war. He and Willy reached an agreement wherein the Reisinger family could use Schumpeter's mother's plot to bury its family members; in return, the Reisingers would take care of her grave, which had deteriorated over the years. Since Annie's death, Schumpeter had been helping the Reisingers financially. During his last years, he also sent money to help the family of Mia Stoeckel, his mistress for several years in Bonn. Her sister, Therese Dautzenberg, had contacted Schumpeter after the war to explain that she was raising Mia's two children, whose parents had been killed during the war, but, as were many Germans, she was in a desperate economic plight. She asked for Schumpeter's help, and she received it.

He offered this kind of support even though he sometimes worried about his own financial situation. He expressed his concern in September 1949 in a diary entry addressed to God and his *Hasen*: "O God and my dear departed, has the end to be in poverty and illness." Although Elizabeth owned the home in Taconic and the one at 7 Acacia Street in Cambridge, most of her money was in stocks and bonds—her inheritance from her parents. She did not need to work, but she still dabbled in her nursery business and enjoyed teaching occasionally, offering a course at Wheaton College in Norton, Massachusetts for the spring term of 1949. Schumpeter had no savings and little income except his salary, yet he seemed generally unconcerned about money management since whatever money he earned he turned over to Elizabeth. She handled all financial matters, giving Schumpeter whatever money he asked for, usually only for lunches, cigarettes, and an occasional book. As one of the most respected senior professors at Harvard, Schumpeter received the highest Harvard salary: $14,000. But his writing never earned him much money. Between 1939 and 1950, for example, his income from royalties amounted to $12,391.19, with about two-thirds of this amount coming in the last half of the decade. Most of his royalty earnings resulted from *Capitalism, Socialism and Democracy*. His other writings, including *Business Cycles* and the *Theory of Economic Development*, brought in almost nothing.[25] But whatever Schumpeter earned was of little interest to him since he saw none of it and personally spent almost none of it. He knew that Elizabeth was conservative in her spending and more careful financially than he. In fact, when she died in 1953, her estate of about $150,000 was intact and went to Harvard's Economics Department to benefit future graduate students in her husband's name.

Despite his good income and Elizabeth's assets and income, Schumpeter thought, abetted by Elizabeth, that his retirement prospects were dim. When he first joined the faculty in 1932, Harvard had agreed to pay him $4,000 a year on retirement after fifteen years, that is, beginning in October 1948. In early 1948, he and Elizabeth had discussed his retirement: "I brought topic of retirement and asked E. whether she still considered it possible. But hesitatingly she said retirement is possible only if Taconic is sold. But that amounts pretty much to No." Always cautious in money matters, Elizabeth did not want to touch her capital. He addressed the subject again in June 1948, when he wrote, "look how impossible retirement is. Even when no further inflation is threatening, I even could not keep up sending [Care] checks [to Austria and Germany]." (He was referring to his help in the support of the Reisinger family in Vienna and Mia's children in Germany).

If he retired, the Schumpeters believed they would have to keep their Cambridge home in order to retain access to research materials and the libraries. But if they kept the Cambridge place, Elizabeth felt they would have to sell Windy Hill, and Schumpeter would not consider giving up Taconic. Although he again considered retirement in 1949 because he was unusually tired, he still rejected it as an option. He would not leave his teaching post at Harvard until retirement became mandatory in 1953, when he turned seventy. Even then, he would not retire from research and writing since the projects he had on the drawing board would have occupied him well beyond his century mark. Despite his weakness for detective novels and sitting beside Twin Lakes, the idea of not working appalled him. Many more doors remained to be opened.

Schumpeter also felt no urgency to retire since he was still a vital man who enjoyed his teaching. Yet he continued to worry about his health. To his friends and colleagues, he complained of being tired, working too hard, and suffering from ill-defined physical problems. In his letters to friends, he commented on his low level of energy, saying he felt like a "washed out rag" and wondering how others got their work done. He still worked long hours and was productive, but he was never satisfied with what he accomplished. In a July 1949 diary entry, he speculated about how much more he could have accomplished if he had worked exclusively on theory in the previous decade, rather than working on the history. He then wrote "but I am definitely old and mude [tired]... I just long for a place of public charity where I could sit down *and stare,* stare into nothing."

8

Although exaggerated, his complaints of physical problems were not completely unfounded. In May 1949, he complained of backaches and suspected kidney problems, perhaps kidney stones. But X-rays taken earlier did not indicate anything serious. In the last few years of his life, he had put on weight and suffered from high blood pressure. He was under the medical care of Dr. Clark Peterson of Lakeville, Connecticut, who was also Elizabeth's doctor, but Schumpeter apparently took no medicine systematically. Dr. Peterson did, however, strongly recommend that Schumpeter, who smoked a pack of cigarettes a day, quit smoking and restrain his cocktail hour. Schumpeter did not consider himself a heavy drinker—usually having two, sometimes more, drinks before supper. Schumpeter joked with his colleagues about his effort to find a doctor who would not frown on his drinking.[26] Dr. Peterson also recommended that Schumpeter reduce his work load. At age sixty-six, he should have been slowing down and taking better care of himself, but he ignored all of the doctor's recommendations and continued doing as much as he had done twenty and thirty years earlier, probably working even more than earlier.

Schumpeter's diary provides evidence of his health concerns, but it also shows his continuing vitality, even in the face of his chronic depression. For example, on his sixty-sixth birthday, his last, he wrote, "A real surprise for my birthday—without misery, tiredness, or hopelessness... Do your duty. What is the duty? The necessity of the day. Strange, Goethe said that." Three months later, on 29 May 1949, he expressed his enthusiasm for teaching:

Professorship the second semester was terrific. It is true that teaching gives me joy. As some Greek students remarked 'you are enjoying yourself.' But it is not the less true that in the last years it has become different.

Illustrating the contradictory pull between contentment and despair, he then continued in a pessimistic vein: "My belief in the world's values and sense of things dies." A few months later, the polarity of emotions again fused within one diary entry when he wrote on Labor Day:

> Tired. I have had a free and cheerful day... It is true that Elizabeth is sick and after the operation everything has become different... Polly Anna feeling... In September I am happy that again the new acad. year begins and I hope to use it well. H.s.D. [Hasen sei Dank].

The emotional roller-coaster Schumpeter travelled on for much of his life must have been, if nothing else, exhausting.

Still, he continued. He had chastized himself, in the summer of 1949, for reading Ellery Queen mystery novels and not using his time more productively, yet his detective stories provided a necessary form of relaxation and escape from an otherwise grueling schedule. He used Cambridge as his base of operations for teaching, researching in the library, attending meetings, and conducting examinations, but at every opportunity the Schumpeters left Cambridge for Taconic. His classes for years had met on either Monday and Wednesday, or occasionally on Tuesday and Thursday. Elizabeth would drive him down to Taconic on Wednesday afternoon or Thursday, bringing him back the following Sunday or Monday. Although Taconic provided some peace, going to Windy Hill did not signify resting. He worked just as hard, or harder, there as he did in Cambridge, but both Schumpeters preferred Taconic's more relaxing environment. He loved his walks, his grounds, his flowers, the lakes, feeling the atmosphere to be more homey, isolated, and closer to nature.

Neither in Cambridge nor in Taconic did the Schumpeters lead an active social life. Elizabeth's illness and operation in the fall of 1948 brought the two of them closer together, so much so that they tended to exclude the rest of the world. Occasionally, they would visit friends or attend a cocktail party now and again in Cambridge, but mainly, Joseph spent his time reading and writing. In Taconic, he still took walks down between the Twin Lakes and around Windy Hill, but his tennis playing had dropped off to almost nothing. Elizabeth began to spend more time working at her nursery in Taconic, selling trees and shrubs in the community and occasionally even in Cambridge. Although her illness precluded much vigorous physical activity, she loved working in her yard and among her flowers, plants, and shrubs. Their Windy Hill home was always beautifully landscaped, largely through her efforts.

9

The frequent escapes to Taconic partly stemmed from the fact that Schumpeter was no happier with the Harvard Department of Economics in 1949 than he had been earlier. He still complained about his colleagues' lack of serious work and lamented the absence of intellectual stimulation from them. Nor did he personally respect and admire more than a few of his colleagues, although he treated all with great respect. As he explained to his Japanese student and friend, Shigeto Tsuru, in the summer of 1949:

> I who am near enough to Harvard cannot say I experience very much stimulus from my surroundings. Scientifically, Leontief is the only man who is really alive and even he is so much buried in administrative work... that not so very much of him remains either.[27]

As for Harvard as an institution, Schumpeter was completely disenchanted, regarding its atmosphere as "stifling." Most of the faculty, he felt, were narrow specialists and much too discipline-oriented, with little interest outside their own restricted worlds. Expressing his dissatisfaction, he wrote in July 1949: "I give up Harvard. In this soil no more do any of my roses blossom." Much of this alienation was Schumpeter's fault. For many years he had isolated himself, sticking to his office, the library, and the study of his Cambridge home, and fleeing to Taconic at every opportunity. Not really knowing Harvard, he judged it by casual encounters and found it to be much less satisfying than it in the 1920s and early 1930s when he had enjoyed it so much.

By late 1940s, many changes had transformed Harvard. Abbot Payson Usher, with whom Schumpeter had not been close in recent years, had retired, replaced by Alexander Gerschenkron, another leading economic historian. Leonard Crum had resigned in 1947 to go to the University of California-Berkeley, and Edmund Wilson was long gone, as was Albert Monroe. But while some friends left, others returned. Schumpeter's former student, Arthur Smithies, had come to Harvard in 1948, hired away from the University of Michigan. John Kenneth Galbraith was also back, this time as a full professor, and John T. Dunlop, later dean and sometime secretary of labor, had become a regular member of the department. In addition, "Nat" Taylor had settled in as a permanent lecturer. Some new younger people were still around. Walter Isard was serving as a lecturer, while James Duesenberry and Thomas Schelling showed promise as young newcomers. Nicholas Georgescu-Roegen, a special friend of Schumpeter and Rockefeller fellow in the 1930s and brilliant mathematical economist, had made a daring shipboard escape from Rumania and was a visiting professor at Harvard. Among the regulars on the Harvard faculty, Schumpeter was closest to and thought most of Leontief, Haberler, Mason, and Smithies, both personally and professionally. He missed greatly the coterie of stimulating young people. In the 1930s, he was surrounded by the eager young scholars who vanished in wartime. After the war, too many young students enrolled in the department to suit Schumpeter's taste. Harvard, in the postwar years, admitted large numbers of students to make up for the war years, but it still managed to continue the golden years of high intellect, begun in the mid-1930s, by refusing to lower standards. Yet the new breed of students seemed less exciting than those of the 1930s. Many were married and most were intensely career oriented, in a hurry to get started. With only a practical interest in theory, they viewed economics as a means to play a role in the country's life, a view that Schumpeter abominated. For Schumpeter there were no Samuelsons, Margets, Smithies, Hoovers, Metzlers, Masons, Harris, Chamberlins, Sweezys, Stolpers, or others of their caliber. Such quality students existed, of course, but the atmosphere was so different that he could not establish the same kind of rapport with them. Everybody, including faculty and students, worked in their own little niches, with less togetherness then when the department was smaller. And Schumpeter himself hid away in Taconic, out of sight and largely out of contact with students and colleagues.

10

Scheduled to teach his usual advanced economic theory course, the history and literature of economics, and the economics of socialism in the spring of 1950, Schumpeter was looking forward to the new semester. Though he was past retirement age, his teaching load exceeded that of most younger professors. In addition to his many writing projects, he planned to take some time in 1950 to write his presidential address for the International Economic Association meeting in August in Paris. He also had promised an article to *Foreign Affairs*, which, considering that journal's prestige, would have required some time. With the trip to Chicago and these plans in mind, he set out for the American Economic Association meeting held in late December 1949, in New York City. Friends there reported he was outwardly in good spirits and did not seem unwell. As usual, he complained of being tired, but since that was such a standard complaint, people had grown used to it. He gave his paper, "The March into Socialism," at a session presided over by Frank Knight of the University of Chicago. Seymour Harris twitted Schumpeter about his fear of socialism in America, saying that the New Deal had not achieved a significant degree of egalitarianism. Elizabeth had accompanied him to New York, so on 31 December the two rode the train back to Lakeview and then went by car on to Taconic.

During the next few days, he had two tasks. One was to prepare for the Walgreen Lectures scheduled to begin in Chicago on 9 January. Having written detailed notes for each of the six lectures, he knew what he wanted to say; still, the first few days of January 1950 were filled with additional preparation for the Chicago lectures. He planned to take the train there on Sunday, 8 January. His other task was to convert his notes on his last association paper into an article for the *Proceedings of the American Economic Association* to be published in May. He was writing the paper on yellow foolscap, as was his custom, at the end of the first week of January. On Saturday night, 7 January 1950 while working in his favorite study at Windy Hill, Schumpeter wrote the following sentence: "In other words, price control may result in a surrender of private enterprise to public authority, that is, in a big stride toward the perfectly planned economy."[28] Since that sentence seemed to be a good stopping point, he put down his pencil, emptied his pockets, changed into his pyjamas, and went to bed.

Several hours later, while asleep, he suffered a massive stroke. Although he was immediately rendered unconscious, he remained alive for about two hours. Then, in the early morning hours of 8 January 1950, he joined his *Hasen* forever. On his night stand, an open copy of Euripides's plays in Greek, with which he had read himself to sleep, lay next to a picture of his Annie. He had felt no pain and never knew what happened. Dr. Clark Peterson of Lakeville, the attending physician, could do nothing to save his life. At the beginning of 1949, Schumpeter had written in his diary that he had only a little more than a year left. His prediction turned out to be true.[29]

Nothing short of a radically different lifestyle in the preceding thirty or forty years could have perhaps prevented Schumpeter's fate. Yet it is improbable that he would have lived his life any differently in order to live longer. And if Schumpeter had been able to choose a way to die, he would have chosen what happened—a death without warning and without pain. Nothing would have distressed him more than a lingering illness, visits to his bedside from friends, colleagues, and neighbors, becoming a burden to Elizabeth, and being unable to work. He had been asking his *Hasen* to prevent that dismal destiny, and the fear of such a fate may have wrung from him his earlier words about voluntary death. For Schumpeter, the best possible death would be to go as he did—quickly, virtually with pen in hand, in his beloved Taconic.

The word spread quickly in Taconic and Cambridge. I remember receiving and making telephone calls that Sunday morning, learning of his death and telling others. The entire Harvard community was stunned. Old Harvard professors aren't supposed to die; they just retire and write more books.

Schumpeter had seemed strong and vigorous, good for another decade or two. Long obituaries appeared in newspapers in Boston, New York, and most other major cities. The *Harvard Crimson* account was the most detailed, but even the *Christian Science Monitor*, which usually ignored such matters, honored Schumpeter with an obituary. The *New York Times* ran a long and factual article, recounting his life and work and including a photograph. The news also appeared in the European press, especially in London, Bonn, Berlin, and Vienna. Even the Tokyo papers gave front-page coverage to his death. By 1950, Schumpeter was among the most well-known of economists, with his work cited more frequently than any other.

On Tuesday, 10 January, his funeral service was held in St. John's Episcopal Church in Salisbury, Connecticut, a few miles from Taconic. Father Chiera, who is now buried a few yards from Schumpeter, officiated. A snowstorm struck western Connecticut and Massachusetts that day, blanketing the Berkshires and surrounding region, so only a few carloads of the most hardy and some local people could attend. Many from New York, Boston, New Haven, and other cities could not get through the impassable roads. Schumpeter was buried in the Salisbury Cemetery, only about three miles from Windy Hill in Taconic. Elizabeth bought a modest marker that reads simply

Josef Aloys Schumpeter
1883-1950

A final paradox: he will rest in eternity under a stone bearing his misspelled name.

A month later, on 10 February, Professor Edward Mason delivered the eulogy at a memorial service held in the Memorial Church of Harvard Yard. Most of the Department of Economics faculty and many graduate students attended. Professor Mason also chaired the group, which included Professors Harris, Leontief, and Haberler, responsible for writing the minute that was placed upon the records of the Harvard Faculty of Arts and Sciences on 7 February 1950. The minute in part reads:

> Joseph Alois Schumpeter, who died January 8, 1950, in Taconic, Connecticut, was one of the three or four leading economists of his generation and one of the great figures of this University. His erudition was immense and his interests and achievements were by no means limited to economics. The eighteen years he spent at Harvard were years of intense intellectual activity which have left a permanent impress on his colleagues, on hundreds of students, and on his chosen field of study.

Gifted with apparently boundless energy, Schumpeter expended it lavishly. He was always available for consultation by students and devoted a great amount of time to advising and guiding young scholars in all parts of the world. His intemperance in the giving of himself to others may well have contributed to his death. Returning to his country home in Connecticut from meetings of the Economic Association in New York, he was in the course of preparing a series of lectures to be given at the University of Chicago when he died peacefully in his sleep. But neither he nor his friends would have wished him to live differently. Vitality was part of him and the lavish expenditure of it his characteristic way of life.[30]

Notes

1   Friends and colleagues remember how worried and solicitous Schumpeter was about Elizabeth in 1948 and 1949.
2   Schumpeter's diary in this period had many reports on his activities and on his plans for the future. He had lecture commitments in Chicago and Philadelphia at the beginning of 1950.
3   *Capitalism, Socialism and Democracy*, 3rd edition (New York: Harper and Row, 1950) 410-11.
4   *Journal of Political Economy* 57 (June 1949): 199-212.
5   I found these papers, along with other papers, including the Erika Gerschenkron report, in some boxes containing material about the fellowships named after Schumpeter in the Harvard Department of Economics. Probably they were found in the office of the late Arthur Smithies and, since they dealt with Schumpeter, were placed with the Schumpeter fellowship papers.
6   *Journal of Political Economy* 57 (October 1949): 371-82.
7   *Ibid.*, 382
8   *Change and the Entrepreneur*, prepared by the Research Center in Entrepreneurial History, Harvard University (Cambridge: Harvard University Press, 1949), 63-84.
9   *Ibid.*, 64.
10   Proceedings of Universities-National Bureau Conference on Business Cycle Research, New York, 25-27 November 1949.
11   *Quarterly Journal of Economics* 64 (February 1950), 139-55.
12   *Journal of the American Statistical Association* 45 (March 1950): 140-2.
13   *Quarterly Journal of Economics* 63 (May 1949): 147-73.
14   The letter to Spahr is in the correspondence file of the Schumpeter papers in the Harvard University Archives.
15   The correspondence concerning Schumpeter's nomination to the presidency of the International Economic Association is in the Schumpeter papers in the Harvard University Archives.
16   This letter was among those placed in the Schumpeter papers at Harvard by Arthur Smithies.
17   It is possible but highly unlikely that Schumpeter destroyed manuscript. So far as is known, he never destroyed any manuscript.
18   These plans were reported in the essays by Arthur Smithies and Paul Samuelson in Seymour Harris, ed., *Joseph Schumpeter, Social Scientist*. R. M. Goodwin, in a paper "The Schumpeter I Knew" (1982 typescript), indicates that Schumpeter in

those days had plans for five books, including books on cultural history, economic sociology, and a book relating economic to social phonomena.

19   *Zeitschrift fuer die gesamte Stattswissenschaft* 139, no. 2 (June 1983): 191-5.

20   *American Economic Review* 40 (May 1950): 446-56.

21   *Capitalism, Socialism and Democracy*, 3rd edition (New York: Harper and Row, 1950), 422.

22   Ibid., 424.

23   Warren Samuels, editor, *Research in the History of Economic Thought and Methodology* (Greenwich, Conn.: JAI Press, 1987), 115.

24   Schumpeter used the expression "Keynesian nursery" in classes and told his classes that Keynesian economics in the late 1940s could be learned in a couple of weeks. Paul MacCracken in "Can Capitalism Survive?" in H. V. Procknow, editor, *Dilemmas Facing the Nation* (New York: Harper and Row, 1979) mentions Schumpeter's references to the "Keynesian nursery."

25   A report of Schumpeter's earnings from writings is in the Schumpeter papers in the Harvard University Archives.

26   This was reported to me by Gottfried Haberler.

27   This letter is in the correspondence file in the Schumpeter papers in the Harvard University Archives.

28   *Capitalism, Socialism and Democracy*, 3rd edition (New York: Harper and Row, 1950), 424.

29   His death certificate, on file in the Salisbury Town Hall indicates he died of a stroke two hours after its beginning. The certificate also indicated that he had arteriosclerosis for a year.

30   The Minute was reproduced in Seymour Harris, ed., *Joseph Schumpeter, Social Scientist*.

13

Epilogue

Scholars customarily honor the passing of illustrious members of their calling by writing obituaries for publication in professional journals. These articles not only provide some biographical information but also assess the meaning and importance of the fallen colleague's work. Schumpeter had written many such articles, beginning with one in honor of Professor Rudolph Auspitz of the University of Vienna. Published just months after Schumpeter completed his university education in 1906, this was his first piece written in English. His last memorial article, about Wesley Clair Mitchell, was not published until after Schumpeter's own death. It was not long before evaluations and accolades in honor of Schumpeter's life and work began appearing in the leading economics journals the world over.

1

In the most detailed biographical essay, published in Harvard's *Quarterly Journal of Economics*, his good friend and colleague, Gottfried Haberler, wrote a moving tribute.

Joseph A. Schumpeter was one of the great economists of all time. His claim to that rare title ... rests as much on the fact that he was much more than an economist as on his achievement in the economic field itself.... There are in economics more refined and versatile mathematical theorists, there are more resourceful statisticians, and economic historians who know more about certain periods and certain subjects than he did. But as a master of all branches of economics and as a universal scholar, Schumpeter held a unique position among contemporary economists.

Schumpeter was not only a great scholar and original thinker, but he was also a strong, colorful, and exceedingly complex personality. A quite unusual capacity for understanding the minds and view of others, a strong touch of irony, which, at times, seemed to verge on cynicism, and a wonderful sense of humor were combined with deep moral convictions, absolute devotion to his friends, and intense likes and aversions.[1]

Schumpeter was genuinely fond of and close to only a few people. Haberler was one of them; Arthur Smithies was another. Both were therefore in positions to comment on Schumpeter's life, looking at the man as well as his work. In his memorial to Schumpeter, published in the *American Economic Review*, Smithies asserted:

I have not succeeded in bringing out many of the most admirable traits of Schumpeter's character. The liveliness of his wit and the elegance of his manner and the sincerity of his nature. His successes in the lecture hall, the classroom, or the drawing room were no greater than his successes in winning the affection of children. He could meet them on terms of complete equality and they blossomed under his influence. His warm and generous friendship once given was never withdrawn. It is not for his spectacular qualities that he will live in the hearts of his friends.

But most of his later life was that of the solitary and reflective, but impatient, scholar; and no one was invited to share it. His work was too much his own to be discussed. While he sometimes overloaded himself with equipment furnished by others, he made his intellectual journey alone. His study was the workshop of the individual craftsman. By tearing pages out of periodicals, collecting reprints, and limiting himself to the books he really used, he was able to keep most of the tools he needed within easy reach.... Thus he pursued his craft among the hills of Connecticut unimpeded by computing machinery, research staffs, and other instruments of mass production.[2]

Wassily Leontief, another long-time colleague and friend, wrote one of the most perceptive evaluations of Schumpeter's character and work.

The strongest single impression with which one was left after having spent an hour with him in the classroom or at a scientific meeting, or even better on a leisurely walk along the wooded shores of the lake near his Taconic, Connecticut, country home, was that of the astounding width of Schumpeter's intellectual horizon. He was equally at home in early Greek philosophy, English parliamentary history, Italian literature, and French romanesque architecture. One wonders whether, if he had pushed his roots in one single country, Schumpeter would have still become the spiritual citizen of the world that he was.

To economics and to the social sciences in general Schumpeter brought a remarkable combination of imaginative vision and uncommon critical acumen. The vision led him to the formulation of his well-known notion of economic development. However significant, that contribution alone cannot account for the influence which Schumpeter exerted on the fortunes of our discipline during the last four decades. What was it then that made his position so prominent and his departure now so keenly felt?

It was Schumpeter's peculiar concern with the science, with the process of knowledge itself. The intellectual adventure meant more to him than the ultimate discovery. To prepare the ground for new ideas, to watch and protect their growth, gave, I suspect, more satisfaction to him than even the final harvest; and he was wise enough—some will say skeptical enough—to realize that in the field of intellectual endeavor no harvest is final, all fruit is perishable and only as good as the new seed it might contain.

While most economists, including those in the first ranks of the profession, devote today much of their time and energy to the practical task of oiling the creaking wheels of our economic machine, strain their shoulder in helping to heave it out of the rut of whatever current crises it finds itself in, or at least join the circle of eager onlookers supplying gratuitous advice from the sidelines, Schumpeter shied away from the practical attitude. By conviction, as well as by temperament, he was a thinker rather than a doer.... A pessimist and a skeptic in his view on the future of our western civilization which he cherished so much, Schumpeter was an optimist in his belief in the boundless progress of the inquiring mind.[3]

Oskar Morgenstern, a Viennese who first became acquainted with Schumpeter in that city at the time of the first war, summed up his prestige and position when he stated:

Few economists will venture to judge Schumpeter at present and to assign a definite place to him in the development of the science. It is likely, however, that all will agree that he belongs to that small group where a further ranking becomes almost impossible.[4]

In yet another evaluation of Schumpeter's career, Paul Samuelson, the brightest of his students, paid tribute to his old professor with the following words:

Though Schumpeter left behind no band of zealots bent on differentiating his views from those of traditional economic theory, he did leave behind him the only kind of school appropriate to a scientific discipline—a generation of economic theorists who caught fire from his teachings.[5]

Paul Sweezy, Schumpeter's friend and former teaching assistant, offered one of the best illustrations of Schumpeter's impact on those whom he taught. Alan Sweezy, who had also studied under Schumpeter in the early 1930s, wrote to his brother, Paul:

> As I was going to my 10 o'clock class this morning, one of the younger instructors here [at the California Institute of Technology] stopped me and said: "I see we've lost Schumpeter." At first I didn't quite take it in; and then suddenly as I realized what he meant, a whole flood of memories rushed in on me and for a few minutes I had a hard time holding on to myself. It seemed just as though I were hearing about the death of part of my own life. I didn't think of the Schumpeter of recent years, whom I had grown away from and had rarely seen, but was living over again those years at Harvard when Schumpeter was the center in our group of graduate students and young instructors. That they were such good years—so lively and interesting and enjoyable—was largely the result of Schumpeter's personality and influence.[6]

2

Joseph Schumpeter always had as his principal ambition to be the greatest economist in the world. One of those absolutely convinced that he had achieved this goal was Elizabeth Schumpeter, and no sooner had she put her husband in his grave than she set about to add to and polish his reputation. In the early spring of 1950, she began to hunt down the manuscript of the *History of Economic Analysis*, which she discovered all over the houses in Cambridge and in Taconic as well as in his Littauer office. For more than three years she worked on the task of editing and preparing it for publication. Because the earlier cancer returned and gradually destroyed her health, she never saw the book in print, but she did live long enough to see it in the galley proof. For nearly fourteen years, Elizabeth had devoted her life to her husband and his work. Even after his death this devotion continued, consuming her last four years and leaving her little time for herself.

In other ways, she set out to insure the luster of the memory of her husband. After selling the Cambridge house and finding herself with more books than she could handle, she donated about 3,500 of them to the Hitotsubashi University in Tokyo, where Schumpeter had lectured in 1931. The Schumpeter Library there remains an integral part of the university library.[7] When Professors Nakayama and Tobata of Hitotsubashi University visited Taconic, Elizabeth gave them the manuscript of *Capitalism, Socialism and Democracy*. She also donated about three hundred books, used and marked by Schumpeter in the writing of the *History of Economic Analysis*, to the Kress Collection of Economics at Harvard's Baker Library. Most of her husband's papers she deposited at the Houghton Rare Book Library, but they were later transferred to the Harvard University Archives where they remain, stored in about one hundred fifty boxes.

Elizabeth tried unsuccessfully to persuade the Department of Economics to set aside a room in Littauer Center, to be called the Schumpeter Room in honor of her husband. Many years later, the department did honor Alvin Hansen and Edward Mason by naming the lounge and seminar room on the top floor of Littauer after them, but no Schumpeter Room exists anywhere. The department did, however, establish the Schumpeter Prize, which is awarded each year to a promising graduate student. Elizabeth's estate, willed to the department, provides the money for the prize. It is certain that Schumpeter would have preferred to have a research fellowship named after him rather than a room because in this way he could have continued to open doors for graduate students. Schumpeter's own estate was negligible; his net assets were worth only $18,000, of which $8,000 represented copyrights of dubious real value.[8]

In 1951, Elizabeth was also instrumental in the publication of a memorial volume honoring her husband. She persuaded Professor Seymour Harris to edit *Joseph Schumpeter, Social Scientist*, published by Harvard University Press, which contained the Faculty Minute, the obituaries by Smithies and Haberler, and essays written by a dozen of Schumpeter's colleagues and students. Officially, Elizabeth had nothing to do with this volume, but, in fact, she strongly urged its publication and helped to select the contributors.

3

In the more than thirty-five years since Joseph Schumpeter last strode the Yard and stirred his students with his lectures in Emerson Hall, his star has found a permanent and prominent place in the firmament of economics and social science. His reputation at first seemed to dim a bit, with many regarding the theories he taught as old hat, superseded by mathematical formulations that Schumpeter urged but did not produce or teach, and the Keynesian analysis that he rejected. Because it was historical and sociological, not exclusively quantitative and mechanical, his theory of development and cycles didn't seem appropriate to the world of huge corporations, giant governments, and underdeveloped lands. Turning their backs on Schumpeter, economists went chasing after the illusory advantages of mathematical growth models, such as the Harrod-Domar extension of Keynesian analysis, which were so neat, so simple and precise, and ultimately so useless and misleading.

The notion that the economist should remain aloof from the policy fray appeared quaint to the many young economists of the 1950s and 1960s eager to straighten out Washington, the state house, the local corporations, and the world. Most economists embrace economics because they want to change things. Many fear that concentrating on economic science exclusively could mean denying the impulse that makes economics interesting; it could also make economists seem useless and silly. In the decade before and after Schumpeter's death, many economists felt that at last with Keynesian analysis they were on the verge of making a tremendous contribution to public and private policy. In the 1950s, the economist began to feel that not only could he tell the policy maker what policy was appropriate to achieve a given result, he could also suggest the combination of policies to obtain multiple goals. He could even "fine tune" the economy, shifting this or that policy in order to change some aspect of the economy. So great was his knowledge of policy— he thought—that the economist sometimes became a policy maker. Even more, he became the engineer capable of making the policies work in Washington and of boosting the profits of companies.

Just tell the economist that the nation wanted full employment, price stability, economic growth, and income redistribution sufficient to eliminate poverty and he would build models, develop equations, crank out numbers, and recommend just the right policies needed to deliver the results. He would tell the government how to manipulate spending and taxes, help build the Great Society, eliminate poverty, advise on the Vietnam war, and convince everybody that business cycles were things of the past. The economy was putty in the hands of this new breed of economists.

Although some of them had studied under Schumpeter, they had not taken to heart his precept that "economics was getting better and better and economists were getting worse and worse." These economists got their comeuppance in the 1970s and 1980s when nothing seemed to go right. Belief in the business cycle returned with a vengeance as prices, the balance of trade and payments, government revenues and expenditures, unemployment, productivity, and growth all got out of hand. Economic variables performed perversely, with inflation persisting even during depression. Deficits destabilize the financial system and undermine the economy, but eliminating them could induce a depression. The predictions of economists went awry, and their models were exposed as made of sand.

First and last, Schumpeter had urged the use of mathematics in economics, and time has proven him right. Since his death, the theoretical part of economics has become almost a subdiscipline of mathematics. Where economics, in its pell-mell rush toward mathematics, may have gone wrong was in failing to heed the other part of Schumpeter's advice: The mathematics must be hitched to economic and social facts, to the numbers and relationships that reflect the economy's and society's reality. But economists' heads often seemed to be filled only with a jumble of equations rather than with facts and unpretentious common sense. As it turned out, many of the models were held up by skyhooks anchored firmly in the clouds.

In the meantime, back in the real world, the economy continued to defy economists. Slow growth, high unemployment, low productivity gains, chronic inflation, troublesome energy and environmental sectors, high interest rates, government spending resistant to reduction, mounting deficits—none of which were on the economist's agenda—proved recalcitrant to the mathematical models. At the same time, Keynesian analysis has been found wanting in imparting an understanding of the economy, and Keynesian policy has failed to do the job. His attack on savings, and policies that undermined savings, now deprives the economy of the resources it needs for economic progress. Economists have begun returning to basics, looking at how the economy operates and what makes it tick. As the Keynesian star began to recede, the older economics of Schumpeter began to make a comeback, and the role of the entrepreneur and innovation in progress began to be perceived as more important. The general-equilibrium model and adjustment mechanisms of fundamental neoclassical economics began to ring true, making some economists more humble and unsure, a role Schumpeter would have thought appropriate.

With the pendulum of economics swinging back, Schumpeter's star has begun to rise. Gone forever, of course, is some of his classroom economic theory, as the modern economist has the advantage of recent improvements and possesses a thorough grounding in mathematics and the ability to use it in theory. But his work in the history of economics continues to occupy a secure position. Although not fully accepted, his theory of economic development is alive and well and has become increasingly relevant, not only for developed countries of Europe and the United States but also for the new, less-developed countries. The economy does indeed seem to dance to the tune of new ideas, products, and methods introduced by energetic men, and the entrepreneur as innovator today looms large as a vital economic actor. Sober thought demands in these days a reappraisal of where capitalism stands, where it is going, and what might come next. Schumpeter's dictum that capitalism requires an oxygen tent to survive has become more than a clever metaphor. Although the concept of the substitution of socialism for capitalism is still not widely accepted, many now believe that past policies have hastened irreversible and destructive changes that might be remedied by a return to the old liberalism. Economic sociology, one focus of Schumpeter's thinking, seems to describe better the way the world turns than most of the cut-and-dried models developed by the new breed of mathematical economists.

Schumpeter cannot go down as the world's greatest economist in this or any other century. He was much bigger than that. He must go down as one of the world's great economists, as one of the most thoughtful social scientists, as a profound commentator on the social and economic scene, and, perhaps most important, as one of the great teachers of economics and social science.

4

For many economists, Schumpeter's centennial year, 1983, marked a time for thoughtful reappraisal. That year celebrated a great historical nexus, as the centennials of three great men of economics were joined together. Karl Marx died in 1883 while John Maynard Keynes and Joseph Alois Schumpeter were both born in 1883. Meetings were held all over the world to evaluate once again the work of these men. Special meetings to discuss Schumpeter convened in Graz, Vienna, Bonn, Amsterdam, Paris, Milan, Groningen, Goettingen, and many other places. Academic meetings were sponsored by professional associations, including the American Economic Association and the History of Economics Society, as well as regional economic groups. Newly published books evaluated his work while articles discussing Schumpeter appeared in scholarly journals. Schumpeter's name even began to crop up more and more in the popular press—the *Economist, Forbes Magazine*, the *Wall Street Journal,* the *Christian Science Monitor*, and the *New York Times*. In honor of the centennial, the University of Vienna, which had never honored Schumpeter in life, created an honorary Schumpeter Professorship, to be filled each year by a different illustrious economist. In 1981, the University of Vienna appointed Professor Martin Feldstein of Harvard, later President Ronald Reagan's economic advisor, as the first Joseph Schumpeter lecturer and honorary professor. In September 1986, the newly established International Schumpeter Society, whose membership includes not only many of Schumpeter's students but also outstanding Schumpeterian scholars, met in Augsburg, Germany and elected Wolfgang Stolper of the University of Michigan its first president. The society continues to prosper under the leadership of Arnold Heertje of Holland and sponsors annual meetings.

Although it gave Keynes more than three times the space, the *Economist* of London, on 17 December 1983, remembered Schumpeter with these words, among others:

The range and spread of his work was startling. He made significant contributions to analytical methodology, emphasizing the critical importance of marginal analysis. He evolved a theory of business cycles, pondered what he called "fiscal sociology," and had an overriding vision of the collapse of the capitalist system.

To a present-day reader, the most striking features of Schumpeter's thinking remain its rigor, novelty, and clarity. His synthetic skills were outstanding. The breadth of his understanding, the confidence of his grasp of ideology, philosophy and economic method are still thrilling today. There are few economists now writing who would chance their arms so far....

In his centenary year, Schumpeter's preoccupations can be seen to have been the right ones. Innovation and the scope of the public finances remain as central as ever to the successful functioning of the mixed economy. The sources of growth are still opaque; his descriptions of the innovative process have not often been bettered. And many countries await their definitive tax historian. His two interests outside economics, women and horses, also still have their supporters—and, some would say, remain as dimly understood as the economy.

A reproduction of the portraits of Schumpeter and Keynes graced the cover of *Forbes Magazine* on 23 May 1983. Symbolically, ten votive candles stood before the Keynes portrait, but only a single candle burned before Schumpeter. Still, Peter Drucker in his article in the magazine wrote:

In some ways, Keynes and Schumpeter replayed the best-known confrontation of philosophers in the Western tradition—the Platonic dialog between Parmenides, the brilliant, clever, irresistible sophist, and the slow-moving and ugly, but wise, Socrates. No one in the interwar years was more brilliant, more clever than Keynes. Schumpeter, by contrast, appeared pedestrian—but he had wisdom. Cleverness carries the day. But wisdom endureth.

The sum of all the recent evaluations of Schumpeter rejects his placement on the shelf, calls for continued study of his work, and voices the growing sentiment that his thinking was not only important but also still relevant and likely to be so for a long time. Schumpeter has finally achieved his deserved place in the select company of Marx, Keynes, Smith, Walras, and Marshall. He has even been called "America's most brilliant economist" by Tibor Scitovsky of Stanford in his 1979 Ely lecture evaluating capitalism and its future before the American Economic Association.[9] Dozens of papers in the last few years, many of them noted in this book's bibliography, treat Schumpeter and his contributions as a living and vital force in economics, neglected until recently but sure to be of mounting weight. For example, Wolfgang Stolper in his paper at the Congress of the International Institute of Public Finance in Tokyo in 1981, applied the Schumpeterian approach to the current economic malaise.

The number of times Schumpeter is cited in books and articles is high—much higher than that of another great U.S. economist, Irving Fisher. Hardly a basic textbook has been written in the last twenty years that does not cite Schumpeter, usually many times and in many different connections. No book dealing with economic development, growth, technology, the state of capitalism, socialism, economic system, the history of economics, and many other topics can be published without mentioning Schumpeter, again usually several times. In addition, many research books are grounded in Schumpeter's ideas. For example, Christian Seidl, who, before he went to the University of Kiel, held the same post Schumpeter once held at the University of Graz, applied Schumpeter's analysis to present economic conditions in studies contained in his recent book.[10]

The bibliography at the end of this book, although extensive, includes only a few of the publications dealing in a central way with Schumpeter or his work. Michael Stevenson's work, *Joseph A. Schumpeter: A Bibliography, 1905-1950*, includes not only a careful updating of Schumpeter's own bibliography, so carefully begun by Elizabeth Schumpeter in the *Quarterly Journal of Economics*, but also annotates a large number of critical studies of Schumpeter's work.[11]

5

Looking ahead to predict the direction of economics and the social sciences, we can also speculate on Schumpeter's impact over the long haul. If economics continues to emphasize sterile mathematical models and to focus primarily on technique, then Schumpeter will probably play a modest role. Yet, so will economics, having specialized itself into desuetude. Although much of economics seems to have that orientation today, the level of discontent among economists is rising. On the other hand, if economics, though continuing to use mathematics when and as it can, zeroes in on the basic issue of understanding the changing economy, concerns itself with the historical and social framework of the economy, and examines the economy's institutions, structure, and dynamics, then Schumpeter may well be the forerunner of many things yet to come. For example, a new field in economics called public choice, now honored by one of its proponents receiving the Nobel Prize in Economics—James Buchanan—proposes to use and apply the methods of economics to all kinds of decision-making groups, both in the public and private sectors.[12] Schumpeter's analysis of democracy in *Capitalism, Socialism and Democracy* has great relevance to this approach. Although the field of public choice did not originate in Schumpeter's writings, many public choice analysts recognize that Schumpeter was the precursor with many insights to offer.[13]

Schumpeter's increasing impact can be seen in other areas as well. Research in the last decade suggests that his theory of development may yet become the scientific building block Schumpeter hoped it would be. Erik Dahman, one of those who held the Schumpeter Fellowship, in presenting an historical and econometric analysis in his book, *Entrepreneurial Activity and the Development of Swedish Industry, 1919-1939*, explicitly tries to test propositions from *Business Cycles*.[14] *Market Structure and Innovation* by Morton Kamien and Nancy Schwartz also attempts to test Schumpeterian propositions.[15] Another such test is contained in *Unemployment and Innovation* by Christopher Freeman, John Clark, and Luc Soete.[16] Then we have the group of reprinted papers in F. M. Scherer's *Innovation and Growth: Schumpeterian Perspectives*.[17] Finally, a major effort to build on the Schumpeterian theory of development has been undertaken by Sidney Winter and Richard Nelson of Yale. In articles for the *American Economic Review* and in their book, *An Evolutionary Theory of Economic Change*, they attempt to test Schumpeter's analysis.[18] They also attempt to extend his theory and make it mathematical by using the theory of Markov chains (a mathematical method developed since Schumpeter's time) to project the probabilities of future events with transition probabilities over the course of time.

Schumpeter's theory and influence may also extend into the unexplored area of comparative dynamics. Dynamic economic models, only beginning in Schumpeter's later days, typically base their solution for all future time periods on initial and historical conditions only. Comparative dynamics endeavors to compare time paths that differ in some aspect of those conditions. Until recently comparative dynamics has had limited usefulness because of computation problems. But with high-speed computers and the ability to program detailed instructions into them, it becomes possible to calculate many solutions quickly, linking different solutions together by using the solution in each time period as the data for future time periods. Not only can the initial and historical conditions be changed many times, the solution determined in a specified time period can also produce data that forms the basis for new initial and historical conditions. These new data can then be used to calculate solutions in subsequent time periods. In this way, comparative dynamics may be able to imitate evolutionary analysis, at least in part. Winter and Nelson have suggested similar methods for extending Schumpeter's analysis. If this approach is successful, his theory may one day provide the basis for the science of a changing economy.

Some recent work in mathematics, chronicled in James Gleick's *Chaos: Making a New Science* (New York: Penguin, 1987), may also contribute to the resolution of Schumpeter's problem of the indeterminacy of evolutionary paths and his inability to find a new and dynamic theory of economic development. This is a new form of mathematics in which nonlinear dynamic systems of equations can be examined with the aid of computers. It can discover patterns and structure in the behavior of variables—such as a heart suffering from arrhythmia—that had heretofore been thought to be without order. The chief applications so far have been in medicine and biology, but it is possible that the prices and quantities behaving in what is now thought to be an indeterminate manner may turn out to display a pattern discoverable by these new techniques. This new mathematics, which finds determinacy where it was not thought to exist before, may offer a fertile field for investigation in economic theory and approximate a resolution to Schumpeter's problem.

Less formalized than Schumpeter's theory of development, but also important, was his theory of the role of money in the economy. In recent years, his ideas about money have been viewed as an extension and qualification of the quantity theory of money. Although Schumpeter never produced the book he wanted on money, portions of the manuscript he was revising in the 1930s and 1940s were published in 1970. Mrs. Schumpeter gave a portion of the money manuscript to Arthur Marget, a student of Schumpeter during the 1920s. Marget's task was to translate this version, but he died in 1962 before completing the project. The German version, however, was reproduced, and found its way into many hands, including those of Fritz Karl Mann. He took it upon himself to have this incomplete German version published as *Das Wesen des Geldes* by Vandenhoeck & Ruprecht in Goettingen in 1970. The 341-page book, divided into twelve chapters, does not represent an advance in monetary theory and is not even a complete statement of Schumpeter's ideas. At least another chapter remains in his papers in the Harvard Archives, along with many notes for revision of all parts of the book. Still, Schumpeter's idea that the purpose for which money comes into existence (that is, is loaned and borrowed) determines whether prices or output changes continues to raise doubts about the quantity theory of money.

6

A professor is measured not only by the lasting quality and influence of his work, but also by the stature and accomplishments of his students. Schumpeter was only one of several professors at Harvard and Bonn, but at both institutions he was the vital center for the study of economic theory. He taught theory and ate, drank, talked, and lived theory. Most of his former students acknowledge a great debt to Schumpeter not only for what he taught but also for being an inspiration to study and master those things he did not teach—in other words, for pointing out the doors that could be opened. The stature and accomplishments of his former students indicate clearly that Schumpeter's influence lives on in those students and is, in turn, passed down to their students. Schumpeter taught scores of students at Bonn, and more than four hundred earned their doctorates at Harvard during his tenure. Among them are the leaders in economics in universities, business, and government. To mention only a few does an injustice to the remainder, so I will mention only one, primarily because he has often explicitly credited

Schumpeter with playing a role in his career. As the first American to win the Nobel Memorial Prize in Economics, Paul Anthony Samuelson is undoubtedly Schumpeter's most famous and meritorious student. But there are dozens more of great fame and merit.

Despite the large ranks of former students who regard him highly, there is still no Schumpeter school, and it seems unlikely there will ever be one despite the international society recently formed in his honor. That society exists to learn from the works of Schumpeter, not to nurture a school in his name. No one believes passionately in a theorem learned at Schumpeter's knee or gleaned from his writings. He wished to be regarded as just one of those few who nudged economics along a bit. His many admirers do not include followers, nor do the honors bestowed on him include worship. A generation after his death, his work remains relevant and is studied by many serious scholars, but still no school exists. Schools form around those who live long in one place. Schumpeter taught in four universities and nowhere more than his eighteen years at Harvard (two years at Czernowitz, eleven years at Graz, and seven years at Bonn). The ideal spawning ground for a Schumpeter school would have been the University of Vienna, but he never taught there. By the time he reached Harvard, he was too long and too far away from his roots to create a school even if he had been so disposed, which he was not.

But the strongest reason for the absence of a Schumpeter school was the general attitude that undergirded his thinking. Universally-oriented and open-minded, he constructed a complex economic model and then went on to transcend economics. Gottfried Haberler expressed it best.

> *Tout comprendre c'est tout pardonner* is not a powerful rallying cry.... "I never wish to say anything definitive; if I have a function it is to open doors, not to close them"—he said in the informal farewell address to his students in Bonn.... The construction of ... a simplified system is evidently necessary for the formation of a compact group of disciples. But above all, unlike Marshall and Keynes, Schumpeter was constitutionally unable "to give his readers exactly what they craved—a message which was both high-minded and comforting—and at the same time to answer to the call of his conscience."... The main reason why no Schumpeter school developed is that Schumpeter was neither a reformer nor an enthusiastic partisan of capitalism, socialism, planning, or any other "ism;" he was a scholar and an intellectual.[19]

This judgment still holds true. Schumpeter's writings, if they are taken seriously, will themselves prevent their students from raising the flag of loyalty to Schumpeterian ideas. His writings may be interesting, useful, enlightening, and stimulating. Some of his ideas may even be true, but he never presented them as everlasting truth. At best, they only point in that direction. With Schumpeter, the student would always be prepared to tear off one intellectual garment in order to put on another at a moment's notice. He has to agree with the sentiment Schumpeter expressed in his Bonn farewell address: "Economics is not a philosophy but a science. Hence there should be no 'schools' in our field.... I for my part accept the judgment of future generations."[20]

7

Much of the judgment passed in recent days on Schumpeter relates to the policy recommendations that many believe originate in his theories, rather than the theories themselves. Although never forgetting his own warning that the link between theory and policy is tenuous at best, Schumpeter was a conservative in his economic policy thinking, favoring modest government intervention in the economy. The question naturally arises: Would Schumpeter agree with the policies proposed by supply-side economists today? The phrase "supply-side economics," which has recently come into vogue, does not have a technical economic meaning. It is used as a code word to distinguish a certain set of policies from those implied by demand-side economics (which are characterized by Keynesian economic analysis) and the policy of government spending to stabilize the economy. In reality, there is no such thing as supply-side economic theory, unless the user of that term means all of neoclassical economics that is not Keynesian economics. There are, however, supply-side *policies*.

Supply-side policies denote those measures designed to stimulate production through direct and indirect influences on producers—but without government intervention or increases in government demand. Instead of stimulating increased production by increasing government demand (the Keynesian solution), supply-siders would endeavor to influence those responsible for production decisions. They usually recommend lower taxes, accompanied by lower government spending, and less government regulation on producers; this constitutes a general withdrawal of the government from the economy. Despite all the rhetoric, the "fit" of supply-side policies with the stance or the performance of any political party or any administration is highly imperfect. In the early 1980s, some economists anticipated that fiscal policy retrenchment would so stimulate the economy that it would grow sufficiently to produce balanced budgets and full employment. It did grow somewhat, but unemployment remained high, despite a huge and growing deficit. The inflation retreated, but not thanks to supply-side policies; rather, tight monetary policies must receive credit for the defeat of inflation. Although time has dealt harshly with the earlier expectations, many economists still believe that supply-side policies merit serious attention.

Schumpeter's policy recommendations are scattered throughout writings that span a forty-five-year period. He never felt compelled to make a systematic policy statement or appeal, choosing instead to treat policy matters as obiter dicta—private political sentiments germane only to a given time and place and of no permanent importance. Even though he considered his policy ideas important and relevant, he remained aloof from policy making, mainly because policies stem from values and nonanalytical opinions, not scientific results. To the end, he refused to masquerade his policy opinions as scientific judgments.

Still, it is possible to piece together the economic policies that Schumpeter probably would have supported and opposed for the 1980s and 1990. First and foremost, he would uphold the sanctity of the entrepreneur and the holiness of innovation. The government should in no way interfere with the entrepreneur's desire or ability to innovate, including everyone from basement tinkerer to Bell Laboratory researchers. Beyond this, the government should do all it can to encourage innovation. All economic and social policies must be judged in light of their effect on this central dynamo of capitalism because innovation has given rise to the progress of the U.S. economy and the economic welfare of its people. Schumpeter would ask for a probusiness government on grounds that it is the private sector that moves the economy ahead and benefits everybody. Schumpeter would probably favor government efforts to support scientific, education, and research programs that encourage innovations. But government research programs would only supplement private research that would be stimulated by favorable tax treatment and a congenial environment.

Some aspects of Schumpeter's thinking will help to place him properly in the policy spectrum. Bear in mind that Schumpeter, having little confidence in democratic politicians, was a creature of and believed in paternalistic aristocracy. He was also convinced that each group within the electorate in a democracy will seek programs beneficial to it and oppose programs that might damage it. Combine these two propositions and we get a powerful argument in favor of automatic mechanisms that treat all groups equally wherever possible in the economy. Add to this Schumpeter's judgment that maximum economic welfare comes from unrestrained entrepreneurial initiative and innovation, as well as adequate savings to implement them, and the prescription for primary reliance on markets is complete.

Schumpeter's intolerance of politicians who print money to support programs that gain the favor of self-serving voting blocs made Schumpeter tolerant of those favoring the gold standard. Still, he did not accept the commodity theory of money underlying the gold standard, nor was he really a laissez-faire man. He might even agree with a legislation or a constitutional amendment to limit government spending, though he would doubt the ability of politicians to abide by it. A child of the autocratic imperialism of a monarchy long gone, he had less than boundless faith in democracy. Yet he believed the government could play a positive role in encouraging innovation, providing emergency help to those economically damaged by depression, and assisting in the adjustment processes. Such intervention would be great or small, depending on circumstances, not doctrine.

He preferred money managed by a fully independent central bank and politically neutral banking system. An independent Federal Reserve could forestall the aims of politicians from presidents to petty bureaucrats, especially if it limited to increasing the money supply for its two legitimate purposes only. The first purpose is to provide sufficient money for the needs of business. This kind of new money has no effect on the economy; it simply oils the economic machinery to keep it functioning properly. The second purpose of new money is to assist the process of innovation. An increase in money supply supports entrepreneurs when they borrow, enabling them to introduce innovations into the economy and subsequently to expand production. In line with this, Schumpeter rejected the quantity theory of money, which states that increases in the money supply necessarily yield price increases. In contrast, he saw that new money earmarked for innovations has only a minor price effect that is self-limiting and reversible, yet it does boost production by permitting new products and processes in the wake of innovation.

With regard to public finance, Schumpeter would favor a balanced budget most of the time, with modest government expenditures. Any program for the benefit of special groups, if such programs existed at all, would have to be fully funded by taxes, not borrowing. Under no circumstances would he use taxes or government spending to stimulate, suppress, or manipulate the economy as a whole. Stated simply, government should spend what it must to fulfill its obligations, and taxes should pay the bill. Always, both spending and taxes should encourage the entrepreneur, or at least not inhibit him.

There is no way to estimate Schumpeter's opinion of specific items in today's budget. But, based on his stated views, he would probably regard expenditures of federal social programs and programs for favored sectors— such as agriculture and medicine (through subsidies) and higher education (through student aid)—as excessive. He believed in an emergency safety net, to be sure, but not a net so high and so imperfect as to benefit people who do not require assistance while the truly needy slip through. Incentives, both reward and punishment, play a vital role in Schumpeter's thinking; he would look askance at any program that threatens incentives or withholds penalties.

He would therefore regard the mania for new social programs in the last few decades as sheer lunacy, reflecting the irresponsibility of political authorities who surrender to the cries, real or feigned, of every group wishing to slop from the federal trough. He feared that democratic leadership would one day cease to lead and instead start to follow the interest groups. He would fiercely resist this trend. He also feared Russia, and later the Soviet Union, long before most Americans began to worry about a potential threat. But the present burden of defense and the escalation of armaments are so far beyond anything in his experience that it is hard to guess what he might think. Because he believed in the efficacy of negotiations during both peacetime and war, it seems unlikely that he would approve of current defense spending levels.

He would regard the idea of indexing spending programs or taxes (that is, adjusting taxes and government benefits automatically to changes in prices) as a gross governmental abdication of responsibility. What pressures would coerce presidents and congressmen to confront and conquer inflation if taxpayers and recipients of government benefits see that government has blunted inflation's cutting edge?

Schumpeter's greatest fear concerning high government expenditures and consequent high taxes was their effect on entrepreneurs, innovation, and savings. High taxes depress the entrepreneur and discourage him from undertaking new ventures. But, if taxes must be high, then the key promoter of economic progress must receive a break or there won't be any production to tax. Taxation of enterprise income—and even worse, progressive taxation—in effect penalizes those who make development possible. Heavy taxation of savers in the form of income taxation similarly punishes those who provide the sinews of economic progress. Schumpeter would use taxes to encourage entrepreneurs and savers by taxing only the consumption part of income, rather than total income. He might also favor a value-added tax or a national sales tax, if their implementation would not burden the poor unduly.

In Schumpeter's day, social security and other social programs were still in their infancy, but he perceived the danger in their expansion, fearing they would undermine incentives and distort the economy because of the way they are financed. Payroll taxes raise labor costs and encourage the substitution of capital for labor at a time when high labor costs, underwritten by minimum wages, unemployment compensation, and other social programs, may contribute to unemployment. To Schumpeter, high involuntary unemployment signified, among other things, that wages were too high and government should not support efforts to keep them that way.

Nor could Schumpeter countenance a deficit with its intolerably pernicious effects. He would probably apply draconian measures to eliminate large chronic deficits, partly because the Federal Reserve cannot be free of political domination as long as the deficit exists and partly because the deficit represents society's unwholesome goal of trying to get something without paying for it. As the government's banker, the Federal Reserve must honor the government's checks, even when the treasury is overdrawn. But, in honoring government expenditures, the Federal Reserve must absorb government securities sold by the treasury at interest rates attractive enough to find lenders and then permit banks to expand credit. Because interest rates reflect the government's need to borrow, they are higher than they would be without deficits. Entrepreneurs with innovations in the wings face higher start-up costs and may even be crowded out of the market as they compete for funds necessary to initiate innovations. They also face uncertainty about the political management of money. Confronted with the ambiguity of the U.S. economy in the 1980s, wherein deficits simultaneously underlie a shakily prosperous economy and pose a serious threat to long-run economic prospects, Schumpeter would not hesitate. He would eliminate the deficit and let the economy adjust, allowing it to suffer whatever short-run pangs of anguish are necessary in order to achieve long-run stability.

Schumpeter would not follow the Keynesian policy of using government expenditures and taxation to try to manipulate and guide the economy to continuous full employment. He feared, justifiably, that each spending program would produce a constituency, which would combine with similar constituencies to perpetuate and enlarge government spending programs. He felt Keynesian short-run thinking would produce, in the long run, monstrous government spending and government planning. He also feared the high taxes needed to sustain the spending programs, especially those taxes that burdened entrepreneurs and savers. Even before his death, he saw the failure of the new Keynesian economics, which began to unfold in the 1960s, as inevitable.

With certainty, Schumpeter would also eliminate most latter-day government regulation. In many cases of regulation, he would regard either fiscal or property-rights solutions as more efficient. In his lifetime, pollution and environmental concerns were not the problems they are today, but surely Schumpeter would favor assigning environmental property rights to individuals and governments, enabling them to charge, through prices and taxes, for the use of the environment they own, rather than attempting to regulate hundreds of thousands of enterprises. Exceptions exist, but in most cases he would argue that the price system is a better regulator, and competition is an efficient if ruthless overseer.

8

With this in mind, then, how do we judge Schumpeter as an economist in policy matters? He was no monetarist, no laissez-faire enthusiast, and no libertarian; nor was he a gold bug. He did not accept Keynesian economic policies, nor was he a supply-sider in the way those words are currently used in the Washington lexicon of the 1980s. Today's supply-siders seem to want policies with little regard for analytical foundation, often calling for across-the-board tax reductions, selective spending cuts (particularly in the social part of the budget), large and increasing military expenditures, huge deficits, and deregulation devoid of direct stimulus to innovation, production, and savings. Schumpeter would argue that this political position is an anemic, poorly analyzed, and inept mixture of Keynesian and neoclassical economics with ideological and militaristic overtones. It is therefore alien to a politically neutral union of the old economics and his own vision and analysis of economic development.

But if supply-side economics is broadened to mean the acceptance of neoclassical economics and Manchesterian liberalism as the basis for policy, and narrowed to exclude its purely political and military overtones, then perhaps Schumpeter was a kind of supply-sider. Add the ideas that economic progress originates with innovating entrepreneurs and that policy should marshal all measures to encourage them, and Schumpeter becomes not only a supply-sider but one of its progenitors. Schumpeterian economics and values, which stress the importance of economic progress contributed by private, decentralized decision making, may provide a basis for resolving the current economic malaise. Although Schumpeter would argue that nothing can save capitalism, sensible policies can forfend its eventual demise. Still, in justice to Schumpeter, remember that he wore his policy cloak loosely, ready to don another garment when facts or circumstances changed.

And what can be said of Schumpeter's oft-cited prophecy of the demise of capitalism and the appearance of socialism in its stead? The economic history of the post-World War II period, as well as the conservative resurgence of the 1980s, suggests that there is still life in capitalism and that Schumpeter was wrong. Most economists are not prepared to write off capitalism, but many would add the word "yet." Schumpeter put no firm date on the succession of socialism and even waffled on just what constituted socialism. Certainly, many of the elements that he argued were undermining capitalism and favoring socialism are still at work and may one day bring the predominance of the public economy. And perhaps, as time passes, we will change our minds as to what constitutes capitalism and socialism, calling one the other.

9

Schumpeter wore many garments in the course of his life, and, as disparate as they were, all seemed somehow tailor-made. His sixty-seven years saw him play countless, yet natural, roles: those of inspired student, enfant terrible, government minister, bank president and businessman, and above all, professor; pretender to aristocracy, true elitist, and gentleman of manners; public speaker, scholar, writer, and counsellor; art historian, horseman, and traveller; complainer, sufferer from depression, critic, and ebullient entertainer; historian, theoretician, and secret worshipper to a private god. All these roles intertwined to make him a multifaceted man of paradox.

His life raises questions as to how a man can persevere in the face of repeated tragedy and disappointment; how a great romanticism can coexist with a deep commitment to science; how a man eaten up with grief, guilt, and inner torment can produce a life's work that overwhelms in sheer volume, erudition, and span of knowledge; and how a man who viewed himself as a failure could reach the pinnacle of his profession and still be haunted by the belief that it wasn't enough. A deep melancholy pervaded Schumpeter's life and character, self-doubt dogged his every turn, and his quest for knowledge left him frustrated and despairing.

Yet, he suffered silently so that he could do what he did best: teach. Committed to opening doors, he devoted himself to unlocking that "sacred decade" within others, always convinced that answers to the mysteries of how and why the world works as it does could be found, understood, and acted upon. Schumpeter's work is there for anyone to study, confirming his reputation as one of this century's great social scientists and economists. His public life stands as an open testament to the rewards of seemingly boundless energy and deep conviction. His internal life, however, must remain in the shadows, illuminated here and there, but ultimately so paradoxical that it confounds and confuses. This is, perhaps, the way Schumpeter would have wanted it.

Notes

1   *Quarterly Journal of Economics* 64, no. 3 (August 1950): 333-372.
2   *American Economic Review* 40, no. 4 (September 1950): 628-648.
3   *Econometrica* 18 (April 1950): 103-110.
4   *Economic Journal* 61, no. 241 (March 1951): 197-202.
5   *Review of Economics and Statistics* 33 (1951): pages.
6   Paul Sweezy quotes this letter from his brother in the Editor's Introduction in *Imperialism and Social Classes* (New York: Augustus Kelley, 1951), xxiv-xxv.
7   The complete listing of the holdings given by Mrs. Schumpeter was published in *The Catalogue of Prof. Schumpeter Library* (Tokyo, Japan: Hitotsubashi University Library, 1962).
8   His will, in Book 45, pp. 274-8 and Book 46, pp. 73-74, Town Hall Records, Salisbury, Connecticut, gave European assets (having no value) to Annie's family in Vienna and Mia's family in Bonn, and other assets to Elizabeth.
9   *American Economic Review* 70 (March 1980): 1-13.
10 Christian Seidl, ed., *Lectures on Schumpeterian Economics* (Berlin, Germany: Springer-Verlag, 1984). See also his "Supply-side Economics in Democratic Management," *Austria Today* January 1983: 6-10.
11 The Stevenson study was published by Greenwood Press (Westport, Conn., 1985), and Elizabeth Schumpeter's bibliography was published in the *Quarterly*

Journal of Economics 64, no. 3 (August 1950): 373-384.

12 James Buchanan of George Mason University won the Nobel Prize in 1986.

13 Bruno Frey, "Schumpeter, Political Economist," 126-42.

14 Translated by Axel Leijonhufvud and published by Richard Irwin for the American Economic Association, Homewood, 1970.

15 Published by Cambridge University Press, New York, 1982.

16 Published by Greenwood Press, 1982.

17 Published by MIT Press, Cambridge, 1984.

18 *American Economic Review* 67, no. 1 (1977); 72, no. 1 (1982); 73, no. 2 (1983); and Harvard University Press, Cambridge, 1982.

19 *Quarterly Journal of Economics* 64, no. 3 (August 1950): 333-372.

20 "Das Woher und Wohin unserer Wissenschaft," Schumpeter's final address to his Bonn students, 20 July 1932.

Appendix A

Chronology
Joseph Alois Schumpeter

1883	Born 8 February 1883 in Triesch (Třešť) Moravia, part of the Austro-Hungarian monarchy (now Czechoslovakia).
1887	Father (Josef Alois Karl Schumpeter) died.
1888-1893	Attended public school in Graz, Austria.
1893	Mother married Lieutenant Field Marshal Sigmund von Kéler.
1893-1901	Attended the Theresianum (Gymnasium) in Vienna.
1901-1906	Attended the University of Vienna. Received a Dr. juris in 1906.
1906-1907	Visited Berlin and London.
1906-1950	Published 200 articles in such journals as *American Economic Review, Der deutsche Volkswirt, Quarterly Journal of Economics, Der oesterreichische Volkswirt, Economic Journal, Review of Economics and Statistics, Schmollers Jahrbuch, Journal of Economic History, Journal of Political Economy, Econometrica, Economica, Zeitschrift fuer Volkswirtshaft,* and *Archiv fuer Socialwissenschaft.*
1907	Married Gladys Ricarde Seaver in England, November 5.
1907-1908	Worked as a trial attorney for the International Mixed Tribunal in Cairo, Egypt.
1908	*Das Wesen und der Hauptinhalt der theoretischen Nationaloekonomie* (The Nature and Principal Contents of Economic Theory) was published by Duncker and Humblot, Munich and Leipzig.

1909	Received his habilitation in political economy from the University of Vienna.
1909-1911	Worked as an associate professor at the University of Czernowitz.
1911	*Die Theorie der wirtschaftlichen Entwicklung* (The Theory of Economic Development) was published by Duncker and Humblot, Leipzig.
1911-1921	Worked as a professor at the University of Graz.
1913	Separated from Gladys Ricarde Schumpeter.
1913-1914	Worked as the Austrian exchange professor at Columbia University in New York City.
1913	Received a Doctor of Letters (Litt.D.) honorary degree from Columbia University.
1914	*Epochen der Dogmen- und Methodengeschichte* (Grundriss der Sozialoekonomik) (Epochs of Dogmatic and Methodological History [Outline of Social Economy]), J. C. B. Mohr (Paul Siebeck), Tuebingen.
1917	"Das Sozialprodukt und die Rechenpfennige" (The Social Product and Monetary Calculation), *Archiv fuer Sozialwissenschaft*, 44, 627-715.
1918	*Die Krise des Steuerstaats* (The Crisis of the Tax State), Leuschner Lubensky, Graz und Leipzig.
1919	"Zur Soziologie der Imperialismen" (The Sociology of Imperialisms), *Archiv fuer Socialwissenschaft und Sozialpolitik*, 46, 1-39, 275-310; also, J. C. B. Mohr (Paul Siebeck), Tuebingen.
1919	Served as a member of the German Socialization Commission, Berlin.
1919	Served as state secretary of finance, Republic of Austria, March-October.
1921-1924	Served as president of the Biedermann Bank, Vienna.
1925	Married Annie Reisinger November 5.
1925-1932	Worked as professor of economics at the University of Bonn, specializing in public finance.
1926	Mother, Frau von Kéler, died in June; wife, Annie, and child died in childbirth in August.
1927	"Die sozialen Klassen im ethnisch homogenen Milieu" (Social Classes in an Ethically Homogeneous Milieu), *Archiv fuer Sozialwissenschaft und Sozialpolitik 57, 1-67.*
1927-1928	Worked as visiting professor of economics at Harvard University.

1930	Worked as visiting professor of economics at Harvard University.
1930-1950	Was a founding member (1930) and council member of the Econometric Society.
1931	Was a visiting lecturer at Tokyo College of Commerce (Hitotsubashi University) and other universities in Japan.
1932-1935	Worked as a professor of economics at Harvard University.
1934	*Theory of Economic Development* (translation of 1911 book published in German) was published by Harvard University Press, Cambridge.
1935-1950	Was appointed to the position of George Baker professor of economics at Harvard University, specializing in teaching economic theory, money, cycles, and the history of economics.
1937	Married Elizabeth Boody Firuski in New York City.
1938	Received a Doctor of Philosophy (D. Phil) honorary degree from the University of Sofia.
1938-1939	Was elected to be vice-president of the Econometric Society.
1939	Became a naturalized U.S. citizen, 3 April
1939	*Business Cycles* was published by McGraw Hill, New York, in two volumes.
1940-1941	Served as president of the Econometric Society.
1942	*Capitalism, Socialism and Democracy* were published by Harper and Row, New York.
1942	Received a Master of Arts (M.A.) honorary degree from Harvard University.
1948	Was elected president of the American Economic Association.
1950	Named president designate of the International Economic Association.
1950	Died in Taconic, Connecticut, 8 January.
1951	*Ten Great Economists from Marx to Keynes*, a collection of articles edited by his widow, was published by Oxford University Press.
1954	*History of Economic Analysis,* edited by his widow, was published by Oxford University Press.
1970	*Das Wesen des Geldes* was published by Ruprecht, Goettingen, Germany.

Appendix B

Bibliographies of Schumpeter's Writings

The earliest bibliography of Schumpeter's work and works about him was prepared by his student, Klaere Tisch, in Bonn in 1933. Titled *Verzeichnis der Schriften und Rezensionen von Joseph Schumpeter*, it is a paperbound typescript of twenty-six pages. Christa Hasenclever of Bonn gave me the copy that I have. The number of titles dealing with Schumpeter's works—primarily book reviews—was limited.

Schumpeter's widow prepared an exhaustive bibliography of Schumpeter's own works shortly after his death. Entitled "Bibliography of the Writings of Joseph Alois Schumpeter," it was published in the *Quarterly Journal of Economics*, (64 [August 1950]: 373-84).

Michael I. Stevenson of the University of Nebraska compiled a more complete bibliography than that of Mrs. Schumpeter and has brought it up to date as a part of his *Joseph Alois Schumpeter: A Bibliography, 1905-1950* (Westwood, Conn.: Greenwood Press, 1985). It is a valuable reference work since many of the entries are annotated and it includes items by Schumpeter published since his death. Stevenson's bibliography is also a detailed bibliography of works dealing with Schumpeter—although there are probably more entries below—and its annotation makes it a valuable addition to Schumpeter literature despite its organization by date, then author.

In addition to the Tisch and Stevenson bibliographies and the one by Mrs. Schumpeter, another bibliography of Schumpeter's own writings, originally published in 1983, has been prepared by Motoi Kanazashi of Japan, showing especially the material translated into Japanese. It also includes material by

Schumpeter published since his death. The third edition, dated 1987, has 243 entries.

Schumpeter never prepared a formal vita of the kind maintained by professors today, kept no systematic record of what he wrote, and did not even possess copies of much that he had written. When the Walgren Foundation asked him for a vita in preparation for the lectures he was to give in Chicago in 1950, he replied with a list of six works, including his four major books and his articles on imperialisms and social classes. A few items attributable to Schumpeter, as noted in the text, have been published since 1950, including a part of his money book, *Das Wesen des Geldes* (1970). I arranged to have published two of his Japanese lectures: "The 'Crisis' in Economics—Fifty Years Ago" (*Journal of Economic Literature* XX [September 1982]: 1049-1059) and "Recent Developments of Political Economy" (*Kobe University Economic Review* 28 [1982]: 1-15), as well as some other minor items, including a part of a 1937 rationality paper that I found in the archives and the notes for the Wahlgren lectures, both published in recent issues of *Zeitschrift fuer die gesamte Staatswissenschaft*. A different version of the first part of *History of Economic Analysis*, which I found in the Schumpeter papers in the Harvard University Archives, was published in a book edited by Warren Samuels and called *Research in the History of Economic Thought and Methodology* (Greenwich, Conn.: JAI Press, 1987). There probably remains in the Schumpeter papers other material worthy of publication.

Schumpeter's papers in the Harvard University Archives still include several papers and other unpublished material, including a part of the manuscript of his book on money, which have never been published. For example, there is a six-page typescript on the sales tax, an essay on welfare economics, some typescript on savings, a German typescript on business cycles, a typescript of notes for five lectures on wage and tax policy (delivered in Mexico), and many other unidentified pieces. Only a limited amount of this may be worthwhile publishing at this time, although, at some later date, scholars may decide that anything Schumpeter wrote should be published. I have searched in vain for any manuscript of Schumpeter's projected book on economic theory, *The Theoretical Apparatus of Economics*. I found scraps that might have been notes or preliminary drafts, including a proposal he made to Dr. Nicholas Georgescu-Roegen for a book on economic theory that they might write together, but nothing seemed to contain anything that cried out for publication.

One of the most important of the new Schumpeterian writings are the three World War I political memoranda found by Christian Seidl in the National Library of Austria. They are published in Wolfgang F. Stolper and Christian Seidl's *Aufsaetze zur Wirtschaftspolitik* (Tuebingen, Germany: J.C.B. Mohr [Paul Siebeck], 1985).

The International J. A. Schumpeter Society plans to sponsor the republication of the original (1911) *Die Theorie der wirtschaftlichen Entwicklung* with a comparison with subsequent editions by Wolfgang Stolper. Dr. Stolper also has the German notes, prepared by Klaere Tisch, to the class in Finanzwissenschaft (Public Finance) that Schumpter gave in the winter semester 1928/1929 at the University of Bonn, but it is unlikely that these are publishable. Notes of his class in public finance at the University of Graz also exist in the hands of Dr. Christian Seidl.

Schumpeter's own works offer no explicit autobiographical references and little factual material that is helpful from the point of view of his biography. Still, his writings team with the pattern and course of his thinking. As quoted in the text, Simon Kuznets wrote that his *Business Cycles* seemed like the diary of an intellectual journey. On substantive issues he often tells his readers what he thinks, why he thinks it, the process by which he arrived at what he thought, and the qualms he has about what he thinks, all the while never departing from the substance of what he is writing about. His writings show skill in presenting pros and cons and leading the reader to the conclusion he wants the reader to believe.

Schumpeter must be read with care, however, not only because he presumes intelligence and diligence by the reader but because he is sometimes playful, presenting, for example, elaborate arguments in favor of a position he does not necessarily agree with and sometimes leaving the reader in doubt about his own position.

Appendix C

Personal Interviews

I have benefitted immensely from many people with whom I have talked and corresponded about Schumpeter. Mostly these are people who knew Schumpeter personally in life and were either students or colleagues. To my great sorrow, some of them died between the time I talked to them and the present. Although no one still alive knew Schumpeter in his first twenty years, many knew Schumpeter well and talked to me of his early years.

Among those to whom I am greatly indebted are:

Gottfried Haberler, American Enterprise Institute in Washington,
Toni Stolper, the widow of Gustav Stolper who lived in Alexandria, Virginia until she died recently,
Herbert Furth, American-Austrian, retired official of the Federal Reserve System,
Paul Rosenstein-Rodan of Boston University, now deceased,
Eduard Maerz, now deceased, of the University of Vienna,
Wolfgang Stolper, professor emeritus, University of Michigan,
Arthur Smithies, Fritz Machlup, and Redvers Opie, all three now deceased,
Edward Mason, professor emeritus, Harvard University,
Wassily Leontief, New York University,
Dr. Steffy Browne of Brooklyn College,
Nicholas Georgescu-Roegen, Vanderbilt University,
John Kenneth Galbraith of Harvard University, who frequently mentions Schumpeter in his writings,

Christian Seidl, University of Kiel, Germany,
Guenther Harkort, now deceased, Paul Samuelson of MIT, and Christa
    Hasenclever, both of Bonn,
Paul Sweezy of the *Monthly Review*,
Alex Balinky of Rutgers University, and
Juergen Backhaus of The Netherlands.

Ms. Lucia Krassnigg, niece of Schumpeter's second wife, also helped me a
great deal in conversation in Vienna and in correspondence. I enjoyed
conversations with Mrs. Emilie Schumpeter of Vienna, the widow of Karl
Schumpeter, the son of the brother of Schumpeter's father. She had stories of
the family as well as pictures. I have also talked to many Schumpeter
students, including Joseph P. McKenna (University of Missouri-St. Louis),
Hyman Minsky (Washington University), Alfred Kahn (Cornell University),
as well as those already mentioned and many others. Among the
noneconomists I talked to at length about Schumpeter is Dr. Richard
Swedberg of the Department of Sociology of the University of Stockholm, a
specialist in economic sociology.

Wolfgang Stolper, Christian Seidl, and Eduard Maerz were most helpful in
providing me with newspaper clippings from the Vienna press and other
documents concerning Schumpeter's period as state secretary of finance and
president of the Biedermann Bank. There are only a few left with whom I
talked who knew Schumpeter in Vienna days. One was Professor Paul N.
Rosenstein-Rodan, now deceased, of Boston University. Mrs. Toni Stolper,
Schumpeter's friend in Vienna and Bonn, also reminisced with me about her
days in Vienna and Berlin. Dr. Herbert Furth probably knows more about the
political and economic events and circumstances of this period in Vienna than
anyone else. Dr. Steffy Browne, retired professor of economics, Brooklyn
College, knew Schumpeter in Vienna and later and knows every American
Austrian who has lived since her days in Vienna. Many of Schumpeter's
colleagues, including Wassily Leontief and Edward Mason, remember
Schumpeter's comments about the early part of his life.

Additional information about Schumpeter's Bonn period comes from
letters Schumpeter wrote between 1925 and 1932, some of which were
published in Eduard Maerz's *Joseph Alois Schumpeter—Forscher, Lehrer
und Politiker* (Wien, Austria: Verlag fuer Geschichte und Politik, 1983).
These and other letters were originally in the possession of Dr. Gottfried
Haberler, who provided me with copies. The late Dr. Redvers Opie also
kindly gave me copies of his correspondence with Schumpeter.

The people most closely associated with Schumpeter in the 1930s and
1940s and with whom I talked are Wolfgang Stolper, Paul Sweezy, Edward
Mason, Gottfried Haberler, John Kenneth Galbraith, Wassily Leontief, Paul

Samuelson, Fritz Machlup, and Herbert Zassenhaus. I am also most grateful to Haberler, Leontief, Zassenhaus, and Mrs. Sweezy. I also corresponded with many others, including Shigeto Tsuru, Kei Shibata, Robert Bryce, Herbert Furth, Martin Bronfenbrenner, James Earley, and many others.

Appendix D

The Schumpeter Papers

After Schumpeter died, his widow organized his papers and presented them to the Harvard University Houghton (Rare Book) Library, although the Harvard University Archives usually is the custodian of the papers of professors at Harvard. The library later turned over all Schumpeter material to the archives. It may be that she held out some papers and destroyed some parts of the Schumpeter diary, especially during the late 1940s, since there are some missing unexplained dates as well as other material. She also gave some manuscripts of published material to admirers of Schumpeter and perhaps threw away some scraps of paper on which Schumpeter had scribbled notes. For example, the manuscript of *Capitalism, Socialism and Democracy* is missing, and Japanese sources believe that she gave that manuscript to Professors Nakayama and Tobata. Twenty-seven of the boxes are unidentified notes—the bits of paper on which Schumpeter made notes—but the amount of material contained in those boxes could not contain all the voluminous notes he made over the years, even in the United States.

In the 1960s, all the Schumpeter papers (except for 115 books that Schumpeter and later Mrs. Schumpeter used most) that Mrs. Schumpeter gave to the Kress Economics Library of the George Baker Library of the Harvard School of Business Administration were collected and organized in the archives in Pusey Library. I am most grateful to Mr. Hanley Holden, curator of the archives, and his staff for their unfailing helpfulness, as well as to Ms. Ruth N. Rogers, curator of the Kress Library of Business and Economics, where Schumpeter worked in the 1940s.

Since there are no relatives of either Schumpeter or Mrs. Schumpeter, there are no restrictions on the use of the Schumpeter papers. They belong to the Department of Economics at Harvard University, whose chairmen in recent years, Professors Zvi Griliches and Jerry Green, have been helpful in making material available and in granting permission for publication.

One general biographic folder appears under the archives classification number HUG 300 in the Harvard University Archives. In the classification HUG(B), there are four boxes—S276.2, S276.10, S276.50, and S276.90—all under Schumpeter's name. These are mainly photographs. There are also two boxes of his published writings, listed as 53M-34(8), but there is no collection of all of Schumpeter's writings in one place at Harvard. The main body of Schumpeter papers is in the classification HUG(FP). Under Schumpeter's name are ten boxes HUG(FP) 4.1, "Brief Daily Records, ca. 1931-1948." This is where most of Schumpeter's diary appears. Although some parts of the diary are in bound notebooks, much of the material consists of loose bits of paper, many undated. HUG(FP) 4.15 consists of one box of papers, manuscripts, and correspondence with August Loesch. 1937-1940. Most of it is Loesch's own work. HUG(FP) 4.2 is one box labelled "Mostly Annie's Diary," and consists of the notebook that is the first copy Schumpeter made of his wife's diary. HUG(FP) 4.20, 4.21, 4.25, and 4.29 consist of five boxes of correspondence concerning the American Economic Association and the Econometric Society, as well as a card file of 1940 addresses.

HUG(FP) 4.3 and 4.4 are each one box of miscellaneous personal writings and correspondence, including letters from Annie as well as Elizabeth to Joseph. HUG(FP) 4.42 is eight boxes of notes—mainly speeches and papers he gave on various occasions in Europe and the United States—while HUG(FP) 4.5 is two boxes of letters from Mia (Maria Stoeckel) to Joseph after he had left Bonn in 1932. HUG(FP) 4.50 is a single box containing drafts of speeches and papers. In HUG(FP) 4.51 is a box containing Schumpeter's Lowell lectures and drafts. Correspondence related to Schumpeter's death fills the three boxes numbered HUG(FP) 4.6. HUG(FP) 4.62 consists of twelve boxes containing Schumpeter's class notes for the 1930s and 1940s.

Schumpeter's general correspondence from the 1920s to 1950 is in nine boxes called HUG(FP) 4.7. The series HUG(FP) 4.71, 4.72, 4.73, 4.74, and 4.75 is nine boxes of notes and manuscript concerned with Mrs. Schumpeter's bibliography, and Schumpeter's manuscripts on socialism, *Rudimentary Mathematics...*, *Ten Great Economists*, and *Business Cycles*. There are two boxes in HUG(FP) 4.75.5, one containing notes and the manuscript of *Business Cycles* and the other miscellaneous correspondence. The manuscript and notes both by Schumpeter and Elizabeth Schumpeter of the book *History of Economic Analysis* appear in twenty-five boxes under the number

HUG(FP) 4.76. HUG(FP) 4.77 consists of eleven boxes (but one box, designated Money book, is missing) of miscellaneous manuscripts and typescripts, including some of his money manuscript. In HUG(FP) 4.7.8, a single box, is correspondence of Schumpeter with Arthur Smithies, given to the archives by Smithies. HUG(FP) 4.78 is a box of articles, speeches, and notes. Correspondence between 1932 and 1940 fills the four boxes numbered HUG(FP) 4.8. The largest section consists of twenty-seven boxes of unidentified notes, numbered HUG(FP) 4.80, while HUG(FP) 4.90 is the manuscript of Haberler's biographical obituary.

The quality of much of the material in the archives is not good, and the personnel of the Archives had not yet undertaken a systematic culling of the papers. For example, in HUG(FP) 4.80 (the unidentified notes), box after box is a jumble of unsorted and disorganized notes. Some are diary-like. Some are notes dealing with economic and historical matters. Some are classroom notes or notes of speeches. But mostly, these are those little bits of paper on which Schumpeter jotted down something and put it in his pocket. Scraps of paper appear in many of the folders in other boxes as well.

Schumpeter did not keep a file of incoming correspondence; much of the incoming correspondence he simply tossed in the wastebasket. Some incoming letters he tore into fourths and eighths, using the back to write notes on. Much of the Schumpeter outgoing correspondence was handwritten. That for which carbons do remain is often trivial and contains little professional discourse.

Some items are strangely missing from the Schumpeter papers. For example, neither his honorary M.A. from Harvard nor the honorary degree from the University of Sofia are in the papers, nor is the certificate of his marriage to Elizabeth Boody. The only passport is a German passport issued when he was in Bonn. It is possible he never had a U.S. passport. Nor are there any financial papers, checkbooks, or bank statements. It is also possible that Elizabeth kept some of Schumpeter's papers or possessions, but the items do not appear in the papers Mrs. Schumpeter left.

Mrs. Schumpeter's papers are on deposit at the Schlesinger Library of Radcliffe College in Cambridge, Massachusetts. The three boxes consist primarily of her professional correspondence, documents concerning her life, and material concerning Schumpeter and his work both while he was alive as well as during the period when she survived him and tried hard to secure and increase his reputation. Undoubtedly more of her personal papers existed, but her Radcliffe classmates, who placed the papers in the library, must have held out or destroyed some papers.

Appendix E

Bibliography

This bibliography contains most of the important comments on the life and works of Joseph Schumpeter, but is still far from complete. It does not include Schumpeter's own works. A bibliography containing all books and journal articles dealing with Schumpeter in a significant way would be so large and diffuse that it would not be useful, since a large share of economics books published each year at least refer to Schumpeter and his work and some devote some space to describing his work. And the Social Science Citation Index each year lists another hundred or more articles in which Schumpeter's name and a reference to his work appear. Some of these deal centrally with Schumpeter's work.

Work continues all over the world on various aspects of Schumpeter's work. To keep tabs on what is being published about Schumpeter, it is necessary to follow several subcategories of economics, such as economic theory, history of economics, economic history, business cycles, economic growth and development, money and banking, and industrial organization in the *Journal of Economic Literature*. The economic literature, as well as the large literature in sociology and political science, is the best place to find detailed and sometimes conflicting evaluations of particular studies of Schumpeter. The contemporary writer most familiar with the broad range of Schumpeter's work is probably Wolfgang Stolper.

Abeken, Gerhard. "Der Kapitalprofit in der fortschreitenden Volkswirtschaft" dissertation, University of Rostock, Germany, 1927.

Adams, Arthur B. *Economics of Business Cycle*, New York, N.Y.: McGraw-Hill, 1925.

Adams, Walter, and Herbert Kisch. "Joseph Schumpeter." In *Encyclopedia of American Biography*, 969-71. New York, N.Y.: Harper and Row, 1974.

Adams, Walter, and J. B. Dirlum. "Big Steel, Invention and Innovation." *Quarterly Journal of Economics* 80, no. 2 (May 1966): 167-89.

Adelman, Irma. "Schumpeter." In *Theories of Economic Growth and Development*, edited by Irma Adelman, 94-108. Palo Alto, Calif.: Stanford University Press, 1961.

Albach, H. "Zur Wiederentdeckung des unternehmers in der Wirtschaftspolitischen Diskussion." *Zeitschrift fuer gesamte Staatswissenschaft* 135, no. 4 (1979): 433-53.

Aldrup, Dieter. "Schumpeter und der Marxismus." *Jahrbuch fuer Sozialwissenschaft* 22, no. 1 (1971): 12-17.

Ames, Edward. "Research, Invention, Development, and Innovation." *American Economic Review* 51(1961): 370-81.

Amonn, Alfred. "Die Probleme der wirtschaftlichen Dynamik." *Archiv fuer Sozialwissenschaft* 38 (1914): 83-114.

Anderson, B. M., Jr. "Schumpeter's Dynamic Economics." *Political Science Quarterly* 30 (July 1915): 645-60.

Angell, J. W. *Investment and Business Cycles*. New York, N.Y.: McGraw-Hill, 1941.

Anonymous. "In Memoriam Joseph A. Schumpeter." *Cavalcade* (Viennese magazine), 1950.

——— "Jos. Schumpeter: Wesen," Kurse Besprechung im *Archiv fuer Sozialwissenschaft* 28 (1909): 339.

——— Review of *Aufsaetze zur Sociologie, Journal of Economic History* 16 (1956): 4.

——— Review of *Das Wesen und der Hauptinhalt der theoretischen Nationaloekonomie, Political Science Quarterly* 24 (1953): 19.

——— Reviews of *Business Cycles. American Historical Review* 46 (1940): 96; *Annals* (American Academy of Political and Social Science) 208 (1940): 205; *Review of Politics* 3 (1941): 261.

——— Reviews of *Capitalism, Socialism and Democracy. American Political Science Review* 37 (1943): 523; *American Scholar* 17 (1947-48): 114 and 41 (1971): 484; *Booklist* 15 (January 1943): 194; *British Journal of Sociology* 28, no. 4 (1977): 526; *International Affairs* 25 (1949): 330; *Journal of Economic History* 3 (1943): 238; *Manchester Guardian* 1 December 1943: 3; *New Republic* 20 December 1975: 31; *Political Quarterly* 21 (1950): 418; *Political Science Quarterly* 58 (1943): 265; *Review of Politics* 5 (1943): 120;

Social Research 20 (1953): 55; *Sociological Review* ns 26 (1978): 177-78; *Times Literary Supplement* 16 October 1943: 501.

—— Reviews of *Die Theorie der wirtschaftlichen Entwicklung. Political Science Quarterly* 30 (1915): 645.

—— Reviews of *Economic Doctrine and Method. American Journal of Economics and Sociology* 16, no. 1 (1956): 105; *Economic History Review* ns 8 (1955): 411; *Journal of Economic History* 15 (1955): 44; *Social Sciences* 31 (1956): 125; *Times Literary Supplement* 18 March 1955: 168.

—— Reviews of *History of Economic Analysis. Business Week* 20 March 1954: 90; *Foreign Affairs* 32 (1954): 670; *Freeman* 5 (1954-55): 190; *Journal of Economic History* 15 (1955): 323; *Saturday Review of Literature* 22 May 1954: 33; *Science and Society* 19 (1955): 71.

—— Reviews of *Imperialisms and Social Classes. American Journal of Sociology* 57 (1951-52): 198; *Economic History Review* ns 4 (1952): 403; *International Affairs* 28 (1952): 196; *Journal of Politics* 14 (1952): 541; *Rural Sociology* 16 (1951): 412; *Social Service Review* 25 (1951): 263; *Times Literary Supplement* 20 July 1951: 454; *World Politics* 4 (1951-52): 402.

—— Reviews of *Ten Great Economists from Marx to Keynes. American Journal of Economics and Sociology* 13, no. 2 (1954): 224; *Canadian Forum* 31 (1951): 138; *International Affairs* 29 (1953): 87; *Journal of Economic History* 15 (1955): 191; *Political Science Quarterly* 67 (1952): 150; *San Francisco Chronicle* 22 July 1951: 20; *Twentieth Century* 152 (1952): 189.

—— Reviews of the *Theory of Economic Development. Political Science Quarterly* 30 (1915): 645; Political Science Quarterly 42 (1927); *Books* (28 July 1935): 14; *Social Research* 2 (1935): 393; *Social Research* 20 (1953): 19.

—— "Schumpeter Centenary: The non-Marxist Revolutionary." *Economist* 19-20 (19 November 1983).

Aufricht, Hans. "The Methodology of Schumpeter's History of Economic Analysis." *Zeitschrift fuer Nationaooekonomie* 18 (1958): 384-441.

Ayres, C. E. "Capitalism in Retrospect: with a Comparison of Two Recent Works: J. A. Schumpeter's Capitalism, Socialism and Democracy and H. von Beckerath's In Defense of the West." *Southern Economic Journal* 9 (1943): 293-301.

Ayzenshtadt, A. "The Learned Handmaidens of American Capital." *Planovoye Khozyaystvo* 4 (1947). Translated by E. D. Domar and published in *American Economic Review* 39 (1949): 933-34.

Bachrach, P. *The Theory of Democratic Elitism: A Critique.* Boston, Mass.: Little Brown, 1967.

Bagotti, T. "Joseph Alois Schumpeter." *Revista Internationalize di Scienze Economische e Commerciali* 7 November 1960): 1069-75.

Balabkins, Nicholas W. "Repressed Inflation and Pseudo-Innovations." *Technovation* 3 (1985): 187-97.

———— "Schumpeter, Keynes, and Marx: A Centennial Celebration." Three lectures given by Nicholas W. Balabkins, Jon T. Innes, and J. Ralph Lindgren. Fairchild-Martindale Center, Lehigh University, Bethlehem, Pennsylvania. 1983.

Balinky, Alexander. *Marx's Economics: Origin and Development.* Lexington, Mass.: D. C. Heath, 1970.

Bandaloukas, Claude B. "The Destiny of Capitalism according to Marx and Schumpeter." *Greek Quarterly Review of Economics and Political Science* 8 (1953): 1.

Barnett, H. G. *Innovation: The Strategy of Economic Development.* New Haven, Conn.: Yale University Press, 1953.

Bauer, Otto. *Die oesterreichische Revolution.* Vienna, Austria: Wiener Volksbuchhandlung, 1923. Translated as *The Austrian Revolution* (London, England, 1925) and reissued by Burt Franklin, New York, N.Y., 1970.

Baumol, William J. "Entrepreneurship in Economic Theory." *American Economic Review* 53 (2 May 1968): 64-71.

———— *Economic Dynamics*, 3rd ed. New York, N.Y.:MacMillan, 1970. Chapter 3: "Dynamics of Marx and Schumpeter".

Bayer, Hans. "J. Schumpeter et l'école economique autrichienne." *Economie Appliquée* 4 (1951): 167-90.

Beach, E. F. "A Modified Schumpeterian Process." *Indian Economic Journal* 28, no. 3 (1981): 51-62.

Becker, H. M. "Joseph Alois Schumpeter (1883-1950)." *ESB* (Rotterdam, Holland) 61, no. 3077 (1976): 1069-71.

Becker, James F. "Joseph A. Schumpeter: Historian of Professional Economics." In *Research in the History of Economic Thought and Methodology: A Research Annual*, edited by W. J. Samuels, 131-45. Greenwich, Conn.: JAI Press, 1983.

Becker, James, and Mark Perlman. "Joseph Schumpeter." In *Research in the History of Economic Thought and Methodology*, edited by Warren J. Samuels. Greenwich, Conn.: JAI Press, 1983

Beckerath, Herbert von. "Joseph A. Schumpeter as a Sociologist." *Weltwirtschaftliches Archiv* 65 (1950): 200-214. Reprinted in Seymour Harris, ed., *Joseph A. Schumpeter, Social Scientist*, 110-19.

Beckerath, Irwin von. "Einige Bermerkungen zu Schumpeters Theorie der wirtschaftlichen Entwicklung." *Schmollers Jahrbuch* 53 (1929): 2.
―――― Review of *Capitalism, Socialism and Democracy. Zeitschrift fuer die gesamte Staatswissenschaft* 106 (1950): 193-222.
Bell, Daniel, and Irving Kristol, eds. *Capitalism Today.* New York, N.Y.: Basic Books, 1971.
Bell, Daniel. "The Prospects of American Capitalism: On Keynes, Schumpeter, and Galbraith." In *The End of Ideology*, edited by Daniel Bell. Glencoe, Ill.: Free Press, 1960.
―――― *The Coming of Post Industrial Society.* New York, N.Y.: Basic Books, 1973.
Below, G. Review of *Die Krise des Steuerstaats, Kurze Besprechung, Conrads Jahrbuch* 121 (1923): 302.
Benguigu, G. Review of *Imperialism and Social Classes. Sociologie du Travail* 1 (1973): 95-96.
Bennion, E. G. "Unemployment in the Theories of Schumpeter and Keynes." *American Economic Review* 33 (June 1943): 336-47.
Bergson, Abram, et al. "Essays in Honor of Joseph A Schumpeter." *Review of Economic Statistics* 25, no. 1 (February 1943): 2-100. Essays by Bergson, Goodwin, Haavelmo, Lange, Machlup, Marschak, Metzler, Samuelson, Smithies, Staehle, Stolper, Sweezy, Wilson, and Worcester.
Berliner, Joseph. *The Innovation Decision in Soviet Industry.* Cambridge, Mass.: MIT Press, 1976.
Bernhauer, Ernst. "Die Konjunkturtheorie Joseph Schumpeters." *Zeitschrift fuer die gesamte Staatswissenschaft* 115, no. 4 (1959): 626-55.
Bissell, Richard. *You Can Always Tell A Harvard Man.* New York, N.Y.: McGraw-Hill, 1962.
Bladen, W. W. "Schumpeter's History of Economic Analysis and Some Related Books." *Canadian Journal of Economics and Political Science* 22 (1956): 103-15.
Bliss, C. P. "Schumpeter, the Big Disturbance and Retailing." *Social Forces* 39 (1960): 72-76.
Blodgett, R. H. Review of *Capitalism, Socialism and Democracy. American Academy of Political and Social Science Annals* 228 (1943): 126.
Boehm, Stephan. "Schumpeter's Theory of Economic Change." Paper presented at History of Economics Meeting, Charlottesville, Virginia, 24-26 May 1983. 16 pages.
Boehm, Stephen, ed. *Joseph A. Schumpeter: Beitrage zur Sozialoekonomik* (Schumpeter's Essays in German). Vienna, Austria: Bohlau, 1987.
Boehm-Bawerk, Eugen. "Ein 'dynamische' Theorie des Kapitalizinses." *Zeitschrift fuer Volkswirtschaft* 22 (1913): 640-56.

Boes, Dieter, and Hans-Dieter Stolper, editors. *Schumpeter oder Keynes? Zur Wirtschaftspolitik der neunziger Jahre.* Berlin/New York: Springer Verlag, 1984.

Bonne, Alfred. "Towards a Theory of Implanted Development in Underdeveloped Countries." *Kyklos* 9 (January 1956): 1-24.

Bottomore, Tom. "The Decline of Capitalism, Sociologically Considered." In *Schumpeter's Vision,* edited by Arnold Heertje (see), 22-44.

Bourricaud, F. "Democratie et Polyarchie. Une Forme nouvelle de Pouvoir." *Esprit* 27, no. 5 (1959): 772-88.

Bousquet, G. H. "L'oeuvre scientifique de quelques economistes étrangers." *Review d'économie politique* 43 (1929): 1017-49.

——— "Souvenirs et Reflexions sur Schumpeter (1883-1950)." *Revue d'economique politique* 92 (February 1982): 240-44.

——— "Trois etudes sociologiques de J. Schumpeter." *Cahiers Vilfredo Pareto* issue 19, vol. 59 (1981): 149-59.

Bowman, R. T. Review of *Rudimentary Mathematics for Economists and Statisticians. American Economic Review* 36 (1949): 925-927.

Brahmananda, P. R. "Joseph Alois Schumpeter: A Centennial Appraisal." *Indian Economic Journal* issue 31, vol. 2 (December 1983): 1-26.

Brandt, J. "Growth and Creative Destruction." *Revue d'économie politique* 74 (March 1964): 603-41.

Breton, Y. "La theorie schumpeterienne de l'entrepreneur ou le probleme de la connaissance economique." *Review economique* issue 35, vol. 2 (March 1983): 247-66.

Brittan, S. "Can Democracy Manage an Economy (Capitalism, Socialism and Democracy)." In *The End of the Keynesian Era: Essays on the Disintegration of Keynesian Political Economy,* edited by Robert J. A. Skidelsky. New York, N.Y.: Holmes and Meier, 1977.

Brogan, D. W. Review of *Capitalism, Socialism and Democracy, Spectator* October 1943: 412.

Bronfenbrenner, Martin. "A Reformulation of Naive Profit Theory." *Southern Economic Journal* 26 no. 4 (1960): 300-309.

——— "Schumpeter's Contributions to the Study of Comparative Economic Systems." In *Schumpeterian Economics,* edited by Helmut Frisch (see), 95-112.

Bruche, G. Review of *Die Krise des Steuerstaats. Argument* 19 (1977): 616-18.

Bruck, F. W. *Social and Economic History of Germany from William II to Hitler.* New York, N.Y.: Oxford University Press, 1938.

Buck, Paul, ed. *Social Sciences at Harvard, 1860-1920.* Cambridge, Mass.: Harvard University Press, 1965.

Budge, Siegfried. "Waren-oder Anweisungstheorie des Geldes?" *Archiv fuer Sozialwissenschaft* 46 (1919): 732.

Buelow, Friedrich. Review of *Capitalism, Socialism and Democracy. Weltwirtschaftliches Archiv* 67 (January 1951): 42-46.

Burchardt, Fritz. "Beitrage zum Problem der Static bei Schumpeter." Ph.D. dissertation, Universitaet Kiel, 1925. Machineschrift.

Burke, William. "Mitchell-Schumpeterian Criticism." *Social Science* 36 (March 1961): 177-82.

Burns, Arthur F., ed. *Wesley Clair Mitchell, the Economic Scientist.* New York, N.Y.: National Bureau of Economics Press, 1952.

Burns, Edward McNall. "Twentieth Century Conservatism." In *Ideas in Conflict: The Political Theories of the Contemporary World,* edited by Edward M. Burns. New York, N.Y.: W. W. Norton, 1960.

Calzoni, Guiseppe. *Credito, innovazioni e ciclo economico: un modello di sviluppo schumpeteriano.* Milan, Italy: F. Angeli, 1980

Carlin, Edward A. "Schumpeter's Constructed Type—The Entrepreneur." *Kyklos* 9 (January 1956): 7-43.

Casa-Gonzales, A. "El Concepto 'schumpeteriano' de la formación de capital y los paises en vías de desarrollo." *Trimestre Económico* 33 (1966): 132.

Casson, Mark. *The Entrepreneur: An Economic Theory.* London, England: Rowman and Allenheld, 1982.

Chabert, Alexandre. "Schumpeter et la methode economique." *Economie Appliquee* 3 (1950): 457-71.

Chakravarty, Sukhamoy. *Alternatives Approaches to a Theory of Economic Growth: Marx, Marshall and Schumpeter.* New Delhi, India: Orient Longman, 1980.

Chalk, A. F. "Schumpeter's Views on the Relation of Philosophy and Economics." *Southern Economic Journal* 24 (June 1958): 271-82.

Chamberlin, Edward Hastings. "The Impact of Recent Monopoly Theory on the Schumpeterian System." *Review of Economics and Statistics* 33 (1951): 133-8; in *Joseph A. Schumpeter,* edited by Seymour Harris (see), 83-88.

Clark, John Bates. "Joseph Schumpeter: Das Wesen und der Hauptinhalt der theoretischen Nationaloekonomie." *Political Science Quarterly* 24 (1909): 721-5.

———— Review of Schumpeter *Theorie der wirtschaftlichen Entwicklung. American Economic Review* 2 (April 1912): 973ff.

Claude, H. "Schumpeter si curental reformist din Franta." *Probleme Economice* (Bucharest) 11, no. 5 (1958): 57-71.

Clemence, Richard V., and Francis S. Doody. *The Schumpeterian System.* Cambridge, Mass.: Addison-Wesley Press, 1950. Reprinted by A. M. Kelley, New York, N.Y., 1966.

Clemens, Helene. "Schumpeter Kapitalzintheorie." Ph.D. dissertation, University of Freiberg, 1929.

Coats, A. W. "History of Economic Analysis." *Economica* 22, no. 5 (1955): 171-4.

Coe, Richard D., and Charles K. Wilbur, *Capitalism and Democracy: Schumpeter Revisited.* South Bend, Ind.: Notre Dame University Press, 1984.

Cole, Arthur H. "Entrepreneurship As an Area of Research." *Journal of Economic History*, supplement 2 (1942): 118-26.

Cole, Arthur H. "Meso-Economics: a Contribution from Entrepreneurial History." *Explorations in Entrepreneurial History* 6 (January 1968): 3-33.

Conrad, Otto, "Der Zusammenbruch der Grenznutzentheorie, eine Auseinandersetzung mit Joseph Schumpeter," *Conrads Jahrbuch* 129 (1928): 481-528.

Cramer, Dale L., and Charles G. Leathers. "Schumpeter and the Leviathan View of Government." Paper delivered at the New York History of Economics Society meeting, 1986.

——— "Schumpeter and the Supply-Siders on Say's Law." Abstract in *Bulletin of the History of Economics Society* 7, no. 1 (summer 1986): 31.

——— "Schumpeter's Corporatist Views—Links among His Social-Theory, Quadragesimo Anno, and Moral Reform." *History of Political Economy* 13 (April 1981):745-71.

——— "Veblen and Schumpeter on Imperialism." *History of Political Economy* 9 (February 1977): 237-55.

Crankshaw, Edward. *The Fall of the House of Habsburg.* New York, N.Y.: Viking Press, 1963.

——— *Vienna: The Image of a Culture in Decline.* London, England: MacMillan, 1938.

Crosser, Paul E. *Economic Fictions: A Critique of Subjectivistic Economic Theory.* New York, N.Y.: Philosophical Library, 1957.

da Empoli, Domenico. "Una lettera italiana di J. A. Schumpeter." *Economie delle Scelte Pubbliche* 1 (March 1983): 199-207.

Dahman, Erik. "Schumpeterian Dynamics: Some Methodological Notes." *Journal of Economic Behavior and Organization* 5, no. 1 (March 1984): 25-34.

Dahmen, Erik. *Entrepreneurial Activity and the Development of Swedish Industry, 1919-1939.* Translated by Axel Leijonhufvud and Richard Irwin. Homewood, Ill.: American Economic Association, 1970.

Dasgupta, Partha, and Joseph Stiglitz. "Industrial Structure and the Nature of Innovative Activity." *Economic Journal* 90 (1980): 266-93.

——— "Uncertainty, Industrial Structure, and the Speed of R and D." *Bell Journal of Economics* 11 (1980): 1-28.

Dass, S. "Professor J. A. Schumpeter on Economic Development." *Indian Journal of Economics* 42 (1962): 237-49.

Date, Kunihari. "Shumpeta moderu ai okeru junkan to susei" (The relation of cycles and trends in Schumpeter's model). *Kikan Riron Keisaigaku* (Tokyo, Japan) 11 (January-February 1960): 35-42.

Date, Kuniharu. "The Relation of Cycles and Trends in Schumpeter's Model." *Waseda Economic Papers* 5 (1961): 22-34.

——— *Shumpeta.* Tokyo, Japan: Keizaigakusha to gendai, 1979.

Davidson, William H. "Factor Endowment, Innovation, and International Trade Theory." *Kyklos* 32, no. 4 (1979): 764-74.

Davies, M. R. "J. A. Schumpeter and the Methodology of the Social Sciences." *Political Science Review* 11, nos. 2-3 (1972): 105-223.

Davis, Horace. B. "Schumpeter As Sociologist." *Science and Society* 24, no. 1 (1960): 13-35.

——— Review of *Imperialism and Social Classes. Political Science Quarterly* 66 (1951): 465-6.

DeKierck, W. "De wegenschappelijkheld van Schumpeters theorie over de essentie en de werking van de kapitalistische economie." *Tijdschrift voor Economie* 15, no. 3 (1970): 272-308.

Demaria, Giovanni. "Les formes de la connaissance chez Schumpeter." *Economie Appliquee* 4 (1951): 141-66.

DeRoover, R. "Joseph A. Schumpeter and Scholastic Economics." *Kyklos* 10, no. 2 (1957): 115-43.

DeSchweinitz, Karl. "Free Enterprise and Democracy." *Social Research* 20, no. 1 (1953): 55-74

Deutsch, K. W. "Joseph Schumpeter As an Analyst of Sociology and Economic History." *Journal of Economic History* 16, no. 1 (1956): 41-56.

Dewey, D. "Professor Schumpeter on Socialism: the Case of Britain." *Journal of Political Economy* 58, no. 3 (1950): 187-210.

Diehl, Karl. "Joseph Schumpeter: Wesen." *Conrads Jahrbuch* 92 (1909): 813.

Dieterlen, Pierre. "Schumpeter, analyse du profit." *Economie Appliquee* 3 (1950): 497-530.

Dorfman, Joseph, ed. "The Seligman Correspondence, No. 4." *Political Science Quarterly* December 1941.

Dorfman, Joseph. Review of *History of Economic Analysis*. *Political Science Quarterly* 69 (1954): 603.

———— *The Economic Mind in American Civilization*, vols. 4 and 5. New York, N.Y.: Viking Press, 1959; August M. Kelley, 1969.

Drucker, Peter F. "Schumpeter and Keynes." *Forbes* 23 May 1983: 124-8.

———— *Adventures of a Bystander*. New York, N.Y.: Harper and Row, 1978.

———— *Innovation and Entrepreneurship*. New York, N.Y.: Harper and Row, 1985.

Duijn, J. J. van *The Long Waves in Economic Life*. London, England: George Allen and Unwin, 1983.

Earley, James S. "Schumpeter's Theory of Money, Credit, and Cycles: A Second Approximation." Paper presented at the History of Economics Society Meeting, May 1983.

Economie Appliquee (Paris, France). Tome 3, no. 3/4 (July-December 1950). Articles by E. Heiman, R. Frisch, R. Triffin, E. Schneider, G. Haberler, G. Leduc, A. Chabert, M. Fanno, P. Sylos-Labini, P. Dieterlen, R. Varga, J. Vullemin, and A. Taymans.

Economie Appliquee (Paris, France). Tome 4, no. 2 (April-June1951). Articles by G. Demaria, Hans Bayer, Yves Mainguy, G. Fain, G.-Th. Guilbaud, F. Perroux, and D. McCord Wright.

Edmondson, C. Earl. *The Heiwehr and Austrian Politics, 1918-1936*. Athens, Ga.: University of Georgia Press, 1938.

Egan, Joseph John. "Qualitative Economic Changes in Secular Inflation: An Examination of Schumpeter's Thesis of Innovation and Autodeflation during Development." Ph.D. dissertation, Georgetown University, Washington, D.C., 1961.

Egidi, M. *Schumpeter: Lo sviluppo come transformazione morfologico*. Milan, Italy: Etas Libri, 1981.

Eisenmenger, Anna. *Blockage: The Diary of an Austrian Middle-class Woman, 1914-1924*. London, England: Constable, 1932.

Eisermann, Gottfried. "Joseph Schumpeter als Soziologe." *Kyklos* 18, no. 2 (1965): 288-315.

Eklund, Klas. "Long Waves in the Development of Capitalism." *Kyklos* 33, no. 3 (1980): 383-419.

Elliott, J. E. "Marx and Schumpeter on Capitalism's Creative Destruction: a Comparative Statement." *Quarterly Journal of Economics* 95, no. 1 (1980): 45-68.

———— "Schumpeter and Marx on Capitalist Transformation." *Quarterly Journal of Economics* 98, no. 2 (1983): 333-6.

——— "Schumpeter and the Theory of Capitalist Economic Development." *Journal of Economic Behavior and Organization* 4, no. 4 (December 1983): 277-308.

Elster, Karl. "Die Grundgleichung der Geldtheorie." *Conrads Jahrbuch* 115 (1920): 1-17.

Endress, Ruth. *Unternehmer, Manager oder Staatsfunctionar, Die Bedeutung der Schumpeterschen Entwicklungprognosen fuer die Gegenwart.* Neuwied, German: Luchterhand, 1971.

Ericson, George. Review of *History of Economic Analysis. Christian Science Monitor* 9 April 1954, 9.

Etherington, Norman. "Reconsidering Theories of Imperialism." *History and Theory* 21, no. 1 (1982): 1-36.

Evans, G. H., Jr. "The Entrepreneur and Economic Theory: A Historical and Analytical Approach." *American Economic Review* supplement (May 1949): 336-48.

Eycken, Henri vander. "Equilibre general et theorie du cycle: Hicks et Schumpeter." *Revue de l'institut de Sociologie* 3 (1955): 479-503.

Fanno, Marco. "Schumpeter et la vitesse de circulation de la monnaie." *Economie Appliquee* 3 (1950): 473-80.

Fellner, William J. "March into Socialism, or Viable Postwar Stage of Capitalism?" In *Schumpeter's Vision,* edited by Arnold Heertje (see), 45-68.

——— "Trends and Cycles in Economic Activity." In *An Introduction to the Problem of Economic Growth.* New York, N.Y.: Henry Holt, 1956.

Fels, Rendigs, editor. *Business Cycles,* by Joseph A. Schumpeter. New York, N.Y.: McGraw-Hill, 1964. Abridged. See in particular the introduction and summary, pp. viii-xiii and 424-39.

Fels, Rendigs. "The Long-Wave Depression, 1873-1897." *Review of Economics and Statistics* 31 (1949): 69-73.

——— "The Theory of Business Cycles." *Quarterly Journal of Economics* 56, no. 1 (1952): 25-42.

——— *American Business Cycles, 1865-1897.* Chapel Hill, N.C.: University of North Carolina Press, 1959.

Fetter, Frank W. "An Early Memory of Joseph Schumpeter." *History of Political Economy* 6, no. 1 (1974): 92-94.

Fisher, F. M., and P. Temin. "Returns to Scale in Research and Development: What Does the Schumpeterian Hypothesis Imply?" *Journal of Political Economy* 81, no. 1 (1973): 56-70.

——— "Schumpeterian Hypothesis: Reply [to Rodriguez 1979]." *Journal of Political Economy* 87, no. 2 (1979): 386-389.

Fisher, Irving Norton. *My Father, Irving Fisher*. New York, N.Y.: Comet Press, 1956.

Fishman, Leo. Review of *History of Economic Analysis*. *American Academy of Political and Social Science Annals* 295 (1954): 164.

Foster, John Bellamy. "The Political Economy of Joseph Schumpeter: A Theory of Capitalist Development and Decline." *Studies in Political Economy* (Canada) 1984.

———— "Theories of Capitalist Transformation: Critical Notes on the Comparison of Marx and Schumpeter." *Quarterly Journal of Economics* 97 (May 1983).

Freeman, C., and M. Jahoki, eds. *World Futures, The Great Debate*. London, England: Martin Robertson, 1978.

Freeman, Christopher. *The Economics of Industrial Innovation*, 2nd edition. London, England: Frances Pintar, 1982.

Frey, Bruno. "Product and Process Innovations in Economic Growth." *Zeitschrift fuer Nationaloekonomie* 29 (1969): 29-38.

———— "Schumpeter, Political Economist." In *Schumpeterian Economics*, edited by Helmut Frisch (see), 126-42.

Frisch, Helmut, ed. *Schumpeterian Economics*. New York, N.Y.: Praeger, 1982.

Frisch, Ragnar. "Propagation Problems and Impulse Problems in Dynamic Economics." In *Economic Essays in Honour of Gustav Cassel*, London, England: Allen and Unwin, 1933, 171-205.

———— "Some Personal Reminiscences on a Great Man." *Econometrica* 19 (1951): 87-91.

Fritz, Richard G., and Clyde Haulman. "The Role of Financial Institutions in Economic Development—the Emergence of Diverse Views in the Early Twentieth Century." Paper presented at the History of Economics Meeting, Charlottesville, Virginia, May 1983. Typescript.

Froehlich, W. "The History of Economic Analysis Reconsidered." *Review of Social Economy* 13 (1955): 100-108.

Furtado, Celso. "Formacao de Capital e Desenvolvimento Economico." *Revista Brasileira de Economie* 6 (1952): 3.

Fusfeld, Daniel. "Joseph Schumpeter." In *World Book* 17: 160, 1962 edition.

Futia, Carl A. "Schumpeterian Competition." *Quarterly Journal of Economics* 95, no. 1 (June 1980): 675-95.

Gainham, Sarah. *The Habsburg Twilight*. New York, N.Y.: Atheneum, 1977.

Galbraith, John Kenneth. *A Life in Our Times: Memoirs*. Boston, Mass.: Houghton Mifflin, 1981.

Gasparini, Innocenzo. "Schumpeter, Demaria e Gerschenkron." *Revista storica italiana* 91, no. 4 (1979): 689-93.

Geiger, Rudolf. *Die Entwicklungstendenzen den Kapitalismus bei Keynes, Schumpeter und Burnham.* Zurich, Switzerland: Schriften des Schweizerischen Wirtschaftsarchives, 1959. Polygraphischer Verlag 13.

Georgescu-Roegen, Nicholas. "General Reflections on the Theme of Innovations." Proceedings of the International Colloquium on Economic Effects of Space and other Advanced Technology, Strasbourg, Austria, 1980.

———— "Methods of Economic Science." *Journal of Economic Issues* 13, no. 2 (1979): 317-28

Gherity, James A. "Schumpeter." In *Encyclopedia of World Biography*, 9:470-1. New York, N.Y.: McGraw-Hill, 1975.

Giersch, Herbert, ed. *Macroeconomic Policies for Growth and Stability: A European Perspective.* Tuebingen, German: Mohr, 1981.

Giersch, Herbert. "Aspects of Growth, Structural Change, and Employment: a Schumpeterian Perspective." *Weltwirtschaftliches Archiv* 115, no. 4 (1979): 628-52

———— "Schumpeter and the Current and Future Development of the World Economy." In *Schumpeterian Economics,* edited by Helmut Frisch (see), 49-59.

———— "The Age of Schumpeter." *American Economic Review* 74 (May 1984): 103-109.

Gilder, George. *The Spirit of Enterprise.* New York, N.Y.: Simon and Schuster, 1984.

Giva, Denis. "Il proceso capitalistico nella theorie di Schumpeter." *Studi storici* 18, no. 4 (1977): 141-52.

Goodwin, Richard. "Schumpeter: The Man I Knew" unpublished typescript, University of Siena, Italy, 1982.

Gordon, Barry J. "Aristotle, Schumpeter, and the Metallist Tradition." *Quarterly Journal of Economics* 75 (1961): 608-14.

Gottlieb, M. "The Ideological Influences of Schumpeter's Thought." *Zeitschrift fuer Nationaloekonomie* 19 (1959): 1-42.

Graziani, Augusto. "Il trattato nulla moneta di J. A. Schumpeter." In *Scritti in onore de Guesseppe de Meo,* 457-66. Rome, Italy: Instituto Demografische e Attuariali, 1978.

Greene, Murray. Review of *Imperialism and Social Classes. Social Research* 19 (1952): 453-63.

Groenwegen, J. "'Capitalism is Change'" Joseph Alois Schumpeter." *Intermediair Infomatie voor Leidinggevende Functionarissen* 17, no. 18 (1981): 13-18.

Grossi, M., et. al. "Il movimento dei prezzi e delle altre quantita economische secondo la teorie delle fluttuazioni economische di Joseph Schumpeter." *Giorgnale degli Economisti e Annali di Economie* 30, no. 11/12 (1971): 895-959.

Guha, A. *An Evolutionary Theory of Economic Growth.* New York, N.Y.: Oxford University Press, 1982.

Guiheneuf, Robert. "Psychologie individuelle et psychologie sociale dans l'oeuvre de Schumpeter." *Revue francaise de science politique* 2, no. 3 (1952): 581-95.

Guilbaud, G. Th. "En marge de Schumpeter: quelques esperances mathematiques." *Economie Appliquee* 4 (1951): 143-70.

Guisada, Juan M. "Joseph Schumpeter y la Teoria del Desarrollo Economico." *Revista de Occidente* 21-22 (1983): 200-218.

Gulick, Charles. *Austria from Habsburg to Hitler.* 2 volumes. Berkeley, Calif.: University of California Press, 1948.

Haavelmo, Trygve. "Statistical Testing of Business-Cycle Theories." *Review of Economic Statistics* 25 (1943): 13-18.

Haberler, Gottfried. "Austria's Economic Development after the Two World Wars." In *Empirische Wirtschaftforschung und Monitare Oekonomik,* edited by Werner Clement and Karl Socher. Berlin, German: Duncker and Humblot, 1979.

———— "Joseph Alois Schumpeter, 1883-1950." *Quarterly Journal of Economics* 64 (1950): 3; in *Joseph A. Schumpeter,* edited by Seymour Harris (see), 333-372.

———— "Joseph Alois Schumpeter." In *Political Economy: A Historical Perspective,* edited by Horst Claus Recktenwald. London, England: Collier-MacMillan, 1973. Extract of "Joseph Alois Schumpeter, 1883-1950," by Gottfried Haberler (see).

———— "Kritische Bermerkungen zu Schumpeters Geldtheorie." *Zeitschrift fuer Volkswirtschaft* 4 (1924): 646-68.

———— "Schumpeter's Capitalism, Socialism and Democracy." In *Schumpeter's Vision,* edited by Arnold Heertje (see), 69-94.

———— "Schumpeter's Theory of Interest." *Review of Economics and Statistics* 33 (1951): 122-8; in *Joseph A. Schumpeter,* edited by Seymour Harris (see), 72-78.

———— "Schumpeter, Finance Minister, March 15 to October 17, 1919." *Economie Appliquee* 3 (1950).

———— *Prosperity and Depression.* 1937. Reprint. Cambridge, Mass.: Harvard University Press, 1960.

——— Review of *Joseph A. Schumpeter: Life and Work of a Great Social Scientist*, translated by W. E. Kuhn (Lincoln, Nebr.: Bureau of Business Research, University of Nebraska-Lincoln, 1975). *Journal of Political Economy* 85, no. 3 (1977): 660.

Haeusserman, Erich. *Der Unternehmer: Seine Function, sein Zeilsensetsung, sein Gewin*. Stuttgart, Germany: Kohlhammer, 1932.

Hainsich, Michael. "Joseph Schumpeter: Wesen. Entwicklung. Eine dynamische Zinstheorie. Entgegnung." *Grunberg Archiv* 5 (1915): 216-23.

Hamazaki, M. "Shumpeta keizaigaku no hohoon-taki iohi kosatsu" (The methodological approach in Schumpeterian economics). *Ritsumeikan Keizaigaku* 2 (1954): 42-71.

——— *Shumpeta keisaigaku no kihon-mondia* (Fundamental problems of Schumpeterian Economics). Kyoto, Japan: Yukonsha, 1955.

Hansen, Alvin H. "Schumpeter's Contribution to Business Cycle Theory." *Review of Economics and Statistics* 33 (1951): 129-32; in *Joseph A. Schumpeter*, edited by Seymour Harris (see), 79-82.

——— *Fiscal Policy and Business Cycles*. New York, N.Y.: Norton, 1941.

——— Review of the *Theory of Economic Development*. *Journal of Political Economy* 44 (1936): 560-3.

Hardach, Gerd. "Joseph Schumpeter." In *Deutsche Historiker*, 6: 55-68. Goettingen, Germany: publisher, 1980.

Hardy, C. O. "Schumpeter on Capitalism, Socialism and Democracy." *Journal of Political Economy* number (1945): 348-56.

Harkner, Heinrich. Review of *Vergangenheit und Zukunft der Sozialwissenschaft, Wie studiert man Sozialwissenschaft. Conrads Jahrbuch* 107 (1916): 105.

Harris, John R. "Entrepreneurship and Economic Development. ," In *Business Enterprise and Economic Exchange*, edited by L. P. Cain and P. J. Uselding, 141-72. Kent, Ohio: Kent State University Press, 1973.

Harris, Seymour E. *Economics of Harvard*. New York, N.Y.: McGraw-Hill, 1970.

——— Review of *History of Economic Analysis*. *New York Times* 18 April 1954, p. 6.

Harris, Seymour, ed. *Joseph A. Schumpeter, Social Scientist*. Cambridge, Mass.: Harvard University Press, 1951.

Hartman, Heinz. "Managers and Entrepreneurs: a Useful Distinction?" *Administrative Science Quarterly* 3, no. 4 (1959): 429-51.

Hartmann, R. S., and D. R. Wheeler. "Schumpeterian waves of innovation and infrastructure development in Great Britain and the United States: the Kondratieff cycle revisited." In *Research in Economic*

History, edited by P. Uselding, 4: 37-85. Greenwich, Conn.: JAI Press, 1979

Hausdorfer, Walter. Review of *Ten Great Economists from Marx to Keynes*. *Library Journal* 15 May 1951, p. 865.

Hayami, T. "Shumpeta to Keinzu no rishi gainen no hikaku." *Hitotsubashi Ronso* 53, no. 6 (1965): 89-96.

Hayek, Friedrich A. "Schumpeter on the History of Economics." In *Studies in Philosophy, Politics, and Economics*, edited by Friedrich A. Hayek. Chicago, Ill.: University of Chicago Press, 1967.

Heaton, Herbert. *Edwin F. Gay, A Scholar in Action*. Cambridge, Mass.: Harvard University Press, 1952.

Heertje, Arnold, ed., *Schumpeter's Vision: Capitalism, Socialism and Democracy after 40 years*. New York, N.Y.: Praeger, 1981.

Heertje, Arnold. "Schumpeter's Model of the Decay of Capitalism." in *Schumpeterian Economics*, edited by Helmut Frisch (see), 84-94.

———— *Innovation, Technology, and Finance*. London, England: Basic Blackwell, 1988.

Heilbroner, Robert L. "Economics and Political Economy: Marx, Keynes, and Schumpeter." *Journal of Economic Issues* 18, no. 3 (September 1984): 681-688.

———— "Was Schumpeter Right?" *Challenge* 25, no. 1 (1982): 57-63.

———— "Was Schumpeter Right?" *Social Research* 48, no. 3 (1981): 456-71; in *Schumpeter's Vision*, edited by Arnold Heertje (see), 95-106.

———— *The Worldly Philosophers*. New York, N.Y.: Simon and Schuster, 1961.

Heimann, E. "L'homme." *Economic Appliquee* 3 (1950): 399-405.

———— "Schumpeter and the Problems of Imperialism." *Social Research* 19 (1952): 177-97.

Heinze, Gerhard. *Statische oder dynamisch Zinstheorie? Versuch einer kritischen Beleuchtung der Casselschen und Schumpeterschen Zinstheorie*. Ph.D. dissertation, University of Leipzig, Germany, 1928.

Henner, H. P. Review of *Capitalism, Socialism and Democracy. Analyse et Prevision* 14, no. 3 (1972): 1139-40.

Hennipman, P. "Van en over Schumpeter." *De Economist* 4 (1952): 284-303.

Hession, Charles. *The Life of John Maynard Keynes*. London, England: MacMillan, 1984.

Hicks, John R. "The Scope and Status of Welfare Economics." *Oxford Economic Papers* 27, no. 3 (1975): 325.

Higgins, Benjamin. *Economic Development*. New York, N.Y.: W. W. Norton, 1968.

Hirschman, Albert O. *The Passions and the Interests.* Princeton, N.J.: Princeton University Press, 1977.

———— *The Strategy of Economic Development.* New Haven, Conn.: Yale University Press, 1958.

Hockwald, Werner. Review of *Joseph A. Schumpeter: Life and Work of a Great Social Scientist,* translated by W. E. Kuhn (Lincoln, Nebr.: Bureau of Business Research, University of Nebraska-Lincoln, 1975). *History of Political Economy* 9, no. 3 (1977): 449.

Hoselitz, B. F. Review of *Imperialism and Social Classes. Journal of Political Economy* 59 (1951): 360.

Howey, Richard S. *A Bibliography of General Histories of Economics, 1692-1975.* Lawrence, Ks.: Regents Press, 1982.

———— Review of *The Theory of Economic Development. American Economic Review* 25 (March 1935): 90-91.

Hug, Rudolf. *Der Gedanke der wirtschaftlichen Entwicklung bei Schumpeter und seine Aufhahme in der oekonomischen Theorie.* University of Heidelberg dissertation, Germany, 1933.

Hughes, Jonathan. *The Vital Few: The Entrepreneur and American Economic Progress.* New York, N.Y.: Oxford University Press, 1986.

Hurwicz, E. "Joseph Schumpeter: Zur Soziologie der Imperialismen." *Zeitschrift fuer Sozialwissenschaft* 11 neue folge (new series) (1920): 213.

Hutchison, Keith. Review of *Economic Doctrine and Method. The Nation* 179 (6 November 1954): 411.

Hutchison, T. W. *A Review of Economic Doctrines, 1870-1929.* Oxford, England: Clarendon Press, 1953.

———— *Knowledge and Ignorance in Economics.* Chicago, Ill.: University of Chicago Press, 1977.

Infantino, Lorenzo. "Schumpeter e la teoria dell'imperialismo." *Revista di Sociologia* 14, no. 1-3 (1976): 31-60.

Innes, H. A. Review of *Business Cycles. Canadian Journal of Economics and Political Science* February 1940: 90-96.

Iwai, Katsuhito. "Towards Schumpeterian Dynamics." New Haven, Conn.: Yale University, 1980. Mimeograph.

Iwasaki, H. "Shumpeta riron no kagaku-toki seikaku" (Nature and characteristics of Schumpeter's economic theory). *Hokei Ronshu* 5, no. 3 (1956): 23-46.

Janeway, Eliot. Review of *Ten Great Economists from Marx to Keynes. New York Times* 8 July 1951, p. 3.

Janik, Allen, and Stephen Toulmin. *Wittgenstein's Vienna*. New York, N.Y.: Simon and Schuster, 1973.

Jaszi, Oscar. *The Dissolution of the Habsburg Monarchy*. Chicago, Ill.: University of Chicago Press, 1929.

Jenks, L. H. *Change and the Entrepreneur*. Cambridge, Mass.: Harvard University Press, 1949.

Jensen, Hans E. "J. A. Schumpeter's Sociology-of-Knowledge Approach to the History of Economics." Paper presented at the meeting of the History of Economics, 1984, Pittsburgh. Typescript. 21 pages.

——— "New Lights on J. A. Schumpeter's Theory of the History of Economics?" In *Research in the History of Economic Thought and Methodology*, edited by Warren Samuels. Greenwich, Conn.: JAI Press, 1987.

Jewkes, J. *Ordeal by Planning*. London, England: MacMillan, 1948.

Jewkes, J., D. Sawers, and R. Stillerman. *The Sources of Invention*. London, England: MacMillan, 1958.

Johnson, Alvin S. "Abstract Economics according to Schumpeter" (review of *Das Wesen und der Hauptinhalt der theoretischen Nationaloekonomie*). *Journal of Political Economy* 17, no. 6, (June 1909): 363-9.

Johnson, William M. *The Austrian Mind: An Intellectual and Social History, 1848-1938*. Berkeley, Calif.: University of California Press, 1972.

Kahn, E. J., Jr. *Harvard*. New York, N.Y.: W. W. Norton, 1969.

Kaiser, Richard. "Zur Kritik der methodischen Ansighten Joseph Schumpeters." Ph.D. dissertation, Universitaet Hamburg, Heidelberg, Germany, 1927. Machineschrift.

Kamien, Martin I., and Nancy L. Schwartz. "Market Structure and Innovation: A Survey." *Journal of Economic Literature* 8 (March 1975): 1-37.

Kamp, M. Ernst, and Friedrich Stamm. "Schumpeter." Bonner Gelehrte, Beitrage zur Geschichte der Wissenschaften in Bonn (Contribution to the History of Science at Bonn), Staatswissenschafter (Political Science) (Bonn: Bouvier u. Co Verlag, 1969), 54-66.

Kanazashi, Motoi. *Bibliography of the Writings of Joseph Alois Schumpeter*, 3rd edition. 1987. Private publication (author's address: 2-14-10 Higashi Tamagawa Gaknen Michida-Shi, Tokyo 194).

Kanbur, S. M. "A Note on Risk Taking, Entrepreneurship, and Schumpeter." *History of Political Economy* 12, no. 4 (1980): 489-98.

Kann, Robert A. *A Study in Austrian Intellectual History*. New York, N.Y.: Frederick A. Praeger, 1960.

Karrer, Hans "Schumpeters Beitrag zur Soziologie." *Kyklos* 5 (1951): 197-211.

Kautsky, J. H. "J. A. Schumpeter and Karl Kautsky: Parallel Theories of Imperialism." *Midwest Journal of Political Science* 5, no. 2 (1961): 101-28.

Kendall, M. G. "Review of Business Cycles." *Journal of the Royal Statistical Society* 104, no. 2 (1941): 177-80.

Kessler, Martin. "Synthetic Vision of Joseph Schumpeter." *Review of Politics* 23 (1961): 334-55.

Khan, Mohamed Shabbir. *Schumpeter's Theory of Capitalist Development.* Aligarh, India: Muslim University Press, 1957.

Kiersted, B. S. *The Theory of Economic Change.* Toronto, Canada: MacMillan, 1949.

Kilby, Peter, ed. *Entrepreneurship and Economic Development.* New York, N.Y.: Free Press, 1971.

Kingdom, Frank. Review of *Capitalism, Socialism and Democracy. Saturday Review of Literature* 28 November 1942, p. 21.

Kirzner, Israel M. "The Entrepreneurial Role in Menger's System." *Atlantic Economic Journal* 6, no. 3 (September 1978): 31-45.

────── *Competition and Entrepreneurship.* Chicago, Ill.: University of Chicago Press, 1973.

────── *Perception, Opportunity, and Profit.* Chicago, Ill.: University of Chicago Press, 1979.

Kisch, Herbert. "Joseph Alois Schumpeter." *Journal of Economic Issues* 13, no. 1 (1979): 141-57.

Klein, Burton. *Dynamic Economics.* Cambridge, Mass.: Harvard University Press, 1977.

Kleinknecht, Alfred. "Observations on the Schumpeterian Swarming of Innovations." *Futures* 13 (1981): 4.

Knight, Frank H. Review of *History of Economic Analysis. Southern Economic Journal* 21 (1955): 261-72.

Kohn, Meir, and John T. Scott. "Scale Economies in Research and Development: The Schumpeterian Hypothesis." *Journal of Industrial Economics* 30, no. 3 (1982): 239-49.

Koopmans, J. G. "De Zin der Bank Politik (Schumpeter and Keynes)." *De Economist* 1925: 798-918.

Kruger, Daniel H. "Hobson, Lenin, and Schumpeter on Imperialism." *Journal of the History of Ideas* 16 (1955): 252-9.

Kuhn, W. E. *The Evolution of Economic Thought.* 2nd edition. Chicago, Ill.: Southwestern Publishing, 1970.

Kuznets, Simon "Schumpeter's Business Cycles." *American Economic Review* 30, no. 2 (1940): 257-71; in *Economic Change: Selected*

Essays in Business Cycles, National Income, and Economic Growth,
by Simon Kuznets (New York, N.Y.: Norton, 1953), 105-24.

Labini, Paolo Sylos. "Le probleme des cycles economiques de longue durée." *Economie Appliquee* 3 (1950): 481-95.

L[achman], L. M. "Joseph A. Schumpeter, 1883-1950." *South African Journal of Economics* 18 (June 1950): 215-8.

Lambers, Hendrick Wilm. "The Vision." In *Schumpeter's Vision,* edited by Arnold Heertje (see), 107-29.

Lampe, Adolf. "Schumpeters System und die Ausgestaltung der Verteilungslehre." *Conrads Jahrbuch* 121 (1923): 417-44, 513-46.

Lange, Oskar. "A Note on Innovations." *Review of Economics and Statistics* 25 (1943): 1.

——— Review of *Business Cycles.* *Review of Economics and Statistics* 23, no. 4 (1941): 190-3.

Laskine, E. "Joseph Schumpeter: Entwicklung." *Revue d'économie politique* 27 (1913): 134.

Laumas, P. S. "Schumpeter's Theory of Economic Development and Underdeveloped Countries." *Quarterly Journal of Economics* 76 (1962): 653-9.

Layton, W. T., and C. Rist. *The Economic Situation in Austria.* Geneva, Switzerland: League of Nations, 1925.

Leahy, William H., and David L. McKee. "A Note on Urbanism and Schumpeter's Theory of Development." *Growth and Change* 7, no. 1 (1976): 45-47.

——— "On Goldfields, Libraries, Cities and Schumpeter." *American Economist* 18, no. 1 (1974): 142-4.

——— "The Schumpeterian View of Regional Economy." *Growth and Change* 3, no. 4 (1972): 23-25.

Leathers, Charles G. "Intellectual Activism: a Schumpeterian Threat to the New Industrial State." *Nebraska Journal of Economics and Business* 10, no. 3 (1971): 3-11.

Leduc, Gaston. "Schumpeter, disciple de Walras." *Economie Appliquee* 3 (1950): 441-56.

Lee, Algernon. Review of *Business Cycles.* *New York Times* 17 December 1939, p. 17.

Leff, Nathaniel H. "Entrepreneurship and Economic Development." *Journal of Economic Literature* 17 (March 1979): 46-64.

——— "Industrial Organization and Entrepreneurship in the Developing Countries." *Economic Development and Cultural Change* 28, no. 4 (July 1978): 661-75.

Lehnis, Felix. *Der Beitrag des spaten Schumpeter zur Konjuntursforschung; Interpretationen und methodologische Wurdugung der Business Cycles.* Stuttgart, Germany: G. Fischer, 1960. Beitrage zur Erforschung der wirtschaftlichen Entwicklung (Contribution to the Exploration of Economic Development), 5.

Lekachman, Robert. *A History of Ideas.* New York, N.Y.: McGraw-Hill, 1959.

Leontief, Wassily. "Joseph A. Schumpeter (1883-1950)." *Econometrica* 18 (April 1950): 103-10.

Lester, R. A. Review of *Economic Doctrine and Method. New Republic* 4 (October 1954): 20.

Lexis, Wilhelm. Review of *Die Theorie der wirtschaftlichen Entwicklung. Conrads Jahrbuch* 46 (1913): 84-91.

Lichtheim, G. *Imperialism.* New York, N.Y.: Praeger, 1971.

Lichtman, Richard. "The Facade of Equality in Liberal Democratic Theory." *Inquiry* 12 (1969): 170-208.

Liebenstein, Harvey. "Entrepreneurship and Development." *American Economic Review* 53, no 2 (May 1968): 72-83

Liebhofsky, H. H. "Institutions and Technology in Economic Progress: Schumpeter's Theory of Economic Development As a Special Case of the Institutionalist Theory." *American Journal of Economic Sociology* 19, no. 2 (1960): 139-50.

Link, A. N. "Firm Size and Efficient Entrepreneurial Activity: a Reformation of the Schumpeter Hypothesis." *Journal of Political Economy* 88, no. 4 (1980): 771-82.

Lipset, Seymour Martin, and David Riesman. *Education and Politics at Harvard.* New York, N.Y.: McGraw-Hill, 1975.

Lisle, E. A. "Croissance et Mode de Vie." *Analyse et Prevision* 7, no, 4 (1969): 223-7.

Little, I. M. D. Review of *History of Economic Analysis. Economic History Review* vol. 2, no. 8, part 1 (1955): 91-98.

Loewe, Adolf. *Zur oekonomischen Theorie des Imperialismus (Wirtschaft und Gesellschaft).* Frankfurt, Germany: Festschrift fuer Franz Oppenheimer zum 60.Geburtstage (Homage Volume for Franz Oppenheimer on his 60th Birthday), 1924.

Lopez, Enrique Hank. *The Harvard Mystique.* New York, N.Y.: MacMillan, 1979.

Loury, Glenn. "Market Structure and Innovation." *Quarterly Journal of Economics* 93 (August 1979): 395-410.

Lowe, A. *Economics and Sociology: A Plea for Cooperation in the Social Sciences.* London, England: Allen and Unwin, 1935.

Lukawer, E. Marks i Schumpeter, o gospodarce socjalistycsnej socjalistycznej." *Ekonomista* (Warsaw, Poland) 2 (1967): 309-30.

Lunn, John E. "Research and Development and the Schumpeterian Hypothesis." *Southern Economic Journal* 49, no. 1 (1982): 209-17.

MacCartney, C. A. *Problems of the Danube Basin.* Cambridge, Mass.: Harvard University Press, 1944.

———— *The Habsburg Empire, 1790-1918.* New York, N.Y.: MacMillan, 1969.

MacDonald, Mary. *The Republic of Austria, 1918-1934: A Study in the Failure of Democratic Government.* New York, N.Y.: Oxford University Press, 1946.

MacDonald, Ronan Gerald. "A Comparison of the Theories of Entrepreneurial Expectations of Keynes and Schumpeter." Ph.D. dissertation, University of Wisconsin-Madison, Madison, Wis.

———— "Schumpeter and Max Weber: Central Visions and Social Theories." *Quarterly Journal of Economics* 79, no. 3 (1965): 373-96.

Machlup, Fritz. "Capitalism and Its Future Appraisal by Two Liberal Economists." *American Economic Review* 33, no. 2 (June 1943): 301-20.

———— "Forced or Induced Savings: An Exploration into its Synonyms and Homonyms." *Review of Economics and Statistics* 25 (1943): 29-39.

———— "Schumpeter's Economic Methodology." *Review of Economics and Statistics* 33 (1951): 145-51; in *Joseph A. Schumpeter,* edited by Seymour Harris (see), 95-101.

MacLaurin, R. W. "The Sequence from Invention to Innovation and its Relation to Economic Growth." *Quarterly Journal of Economics* 67 (February 1953): 97-111.

Madarasz, Aladar. "Economists and Economic Thought." *Acta Oeconomica* (Budapest, Hungary) 25, no. 3/4 (1981): 337-58).

———— "Schumpeter's Theory of Economic Development." *Acta Oeconomica* (Budapest, Hungary) 25, no. 3/4 (1980): 337-57

Maerz, Eduard. "Die Theorie der wirtschaftlichen Entwicklung von Joseph A. Schumpeter in ihrer Besiehung sum marxschen System." *Wirtschaft und Gesellschaft* 6, no. 3 (1980): 253-70.

———— "Joseph A. Schumpeter as Minister of Finance of the First Republic of Austria, March, 1919-October, 1919." In *Schumpeterian Economics,* edited by Helmut Frisch (see), 162-79.

———— "Joseph Alois Schumpeter (1883-1950)." *Neue Oesterreichische Biographie ab 1815, Gross Oesterreicher XX* (New Austrian Biography Since 1815, Greater Austria 20). Wien (Vienna): Amalthea Verlag, 1979/ 67-77.

———— "The Austrian Credit Mobilier in a Time of Transition." In *Economic Development in the Habsburg Monarchy in the Nineteenth Century*, edited by John Komlos. New York, N.Y.: Columbia University Press, 1983.

———— "Zur Genesis der Schumpeterischen Theorie der wirtschaftlichen Entwicklung." In *On Political Economy and Econometrics—Essays in Honor of Oskar Lange*, 363-88. Oxford, England: Permagon Press, 1964.

———— *Austrian Banking and Financial Policy: Creditinstalt at a Turning Point, 1913-1923*. Translated by Charles Kessler. New York: St. Martin's Press, 1984.

———— *Einfuhrung in der Marxische Theorie der wirtschaftliche Entwicklung*. Vienna, Austria: Europaverlag, 1976.

———— *Joseph Alois Schumpeter-Forscher, Lehrer und Politiker*. Vienna, Austria: Verlag fur Geschichte und Politik, 1983.

Mahajan, V. S. "Schumpeter's Theory of Growth." *Indian Journal of Economics* 41 (July 1960): 73-77.

Mainguy, Yves. "Capitalisme, socialisme et neo-liberalisme." *Economie Appliquee* 4 (1951): 211-42.

Majumder, Badiul Alam. "Innovations and International Trade: An Industry Study of Dynamic Competitive Advantage." *Kyklos* 32, no. 3 (1979): 559-70.

Mann, Fritz Karl. "Bermerkungen ueber Schumpeters Einfluss auf die amerikanische Wirtschaftheorie." *Weltwirtschaftliches Archiv* 81 (1958): 149-75.

———— "Life and Work" (review of *Joseph A. Schumpeter: Leben und Werk eines Grossen Sozialoekonomen*, by Erich Schneider), in. *Economic Review* 11, no. 1 (1973): 35; in English in *Finanz Archiv* 30 (1971): 306-10.

———— Review of *Ten Great Economists*. *American Academy of Political and Social Science Annals* 278 (1951): 209.

Mansfield, Edwin. *Industrial Research and Technological Innovation: An Econometric Analysis*. New York, N.Y.: W. W. Norton, 1968.

———— *The Production and Application of New Industrial Technology*. New York, N.Y.: Norton, 1977.

Marget, Arthur W. "The Monetary Aspects of the Schumpeterian System." *Review of Economics and Statistics* 33 (1951): 112-21; in *Joseph A. Schumpeter*, edited by Seymour Harris (see), 62-71.

Markham, Jessie. "Market Structure, Business Conduct, and Innovation." *American Economic Review* 55 (May 1965).

Marschak, Jacob. Review of *Business Cycles*. *Journal of Political Economy* 48, no. 6 (December 1940): 889-94.

Mason, Edward S. "Schumpeter on Monopoly and the Large Firm." *Review of Economics and Statistics* 33 (1951): 139-44; in *Joseph A. Schumpeter,* edited by Seymour Harris (see), 89-94.

Mayer, Hans. "Eine neue Grundlegung der theoretischen Nationaloekonomie." *Zeitschrift fuer Volkswirtschaft* 20 (1911): 181-209.

Mayhew, Anne. "Schumpeterian Capitalism versus the 'Schumpeterian Thesis.'" *Journal of Economic Issues* 14, no. 2 (1980): 583-92.

McCracken, Paul W. "Can Capitalism Survive." In *Dilemmas Facing the Nation,* edited by Herbert V. Prochnow, 134-152. New York, N.Y.: Harper and Row, 1979.

McCrea, R. C. "Schumpeter's Economic System." *Quarterly Journal of Economics* 27 (1913): 520-9.

McNulty, Paul J. "On Firm Size and Innovation in the Schumpeterian System." *Journal of Economic Issues* 8, no. 3 (1974): 627-32.

Medio, Alfredo. "L'interesse nella teorie dello sviluppo economico di Joseph Schumpeter." *Revista internazionale di Scienze economiche e comerciali* 15, no. 10 (1968): 1025-42.

Medow, Paul. "Conceptual and Methodological Problems in Applying Schumpeter's Theory of Economic Development to Non-Market Economies." Ph.D. dissertation, Columbia University, New York, N.Y., 1960.

Meek, R. L. "Is Economics Biased? Heretical View of a Leading Thesis in Schumpeter's History." *Scottish Journal of Political Economy* 4 (1957): 1-17.

Meisel, James N. *The Myth of the Ruling Class.* Ann Arbor, Mich.: University of Michigan Press, 1958.

Meissner, Frank. "The Schumpeters and Industrialization of Třešt." *Zeitschrift fuer die gesamte Staatswissenschaft* 135, no. 2 (June 1979): 256-262.

Meltzer, Allen H., and Scott F. Richard. "Why Government Grows (and Grows) in a Democracy." *Public Interest* 52 (1978): 111-8.

Michaels, James W., and Normal Gall. "A Wagnerian Vision." *Forbes* 23 May 1983: 130-2.

Miller, J. P. Review of *History of Economic Analysis. Yale Review* ns 44 (1954): 123.

Minsky, Hyman P. "Money and Crisis in Schumpeter and Keynes." Working Paper Series No. 58. St. Louis, Mo.: Department of Economics, Washington University, 1983.

Mirkovich, N. "Schumpeter's Theory of Economic Development." *American Economic Review* 30 (September 1940): 580.

Mitchell, Wesley C. "Schumpeter and Public Choice." *Public Choice* 41, no. 1 (1984): 73-88 and 42, no. 2 (1984): 161-74.

Mitchell, Wesley Clair. "Schumpeter." In *Types of Economic Theory*, edited by Joseph Dorfman, 2:375-416. New York, N.Y.: Augustus M. Kelley, 1969.

Mohd, Shabbir Khan. *Schumpeter's Theory of Capitalist Development*. Delhi, India: Muslim University, 1957.

Mommsen, Wolfgang J. *Theories of Imperialism*. Translated by P. S. Falla. New York, N.Y.: Random House, 1980.

Montaner, Antonio. "Schumpeter und die Entwicklung der Wirtschaftsanalyse." *Zeitschrift fuer Nationaloekonomie* 27 (1967): 160-74

Morgenstern, Oskar. "Joseph A. Schumpeter, 1883-1950." *Economic Journal* 61, no. 241 (1951): 197-202.

———— "Review of *Business Cycles.*" *Journal of the American Statistical Association* 35 (June 1940): 423-4.

———— Review of *Business Cycles. New Republic* 6 May 1940, p. 615.

———— Review of *Theorie der wirtschaftlichen Entwicklung. American Economic Review* 17 (June 1927): 281-2.

Morrison, Samuel Eliot. *Three Centuries of Harvard, 1636-1936*. Cambridge, Mass.: Belknap Press of the Harvard University Press, 1965.

Morton, Frederic. *A Nervous Splendor: Vienna 1888/89*. Boston, Mass.: Little, Brown, 1979.

Moynihan, Daniel Patrick. "Address to the Entering Class at Harvard College, 1972 [*Capitalism, Socialism and Democracy*]." In *Coping: Essays in the Practice of Government*, by Daniel P. Moynihan. New York, N.Y.: Random House, 1974.

Mpantaloukas, Klaudios Basileiou. *The Fate of Capitalism according to Marx and Schumpeter*. Athens, Greece: A. Papazeses, 1953. In Greek.

Mukerji, D. P. "Rationality in Economic Science and the Contributions of Robbins, Keynes, Marx and Schumpeter." *Indian Journal of Economics* 35, no. 139 (1955): 295-317.

Mussche, G. "Le systeme de Schumpeter et la sociologie economique." *Annales de la Faculte de Droit et des Sciences economiques de Lille* 1968: 125-65.

Nagatomo, I. "Shumpeta no keiki hendo riron." *Keizai Ronso* 86, no. 6 (1960): 43-57.

———— "Shumpeta no toshi riron." *Keisai Ronso* 89, no. 2 (1962): 37-50.

Nelson, Richard R., and Sidney G. Winter. "Evolutionary vs. Neoclassical Theories of Economic Growth: Critique and Prospectus." *Economic Journal* December 1974: 886-905.

———— "Factor Price Changes and Factor Substitution in an Evolutionary Model." *Bell Journal of Economics* 6 (Autumn 1975): 466-86.

———— "Forces Generating and Limiting Concentration under Schumpeterian Competition." *Bell Journal of Economics* 9, no. 2 (Autumn 1978): 529-48.

———— "Simulation of Schumpeterian Competition." *American Economic Review* 67 (February 1977): 271-6.

———— "Simulation of Schumpeterian Competition." *American Economic Review* 67, no. 1 (1977): 271-6.

———— "Technical Change in an Evolutionary Model." *Quarterly Journal of Economics* 90 (February 1976):, 90-118.

———— "The Schumpeterian Tradeoff Revisited." *American Economic Review* 72, no. 1 (1982): 114-32.

———— "Toward an Evolutionary Theory of Economic Capabilities." *American Economic Review* 63 (May 1973): 440-9.

———— *An Evolutionary Theory of Economic Change.* Cambridge, Mass.: Belknap Press of the Harvard University Press, 1981.

Niehans, Juerg. "Economics, History, Doctrine, Science, and Art." *Kyklos* 35 (1981): 165-77.

———— Review of *History of Economic Analysis. Schweizerische Zeitschrift fuer Volkswirtschaft und Statistik* 92 (1956): 240.

Nitsch, T. O. "Schumpeter and Catholicism: a Comment." *Review of Social Economy* 22 (September 1964):, 104-10.

Nordhaus, W. D. "Some Skeptical Thoughts on the Theory of Induced Innovations." *Quarterly Journal of Economics* May 1973.

Notel, Rudolph. Review of *Ten Great Economists from Marx to Keynes. Kyklos* 6, no. 2 (1952): 183-4.

Nussbaum, F. L. Review of *History of Economic Analysis. American Economic Review* 44 (October 1954): 62-64.

———— Review of *History of Economic Analysis. American Historical Review* 60, no. 1 (1954): 62-64.

O'Donnell, L. A. "Rationalism, Capitalism, and the Entrepreneur: the Views of Veblen and Schumpeter." *History of Political Economy* 5, no. 1 (Spring 1973): 199-214.

O'Neill, Michael Patrick. "An Analysis of Entrepreneurship in Economic Development: A Synthesis of Schumpeter, Hagan, and McClellan." Ph.D. dissertation, University of Oklahoma, 1977.

O'Toole, Laurence, Jr. "Schumpeter's 'democracy': a Critical View." *Polity* 9, no. 4 (1977): 446-62.

Oppenheimer, Franz. "Das Bodenmonopol." *Archiv fuer Sozialwissenschaft und Sozialpolitik* 44 (1918): 487-484; 45 (1921): 866-75.

Orlando, B. "Schumpeter e Hilferding theorici del capitalismo tedesco." *Revista internazionale di Scienze economiche e comerciali* 14, no. 11 (1967): 1118-26.

Ortlieb, Heinz-Dietrich. Review of *Capitalism, Socialism and Democracy. Hamburger Jahrbuch fuer Wirtschafts- und Gesellschaftspolitik* 1956: 147-57.

Osterhammel, Juergen. "Joseph A. Schumpeter and Max Weber," in Wolfgang Mommsen and Juergen Osterhammel, *Max Weber and His Contemporaries* (London: Allen and Unwin, 1987), 106-120.

Pagani, Angelo. "Il 'Center' in Entrepreneurial History' e la teoria Schumpeteriana dell'innovazione." *Quaderni di Sociologie* 12, no. 4 (1963): 375-417.

Pal, S. "Schumpeter and His Ideas of Economic Development," *Indian Journal of Economics* 36 (July 1955): 129-42.

———— "Significance of Schumpeterian Ideas for the Underdeveloped Countries." *Indian Economic Review* 2, no. 4 (August 1955): 89-91.

Palyi, Melchoir. Review of *History of Economic Analysis. Chicago Sunday Tribune* 16 May 1954, p. 62.

———— Review of *Ten Great Economists. Chicago Sunday Tribune* 19 August 1951, 5.

Papanek, Gustav. "The Development of Entrepreneurship." *American Economic Review* 52, no. 2 (May 1952): 46-66.

Paque, Karl-Heinz. "Einige Bermerkungen zur Persoenlichkeit Joseph A. Schumpeter." Paper presented to the Institut fuer Weltwirtschaft, Kiel, Germany, December 1952. Typescript.

Paulsen, Andreas. "Unternehmer und Unternehmerleistungen in Entwicklungstandern" (Entrepreneurship and Entrepreneurial Activities in Developing Countries). *Jahrbucher fuer Nationaloekonomie und Statistik* 5-6 (December 1963): 385-411.

Pellanda, A. Review of *Zur Soziologie der Imperialismen. Revista Internazionale di Scienze Economische e Comerciali* 21, no. 8 (1974): 802.

Perlman, Mark, ed. Proceedings of the first International J. A. Schumpeter Society meeting in Augsburg, Germany, September 1986. To be published.

Perlman, Mark. "Schumpeter as a Historian of Economic Thought." In *Schumpeterian Economics,* edited by Helmut Frisch (see), 143-161.

Perroux, François. "Les trois analyses de l'evolution de la recherche d'une dynamique totale chez Joseph Schumpeter." *Economie Appliquee* 4 (1951): 271-330.

———— *La Pensee Economique de Joseph Schumpeter*. Geneva, Switzerland: Librairie Droz, 1965.

Pick, Robert. *The Last Days of Imperial Vienna*. New York, N.Y.: Dial Press, 1976.

Pohle, Ludwig. "Das Wesen und der Hauptinhalt der theoretischen Nationaloekonomie." *Zeitschrift fuer Sozialwissenschaft* 12 (1909): 332-58.

Pollard, Spencer D. How Capitalism Can Succeed. Harrisburg, Pa.: Stackpole Books, 1966.

Predohl, Andreas. "Gesetz und Gestalt. Methodologische Bermerkungen zur Schumpeters '*Business Cycles*'." *Jahrbuch fuer Sozialwissenschaft* 1, no. 1 (1950): 333-72.

———— "Schumpeter und die Theorie der Wirtschaftlichen Entwicklung." In *Gustav Cassel, Joseph Schumpeter, Berhhard Harms: 3 Richtungsweisende Wirtschaftwissenschaftler: Aufsaetze*, by Andreas Predohl. Goettingen, Germany: Vandenhoeck und Ruprecht, 1972.

Pribrim, Karl. *A History of Economic Reasoning*. Baltimore, Md.: Johns Hopkins University Press, 1983.

Pridavka, Gary M. "Entrepreneur: Undefined or Ill-defined." *Michigan Academician* 12, no. 2 (1979): 164-74.

Prime, Michael G., and David R. Henderson. "Schumpeter on preserving private enterprise." *History of Political Economy* 7, no. 3 (1975): 293-8. Reproduces Joseph Schumpeter's paper, "The Future of Private Enterprise in the Face of Modern Socialist Tendencies" (Comment sauvegarder l'enterprise privee), presented as the Proceedings of the Convention of L'Association Professionelle des Industriels, Montreal, Canada, 1946.

Quick, Paddy. "The Great Depression of 1873-1896: Myth or Reality?" Paper presented to the Union of Radical Political Economists 25 August 1983. Mimeograph.

Raines, J. Patrick, and Clarence Young. "Rationality, Capitalism and Democracy: Views of Schumpeter and Knight." Paper given at the New York History of Economics Society meeting, Barnard College, New York, 1986.

Reclam, Michael. "J. A. Schumpeter's 'Credit' Theory of Money." Ph.D. dissertation, University of California-Riverside (University Microfilms), Ann Arbor, Michigan, 1984.

Redlich, Fritz. "Entrepreneurship in the Initial Stages of Industrialization." *Weltwirtschaftliches Archiv* 75 (1955): 59-103.

———— "The Business Leader in Theory and Reality." *American Journal of Economics and Sociology* 8, no. 19 (1938): 223-37.

———— "Toward the Understanding of an Unfortunate Legacy." *Kyklos* 19, no. 4 (1966): 709-18.

———— "Unternehmerforchung und Weltanschuang." *Kyklos* 8, no. 3 (1955): 277-300.

Rexhausen, Felix. *Der Unternehmer und die Volkswirtschaftliche Entwicklung*. Berlin, Germany: Duncker and Humblot, 1960.

Ricci, D. M. "Democracy Attenuated: Schumpeter, the Process Theory, and American Democratic Thought." *Journal of Politics* 32 (1970): 239-67.

Ricci, Umberto. "Joseph Schumpeter: Uber die mathematische Methode der theoretischen Nationaloekonomie." *Giorgnale degli Economisti* 34 (1907): 320.

Richardson, G. B. Review of *History of Economic Analysis*. *Oxford Economic Papers* ns 7 (1955): 136-50.

Riegger, Roland. *August Loesch: In Memoriam*. Heidenheim, Germany: Verlag der Buchhandlung Meuer, 1971.

Riemersma, J. C. Review of *History of Economic Analysis*. *Canadian Forum* 34 (1954): 186.

Rimmer, Douglas. "Schumpeter and the Underdeveloped Countries." *Quarterly Journal of Economics* 75 (1961): 422-50.

Rist, Charles. "Joseph Schumpeter: Wesen." *Revue d'économie politique* 24 (1911): 494-6.

Robbins, Lionel. "On a Certain Ambiguity in the Conception of Stationary Equilibrium." *Economic Journal* 40 (June 1930): 194-214.

———— Review of *History of Economic Analysis*. *Quarterly Journal of Economics* 69 (1955): 1-22.

Robinson, Joan. Review of *Capitalism, Socialism and Democracy*. *Economic Journal* 53 (1943): 381-3; in *What Are the Questions? and Other Essays*, by Joan Robinson (Armonk, N.Y.: M. E. Sharpe, 1981), 141-3.

Robinson, Sherman. "Theories of Economic Growth and Development: Methodology and Content." *Economic Development and Cultural Change* 21, no. 1 (October 1972): 54-67.

Rodriguez, C. A. "Schumpeterian Hypothesis: Comment." *Journal of Political Economy* 87, no. 2 (1979): 383-5.

Roepke, Wilhelm, and Hans O. Lenel. "Review of C*apitalism, Socialism and Democracy*." *Ordo Jahrbuch fuer Ordunng von Wirtschaft und Gesellschaft* 1 (1948): 277-96.

Rogge, Benjamin A. *Can Capitalism Survive?* Indianapolis, Ind.: Liberty Classics/Liberty Press, 1979.

Rojo, Luis A. "Marx, Schumpeter, Keynes y la Gran Depresion." *Revista Occidente* 21-22 (1983): 23-43.

Ronen, Joshua, ed. *Entrepreneurship*. Lexington, Mass.: D. C. Heath, 1983.

Rosen, G. "Ghandian Economics: A Schumpeterian Perspective." *Journal of Economic Issues* 16, no. 2 (1982): 435-8.

Rosenberg, J. B. "Research and Market Share: Reappraisal of Schumpeter's Hypothesis." *Journal of Industrial Economics* 25, no. 2 (1976): 101-12.

Rosenberg, Nathan, and Claudio Frischtak R. "Technological Innovation and Long Waves." *Cambridge Journal of Economics* 8, no. 1 (March 1984): 7-24.

Rosenberg, Nathan. "Factors Affecting the Diffusion of Technology." *Explorations in Economic History* Fall 1972: 3-33.

——— "Problems in the Economist's Conceptualization of Technological Innovation." *History of Political Economy* 7, no. 4 (Winter 1975): 456-81.

——— "Science, Invention, and Economic Growth." *Economic Journal* 84 (March 1974): 90-108.

——— *Technology and American Economic Growth*. White Plains, N.Y.: M. E. Sharpe, 1972.

Rostow, Walt W. "Kondratieff, Schumpeter, and Kuznets: Trend Periods Revisited." *Journal of Economic History* 35, no. 4 (1975): 719-53.

——— *The British Economy of the Nineteenth Century*. New York, N.Y.: Oxford University Press, 1948.

——— *The Process of Economic Growth*, 2nd edition. New York, N.Y.: W. W. Norton, 1962.

Rothbarth, E. Review of *Business Cycles*. *Economic Journal* 52 (1942): 223-9.

Rothschild, K. W. "Schumpeter and Socialism." in *Schumpeterian Economics*, edited by Helmut Frisch (see), 113-25.

——— *Austria's Economic Development between the Two Wars*. London, England: Frederick Muller, 1947.

Rumyanchev, A. M. "O nekotorii sotsiologicheskii kontseptsiya sovremennogo revizionisma" (Some Sociological Conceptions of Contemporary Revisionism). *Voprosy Filosofii* I, no. 13 (1959): 14-24; II, no. 13 (1959): 45-56.

Ruttan, V. W. "On Schumpeter and Development." *Phillipine Economic Journal* 4, no. 1 (1965): 57-63.

——— "Usher and Schumpeter on Invention, Innovation and Technological Change." *Quarterly Journal of Economics* 73 (1959): 596-606.

Salin, E. "The Schumpeterian Theory and Continental Thought with comments by A. Gerschenkron and S.-C. Kolm" (Proceedings of the Airley Conference given at the Airley House in Warrenton, Va., April 1966). In *The Transfer of Technology to Developing Countries*, edited by Daniel L. Spencer and Alexander Moroniak, 61-91. New York, N.Y.: Praeger, 1967.

—— Review of *Capitalism, Socialism and Democracy. Schweizerische Zeitschrift fuer Volkswirtschaft und Statistik* 80 (1944): 114-32.

—— Review of *Joseph Schumpeter, Social Scientist. Kyklos* 6, no. 2 (1952): 184-6.

Samuels, Warren J. "A Critique of *Capitalism, Socialism and Democracy*." East Lansing: Michigan State University Department of Economics, 1982. Typescript.

—— "The Influence of Friedrich von Wieser on Joseph A. Schumpeter." *History of Economics Society Bulletin* 4, no. 2 (1983): 5-19.

—— Review of *Joseph A. Schumpeter: Life and Work of a Great Social Scientist*, by Erich Schneider, translated by W. E. Kuhn (Lincoln, Nebr.: Bureau of Business Research, University of Nebraska-Lincoln, 1975). *Southern Economic Journal* 44, no. 1 (1977): 192-3.

Samuels, Warren, ed. *Research in the History of Economic Thought and Methodology*. Vol. 5. Greenwich, Conn.: JAI Press, 1987.

Samuelson, Paul A. "1983: Marx, Keynes, and Schumpeter." *Eastern Economic Journal* 9, no. 3 (1983): 166-79.

—— "A Forward: Schumpeter and Marx." In *Marx's Economics: Origin and Development*, by Alexander Balinky, xi-xii. Lexington, Mass.: D. C. Heath, 1970.

—— "Dynamics, Statics and the Stationary State." *Review of Economic Statistics* 25, no. 1 (February 1943): 56-68.

—— "Joseph Alois Schumpeter." In *Dictionary of American Biography*, edited by John A. Garraty and Edward T. James, supplement 4, 720-3. New York, N.Y.: Charles Scribner's Sons, 1974.

—— "Joseph Schumpeter." *Newsweek* 13 April 1970: 75.

—— "Memories." *Newsweek* 2 June 1969: 83

—— "Paradoxes of Schumpeter's Zero Interest." *Review of Economics and Statistics* 53, no. 4 (November 1971): 391-2.

—— "Schumpeter as a Teacher and Economic Theorist." *Review of Economics and Statistics* 33 (1951): 98-103; in *Joseph A. Schumpeter*, edited by Seymour Harris (see), 48-53.

—— "Schumpeter As an Economic Theorist." In *Schumpeterian Economics*, edited by Helmut Frisch (see), 1-27.

—— "Schumpeter's Capitalism, Socialism and Democracy." In *Schumpeter's Vision*, edited by Arnold Heertje (see), 1-21.

——— "The World Economy at Century's End." Paper given at the Sixth World Congress of the International Economic Association, Mexico City, 1980. Typescript.

Sanger, G. P. "Dr. Joseph Schumpeter: Wesen." *Economic Journal* 19 (1909): 112-4.

Santarelli, Enrico. "L'Influsso dell'analisi Schumpeteriana della funzione imprenditoriale e del credito nel pensiero economico italiano tra le due guerre." *Giorgnale degli Economisti e Annali de Economic* 42, no. 7/8 (August 1984): 507-29.

Sartori, Giovanni. "Anti-Elitism Revisited [*Capitalism, Socialism and Democracy*]." *Government and Opposition* 13, no. 1 (1978): 58-80.

Schaeder, Reinhard. "Schumpeter Joseph A." *Handwoerterbuch der Sozialwissenschaften*. Stuttgart, Germany: Gustav Fischer, 1956. 9: 151-8.

Scherer, Frederic M. "Firm Size, Market Structure, Opportunity and the Output of Patented Inventions." *American Economic Review* 35 (1965): 1097-1125.

——— *Industrial Market Structure and Economic Performance*. Chicago, Ill.: Rand McNally, 1970.

——— *Innovation and Growth: Schumpeterian Perspectives* (84 reprinted essays and papers). Cambridge, Mass.: MIT Press, 1985.

Scherf, H. "Marx, Schumpeter, Keynes: gibt es eine zeitunabhaengige oekonomische Krisentheorie?" *Merkur* 37, no. 3 (1983): 292-300.

Schiming, Richard C. "Two Views of the Future of the Entrepreneur." *Akron Business and Economic Review* 13, no. 2 (1982): 22-25.

Schlesinger, Arthur M. Review of *Capitalism, Socialism and Democracy. The Nation* 26 April 1947, p. 490.

Schlesinger, James R., and Phillips Almarin. "The Ebb Tide of Capitalism? Schumpeter's Prophecy Re-examined." *Quarterly Journal of Economics* 73 (1959): 448-65.

Schmoller, G. "Volkswirtschaft, Volkswirtslehre und -Methode." *Handwoerterbuch der Staatswissenschaften* 8 (3 August 1911): 449-50.

Schmookler, Jacob. "Economic Sources of Inventive Activity." *Journal of Economic History* 22 (1962): 1-20.

——— "Invention, Innovation, and Business Cycles." In *Variability of Private Investment*, by the U.S. Joint Economic Committee, part 2, 45ff. Washington, D. C.: U.S. Government Printing Office, 1962.

——— *Invention and Economic Growth*. Cambridge, Mass.: Harvard University Press, 1966.

Schneider, Erich, and Arthur Spiethoff. *Aufsaetze zur oekonomische Theorie* (1952), *Aufsaetze zur Sociologie* (1952), and *Dogmengeschichte und biographische Aufsaetze* (1954). Tuebingen, Germany: J. C. B. Mohr (Paul Siebeck).

Schneider, Erich. "J. A. Schumpeter, der Theoretiker." *Weltwirtschaftliches Archiv* 65, no. 2 (1950): 169-84.

——— "Joseph Alois Schumpeter in memoriam." *Weltwirtschaftliches Archiv* 64, no. 1 (1950): 1-4.

——— "Schumpeter tel que je l'ai connu." *Economie Appliquee* 3 (1950): 417-25.

——— "Schumpeter's Early German Work, 1906-1917." *Review of Economics and Statistics* 33 (1951): 104-8; in *Joseph A. Schumpeter,* edited by Seymour Harris (see), 54-58.

——— "Schumpeter." *Staatslexicon* (Freiburg im Breisbau) 6 (1961): 1172ff.

——— "The Nature of Money: On a Posthumous Publication by Joseph A. Schumpeter" (review of *Das Wesen des Geldes*). *German Economic Review* 8, no. 4 (1970): 348-52.

——— *Joseph A. Schumpeter: Leben und Werk eines Grossen Sozialoekonomen.* Tuebingen, Germany: Mohr (Siebeck), 1970; *Joseph A. Schumpeter: Life and Work of a Great Social Scientist,* translated by W. E. Kuhn (Lincoln, Nebr.: Bureau of Business Research, University of Nebraska-Lincoln, 1975).

Schultz, B. "Three Economists Indicating a Direction: G. Cassel, J. Schumpeter and B. Harms." *Zeitschrift fuer Wirtschafts- und Sozialwissenschaften* 4 (1975): 379-80.

Schumpeter, Elizabeth B. "Bibliography of the Writings of Joseph Alois Schumpeter." *Quarterly Journal of Economics* 64 (1950): 373-84.

"Schumpeter Centenary." *Economist* 19 November 1983, pp. 19-20

Schweinitz, K. D, Jr. "Free Enterprise and Democracy." *Social Research* 20 (1953): 55-74.

Schweitzer, Paul R. Reply with rejoinder to "Usher and Schumpeter on Invention, Innovation and Technological Change," by V.W. Ruttan (see). *Quarterly Journal of Economics* 75 (1961): 152-6.

Scitovsky, Tibor. "Can Capitalism Survive? An Old Question in a New Setting." *American Economic Review* 70 (1980): 1-13.

Seblebusch, Elizabeth. "Die Aufssung von Wirtschaft und Sozialwirtschaft bei Alfred Amonn und Joseph Schumpeter." Ph.D. dissertation, University of Cologne, Cologne, Germany, 1928.

Seidl, Christian, ed. *Lectures on Schumpeterian Economics.* Berlin, Germany: Springer-Verlag, 1984.

Seidl, Christian. "Joseph Alois Schumpeter in Graz." Research Memorandum 8201, University of Graz, Graz, Austria, August 1982.

———— "Schumpeter versus Keynes: Supply-side Economics or Demand Management." Research Memorandum 8304, University of Graz, Graz, Austria; *Austria Today* 1 and 2 (1983).

Seligman, Ben B. "Is the Depression Inevitable." *Commentary* September 1947: 282-289.

———— "The Economics of Joseph Schumpeter." *Dissent* Autumn 1954: 370-384.

———— *Main Currents in Modern Economics: Economic Thought since 1870,*. Glencoe, Ill: Free Press, 1962.

Shackle, G. L. S. *Epistemics and Economics.* London, England: Cambridge University Press, 1972.

Shelby, George Donald. "An Analysis of Schumpeter's Business Cycles Theory." Ph.D. dissertation, University of California-Berkeley, Berkeley, California, 1956.

Shionoya, Yuichi. "The Science and Ideology of Schumpeter." *Revista Internazionale di Scienze Economiche e Comerciali* 33, no. 8 (August 1986): 730-62.

Shonfield, Andrew. *Modern Capitalism: The Changing Balance of Private and Public Power.* New York, N. Y.: Oxford University Press, 1965.

Shreyer, Jorg. "In Memorium J. A. Schumpeter." *Geschichte und Gegenwart* 2, no. 1 (March 1983): 69-65.

Sievers, Allen. *Revolution, Evolution, and the Economic Order.* Englewood Cliffs, N.J.: Prentice-Hall, 1962.

Silk, Leonard. "Capitalism and Crises." *New York Times* 1 September 1982, p. 26. National edition.

———— *Capitalism: The Moving Target.* New York, N.Y.: Praeger, 1974.

———— *The Economists.* New York, N.Y.: Basic Books, 1976.

Simpson, David. "Joseph Schumpeter and the Austrian School of Economics." *Journal of Economic Studies* 10, no. 4 (1983): 15-28.

Singer, Hans W. "Obstacles to Economic Development." *Social Research* 20 (1953): 19-31.

Smithies, Arthur. "Memorial: Joseph Schumpeter." *American Economic Review* 40 (1950): 628-48.

———— "Schumpeter and Keynes." *Review of Economics and Statistics* 33 (1951): 163-9; in *Joseph A. Schumpeter,* edited by Seymour Harris (see), 136-42.

———— "Schumpeter's Predictions." in *Schumpeter's Vision,* edited by Arnold Heertje (see), 130-49.

Sobel, Robert. *The Worldly Economists.* New York, N.Y.: Free Press, 1980.

Sohn-Rethel, Alfred. "Von der Analytik des Wirtschaftens zur Theorie de Volkswirtschaft. Methodologische Untersuchnung mit bisonderem Bezug auf die Theorie Schumpeters.": Ph.D. dissertation, University of Heidelberg, Germany, 1936.

Solo, Carolyn S. "Innovation in the Capitalist Process: A Critique of Schumpeterian Theory." *Quarterly Journal of Economics* 65 (1951): 417-28.

Solterer, J. "Natural Law and Economics: Reflections on Desan, Rahner, and Schumpeter." *Review of Social Economy* 34, no. 1 (1976): 53-62.

———— "Quadragesimo Anno: Schumpeter's Alternative to the Omnipotent State." *Review of Social Economy* 9 (March 1951): 12-23.

Soltow, James H. "The Entrepreneur in Economic History." *American Economic Review* 53, no. 2 (May 1968): 84-92.

Spann, Othmar. "Die mechanisch-mathematische Analogie in der Volkswirtschaftlehre." *Archiv fuer Sozialwissenschaft* 30 (1910): 786-824.

Spiegel, Henry William. *The Growth of Economic Thought.* Englewood Cliffs, N.J.: Prentice-Hall, 1971.

Spiethoff, Arthur. "Josef Schumpeter: Im Memorium." *Kyklos* 3, no. 4 (1950): 289-93.

St. Clair, David S. "Schumpeter's Theory of Capitalist Development: Revisited and Revised." *Economic Forum* 11, no. 1 (Summer 1980): 62-78.

Stadler, Karl R. *Austria.* New York, N.Y.: Praeger, 1971.

———— *The Birth of the Austrian Republic,* 1918-1921. Leyden, Netherlands: A. W. Sijtoff, 1966.

Stahl, I. "Wicksell, Bowley, Schumpeter and Doll's Eyes." *Scandanavian Journal of Economics* 80, no. 2 (1978): 168-80.

Staley, Charles E. "Schumpeter's 1947 Course in the History of Economic Thought." *History of Political Economy* 15, no. 1 (1983): 25-37.

Stanfield, Ron. "Kuhnian Scientific Revolutions and the Keynesian Revolution." *Journal of Economic Issues* 8, no. 1 (1974): 97-109.

Stark, Werner, "Joseph Schumpeters Umvertung der Werte." *Kyklos* 8, no. 3 (1955): 225-47.

Stevenson, Michael I., compiler. *Joseph Alois Schumpeter: A Bibliography, 1905-1984.* Westport, Conn.: Greenwood Press, 1985.

Stigler, George J. Review of *History of Economic Analysis. Journal of Political Economy* 62 (1954): 344-5.

Stolper, Toni. *Ein Leben in Brennpunkten Unserer Zeit: Gustav Stolper, 1888-1947.* Stuttgart: Klett-Cotta, 1960.

Stolper, Wolfgang F. "Aspects of Schumpeter's Theory of Evolution." In *Schumpeterian Economics,* edited by Helmut Frisch (see), 28-48.

—— "Fiscal and Monetary Policy in the Context of Development: A Schumpeterian Approach." In *Public Finance and Economic Growth* (proceedings of the 37th Congress of the International Institute of Public Finance, Tokyo, Japan,1981), 127-47. Detroit, Mich.: Wayne State University Press, 1981.

—— "Joseph A. Schumpeter." In *International Encyclopedia of the Social Sciences*, 14: 67-72. New York, N.Y.: MacMillan and Free Press, 1968.

—— "Joseph Alois Schumpeter—A Personal Memoir." *Challenge* 21, no. 6 (January-February 1979): 64-69.

—— "Monetary Equilibrium and Business Cycle Theory." *Review of Economic Statistics* 25 (1943): 88-92.

—— "Reflections on Schumpeter's Writings." *Review of Economics and Statistics* 33 (1951): 170-7. Reprint in Harris (1951), 102-9.

—— "Schumpeter and the German and Austrian Socialization Attempts of 1918/1919." Paper given at the meeting of the History of Economics Society, Pittsburgh, Pa., May 1984. Typescript.

—— "Schumpeter: Der politische Oekonom fuer die Neunzigar Jahre? Schumpetersche Wirtschaftspolitik—Schumpeter vs. Keynes order Schumpeter und Keynes?" Manuscript contributed to the Bonn-Harvard Kolloquium of the 100th anniversary of the birth of J. A. Schumpeter, September 1983. Typescript with English translation.

—— "Schumpeters Theorie der Innovation." *IFO Studie, Zeitschrift fuer empirische Wirtschaftforschung* 28 (1982): 4 (English summary 239-70).

—— "The Role of Government." Manuscript contributed to the International Colloquium on J. A. Schumpeter-J. M. Keynes, Paris, France, September 1983. Typescript.

—— "The Schumpeterian System." *Journal of Economic History* 11, no. 3 (1951): 272-7.

Stolper, Wolfgang F., and Christian Seidl. *Aufsaetze zur Wirtschaftpolitik*. Tuebingen, Germany: J. C. B. Mohr (Paul Siebeck), 1985.

Stoneman, Paul. *The Economic Analysis of Technological Change*. New York, N.Y.: Oxford University Press, 1983.

Strasser, Hermann. "Der Beitrag Joseph A. Schumpeter zur funktionalistischen Schichtungs theorie." Unpublished manuscript, 1982. Typescript.

Strausz-Hupe, Robert. Review of *Capitalism, Socialism and Democracy. New York Times* 30 March 1947, p. 6.

Streissler, E. "Schumpeter's Vienna and the Role of Credit in Innovation." In *Schumpeterian Economics*, edited by Helmut Frisch (see), 60-83.

Sugiyama, Ch. "Schumpeter's Lecture in Japan." *Journal of Economic Literature* 21 (1983): 551.

Suval, Stanley. *The Anschluss Question in the Weimar Era.* Baltimore, Md.: Johns Hopkins, 1974.

Sweezy, Paul M. "Professor Schumpeter's Theory of Innovation." *Review of Economic Statistics* 25 (1943): 93-96.

——— "Why Stagnation?" *Monthly Review* 72 (1972): 1-11.

——— Introduction to Schumpeter's *Imperialism and Social Classes.* New York, N.Y.: Augustus M. Kelley, 1951.

——— Review of *Business Cycles. The Nation* 3 February 1940, p. 133.

Sylos-Labini, Paolo. *The Forces of Economic Growth and Decline.* Cambridge, Mass.: MIT Press, 1984.

Synnott, Marcia Graham. *The Half-opened Door: Discrimination and Admissions at Harvard, Yale, and Princeton, 1900-1970.* Westport, Conn.: Greenwood Press, 1979.

Taylor, A. J. P. *The Habsburg Monarchy, 1809-1918.* London, England: Hamish Hamilton, 1967.

Taylor, Overton H. "Schumpeter and Marx: Imperialism and Social Classes in the Schumpeterian System." *Quarterly Journal of Economics* 65 (1951): 525-55.

——— "The Economics of a 'Free' Society." *Quarterly Journal of Economics* 62 (November 1948): 641-670.

——— *Economics and Liberalism.* Cambridge, Mass.: Harvard University Press, 1955.

——— Review of *History of Economic Analysis. Review of Economics and Statistics* 37 (1955): 12-22.

Taymans, A. C. "De Ondernemerstheorie van Prof. Joseph A. Schumpeter (1883-1950)." *Economisch en Sociaal Tijdschrift* 34, no. 3 (1980): 177-291.

——— "George Tarde and Joseph A. Schumpeter: a Similar Vision." *Explorations in Entrepreneurial History* 1, no. 4 (1949): 9-17.

——— "Tarde and Schumpeter: a Similar Vision." *Quarterly Journal of Economics* 64, no. 4 (November 1950): 611-22.

——— Le 'Research Center in Entrepreneurial History'." *Economie Appliquee* 3 (1950): 615-35.

The Catalog of Prof. Schumpeter Library. Tokyo, Japan: The Hitotsubashi University Library, Hitotsubashi University, 1962.

Thorp, W. L. "The Business Depression of Nineteen Hundred Thirty-Six: Discussion." *American Economic Review*, supplement (1931): 196-8.

Tinbergen, Jan. "Schumpeter and Quantitative Research in Economics." *Review of Economics and Statistics* 33 (1951): 109-11; in *Joseph A. Schumpeter*, edited by Seymour Harris (see), 59-61.

Tisch, Klaere. "Verzeichnis der Schriften und Rezensionen von Joseph Schumpeter." Bound typescript of 26 pages issued in Bonn in 1933 with the name Klaere Tisch written in handwriting.

Tortella, Gabriel. "La Magna Dinamica: Tres Grandes Economistas ante el Futuro del Capitalismo." *Revista de Occidente* 21-22 (1983): 7-21.

Treviranus geb Reissert, Margarete. *Die Kapitalzintheorie Joseph Schumpeters*. Dissertation. Marburg University, Marburg, Germany, 1937.

Triffin, Robert. "Schumpeter, souvenirs d'un student." *Economie Appliquee* 5 (1950): 413-6.

Tsuru, Shigeto. "A Peripatetic Economist." *Quarterly Review* (Banca Nazionale del Lavaro, Rome, Italy) 142 (September 1982): 227-44.

———— "Business Cycles and Capitalism: Schumpeter versus Marx." *Hitotsubashi Academy Annals* 2 (1952): 134-47; *Towards a New Political Economy*, by Shigeto Tsuru (Tokyo: Kodansha, 1976) 13.

Tu, Yien-I. "Some Tests on the Dynamic Properties of the Schumpeterian System." Paper delivered at the Missouri Valley Economic Association, St. Louis, Mo., February 1977.

———— "The Dynamic Properties of the Schumpeterian System." *Journal of Economics* 2 (1975): 35-39.

Ulam, Adam. "Remembering Three Teachers." *Encounter* 39, no. 6 (1972): 43-48.

Usher, Abbott Payson. "Historical Implications of the Theory of Economic Development." In *Joseph A. Schumpeter*, edited by Seymour Harris (see), 125-9.

Van der Haag, Ernest ed. *Capitalism: Sources of Hostility*. Washington, D.C.: Heritage Foundation, 1979.

Van Duijn, J. J. *The Long Waves in Economic Life*. London, England: George Allen and Unwin, 1983.

Varga, Etienne. "Schumpeter et le probleme du risque." *Economie Appliquee* 3 (1950): 531-69.

Vercelli, Alessandro. "Technological Flexibility, Financial Fragility and the Recent Revival of Schumpeterian Entrepreneurship." Working Paper Series, no. 102. St. Louis, Mo.: Washington University, 1987.

Verosta, Stephen. "Joseph Schumpeter gegen das Zollbundnis der Donaumonarchie mit Deutschland und gegen die Anschlusspolitik Otto Bauers, 1916-1919." In *Festschrift fuer Christian Broda*, edited by M. Neider, 373-404. Vienna, Austria: Europa Verlag, 1976.

Vestuti, Guido. "Schumpeter theorico dell'ecibinua." *Cleo: trimestral di studi storici* 4, no. 2 (1968): 230-71.

Viner, Jacob. Review of *History of Economic Analysis. American Economic Review* 44 (1954): 894-910.

—— *The Long View and the Short.* New York: Free Press, 1958.

Vogelstein, Theodor M. "Joseph A. Schumpeter and the Socialisierungsfommission: An Annotation to Gottfried Haberler's Memoir of Schumpeter." Unpublished typescript found in the Harvard University Archives, n.d., 7 pages.

Vuillemin, Jules., "Les classes sociales chez Schumpeter et dans la realite." *Economie Appliquee* 3 (1950): 571-614.

Wagener, H.-J., and J. W. Drukker, eds. *The Economic Law of Motion of Modern Society: A Marx-Keynes-Schumpeter Centennial.* New York, N.Y.: Cambridge University Press, 1986.

Walker, C. R. Review of *Capitalism, Socialism and Democracy. Yale Review* ns 32 (1943): 597.

Wallich, Henry C. "Some Notes Towards a Theory of Derived Development." In *The Economics of Underdevelopment*, edited by A. N. Agarwala and S. P. Singh, 189-204. Bombay, India: Oxford, 1958.

Warburton, Clark A. " Money and Business Fluctuations in the Schumpeterian System." *Journal of Political Economy* 61 (December 1953): 509-22.

Warriner, Doreen. "Schumpeter and the Conception of Static Equilibrium." *Economic Journal* 41(1931): 38-50.

Waters, William R. "Entrepreneurship, Dualism and Causality: An Appreciation of the Work of Joseph A. Schumpeter." Ph.D. dissertation, Georgetown University, Washington, D.C., 1953.

—— "Schumpeter's Contributions and Catholic Social Thought." *Review of Social Economy* 19 (September 1961): 133-41.

Weber, Wilhelm. "Joseph Alois Schumpeter + 8–1–1950." *Zeitschrift fuer Nationaloekonomie* 13, no. 2 (1951): 153-7.

Wechsberg, Joseph. *The Vienna I Knew.* Garden City, N.J.: Doubleday, 1979.

Werner, Josua. "Das Verhaeltnis von Theorie und Geschichte bei Joseph A. Schumpeter." *Zeitschrift fuer die gesamte Staatswissenschaft* 114, no. 1 (1958): 99-118.

Whitaker, J. K. "The Schumpeterian Stationary State Revisited." *Review of Economics and Statistics* 53, no. 4 (1971): 389-91.

Whittaker, Edmund. *A History of Economic Ideas.* New York, N.Y.: Longman, Green and Company, 1940.

Wieser, Friedrich. "Das Wesen und der Hauptinhalt der theoretischen Nationaloekonomie. Kritische Glossen" (review). *Schmollers Jahrbuch* 35 (1911): 909-31

Wiles, Peter. "A Sovietological View." In *Schumpeter's Vision*, edited by Arnold Heertje (see), 150-69.

Wiles, Richard C. "Professor Joseph Schumpeter and Underdevelopment." *Review of Social Economy* 25 (1967): 196-208.

—— "Schumpeter and Underdeveloped Countries: Comment." *Quarterly Journal of Economics* 77 (November 1963): 697-9.

Winslow, E. M. "Marxism, Liberal, and Sociological Theories of Imperialism." *Journal of Political Economy* 3, no. 6 (1931): 713-58.

Winterberger, G. *Ueber Schumpeters Geschichtsdeterminismus.* Tuebingen, country: J.C.B. Mohr/Paul Seibeck, 1983.

Wolff, Jacques. "Schumpeter and Marx of the Transitional Period from Capitalism to Socialism." Paper presented at the History of Economics Society meeting, East Lansing, Mich., 1982.

Wolfson, Robert J. "The Economic Dynamics of Joseph Schumpeter." *Economic Development and Cultural Change* 7, no. 1 (October 1958): 31-54.

Wood, Lewis. Review of *History of Economic Analysis.* New Republic 2 August 1954, p. 21.

Wright, David M. "Schumpeter and Keynes." *Weltwirtschaftliches Archiv* 65, no. 2 (1950): 185-96

—— "Schumpeter's Political Philosophy." *Review of Economics and Statistics* 33 (1951): 152-7; in *Joseph A. Schumpeter*, edited by Seymour Harris (see), 130-5.

Wurzer, Lothar. "Die Zukunft der Markwirtschaft: eine Auseinandersetzun mit J. A. Schumpeter." Ph.D. dissertation, University of Koln, Germany, 1965.

Xenos, Nicholas. "Democracy as Method: Joseph A. Schumpeter." *Democracy* 1, no. 4 (1981): 110-23.

Yamabe, N. "Shumpeta taikei ni okera to keizai hendo" (Money and the economic cycle in Schumpeter's system). *Banking* (Tokyo, Japan) 73 (1954): 42-50.

Yamada, Y. "Riron-keizai-gaku: Shumpeta" (Review of *History of Economic Analysis*). *Hitotsubashi Ronso* 35, no. 4 (1970): 16-34.

Yoshida, S. "Keinzu to Shumpeta." *Keizai Riron* 30 (1956): 1-26.
———— *Shumpeta no Keizai-gaku* (The Economics of Schumpeter). Kyoto, Japan: Horitsu Bunkasha, 1956.

Zald, Mayer N., and John D. McCarthy. "Organizational Intellectuals and the Criticism of Society." *Social Service Review* 49, no. 3 (1976): 344-62.
Zaldueno, Eduardo Andes. "El empresario en la obra de Joseph Alois Schumpeter." *Revista de Ciencias Económicas* 48, no. 9 (1960): 69-84.
Zassenhaus, Herbert K. "Capitalism, Socialism and Democracy: the 'Vision' and the 'Theories'." In *Schumpeter's Vision,* edited by Arnold Heertje (see), 170-202.
Zebot, Cyril A. "La posizione di J. Schumpeter su alcuni problemi methodologici delle scienze sociali." *Revista internazionale di Scienze Sociali* 63, no. 2 (1955): 135-40.
Znaniecki, Florian. "Spoleczne Role Uczonych a Historyczne Cechy Wiedzy" (Social Roles of Scholars and the Historical Qualities of Knowledge). *Przegla Socjologiczny* 28 (1976): 110-53.
Zottmann, Anton. Review of *Aufsaetze zur Oekonomischen Theorie. Weltwirtschaftliches Archiv* 70, no. 2 (1953): 41-48.
Zweig, Stefan. *The World of Yesterday.* New York, N.Y.: Viking Press, 1943.
Zwiedeneck-Sudenhorst. "Joseph Schumpeter: Wesen." *Zeitschrift fuer die gesamte Staatswissenschaft* 47 (1911): 142.

Name Index

Alexander, Sidney 2-96
Allais, Maurice 1-85
Allen, R. G. D. 2-162-3
Amonn, Alfred 1-111
Amorosa, L. 1-269
Anderson, Benjamin 1-110
Anderson, Oskar 2-97
Angell, James W. 1-260
Araki, Kotaro 1-270
Aris, R. 2-204
Aristotle 1-52
Ashton, T. S. 2-30
Auspitz, Rudolph 1-58, 1-262
Ayres, Clarence E. 2-131

Babbage, Charles xii
Backhaus, Juergen 2-273
Bain, Joe 2-148
Balinky, Alex 2-274
Baran, Paul 2-43
Barbora of Hladova 1-8
Barone, Enrico 1-231, 2-126
Baster, A. S. J. 2-224
Bastiat, Claude-Frederic 2-213
Baudelaire, Pierre Charles 1-22-23
Bauer, Otto 1-39, 1-161, 1-165,
    1-167, 1-169-77, 1-179, 1-183
Becker, Carl Heinrich 1-289

Becker, Gary 2-133
Beckerath, Herbert von 1-203, 1-205,
    1-235, 1-193, 2-143
Beckerath, Irwin von 1-203
Beebe, Lucius 2-170
Bell, James Washington 2-166
Berchtold, Count 1-186
Berg, Alban 1-54
Bergson, Abram 2-96, 2-98, 2-145,
    2-148
Bernstein, Edward 2-154
Beveridge, Lord 2-149
Bicanski, Stojan 2-44, 2-176
Biedermann, Baron 1-185
Biedermann, Michael Lazar 1-185
Bigelow, Karl 1-247
Billroth, Theodor 1-54
Birkhoff, Georg 1-301, 2-66
Bishop, Robert L. 2-96
Bismarck, Otto von 1-123, 1-150
Black, John D. 1-244, 2-4, 2-139
Bladen, Vincent 2-215
Blake, Robert 1-247, 2-7
Blaug, Mark 2-215
Bode, Karl 1-283
Boehm-Bawerk, Eugen von 1-38-39,
    1-42, 1-51-2, 1-61, 1-74, 1-87,
    1-90-2, 1-109-10, 1-120-1, 1-128,
    1-135, 1-141-2, 1-196, 1-202,

1-205, 1-262, 1-311, 2-42, 2-159,
2-214
Boltzman, Ludwig 1-54
Boody, Maurice and Hilda 2-28
Boody, Romaine Elizabeth 2-28
Bortkiewicz, Ludwig von 1-259,
1-269, 1-289
Boulton, William 1-115
Bourneuf, Alice 2-72
Bouvier, Emile 2-163
Bovary, Madame 1-32
Bowles, Samuel 2-133
Bowley, A. L. 1-269, 2-63
Bowman, R. T. 2-163
Bradley, P. D. 2-97
Bratt, Elmer 2-225
Braun-Stammfest, Richard M.
1-187-9, 1-236, 1-240
Brazda, Dr. Karel xx
Brinton, Crane 2-7
Bronfenbrenner, Martin 2-116-7,
2-275
Brooks, Van Wyck 2-153
Brown, Douglas 1-247, 1-260, 1-267,
1-308
Browne, Steffye xix, 1-142, 2-273-4
Bryce, Robert B. 2-21, 2-41, 2-43,
2-275
Buchanan, James 2-252
Bullock, Charles J. 1-243-4, 1-267,
2-4, 2-26
Burbank, Harold 2-4, 2-139, 2-154
Burian, Methodej xix
Burian, Count Stephan 1-151
Butler, Nicholas Murray 1-129-31,
1-307

Cairnes, John Eliot 1-61
Cantillon, Richard 2-210-1
Carver, Thomas Nixon 1-243-4,
1-267, 2-26
Cassel, Gustav 1-74, 1-231, 1-239,

1-243, 1-255-6, 1-295, 2-58,
2-159
Chamberlin, Edward 1-244, 1-247,
1-247-8, 1-304, 1-308, 2-38, 2-62,
2-64, 2-134, 2-148, 2-160, 2-171,
2-238
Chantler, Phillip 2-32
Chiera, Father 2-240
Child, Sir Josiah 2-211
Christie, Agatha 2-61
Churchill, Winston xv
Clark, John 2-253
Clark, John Bates 1-57-8, 1-65, 1-74,
1-84, 1-100, 1-104, 1-109-10,
1-129-30, 1-208, 2-159, 2-176,
2-183
Clark, Tom 2-226
Cochran, Thomas 2-183
Coe, Richard D. 2-133
Cole, Arthur H. 1-244, 1-247, 1-267,
2-6, 2-165, 2-176, 2-183
Cole, Margaret 2-226
Collado, Emilio 2-154
Conant, James Bryant 1-304, 2-44,
2-65, 2-95, 2-97
Cournot, Antoine Augustin 1-146,
2-4, 2-39, 2-107, 2-211, 2-217
Crum, William Leonard 1-244,
1-310, 2-6, 2-139, 2-151, 2-162,
2-165, 2-237

Dahman, Erik 2-252
Darwin, Charles 1-1
Dautzenberg, Therese 2-233
Dean, Joel 2-110
Debreu, Gerard 1-78
DeGaulle, General Charles 1-84
Dempsey, Father Bernard 2-143,
2-148
deSismondi, John Charles 2-213
Dietzel, Karl Heinrich 1-201-3,
1-205

Disraeli, Benjamin 1-285, 2-54
Divisia, F. 1-269
Dollfuss, Engelbert 2-12
Drucker, Peter 2-251
Duesenberry, James 2-237
Dulles, Eleanor 2-154
Dunlop, John T. 2-96, 2-237
Dunster, Henry 1-310

Earley, James 2-275
Edelberg, Victor 2-8
Edgeworth, Francis Ysidro 1-62,
    1-196, 1-208, 1-211, 2-216
Edison, Thomas Alva 1-105
Ehrlich, Eugen 1-97
Einstein, Albert 1-1
Ekvau, K. 1-283
Elliott, William Yandell 1-301,
    2-233

Federn, Walter 1-212
Fels, Rendig 2-84-5
Feldstein, Martin 2-250
Fetter, Frank Albert 1-100, 1-133-4
Firuski, Elizabeth Boody 2-18, 2-27,
    2-29-32, 2-35-6, 2-38, 2-42,
    2-46-7, 2-267
Firuski, Maurice 2-29
Fisher, Irving 1-74, 1-100, 1-33-4,
    1-208, 1-241, 1-248, 1-256,
    1-262, 1-265, 1-268-9, 1-305,
    1-307-9, 1-310, 2-36-7, 2-42,
    2-45, 2-62, 2-64, 2-95, 2-159,
    2-167, 2-175-6, 2-208, 2-214,
    2-251
Frank, Sir Oliver 2-224
Franz I 1-117
Franz, Joseph 1-10, 1-43, 1-88,
    1-81-2, 1-52-3, 2-110
Freeman, Christopher 2-253
Frickey, Edwin 1-244, 2-7, 2-161
Frisch, Ragnar 1-262, 1-268-9,

    1-295, 1-309, 2-37, 2-44, 2-62,
    2-64, 2-83, 2-108, 2-144, 2-149,
    2-167, 2-176
Fullerton, George Stuart 1-129
Furth, Herbert xix, 2-66, 2-273-5
Furuutchi, Hiro 1-283

Galbraith, John Kenneth 1-123,
    2-237, 2-273-4
Gay, Edwin F. 1-147, 2-26, 2-29,
    2-194
George, Henry xix
Georgescu-Roegen, Nicholas 2-43,
    2-237, 2-270, 2-273
Gerschenkron, Alexander 2-237
Gervaise, Isaac 2-211
Gilboy, Elizabeth W. 2-30
Gladstone, William E. 2-54
Gleick, James 2-253
Goessl, Alfred xix
Goethe, Johann 2-235
Goldscheid, Rudolf 1-167
Goodwin, Richard M. 2-97, 2-145,
    2-205
Gordon, Aaron 2-32
Gossen, Herman Heinrich 1-35
Green, Jerry 2-278
Griliches, Zvi 2-278
Grimme, Adolf 1-289-91
Gruener, Dr. Franz Julius 1-10, 1-11,
    1-13
Gruener, Dr. Julius G. 1-8, 1-10,
    1-11, 1-13
Gruener, Friedrich 1-11
Gruener, Johanna Marguerite See
    Schumpeter, Johanna Marguerite
Gruener, Wilhelmine 1-11
Grunberg, Karl 1-120
Gutmann, Franz 1-203

Haavelmo, Trygve 2-108, 2-144-5
Haberler, Friedl 2-147

Haberler, Gottfried xix, 1-227, 1-247,
   1-260, 1-281, 1-305, 2-6, 2-36,
   2-38, 2-43, 2-45, 2-65, 2-72, 2-98,
   2-110, 2-132, 2-140, 2-160,
   2-194, 2-205, 2-238, 2-240,
   2-243-4, 2-247, 2-255, 2-273-5
Hahn, F. H. xvi
Hanausek, Gustav 1-119
Hance, Wendell 2-97
Hansen, Alvin 1-309, 2-10, 2-24,
   2-65, 2-94, 2-123, 2-154, 2-176,
   2-247
Harkort, Guenther xx, 1-282, 1-284,
   2-274
Harris, Harvard Square bootlegger
   1-245
Harris, Seymour H. 1-244, 1-247,
   1-267-8, 1-304, 1-308, 1-310, 2-5,
   2-7, 2-161, 2-192, 2-228, 2-238,
   2-240, 2-247
Harrod, Roy x, 2-224
Hart, Albert 2-227-8
Hasenclever, Christa xx, 1-282,
   2-269
Hauke, Professor 1-118
Hayek, Friedrich A. von ix, 1-38,
   2-149
Heertje, Arnold 2-132, 2-250
Henderson, Pink Whiskers 1-248
Herbst, Aloisia 1-11
Herzl, Theodor 1-41
Heuser, Heinrich 2-97
Hicks, John R. 1-84, 2-44, 2-149,
   2-208, 2-225-6
Hicks, Ursula Webb 2-8
Higgins, Benjamin 2-96
Hildebrand, Richard 1-118-20,
   1-123-7, 1-147
Hildebrand, Bruno 1-118
Hilferding, Rudolf 1-39, 1-162,
   1-165, 1-179
Hitler, Adolph 1-284, 1-286-8,

   1-292, 2-1-2, 2-12, 2-42, 2-46,
   2-66, 2-90-2, 2-101, 2-138, 2-184,
   2-192
Hoefflinger, Heinrich 1-90, 1-197
Hofmannsthal, Hugh von 1-54
Holden, Harley 2-277
Holley, Julian 2-97
Hoover, Edgar 1-268, 2-79, 2-238
Hoover, Herbert 1-305
Hoover, J. Edgar 2-93
Howey, R. S. 2-10
Hume, David ix, x, xiii, xvi. 2-211

Inama-Sternegg, Karl Theodor von
   1-38
Isard, Walter 2-237

Jenke, Leland 2-183
Jevons, William Stanley 1-35-7, 1-57,
   1-61, 1-64, 1-146, 1-256, 2-213,
   2-216-7
Jewkes, John 2-224
Johnson, Alvin 1-291
Johnson, Harry 2-194
Joseph II, Emperor 1-117
Juglar, Clement 2-76-7, 2-79
Jurachek, Franz von 1-38

Kahn, Alfred 2-274
Kahn, R. F. (Lord) 2-2, 2-21-2
Kaldor, Nicholas (Lord) 2-8, 2-43
Kamien, Morton 2-253
Kanazashi, Motoi 2-269
Karl I, Emperor 1-153, 1-155, 1-166
Kautsky, Karl 1-162
Kéler, Johanna von 1-17-20, 1-23,
   1-63-4, 1-68, 1-90-1, 1-193-5,
   1-200, 1-217-8, 1-221-2, 1-224-8,
   2-59-61, 2-108, 2-199, 2-266
Kéler, Sigmund von 1-17-20, 1-23,
   1-54, 1-63-4
Kelsen, Hans 1-127, 1-197

Keynes, John Maynard (Lord) x, xvi,
    xix, 1-3, 1-256, 1-264-6, 1-282,
    1-312-3, 2-2, 2-17-8, 2-21-6,
    2-44, 2-46, 2-53, 2-58, 2-63,
    2-71, 2-79-80, 2-84, 2-140, 2-154,
    2-157, 2-159-60, 2-167-9, 2-178,
    2-198, 2-212, 2-215-7, 2-227,
    2-248-51, 2-55-6, 2-260
Keynes, John Neville 2-203
Killian, Franc 1-13
Killian, Franziska 1-13
Kitchin, Joseph 2-76-7
Kittridge, George Lyman 1-301
Klein, Artur 1-185-7
Klimt, Gustav 1-54
Knapp, G. F. 1-212
Knight, Frank 2-182, 2-208, 2-215,
    2-238
Koellner, Lutz 2-269
Kola, Richard 1-175-6
Kondratieff, Nikolai 2-76-9
Koopmans, Tjalling 2-195
Krassnigg, Lucia xx, 2-274
Kraus, Karl 1-41
Kun, Bela 1-174
Kunwald, Gottfried 1-189, 1-255
Kuschman, H. 1-283
Kuznets, Simon 2-82-3, 2-183

Lakatos, Imre 2-203
Lammasch, Heinrich 1-152-5
Lange, Oskar 2-25, 2-43, 2-110,
    2-126
Laski, Harold 1-301, 2-150
Layer, Professor 1-118
Lederer, Emil 1-39, 1-162, 1-290-1
Lekachman, Robert 2-132
Lenz, Adolf 1-120, 1-127
Leontief, Wassily xix, 1-85,
    1-259-60, 1-305, 1-308, 2-3-4,
    2-6-7, 2-9, 2-36, 2-38, 2-62,
    2-63-5, 2-79, 2-98, 2-148, 2-153,

2-161, 2-170, 2-172, 2-188,
    2-194, 2-205, 2-208, 2-224,
    2-237-8, 2-240, 2-244, 2-273-4
Leopold II 1-45
Lerner, Abba 2-8, 2-43
Liechtenstein, Prince Franz 1-152
List, Friedrich 2-213
Loesch, August 1-254, 1-256, 1-281,
    2-43
Loos, Adolph 1-54
Lotz, Walter 1-204
Lowell, Abbott Lawrence 1-303-4,
    1-310
Loyo, Gilberto 2-185

Mach, Ernst 1-54, 1-145
Machlup, Fritz xix, 2-41, 2-43,
    2-131-1, 2-145, 2-187, 2-203,
    2-275
Maerz, Eduard xix, 2-273-4
Malthus, Thomas Richard ix, xii,
    1-35, 1-42, 2-212
Mann, Fritz Karl 1-203, 2-254
Marget, Arthur 1-245, 1-247, 2-205,
    2-238, 2-254
Maria Theresa 1-45-6
Marschak, Jacob 2-43
Marshall, Alfred x, xiii, xv, xvi,
    1-34, 1-61, 1-74, 1-80, 1-82,
    1-101, 1-125, 1-135, 1-208,
    1-211, 1-255-6, 1-266, 1-295,
    1-302, 2-39-40, 2-58, 2-107,
    2-208, 2-214, 2-216-7, 2-251,
    2-255
Marx, Karl ix, x, xii, xvi, 1-25, 1-39,
    1-41, 1-46, 1-52, 1-59, 1-74,
    1-110, 1-205, 1-232, 1-249,
    1-264, 1-286, 2-2, 2-226-20,
    2-133-4, 2-211, 2-223, 2-250-1
Mason, Edward S. xix, 1-244,
    1-246-7, 1-260, 1-267-8, 1-281,
    1-304, 1-308, 1-310, 2-2, 2-7,

2-36, 2-38, 2-97, 2-100, 2-134,
2-160, 2-194, 2-203, 2-238,
2-240, 2-247, 2-273-4
Matthews, R. C. O. xvi
McCrea, Roswell C. 1-111, 1-134
McGranahan, D. V. 2-98
McHugh, Laughlin 2-96
McKenna, Joseph P. xix, 2-274
Meade, James Edward 2-224
Medwar, Sir Peter ix
Meek, Ronald 2-216
Meinl, Julius 1-153-4
Menger, Anton 1-34
Menger, Carl 1-34-39, 1-42, 1-51-2,
    1-59, 1-61, 1-74, 1-80, 1-125,
    1-142, 1-191, 1-201, 1-256, 2-213
Metzler, Lloyd 2-97, 2-110, 2-145,
    2-238
Meyer, B. H. 1-133
Mill, John Stuart ix, x, xii, xvi, 1-35,
    1-52, 1-61, 1-64, 1-104, 2-211,
    2-213
Minsky, Hyman 2-274
Mises, Ludwig von 1-39, 1-203-4
Mitchell, Wesley Clair 1-132, 1-134,
    1-204, 1-262, 2-167, 2-195-6,
    2-204, 2-225, 2-243
Monroe, A. E. 1-244, 2-237
Montgomery, Field Marshal 2-137
Moore, H. L. 1-310
Morgan, J. P. 2-170
Morgan, Theodore 2-171
Morgenstern, Oskar 1-85, 1-149,
    1-191, 1-211, 2-43, 2-245
Morrison, Charles Eliot 1-301
Musgrave, Richard A. 2-96
Mussolini, Benito 2-42, 2-46
Myrdal, Gunnar 2-149

Nakayama, Ichiro 1-270, 1-273,
    2-246, 2-277
Naumann, Friedrich 1-151

Naymier, L. B. 1-110
Neisser, Hans 2-10
Nelson, Richard 2-253
Neurath, Dr. 1-203, 1-259
Nixon, Russell 2-97, 2-148
North, Sir Dudley 2-211

Oglobin, Peter 2-223
Ohlin, Bertil 2-149
Opie, Redvers xix, 1-232, 1-247,
    1-260, 1-265, 1-278-9, 1-292, 2-9,
    2-154, 2-274
Oppenheimer, Franz 1-147

Papandreou, Andreas 2-154
Pareto, Vilfredo 1-208, 1-248, 2-219,
    2-225
Parmenides 2-251
Parsons, Talcott 1-247, 1-267, 2-98
Patton, General George 2-138
Perroux, Francois 2-226
Persons, Warren 1-244
Peter 2-147
Peterson, Dr. Clark 2-220, 2-235,
    2-239
Petschek, Georg 1-97
Petty, Sir William 2-210
Phillipovich, Eugene von 1-37-38
P[imperl] 1-240
Plato 1-52, 2-209
Pohle, Ludwig 1-118-9
Popper, Sir Karl 2-203
Pound, Roscoe 1-301

Queen, Ellery 2-61, 2-236
Quesnay, Francois 1-256, 2-39,
    2-107, 2-210-1

Rae, John xii
Rappard, William 2-149
Rathgen, Karl 1-133
Reagan, Ronald 2-250

Redlich, Josef 1-154-5
Reisinger, Anna 1-192, 1-194, 1-212
Reisinger, Annie 1-192-5, 1-197,
    2-266
Reisinger, Emilie 1-192, 1-197,
    1-218, 1-223
Reisinger, Franz 1-192, 1-194, 1-212
Reisinger, Willy 1-192, 1-197, 2-233
Renner, Karl 1-166-7, 1-174, 1-177,
    2-158
Ricardo, David ix, xii, 1-35, 1-52,
    1-65, 1-144, 1-256, 1-264,
    2-117-8, 2-140, 2-159, 2-198,
    2-206, 2-212, 2-215-7
Richardson, George 2-215
Richter, Dr. 1-289-91
Ripley, William Z. 1-243, 1-267,
    2-26
Robbins, Lord Lionel 2-8, 2-89,
    2-149, 2-167, 2-203, 2-215, 2-224
Robinson, Austin 2-226
Robinson, Joan 1-312, 2-2, 2-41,
    2-64, 2-131, 2-149, 2-167
Rodbertus, Johann Karl 2-213
Roessle, Karl Friedrich 1-213, 1-210,
    1-257
Rogers, Ruth N. 2-277
Roll, Eric 2-43
Rommel, General Erwin 2-137-8
Roos, Charles 1-269
Roosevelt, Franklin Delano 1-305-6,
    2-44, 2-101-3, 2-138, 2-141
Rosenstein-Roden, Paul xix, 1-194,
    2-273-4
Rudolf IV 1-32
Rudolf, Count, of Habsburg 1-7
Rudolf, Crown Prince 1-34
Rueff, Jacques 2-226

Salant, William 2-97
Samuels, Warren 2-133, 2-270
Samuelson, Marion C. 2-97

Samuelson, Paul Anthony xix, 1-303,
    2-38-9, 2-41, 2-66, 2-94-6, 2-110,
    2-132, 2-145, 2-148, 2-150-1,
    2-170-1, 2-182, 2-208, 2-238,
    2-245, 2-255, 2-273, 2-275
Sanger, C. P. 1-84
Say, Jean Baptiste 1-35, 2-19, 2-213
Sayers, Dorothy 2-61
Schachner, Robert 1-118-9
Schaeffle, Alfred 1-109
Schelling, Thomas 2-237
Scherer, F. M. 2-253
Schmitz, H. 1-283
Schmoller, Gustav von 1-58, 1-100,
    1-202, 1-211
Schneider, Erich 1-256, 1-260,
    1-266, 1-281, 1-284, 1-293,
    1-195, 2-226
Schober, Alois 1-122
Schoenberg, Arnold 1-54
Schorr, Marla xix
Schreiner, Gustav Franz 1-118
Schultz, Henry 1-309-10
Schumacher, E. F. (Fritz) 1-257-8
Schumacher, Herman Albert 1-257
Schumpeter, Alois Jacob 1-9, 1-13
Schumpeter, Annie 1-197, 1-207-10,
    1-216-8, 1-221-8, 1-236, 1-250,
    1-287-8, 2-9, 2-35, 2-53, 2-56,
    2-59-61, 2-108-9, 2-199, 2-333,
    2-266
Schumpeter, Baron von 1-7
Schumpeter, Elizabeth Boody 2-47,
    2-51, 2-54, 2-58, 2-62, 2-90,
    2-97-8, 2-102-4, 2-109-10,
    2-147-8, 2-150-1, 2-171, 2-174,
    2-182, 2-186, 2-189, 2-193,
    2-204-5, 2-211, 2-214, 2-229-30,
    2-233-4, 2-236, 2-240, 2-246-7,
    2-252, 2-278-9
Schumpeter, Emily xx, 2-274
Schumpeter, Franz (Frantisek) 1-9

Schumpeter, Gladys Ricarde 1-66,
1-89, 1-122, 1-129-30, 1-139,
1-141, 1-145-6, 1-195, 1-216-7,
1-222, 1-228, 2-266
Schumpeter, Johann 1-8
Schumpeter, Johann Georg 1-12
Schumpeter, Johanna Marguerite
1-8-17
Schumpeter, Josef 1-9, 1-12
Schumpeter, Joseph Alois Karl
1-8-13
Schumpeter, Josef Georg 1-11
Schumpeter, Karl Franz Dominik
(Carl) 1-13
Schumpeter, Ludwig 1-8
Schumpeter, Maria (nee Zdarska) 1-9
Schumpeter, Nelly 1-190
Schumpeter, Nikodema 1-8
Schumpeter, Vaclav (Wenzel) 1-8
Schuschnigg, Karl von 2-12, 2-46
Schwartz, Nancy 2-253
Scitovsky, Tibor 2-251
Seaver, Gladys Ricarde 1-66, 2-265
Seidl, Christian 2-252, 2-270-1,
2-274
Seipel, Monsignor Ignaz 1-189
Seligman, Edwin A. 1-131
Semmelweis, Dr. Ignac 1-131
Sen, Sudhir 1-283
Senior, Nassau 2-213, 2-216
Severn, Marian 2-47
Shapley, Harlow 1-301
Shaughnessy, Peggy 2-32
Shaw, George Bernard 2-21, 2-153
Shibata, Kei 1-272-3, 2-45-6, 2-52,
2-275
Shionoya, Yuichi 1-273
Silva-Tarouca, Count Ernst 1-154
Simons, Henry 2-182
Singer, Hans xx, 1-282
Sixte, Prince 1-155
Skidelsky, Robert x

Slichter, Sumner 1-267, 2-54, 2-94,
2-145
Slitor, Richard E. 2-97
Slutsky, Eugen 2-76
Smith, Adam ix, xi-xiii, xvi, 1-1,
1-35, 1-42, 1-52, 1-143-4, 1-157,
1-256, 2-19, 2-159, 2-164, 2-206,
2-208-11, 2-216-7, 2-251
Smithies, Arthur 1-65, 1-245, 1-247,
1-292, 2-9, 2-41, 2-43, 2-110,
2-132, 2-149, 2-154, 2-177,
2-205, 2-222, 2-227, 2-237,
2-238, 2-244, 2-247
Soete, Luc 2-253
Somary, Felix 1-39, 1-90, 1-214
Sombart, Werner 1-212, 1-231,
1-289
Sorokin, Pitrim 1-267, 2-7
Spiegel, Henry 2-150
Spiethoff, Arthur 1-120, 1-152,
1-196, 1-202-5, 1-208-20, 1-232,
1-235, 1-254, 1-259, 1-289-90,
1-292-3, 1-295, 1-312
Spitzmuller, Alexander 1-167
Spott, H. 1-283
Sprague, O. M. W. 1-243, 1-267,
2-26
Springer, J. 1-191
Staehle, Hans 2-110, 2-145
Stalin, Josef 2-101, 2-166
Steinthorsen, Dallas 2-173
Stevenson, Michael I. 2-252, 2-269
Stigler, George 2-143, 2-215
Stoeckel, Maria 1-233-5, 1-242,
1-250, 1-254, 1-261, 1-263,
1-277, 1-293-4, 1-297, 2-2-3, 2-8,
2-12-3, 2-18, 2-42, 2-44, 2-176,
2-233
Stolper, Gustav 1-142, 1-179-80,
1-191, 1-196, 1-204-5, 1-211-2,
1-230, 1-239, 1-249, 1-258,
1-267, 1-280-1, 1-289-90, 2-184

Stolper, Toni xix, 1-230, 2-273
Stolper, Wolfgang xix, 1-256, 1-281,
    2-27, 2-32, 2-96, 2-145, 2-238,
    2-250, 2-270-1, 2-273-4
Stout, Rex 2-61
Sturgkh, Count 1-153
Swedberg, Richard 2-106, 2-274
Sweezy, Alan 2-65, 2-246
Sweezy, Maxine Yaple 2-96, 2-275
Sweezy, Paul xix, 1-142, 2-5, 2-27,
    2-38, 2-41, 2-97-8, 2-134, 2-141,
    2-143, 2-145, 2-149, 2-170-1,
    2-174, 2-205, 2-238, 2-246, 2-274

Takata, Yasuma 1-272
Taussig, Frank William 1-100,
    1-109, 1-133-4, 1-230, 1-241-7,
    1-266-8, 1-292, 1-301-4, 2-3, 2-6,
    2-26, 2-31, 2-38, 2-44, 2-106-7,
    2-214
Taussig, Helen 1-242, 2-31
Taylor, Fred 2-126
Taylor, Harriet ix
Taylor, Overton H. (Nat) 1-244,
    1-247, 1-308, 2-215, 2-237
Thuenen, Johann Heinrich von 1-35,
    1-52, 1-109, 1-146, 2-211, 2-217
Tintner, Gerhard 2-110
Tisch, Klaere 1-282, 2-108, 2-126,
    2-269, 2-271
Tohata, Seiichi 1-270, 1-273, 2-246,
    2-277
Tobin, James 2-96
Tsuru, Shigeto 2-45-6, 2-96, 2-148,
    2-194, 2-275
Tugan-Baranowsky, Mikhail 1-146
Turgot, Anne Robert 2-210-1

Usher, Abbot Payson 1-244, 2-6-7,
    2-237

Vandermeulen, Daniel 2-97

Viner, Jacob 2-215
Vleeschouver, J. E. 1-260
Vydra, Julia 1-11

Wagner, Otto 1-54
Wald, Abraham 1-78
Walker, Roland 2-226
Walras, Léon xi-xiv, 1-35-7, 1-52,
    1-61, 1-73-4, 1-76-80, 1-84, 1-91,
    1-100-1, 1-109, 1-125, 1-146,
    1-157, 1-208, 1-255-6, 1-264,
    2-39, 2-107, 2-159, 2-208,
    2-213-4, 2-225, 2-251
Walsh, J. R. 2-3
Walsh, Raymond 2-65
Watt, James 1-105
Weber, Max 1-143, 1-288
Webern, Anton von 1-54
Wessels, Theodor 1-283
White, Harry D. 2-154
Whitman, Walt 1-40
Wicksell, Knut 1-74, 1-231, 1-295,
    2-39, 2-159, 2-214
Wiebel, Martin 1-283
Wieser, Friedrich von 1-35, 1-37-8,
    1-52, 1-74-5, 1-83-4, 1-86-7,
    1-90-1, 1-104, 1-109, 1-154,
    1-191
Wilber, Charles K. 2-133
Wilhelm, Kaiser 1-205, 1-289
Wilhelms, H. 1-283
Williams, John H. 1-244, 1-247,
    1-267
Wilson, E. B. 1-269, 1-310, 2-3,
    2-45, 2-99, 2-145, 2-237
Wilson, John D. 2-97
Winkler, Wilhelm 1-12
Winter, Sidney 2-253
Wittgenstein, Ludwig 1-54
Wood, Barbara 1-258
Wooley, Herbert 2-97
Worcester, Jane 2-145

Wright, David McCord 2-148

Young, Allyn 1-244, 1-310

Zassenhaus, Herbert xix, 1-283, 2-8, 2-107, 2-126, 2-132, 2-275
Zassenhaus, Mrs. Herbert 1-283
Zawadski, W. 1-269

Zeppelin, Graf 1-43
Zeuthen, F. 1-262
Zola, Emile 1-32
Zuckerkandl, Robert 1-119
Zweig, Stefan 1-20-22
Zwiedeneck-Sudenhorst, Otto von 1-120

Subject Index

Abdication of Karl I 1-166
Abyssinia 2-12
Acacia Street, Cambridge 2-214
Africa 2-138
Agency for International
    Development, U.S. 1-283
Alcohol, use of 2-174
Alexandria 1-66
Alienation 2-141
Allies 1-184
Alpine Mongangesellschaft 1-174-6
America First 2-103
American Economic Association 1-4,
    1-133, 1-248, 1-262, 1-268-9,
    1-312, 2-63, 2-98, 2-100, 2-110,
    2-143, 2-149, 1-164, 1-166,
    1-172, 1-174, 2-287-8, 2-208,
    2-221-2, 2-238-9, 2-251
American Economic Association
    meeting program 2-184, 2-188
American Economic Association,
    presidency 2-181
American Economic Association,
    presidential address 2-196
American Economic Review 2-131,
    2-143, 1-187, 2-244, 2-253
American economists article, 1910
    1-100
American Enterprise Institute 2-65

American Institutions and Economic
    Progress, lectures 2-229
American University (Washington,
    D. C.) 1-203
Amsterdam 1-295
Amsterdam, SS 1-240
Anglo-Austrian Bank 1-189
Anschluss 1-13, 1-172-3, 1-176,
    1-179, 2-12
Anthropolitical Museum 2-185
Anti-semitism 2-66-7, 2-191-2
Anti-utilitarianism 1-61, 1-144
Aphorisms in diary 2-146
Appearance, physical 2-21-2, 1-65-6,
    1-89, 2-30-1, 2-193
Aristocracy, attitude toward 1-46,
    1-55-6
Aristocracy, first society families
    1-45
Aristocracy, low, or second society
    1-33, 1-45-6, 1-64
Aristocratic behavior 1-54-6
Art enthusiasm 2-3
Astoria Hotel 1-186
Atomic Energy Community 1-282
Attitude toward English economists
    1-62
Attitude toward Germany and Japan
    1-204, 2-90-2, 2-101-2

333

Attitude toward mother 1-90-1
Augsburg, Germany 2-250
Australia 1-118
Austria 2-12, 2-43
Austria after World War II 2-158
Austrian educational system 1-15
Austrian Exchange Professor
    1-129-34
Austrian marginal utility school 1-76
Austrian Republic 1-280
Austrian Republic, postwar
    conditions 1-161-2
Austrian Socialization Commission
    1-290
Austro-Hungarian Monarchy 1-10,
    2-24-5, 1-32, 1-42-4, 1-96, 1-127,
    1-140, 2-139, 1-207, 1-285, 1-294
Austro-Marxists 1-183

Bad Godesburg 1-278
Baden-Baden 1-240
Baker Professorship, George F. 2-27
Baker, George, Library, Harvard
    Business School 2-99, 2-142
Bali 1-273
Bank of England 1-189
Bank presidency 1-186-189
Banking concession 1-184-5
Banking crisis, 1933 1-305
Beauvois 2-8
Belief in sub-normals 2-190-1
Benghazi 2-137
Berkshires 2-31
Berlin 1-123, 1-184, 1-277, 2-138
Berlin appointment, discussions
    1-289-91
Berlin, University of 1-33, 1-58,
    1-201, 1-230, 1-274, 1-289
Berliner Boersencourier articles
    1-212
Between the Lakes Road, Taconic
    2-32

Biederman, M. L. and Company
    1-185
Biedermann Bank 1-185, 1-215,
    1-229, 1-240, 1-254, 1-289, 1-290
Biographical studies 1-1-2, 1-5
Boehm-Bawerk 1905-1906 seminar
    1-39, 290
Boehm-Bawerk obituary 1-141
Bohemia 1-7, 1-45, 1-161, 2-90
Bonn 1-277-8, 2-2, 2-8
Bonn activity 1-296-7
Bonn economic education 1-258-9
Bonn Seminar 1-281-3
Bonn, City of 1-206-7
Bonn, City of, History 1-206-7
Bonn, University of 1-2, 1-8, 196-7,
    1-201, 1-241, 1-243, 1-253,
    1-257, 1-277-8, 1-292-3, 2-2,
    2-7-8
Bonn, University of, income 2-215
Bonn, University of, physical setting
    1-205-7
Bonn, University of, student
    population 1-257
Boston 2-2
Boston Economics Club 2-62, 2-107,
    2-165, 2-175
Boston Herald 2-93
Bratislava, Czechoslovakia 1-185
Breast cancer 2-220
Bretton Woods international
    conference 2-154
Brindisi 1-273
British Association for the
    Advancement of Science 1-231
British Commonwealth fellows 2-43
British Museum 1-59, 1-209, 2-2,
    2-29
Brown University 1-312
Brussels 1-282
Budapest, University of 1-33

Buffalo Chamber of Commerce 2-187
Buffalo, University of 1-312, 2-187
Bukowina region 1-96
Bureau of International Studies 2-102
Burgtheater 1-33
Business cycle article in Japan, 1931 1-271
Business cycle article, 1914 1-141
Business cycle article, 1930 1-262
Business cycle article, 1934 2-10
Business Cycles 1-2, 1-108, 1-313, 2-46-7, 2-63, 2-71-85, 2-88, 2-105, 2-111-2, 2-143-4, 2-158, 2-234
Business Cycles, edited by Rendig Fels 2-84-5
Business Cycles, historical analysis 2-78-9
Business Cycles, reviews 2-82-3
Business failure 1-189
Business School, Harvard 1-243
Butler Commission, Columbia University 1-306-7

Cabinet deliberation of *Finanzplan* 1-176
Cabinet resignation 1-177
Cafe Central 1-40
Cairo 1-66-8, 1-123, 1-209
Cambridge University 1-33, 1-61-2, 1-280, 2-2-3
Cambridge, City of 1-5
Cameralists 2-144
Capital levy and political attitudes 1-167, 1-171
Capital levy to stop inflation 1-157-8
Capitalism 1-3
Capitalism article for *Encyclopedia Brittanica*, 1944 2-2-150
Capitalism in Postwar World article, 1943 2-143

Capitalism, belief in 2-182
Capitalism, Socialism and Democracy 1-145, 1-250, 2-28, 2-88, 2-105, 2-111-2, 2-115-34, 2-143-4, 2-149-50, 2-158, 2-160, 2-163, 2-177, 2-246, 2-252
Capitalism, Socialism and Democracy third edition 2-223, 2-230, 2-234
Capitalism, Socialism and Democracy, reviews 2-131-3
Capitalism, Socialism and Democracy, success 2-134
Career possibilities upon graduation 1-53
Cassel article, 1927 1-231
Catholic background, chap. 2
Catholicism 1-10-11, 2-58
Cause of death 2-239
Centennial meetings 2-250
Central bank independence, 1919 1-168
Chameleon in reverse 1-55, 2-231
Chance, Love, and Logic Society 1-267, 2-4
Change and the entrepreneur article 2-224
Chartres, France 2-2
Chicago 2-99
Chicago, University of 1-205, 1-303, 2-194, 2-223
Choate Club 2-225
Christian Science Monitor 2-240, 2-250
Christian Social party 1-166-77
Circular flow 1-143, 2-210
Citation frequency 2-251
Cleveland 2-62, 2-164
Clothes 2-37-8, 2-54, 2-193
Coblenzerstrasse 39 1-208-9, 1-217, 1-254, 1-261
Colby College 2-187

Cologne, City of 1-206
Cologne, University of 1-205, 1-283
Colombo, Ceylon (Sri Lanka) 1-273
Colonial Club 1-242, 1-249
Colorado Springs 2-46
Columbia University 1-34, 1-117,
    1-129-34, 1-303
Committee of Full Professors 1-310,
    2-6
Committee on Mathematical
    Economics 1-310
Communist Manifesto article, 1949
    2-223
Community Church of New York
    2-47
Comparative statics 1-80-1
Comparison with Marshall 1-79, 1-82
Competition, advantages of 2-122
Concentration 1-64-5
Concentration camp 1-282
Concentration, theory of (Marxian)
    2-119
Congress of Vienna 1-185
Conscription and exemption 1-140
Controversy, avoiding 1-311-312
Copenhagen 1-295
Cotuit, Massachusetts 2-43
Cournot Group 2-4
Courtship with Annie 1-194-7
Creative destruction 2-120
Creative response article, 1947 2-184
Crisis in economics article 1931
    (1983) 1-270-1
Cronin's 1-247
Customs union memorandum, 1916
    1-152-3
Cycles book 1-313, 2-8, 2-20, 2-37,
    2-42, 2-44, 2-47, 2-52-3, 2-57,
    2-62, 2-71-2
Czech heritage 1-9-10
Czech National Archives 1-8
Czechoslovakia 1-202

Czechs, attitude toward Germans
    1-11-12
Czernowitz 1-95-6, 1-209
Czernowitz, University of 1-2, 1-32,
    1-92, 1-95-6, 1-119, 1-143, 1-178,
    2-222, 2-262

Daily performance, grades 2-56-7
Damodar Valley Authority (India)
    1-283
Danube Canal 1-19
Deanship, 1916 1-127
Death of Annie and child 1-223
Death of mother 1-221-2
Death, obsession with 2-56
Debate with Paul Sweezy 2-170-1
Debt 1-189, 1-235, 1-240, 2-555
Debt repayment 2-13
Decade of the 1920s article, 1946
    2-164
Democracy and socialism 2-129
Democracy, theory of 2-129-30
Democracy, U.S. 2-1
Department of Agriculture lectures
    2-27
Department of Agriculture, U.S. 2-89
Depressed economy 1-305
Depression article, 1930 1-268
Depression article in Japan, 1931
    1-271
Depression of 1873 1-17
Depression, beginnings, 1926
    1-223-4, 1-227-9, 1-235-6
Depression, chronic 1-239, 1-262,
    1-287, 2-35, 2-55, 2-152, 2-165
Der deutsche Volkswirt 1-212-6,
    1-231, 1-234, 1-258, 1-262, 1-280
Der oesterreichische Volkswirt
    1-142, 1-179, 1-212
Detective stories 2-61, 2-236
Detroit 2-98, 2-99, 1-107
Diabetes 2-219

Diary, Schumpeter 1-197, 1-287-8, 2-53-61
Diary, Annie 1-225, 1-227, 1-287, 2-53, 2-59, 2-109, 2-199
Diplomat Akademie 1-1-19
Dismemberment of Austro-Hungarian Monarchy 1-161
Distribution of the product, 1908 1-56-7, 1-78-80
Distribution theory 1-57
Doblhofgasse 3 1-19, 1-41, 1-63, 1-91, 1-190-1, 1-193, 1-197
Dorotheer Evangelical Lutheran church 1-197
Dressing for dinner in Czernowitz 1-98
Duel in Czernowitz 1-98-9
Duke of Lorraine 1-44
Duke University 1-205
Dunster House 1-310, 2-5, 2-17, 2-31, 2-38, 2-195
Durham, University of 1-278
Dynamic analysis, non-linear 2-253-4

Econometric Society 1-4, 2-36, 2-46, 2-63, 2-67, 2-98, 2-100, 2-175
Econometric Society 2-175
Econometric Society, founding 1-268-9
Econometric Society, presidency 2-63
Econometric Society, vice-presidency 2-62-3
Econometrica article, 1932 1-309
Economic change, sources of, 1-82, 1-103-5
Economic development 1-3, 1-103-5
Economic development theory 2-249
Economic Doctrine and Method 2-204

Economic history 1-2
Economic History Association 2-182
Economic interpretation of history (Marxian) 2-118
Economic Journal 1-62, 2-21, 2-115
Economic policy 2-21, 2-257-61
Economic science, defined 2-206-8
Economic sociology 1-2, 2-249
Economic theory 1-2
Economics as a science 1-144
Economics Club, Detroit 2-107
Economics Department, Harvard 1-88, 1-241, 1-304
Economics Department, Harvard, History of 1-243-4
Economics of Imperfect Competition (Robinson) 2-149
Economics of Imperfect Competition review (Robinson) 1-312, 2-2
Economics of the Recovery Program 2-4
Economics, as pure science 1-61
Economics, classical 1-35-6, 1-143, 1-153, 1-165, 2-201, 2-211-2
Economics, neoclassical 1-35-7, 2-213-5
Economics, study (Vienna) 1-34-39, 1-52
Economist 1-213, 2-171, 2-250-1
Economists National Committee on Monetary Policy 2-225
Educational philosophy 1-255-6
Effect of 1913-1914 U.S. visit 1-134-5
Emerson Hall 2-242
Encyclopedia of the Social Sciences articles 1-262
English economists article, 1949 2-224
English Overseas Trade Statistics, 1698-1808 (Schumpeter-Boody) 2-30

English policy, attitude toward, 1940
   forward 2-101
English visit 1906-1907 1-59-66
English, command of 1-130
Entrepreneurs 1-3, 1-82, 1-100,
   1-103-9, 2-124-6, 2-188
*Epochen der Dogmen- und
   Methodengeschischichte* 1-143,
   2-89, 2-204, 2-243
Equilibrium 1-76-8, 2-19, 2-168
Essays in Biography review
   (Keynes) 1-312
Ethiopia 2-42
Eton 1-18
Eugenics 2-190, 2-192
European Economic Community
   1-282
European socialist parties, history of
   2-130
Exchange Club, Detroit 2-98
Executive Committee meetings
   2-140
Existence of equilibrium 1-78

Faculty Club, Harvard 2-4, 2-38
Faculty Minute, Arts and Sciences
   2-247
Faculty of Law (Vienna) 1-26,
   1-31-34, 1-52-3
Faculty of Law (Czernowitz) 1-96
Faculty of Law (Graz) 1-118
Faculty of Philosophy 1-203
Failure in politics and business 1-222
Family background and heritage
   1-2-14
Family legend 1-7-8
Farewell party, Bonn, 1932 1-295
Fascism 2-192-3
Federal Bureau of Investigation
   2-93-4
Federal Reserve Bank of New York
   1-244

Finanzplan 1-168, 1-280
Finanzplan published, 1919 1-177
First society 1-45
Fisher obituary 2-175-6
Forbes Magazine 1-281, 2-250-1
Foreign Affairs 2-225, 2-238
Foundations of Economic Analysis
   (Samuelson) 2-150
France, Annie's work in 1-193
Frankfurt, University of 1-118, 1-292
Frankfurter Allgemeine Zeitung
   1-283
Freedom of Information Act 2-93-4
Freiberg, University of 1-205, 1-230
French architecture 2-2-3, 2-7, 2-12,
   2-37
Friday Seminar 2-4
Friendships 1-90, 1-260, 2-194,
   2-36-7

Gabelsberger 1-22, 1-41, 2-53-4
General equilibrium analysis 1-76-7,
   2-19
*General Theory of Employment
   Interest and Money* (Keynes)
   2-17-8, 2-21-6, 2-41, 2-46, 2-212
German citizenship 1-207
German Coal Board 1-163
German defeat, World War I 1-162
German historical school 1-58-9,
   1-143, 1-201
German relations memorandum,
   1917 1-154-5
German Socialization Commission
   1-290
German victory at Koeniggraetz
   1-25, 1-44
German-American Bund 2-103
Germans, attitude toward Czechs
   1-11
Germans, attitude toward Hungarians
   1-16

Germans, attitude toward Jews 1-11,
1-16-17
Germany 1-140, 2-1, 2-90-3,
2-101-3, 2-139, 2-145, 2-177
Ghandi 1-283
Gladys's letters, Bonn 2-216
Goals in life 1-117, 1-126-7
Gold standard article, 1927 1-232-3
Golden years at Harvard 1-302,
1-305, 2-161
Grading students 2-41
Graduate Economics Club 1-312,
2-62, 2-175, 2-195, 2-225
Gran rifiuto 1-183, 1-212, 2-87
Graz 1-14, 1-117, 1-122, 1-141,
1-209
Graz, University of 1-2, 1-8, 1-32,
1-101, 1-117, 1-128, 1-178,
1-184, 1-186, 1-204, 1-222,
1-230, 2-7, 2-97, 2-205
Graz, University of, salary 1-122
Great Depression 2-105, 2-123-4,
2-18, 2-27
Greek 1-5, 1-15, 1-20, 2-177, 2-188
Greek and Roman economic thinkers
2-144, 2-153, 2-165
Grenoble, France 2-2
Grief over wife's death 1-224-9
Guadalcanal 2-138

Habilitation 1-60, 1-73, 1-87
Habilitation, 1909, Vienna 1-67,
1-86-7
Habits and behavior 1-89-91
Habsburg dynasty 1-22, 1-43-46,
1-96
Halle, University of 1-133
Hartford 2-31
Harvard Club, Philadelphia 2-225
Harvard Crimson 2-152, 2-240
Harvard dinner honoring Fisher
2-175-6

Harvard Economic Service 1-243-4,
2-29
Harvard Economic Society 1-312
Harvard honorary M.A. 2-97
Harvard Social Science Project 2-188
Harvard Social Science Research
Committee 2-30
Harvard Square 1-242, 1-266, 2-5,
2-38
Harvard Tercentenary (1936) 2-43
Harvard University 1-4, 1-8, 1-253,
1-205, 1-230, 2-239-4, 1-291-3,
1-277, 1-301, 2-29, 2-148,
2-237-8
Harvard University Archives 2-247
Harvard University Press 2-9
Harvard University visit 1-133
Harvard Yard 1-241, 2-301, 2-5
Harvard, attitude toward 1-94-5,
2-139-40, 2-194, 2-237
Hasen 1-226-8, 1-234-5, 1-240,
1-242, 1-261-2, 2-42, 2-53,
2-56-8, 2-60-2, 2-91, 2-108,
2-153, 2-160, 1-287, 1-294, 2-9,
2-198-200, 2-219, 2-221, 2-233,
2-236, 2-239
Hausmacht 1-44
Health 2-55, 2-109, 2-165, 1-276,
2-235-6
Heidelberg, University of 1-201,
1-205, 1-292
Heidenheim, Germany 1-281
Heitzing Cemetary, Vienna 1-222
Historical analysis of business cycle
article 2-224, 2-230
Historical approach to economics
1-119
Historical-evolutionary model 1-109,
1-111
History of Economic Analysis 1-3,
2-144, 2-149-40, 2-189, 2-203-17,
2-226-30, 2-246

History of Economic Analysis,
  beginning 2-89, 2-112
History of Economic Analysis,
  reviews 2-215-7
History of Economic Literature
  course 2-89
History of economics 1-2, 2-165,
  2-221,
History of Economics Society 2-250
Hitler, Sympathy for 1-288
Hitosubashi University, Schumpeter
  Library 1-273
Hitotsubashi Shimbun 1-270
Hitotsubashi University 1-270
Hladov 1-9
Hofrats 1-22, 1-46
Holland 1-295
Holocaust 2-138, 2-166
Holy Roman Empire 1-43, 1-96
Holy Roman Empire of the German
  Nation 1-7
Holyoke House 1-245, 1-302, 2-17,
  2-5, 2-38, 2-42
Hong Kong 1-273
Honolulu 1-270
Honorary Litt.D., Columbia Univ
  1-117, 1-130
Honorary Member Committee,
  American Economic Association
  2-149
Hotel Marseilles, New York 1-130
Houghton Rare Book Library 2-246
Housatonic Book Shop 2-29
House system at Harvard 1-303
Hungarian Communist Party 1-174
Hungarian, political agitation,
  chap. 3
Hungary 1-161
Hyde Park 1-63, 1-209

Ideology in economics 2-196-8
Iglau, Moravia 1-8, 1-10, 1-14

Ikko Simbun 1-270
Illinois, University of 2-98
Imperial Palace 1-33
Imperialism and development
  articles, 1919 1-155-6
Income from royalties 2-234
Index numbers, early study of 1-38
Indian Ocean 1-273
Indirect taxes, increases, 1919 1-169
*Industrialization of Japan, Korea,
  and Manchuria* (Boody
  Schumpeter) 2-102
Inflation article for *Nation's Business*
  2-187
Inflation, 1919-1924 1-184, 1-207
Influence at Harvard 2-6
Inner Circle 2-4
Inner City, Vienna 1-19
Innovation 1-3, 1-82, 1-100, 1-103-6,
  2-73-76, 2-123-5
Innovations and crises, 1910 1-100
Innovator 1-104-5
Inns of Court 1-60
Innsbruck, University of 1-32
Input-Output analysis (Leontief) 2-63
Instability of Capitalism article, 1928
  1-249
Instability paper, 1927 1-230-1
Institute of World Affairs 2-234
Interest 1-78-9
Interest and Usury (Dempsey) 2-143
International Bank for
  Reconstruction and Development
  2-154
International commodity prices 1-38
International Economic Association
  2-226, 2-238
International Institute of Public
  Finance (Tokyo) 2-251
International J. A. Schumpeter
  Society 1-86, 2-250
International Mixed Tribunal 1-67

International Monetary Fund 1-283, 2-154
Invention and innovation 1-105
Italian Riviera 1-195-6
Italian steel interests 1-175
Italy 1-140, 2-8, 2-42, 2-90, 2-138

Japan 1-262, 2-90-2, 2-101-3, 2-139, 2-145-6, 2-151, 2-155, 2-177
Java 1-273
Jena, University of 1-118, 1-203
Jesuits 1-18, 1-117
Jewish influence 1-11
Jews, attitude toward 2-66-7
Jihlava Archives 1-11
Jihlava, Czechoslovakia 1-8
Joseph A. Schumpeter: A Bibliography, 1905-1984 2-252
Joseph Schumpeter, Social Scientist (Harris) 2-247
Journal of the American Statistical Association review, 2-225
Journal of the American Statistical Association, review 2-24-5
Juglar 8- to 11-year cycle 2-76
Justice Department, Criminal Division 2-94

Kaffeehaus in Vienna 1-40-1
Kalksburg, Austria 1-17
Kanematsu Lecture Hall 1-270
Kaufmann Bank 1-187-8, 1-240
Keynes's evaluation 2-167-9
Keynes's obituary 2-167
Keynesian analysis, criticism of 2-24-26
Keynesian nursery 2-232
Keynesian Revolution 2-17
Kiel, University of 1-230, 1-292
King of Poland 1-44
Kingston, Jamaica 1-249
Kitchin 40-month cycle 2-76

Kobe College of Commerce 1-196
Kobe Shodai Shimbun 1-273
Kobe University 1-272
Kobe, Japan 1-272
Koeniggraetz, German victory at 1-44
Koenigsberg, University of 1-203
Kondratieff 50- to 60-year long wave 2-76
Korecnik, Movavia 1-12
Kress Economics Library 2-99, 2-112, 2-141-2, 2-158, 2-174, 2-209, 2-246
Krise des Steuerstaates, Die 1-156, 2-27, 2-115
Kunitachi, Japan 1-271
Kunstler Cafe 1-40
Kyoto 2-138
Kyoto University 2-45

L'art pour l'art 1-40, 1-5, 1-61, 1-86, 1-144
Labor theory of value 1-35, 1-201, 1-213
Labor theory of value (Marxian) 2-119
Laconia, SS 2-3
Laissez-faire policies 1-42
Lakeville, Connecticut 2-31
Land ownership article, 1916 1-147
Landtmann Restaurant 1-40
LaRochelle, France 2-2
Latin 1-15, 1-20
Leadership, lack of 2-140-1
Leeds 1-240
Leverett House 2-187
Librarian incident at Czernowitz 1-98-99
Littauer Center 1-241, 2-171, 2-204, 2-246-7
Littauer Library 1-244
Locarno, Italy 1-197

Lochobers 2-4
Logical positivism 1-42
London 1-123, 1-129, 1-240, 2-138
London School of Economics 1-59,
   1-62, 1-230, 1-280, 2-2-3, 2-8,
   2-29,
London School outing, 1934 2-8
London Times 2-21
London, University of 1-59
Louvre 2-3
Lowell Institute lectures 2-104-7,
   2-111, 2-143
Lund 1-295
Lusitania 1-129
Lutheran church 2-58

Macroeconomic analysis 2-18
Malta fever 1-68, 1-86
March into Socialism paper, 1949
   2-230, 2-232, 2-238
Marginal productivity article 1-231
Marginal productivity theory 1-57-8
Marginal productivity theory article,
   1916 1-147
Marginal utility in economics 1-36-7
Markets 1-3
Markvarek 1-8
Marriage, first, 1907 1-66
Marriage, second, 1925 1-197
Marriage, third, 1937 2-47
Marshall, meeting with 1-61
Marxian economics 2-116-20
Marxian theory of imperialism 1-156
Marxism, a religion 2-117
Mastectomy, radical 2-220
Mathematical approach in economics
   1-36-7, 1-119, 2-231
Mathematical economics proposal
   1-309
Mathematical economics, teaching of
   2-3

*Mathematical Investigations in the
   Theory of Value and Price*
   (Fisher) 2-175
Mathematical method in economics
   1-56-7
Mathematical models 2-230-1
Mathematics 1-2, 1-146-7, 2-142-3,
   2-150, 2-158, 2-177, 2-190,
   2-230-1
McGraw-Hill 2-147
Mediterranean Sea 1-273
Meinl group 1-153
Memorial Chapel 1-301
Memorial Hall 1-247
Menger obituary 1-191
Mercantilists 2-144
Merida 2-185
Merle's 2-5
Methodenstreit 1-59, 1-211
Methological article, 1914 1-141
Mexico City 2-185
Mexico, Universidad Autonoma de
   2-185
Mexico, vacation 2-181
Mia's death confirmed 2-176
Miami Beach 2-45
Michigan, University of 1-268
Millertown, New York 2-31
Ministry of Finance 1-166-80,
   1-184-5
Ministry of Religion and Instruction
   1-120
Minute of Faculty of Arts and
   Sciences 2-240-1
Mississippi River 1-210
Missouri, University of 1-241
MIT 2-95
MIT Graduate Students Club 2-187
Mitchell, W. C. obituary 2-195,
   2-225
Mittleuropa by Friedrich Naumann
   1-151

Monarchy preservation
 memorandum, 1916 1-153
Monetary analysis 1-147-9
Money book 1-2-3, 1-143, 1-165,
 1-211, 2-234-5, 1-278-9, 1-313,
 2-10, 2-37, 2-88-9, 2-228, 1-232,
 1-262-5
Monopolistic competition
 (Chamberlin) 2-64
Montgomery, Field Marshal 2-138
Montreal 2-62, 2-163
Moravia 1-45, 1-161
Moravia 1-7-11, 2-90
Motivation of entrepreneur 1-106
Multiple cycles 2-76-8
Munich soviets 1-174
Munich, University of 1-204-5,
 2-292
Mur, River in Graz 1-14, 2-122

Nara, Japan 1-273
Nassau 1-249
National Bureau of Economic
 Research 1-132, 2-195
National Museum of Mexico 2-185
National Socialism 1-284-7, 2-1
Natural law philosophers 1-52,
 2-144, 2-153, 2-165
Neo-conservatives 1-2
New economics, victory of 2-159
New England Indian Summer
 (Brooks) 2-153
New Hampshire, University of 1-312
New Haven 2-31
New Orleans 2-100
New School for Social
 Research-New York 1-291
New York Academy of Political
 Science 1-248
New York City 2-31, 1-209
New York Times 2-82, 2-250
New York University 2-183

New Zealand 1-118
Nice 2-8
Nikko 2-138
North Africa 2-138
Note-taking 1-16, 2-172-3
Nuremburg 1-7

Office of Strategic Services 2-148,
 2-161
Old Howard 2-4
Olmutz, Moravia 1-11
Opening doors 1-126-7
Opening doors statement 1-295-6
Origins of development theory
 1-109-10
Osaka, Japan 1-273
Oslo 1-295
Oxford University 1-34, 1-62, 1-243,
 1-278, 1-280, 2-2-3
Oyster House 2-4

P.V., (PV), (Prel. Vol.), Preliminary
 Volume 2-111, 2-133, 2-145,
 2-150, 2-165, 2-177, 2-188,
 2-227-8, 2-231, 2-253-4
Pacific theater 2-138
Pacifist beliefs 1-140-1
Pan-German Grossdeutsche 1-166
Paradox 1-4
Paris 1-123, 2-8
Paris, Annie's visit, 1926 1-217
Paris, University of 1-32-3
Parliament 1-33, 1-176, 1-185
Partial equilibrium analysis 1-76,
 2-18-9
Patton, General George 2-138
Pergamon Museum 1-281
Peter, the Irish setter 2-147-8
Ph.D.s granted by Harvard 2-148,
 2-162
Phi Beta Kappa 2-29
Philadelphia 2-98

Physiocrats 1-143, 2-210
Piarist fathers 1-18
Piltenburk, Moravia 1-8
Plans late in life 2-222
Poland 2-90
Policies of Laborism article 2-223
Policy viewpoint, 1925-1932
  2-283-7, 2-213-5
Policy-itis 2-81
Political career, 1916-1917 1-49-55
Political Economy Club, Columbia
  University 2-99
Political goals, 1916-1917 1-150-1
Political Science
  Department-Harvard, 1883 1-241
Poppelsdorf Allee 1-208
Poppelsdorf Cemetary 1-235
Population data, early study of 1-38
Port Said 1-273
Postwar Economic Problems (Harris)
  2-143
Prague 1-8-9
Prague, University of 1-32, 1-119,
  1-128, 1-196, 1-202, 1-230
Prayer, program of 2-199
Preference for independent central
  bank 2-258-9
Preference for indirect taxes 2-259
Preference for monarchy 2-257
Present State of Economics article in
  Japan, 1931 (1983) 1-273
Princeton visit 1-133-4
Princeton, University of 2-187,
  1-303, 1-185, 1-187
Principles of Economics (Marshall)
  2-107
Principles of Political Economy
  (Mill) 2-211
*Principles of Political Economy and
  Taxation* (Ricardo) 2-212
Privatdozent 1-87, 1-91, 1-254

*Proceedings of the American
  Economic Association* 2-239
Professors and their status 1-33-4
Profit 1-79
Prosperity and Depression
  (Haberler) 2-45, 2-65
Protective tariffs article, 1940 2-99
Protestantism 1-43
Prussia 1-206
Prussian Ministry of Education
  1-196, 1-289
Public Choice 2-252
Public finance teaching 2-216
Public speaking 1-142
Purchasing Power of Money (Fisher)
  1-265

Quadregisimo Anno 2-163, 2-232
Quantity theory of money 1-148-9
Quarterly Journal of Economics
  2-151, 2-162, 2-194-5, 2-205,
  2-111, 2-225, 2-243, 2-252
Quebec, University of 2-163

Racial prejudice 2-66-7
Radcliffe College 1-312, 2-7, 2-29,
  2-140, 2-225-6
Radkov, Moravia 1-8
Rasna, Moravia 1-8
Rathaus 1-19, 1-37
Rationality in Economics article,
  1940 2-98
Rationality seminar 2-98
Rationality, cause of capitalist
  decline 2-124-5
Red Sea 1-273
*Reflections on the Revolution of Our
  Time* (Laski) 2-143
Reichstag, German 1-284
Reisinger family 1-192

Religion 1-4-5, 1-225-9, 1-240,
2-261, 1-288, 2-53, 2-58-61,
2-199-200
Research Center of Entrepreneurial
History 2-224
Research Center on Entrepreneurship
2-183
Restoration of private industry, 1919
1-169
Result trend 2-78
Retirement 2-234-5
Review of Economic Statistics 2-145
Review of Economic Studies 2-39
Rhine River 1-206, 1-208, 1-235,
1-282
Ricardian vice 2-212
Ringstrasse 1-19, 1-33
Rivalry with Keynes 1-3
Rockefeller fellows 2-43
Rockefeller Foundation 2-183, 2-188
Role of money 1-107
Roman Catholic church 2-163
Rommel, Erwin 2-137-8
Roose, Benjamin, and Company
1-187
Rotary Club 2-93
Rothschilds 1-185
Rotterdam 1-295
Rouen, France 2-2
Royal Air Force 2-138
Royal court appearance 1-121-2
Royal Economic Society 1-58, 2-226
*Rudimentary Mathematics for
Economists and Statisticians*
2-163
Russia 2-91, 2-101, 2-155
Ruzena, Moravia 1-8

Sacred decade 1-51, 1-145
Salary, Harvard 2-27, 2-110, 2-188-9
Salisbury Cemetary 2-240

Salisbury, Connecticut 2-29, 2-31,
2-240
Samuelson appointment incident
2-94-5
San Juan, Puerto Rico 1-249
Saturday Review of Literature 1-82
Say's Law 2-19
Scandinavia, trip, 1932 1-295
Schmoller article, 1926 1-211
Schmollers Jahrbuch 1-202, 1-212,
1-231
Scholastic doctors 1-52, 2-144,
2-153, 2-165
Schools, attitude toward 2-5, 2-255-6
Schools, attraction and repulsion
2-159-60
Schumpeter Fellowship, Harvard
University 2-247
Schumpeter Necrology 1-8
Schumpeter Prize 2-247
Schumpeter Professorship,
University of Vienna 2-250
Schumpeter Society, International
J. A. 2-250
Science and Ideology speech, 1948
2-196
Scollay Square, Boston 2-4
Scythia, S.S. 2-2
Second society, Austro-Hungarian
monarchy chap. 4
Seltzer water bottle incident 1-23-4
Separation from Gladys 1-139, 1-141
Seven Mountains 1-282
Seven Wise Men 1-308, 2-4, 2-27,
2-62, 2-161,
Sexual life 1-233-4
Shanghai 1-273
Sharon, Connecticut 2-220
Ships in the Fog, unfinished novel
2-10-12
Short-run-itis 2-81
Sicily 2-138

Silesia 1-161
Singapore 1-273
Slovakia 1-161
Small Is Beautiful (E. F.
Schumacher) 1-258
Smith Academy 1-241
Social classes article, 1927 1-231-2
Social classes, theory of (Marxian)
2-118
Social Democrat party 1-166-74
Social economics article, 1909 1-88
Social life 1-190-1, 2-28, 2-30-2
Social Product and Money
Calculations article, 1917 1-147-9
Social Relations Colloquy 2-287
Socialism 1-3
Socialism and democracy 2-129
Socialism, workability of 2-126
Socialist article, 1920 1-191
Socialist substitute for price system
2-126-8
Socialization Commission 1-161-165
Socialization policy, Austrian
1-169-70
Socializations vs. nationalization
1-163
Socratic method of teaching 1-226,
1-302-3
Sofia, University of, honorary degree
2-97
Sombart article, 1927 1-231
Sorbonne 1-59
Soviet Union 2-91, 2-101, 2-166
Speaking engagements 1-128, 1-312,
2-9
St. John's Day 1-8
St. John's Episcopal Church 2-240
St. Katarina's Church 1-12-13
Staatswissenschaft seminar at Berlin
1-58-9
Stabilization loan, 1919 1-172
Stabilizing the exchange rate, 1919

1-168
Stable Money Society 1-248
Stadtpark, Graz 1-122
Stanford University 1-205, 2-283
State Secretary of Finance 1-166-80,
1-190, 2-254, 1-289
State Secretary of Finance, failure as
1-177-8
Stationary state 2-213
Statistiches Handbuch 1-12
Stockholm 1-295
Stopping inflation, 1919 1-168
Stroke 2-240
Student boycott and protest 1-117,
1-123-6
Student consultation 1-126, 1-254,
2-7
Student letter about Yale offer 2-96-7
Styria, Province of Austria 1-16
Sub-normals 2-190-1
Suez Canal 1-273
Supply-side economics and policies
2-256
Surplus value, theory of (Marxian)
2-119
Survival of capitalism 2-120
Sussex, University of 1-282
Switzerland 1-141

Tableau economique 2-210
Taconic, Connecticut 1-5, 2-29,
2-31-32, 2-43, 2-88, 2-108, 2-144,
2-147, 2-189, 2-204, 2-236
Tales of Arabian Nights 1-97
Taussig retirement party 2-44
Tax preferences 1-214
Tax state monograph, 1918 1-156
Taxes and spending, 1919 1-166
Teaching 1-3-4, 1-255-8, 2-171-4,
2-38-41
Technische Hochschule
Charlottenburg 1-230

Telc 1-9
Temple Inn 1-60
Tennis 1-5, 2-32, 2-37, 2-43, 2-108
Testing theory 2-20
Textile factory in Moravia 1-9
The Theoretical Apparatus of Economics, unwritten book 2-52, 2-89, 2-111, 2-133, 2-227
Theoretical problems of growth article, 1947 2-183
Theorie der wirtschaftlichen Entwicklung, Die 1-102-10, 1-250, 2-143
Theorie der wirtschaftlichen Entwicklung, Die, Japanese translations 1-273
Theorie der wirtschaftlichen Entwicklung, Die, English translation 1-277-8
Theorie der wirtschaftlichen Entwicklung, Die, Japanese translation 2-52
Theorie der wirtschaftlichen Entwicklung, Die, reviews 1-110-1, 1-211
Theorie der wirtshaftlichen Entwicklung, Die, revised, 1926 1-211
Theory of Economic Development 1-3, 2-9, 2-71, 2-73, 2-234
Theory of Economic Development, Japanese translation, 1937 2-117
Theory of Economic Development, reviews 2-9-10
Theory of International Trade (Haberler) 2-65
Theory of Money and Banking, unwritten book 2-227
Theory of Price (Stigler) 2-143
Theory of Wages (Hicks) 2-226
Therapeutic nihilism 1-41-2
Theresianstadt, Bohemia 1-17

Theresianum 1-18-26, 1-47, 1-52, 1-146, 1-152, 1-187
Thursday Club 1-312
Time in economic analysis 2-142, 2-253-4
Tobruk 2-138
Tokyo College of Commerce 1-196
Tokyo Imperial University 1-271
Tokyo University of Commerce 1-270
Trade Statistics and Cycles in England, 1698-1825 (Boody) 2-29
Treatise on Money, A (Keynes) 1-265-6, 1-313, 2-22
Trest, Czechoslovakia 1-7-14
Treaty of Versailles 2-12
Trestice, Moravia 1-8
Triesch, Movavia 1-8-9
Turks, Ottoman 1-40-44
Twenty-ninth Infantry Troop Division 1-17
Twin Lakes Road, Taconic 2-32

U.S. citizenship application 2-2
U.S. citizenship, granted 2-90
Undergraduate education 2-6-7
Unemployment in Vienna, 1919 1-165
United Nations Development Agency 1-282
United Nations Educational, Scientific, and Cultural Organization 2-226
Unternehmehmer 1-104
Upper Austrian Porcelain Enterprise 1-187
Utilitarianism 1-61
Utility school 1-143, 1-201

Value and Capital (Hicks) 2-226
Varitionsmethode 1-80-1
Vassar College 2-29

Verbindung 1-32
Vergangenheit und Zukunft der Sozialwissenschaft 1-101, 1-143, 2-204
Vienna 1-10, 1-14, 1-123, 1-184, 1-203, 1-209
Vienna, fin-de-siecle intellectual life 1-53-4
Vienna, fin-de-siecle attitudes 1-25, 1-43-45, 1-53
Vienna, postwar conditions 1-162
Vienna, University of 1-23, 1-26, 1-31-34, 1-101, 1-152, 1-230
Vienna, University of, professor's pay, 1-178
Virginia, University of 2-102
Vision 1-51-2, 1-73-4, 1-81-2
Visitors to Bonn 1-259
Volksschulen in Graz 1-15
Voluntary death 2-56, 2-221, 2-228
Vorechov, Moravia 1-8

Waiver of first marriage 1-195
Waldorf Astoria 2-47
Wall Street Journal 2-250
Walras's obituary 1-100
Walrasian basis of theory 1-76, 1-80
War as atavistic and irrational 1-156
Washington University 1-241
Wealth of Nations (Smith) 2-22, 2-211
Weber obituary 1-191
Wehrmacht, German 2-42
Weimar Republic 1-207, 1-213-4
Wellesley College 2-183
Wesen des Geldes, Das (1970) 2-254
Wesen und der Hauptinhalt der theoretischen Nationaloekonomie, Das 1-65-8, 1-73-5, 2-73, 2-250
Wesen und der Hauptinhalt der theoretischen Nationaloekonomie,

Das, attempted revision 1-279-81
Wesen und der Hauptinhalt der theoretischen Nationaloekonomie, Das, Japanese translations 1-272
Wesen und der Hauptinhalt der theoretischen Nationaloekonomie, Das, reviews 1-83-86
West Indies 1-249
Wheaton College 2-233
White Hart Inn 2-32
White Mountains, New Hampshire 2-43
Widener Library 1-249, 1-301, 2-5, 2-38, 2-42, 2-183, 2-266
Wiedner Hauptstrasse, Vienna 1-19
Wiener Neustadt, Austria 1-10
Windy Hill 2-31-32, 2-147, 2-204, 2-236
Women's rights, University of Vienna 1-23-4
Work, dedication to 1-229
World War I, beginnings 1-140
World War I, effect on Graz 1-149
World War II, beginning 2-90-92
Writing *Capitalism, Socialism and Democracy* 2-99, 2-108, 2-110
Writing style 1-3-4, 1-68, 1-82, 1-100, 1-103, 1-263-5

Yale offer and response, 1940 2-95-97
Yale Review 1-245
Yale teaching 2-95, 2-100, 2-108
Yale University 1-34, 1-205, 1-303
Yale University visit 1-133
Yokohoma, Japan 1-270
Young Republicans 2-187
Yucatan 2-185
Yugoslavia 1-283

Zoegling 1-19